About This Book

Why is this topic important?

Experiential learning strategies make it possible for training to resemble a learner's work environment. This capacity yields greater understanding, retention, and application back on the job than training approaches that are removed from the real world do. People need to process more than facts and concepts to be motivated to perform effectively, to identify what needs to be done, to be skilled at it, and to use it consistently. They must experience it.

What can you achieve with this book?

This handbook is a premier compendium of models, advice, and case examples on how to design and facilitate experiential learning to improve training and performance in the workplace. It brings together the experience, creativity, and wisdom of many of the world's best thinkers and practitioners of experiential learning. Much of the material can also be applied to educational settings.

How is this resource organized?

The handbook contains contributed articles by leading experts in three sections:

I.   The Foundations of Experiential Learning
II.   Experiential Learning Methodologies
III. Training Applications of Experiential Learning

About Pfeiffer

Pfeiffer serves the professional development and hands-on resource needs of training and human resource practitioners and gives them products to do their jobs better. We deliver proven ideas and solutions from experts in HR development and HR management, and we offer effective and customizable tools to improve workplace performance. From novice to seasoned professional, Pfeiffer is the source you can trust to make yourself and your organization more successful.

Essential Knowledge   Pfeiffer produces insightful, practical, and comprehensive materials on topics that matter the most to training and HR professionals. Our Essential Knowledge resources translate the expertise of seasoned professionals into practical, how-to guidance on critical workplace issues and problems. These resources are supported by case studies, worksheets, and job aids and are frequently supplemented with CD-ROMs, websites, and other means of making the content easier to read, understand, and use.

Essential Tools   Pfeiffer's Essential Tools resources save time and expense by offering proven, ready-to-use materials—including exercises, activities, games, instruments, and assessments—for use during a training or team-learning event. These resources are frequently offered in looseleaf or CD-ROM format to facilitate copying and customization of the material.

Pfeiffer also recognizes the remarkable power of new technologies in expanding the reach and effectiveness of training. While e-hype has often created whizbang solutions in search of a problem, we are dedicated to bringing convenience and enhancements to proven training solutions. All our e-tools comply with rigorous functionality standards. The most appropriate technology wrapped around essential content yields the perfect solution for today's on-the-go trainers and human resource professionals.

Essential resources for training and HR professionals

Pfeiffer™

THE HANDBOOK
OF EXPERIENTIAL
LEARNING

---

edited by Mel Silberman

John Wiley & Sons, Inc.

Published by Pfeiffer
An Imprint of Wiley
989 Market Street, San Francisco, CA 94103-1741
www.pfeiffer.com

For additional copies/bulk purchases of this book in the U.S. please contact 800-274-4434.

Pfeiffer books and products are available through most bookstores. To contact Pfeiffer directly call our
Customer Care Department within the U.S. at 800-274-4434, outside the U.S. at 317-572-3985,
fax 317-572-4002, or visit www.pfeiffer.com.

Pfeiffer also publishes its books in a variety of electronic formats. Some content that appears in print
may not be available in electronic books.

Library of Congress Cataloging-in-Publication Data

The handbook of experiential learning / edited by Mel Silberman.
    p. cm.
  Includes index.
  ISBN-13: 978-0-7879-8258-4 (cloth)
  ISBN-10: 0-7879-8258-X (cloth)
  1. Experiential learning. 2. Active learning. 3. Teaching. I. Silberman, Melvin L.
  LB1027.23.H36 2007
  153.1'52—dc22

2006100391

Acquiring Editor: Martin Delahoussaye
Director of Development: Kathleen Dolan Davies
Developmental Editor: Susan Rachmeler

Production Editor: Dawn Kilgore
Editor: Rebecca Taff
Manufacturing Supervisor: Becky Carreño

Printed in the United States of America

Printing 10 9 8 7 6 5 4 3 2 1

CONTENTS

PART III   TRAINING APPLICATIONS OF EXPERIENTIAL LEARNING   239

INTRODUCING *THE HANDBOOK*
OF EXPERIENTIAL LEARNING

*T*HE HANDBOOK OF EXPERIENTIAL LEARNING is a premier compendium of models, advice, and case examples on how to design and facilitate experiential learning to improve training and performance in the workplace. It brings together the experience, creativity, and wisdom of many of the world's best thinkers and practitioners of experiential learning. Much of the material can also be applied to educational settings.

The Handbook of Experiential Learning contains contributed articles by leading experts in three sections:

I. Foundations of Experiential Learning

This section examines the case for experiential learning in the effort to bring about deep levels of learning and change. It also explores the theoretical roots of experiential learning and discusses the ways in which all experiential learning can be "debriefed" so that the experiences teach participants and not merely engage them.

II. Experiential Learning Methodologies

This section presents ten experiential learning methodologies. Each one represents a popular and important strategy to maximize the impact of experiential learning. Each methodology is defined and illustrated with examples that apply to an array of training topics. For example, role playing will be discussed with examples applying to more than one topic. Expert advice will also be given on how to design and facilitate each experiential learning tool.

III. Training Applications of Experiential Learning

This section demonstrates how a variety of experiential methodologies are utilized to form the core training approach in eight different training areas, including both technical and non-technical subject matter. For each area, there is an examination of its critical success factors and the key experiential strategies that the author (and others in the field) have employed to conduct successful training in his or her area of expertise.

Experience and Learning

The major justification for assembling this handbook is simple. It is now well established that the closer training resembles (even metaphorically) a learner's work environment, the greater the understanding, the retention, and the application back on the job. What this means is that people need to process more than facts and concepts to be motivated to perform effectively, to identify what needs to be done, to be skilled at it, and to use it consistently. They must experience it.

This notion is expressed well by the Chinese philosopher, Confucius:

By three methods we may learn wisdom: First, by reflection, which is noblest; second, by imitation, which is easiest; and third by experience, which is the bitterest.

We must, however, not become simplistic about the primacy of experience. Effective education and training is both abstract and concrete. Jean Piaget, the renowned developmental psychologist, taught us that children learn concretely, but become capable of abstract thought as they enter adolescence and adulthood. Unfortunately, many trainers have taken this change in mental capacity to mean that concrete learning experiences can now be curtailed. To the contrary. Learning by direct experience should continue throughout a person's lifespan. For example, participants will understand project management concepts best through actually managing a small project. They will understand supply chains through managing a real or imaginary one. They will understand the problems faced by visually impaired people through participating in a simulation of blindness. The need for concrete experience doesn't diminish, but, with the capacity for abstract thinking, participants can now go from the experience to much higher-order understandings.

Much of the credit for the positive connection between concrete experience and abstract learning goes to John Dewey (1938), the author of *Experience and Education*. Dewey understood that merely having an experience was not the same as learning from it. Action and thought have to be linked. Back in 1916, he posited, "Thinking . . . is the intentional endeavor to discover specific connections between something which we do and the consequences which result, so that the two become continuous. Their isolation, and consequently their purely arbitrary going together, is cancelled; a unified, developing situation takes place."

Because of Dewey, successful practitioners of experiential learning don't just engage participants in activities. They help them derive meaning from those activities. The most widely used term for this is called "debriefing" (perhaps not the best term, as Roger Greenaway will comment on in Chapter 3 of this handbook). Other useful terms might be *reviewing, processing,* or *mining.* Regardless of terminology, the crucial idea is that an experience can lead to learning, and maybe even to change . . . but only if it is harvested, separating "the wheat from the chaff." As Colin Beard and John Wilson (2002), authors of *The Power of Experiential Learning,* put it, "Experience may underpin all learning but it does not always result in learning. We have to engage with the experience and reflect on what happened, how it happened, and why." David Kolb (1983), the author of the classic text, *Experiential Learning,* summed this concept up with his well-known words, "Learning is the process whereby knowledge is created through the transformation of experience."

The Growth of Experiential Learning

With these understandings, facilitators have been using experiential learning in their training efforts for some time. As I observe the field in the first decade of the 21st century, I see not just a steady use of experiential learning activities, but a virtual explosion. More sessions of major training conferences are devoted to experiential learning than ever before. There are also more providers of experiential learning than ever before.

Three major reasons for this tidal wave of experiential learning impress me. One is that new technology provides so many useful tools for experiential training. The experiences can be virtual as well as in physical time and place; some of them are so "high fidelity" that it feels just like the real thing. Games, designed for information acquisition, can be digitized and readily available on anyone's desktop for individual or group play. Augmented reality role-playing exercises are now being designed so that skill practice can be both safe and challenging. A second reason is that the youngest generations of employees prefer experiential learning

hands down over anything didactic. For example, the average age of sales associates in most retail environments is in the early twenties. These young people grew
up on games and technology. Training them on everything from safety procedures
to product knowledge to loss prevention can be done with hands-on methods they
embrace. A final reason is that the best minds in the field are increasingly its most
creative people. They have figured out how to bring high-impact experiential
learning into training in ways that are practical, doable, and affordable. (The contributors to this handbook are outstanding exemplars.) In some cases, the front-
end cost may still be high, but it pays off in the long run. In other cases, the
immediate solutions are far less costly than traditional materials. Moreover,
excellent guides now exist on how to create your own "home-grown" experiential
activities so that thoughtful trainers can customize experiential strategies to their
own unique training context.

"Sticky" Learning

In his book *The Tipping Point*, Malcolm Gladwell (2000) uses the term "stickiness" to
identify why some ideas, practices, and products capture the public's imagination.
Experiential learning is "sticky." When it is done well, it adheres to you. Participants
will usually forget a great presentation, but they often remember a great experience.
For example, I have facilitated countless times The Game of Life, an activity that
resembles the classic competition-cooperation exercise, The Prisoner's Dilemma.
The game is played by six groups of any size, although adjustments can be made to
accommodate fewer groups. Each group has approximately the same number of
players. The objective is for each group "to win as much as you can." Most participants assume that the only way to win as much as possible is to block the win-
nings of others, an assumption known as a "zero-sum" condition.

There are six rounds to the game. For each round, each group chooses either
Y or X (without knowing what the other groups have chosen) and writes its choice
on a slip of paper. All slips are handed to the trainer, who tallies them and announces the results. Each group's payoff depends on the combination of choices
made by the groups. For six groups, there are seven possible combinations (other
payoff schedules can easily be generated for fewer than six groups):

Combinations	*Payoffs*
All choose X	All lose $2
Five choose X; one chooses Y	Xs win $2; Y loses $10
Four choose X; two choose Y	Xs win $4; Ys lose $8

Three choose X; three choose Y	Xs win $6; Ys lose $6
Two choose X; four choose Y	Xs win $8; Ys lose $4
One chooses X; five choose Y	X wins $10; Ys lose $2
All choose Y	All win $2

After the third and fifth rounds, allowance is made for a ten-minute negotiation session between single representatives from any group that wishes to participate. The negotiations, if held, are to be loud enough for everyone in the room to hear. Before these opportunities for negotiation, the trainer announces that the payoff (wins and losses) will be tripled for the fourth round and multiplied tenfold for the sixth (last) round. Rarely, if ever, do groups take advantage of the opportunities to strategize together, build trust, and create win-win solutions.

After experiencing The Game of Life, participants always have many reactions, especially anger at teams that did not cooperate (the six groups rarely choose to cooperate by all choosing Y) and disdain for any groups that used deceit. Some participants will protest, "It's only a game," while others will take it very seriously. It is crucial to obtain these reactions and observations in order to realize the potential of this experiential activity. The biggest mistake is to analyze the game too quickly before allowing feelings to be expressed.

After noting what happened during the game and what participants were feeling, I guide participants to begin to develop many insights. They note that the world is not simply divided into good guys and bad guys. They understand that behaviors could have occurred during the negotiations that would have inspired trust and cooperation. They also observe how groups that were losing heavily often behaved like victims and failed to see that they had the power to turn their fortune around.

After achieving these insights, participants can now be helped to do some generalizing. Among the principles and learnings that might emerge are these:

- All parties in an organization are responsible for creating its ultimate climate.
- The actions of one unit invariably affect the actions of the others.
- Groups with power are reluctant to negotiate.
- Negotiation is most effective when each side acknowledges its needs in a straightforward fashion and acknowledges its differences with others in a non-blaming manner.

At this point, participants are usually motivated to start applying the experience to their own organization. When all participants belong to the same organization, discussion can address the inter-group competition within their own ranks and ways to alleviate it. When participants come from different organizations, individual participants can share case situations for the advice and counsel of peers.

Needless to say, the game "sticks" with participants. I have heard from people years later that they not only remember the experience but also retain what they learned from it.

What Is Experiential Learning?

Sometimes, the term "experiential learning" is used to signify any training that is interactive, with minimal lecture (and slides). While many good methods to design training activities exist, it is important to single out the "sticky" quality that makes a training activity truly "experiential." (In one of my recent books, *Training the Active Training Way*, experiential activity is but one of several bases for making training active and effective.) Let me explain with some examples of active training techniques I would not classify as "experiential," even though they are high on my list of recommended practices.

One of the best ways to make learning concrete is the use of *case studies*. A case study may be as short as a paragraph or as long as ten to twenty pages of text. Typically, a concrete situation is presented that demands analysis (What happened here?) or a solution (How can this problem be resolved?). The situation can be a summary of a real case or one that is contrived to provide important information, raise certain issues, and/or require a decision. Clearly, participating in a good case study can be highly engaging. What may not elevate it to the status of an experiential activity pertains to *how* it is experienced. If the case study remains as written text to be discussed and analyzed by participants, it probably will not engage the emotions along with the intellect. Participants will probably keep some personal distance from the situation(s) imbedded in the case. However, if the cases were imbedded in *action learning problems*, the experience might be different. As you will read in Chapter 5 of this handbook, action learning entails real people resolving and taking action on real problems in real time and learning while doing. The basic requirements for action learning include an important and urgent problem, a diverse group of four to eight people, a reflective inquiry process, implemented action, a commitment to learning, and the presence of an action learning coach. With these ingredients, the "cases" participants wrestle with have an immediacy that brings a range of emotions, beliefs, and ideas to the forefront.

A second example of a highly engaging technique that would not be considered "experiential" is one of my favorites: *jigsaw learning*. Jigsaw learning is one of the best ways to engage participants in team learning, where participants work in small groups, learning from and teaching each other, rather than from the trainer directly. Instead of asking each group to study the same information, as is the case in conventional small group learning, you can give different information to different groups and then form study groups composed of representatives of each of the initial groups. The beauty of jigsaw learning is that every single participant teaches something or brings his or her newly acquired knowledge to the learning task. It is an exciting alternative whenever the material to be learned can be segmented or "chunked" and when no one segment must be taught before the others. Each participant learns something that, when combined with the material learned by the others, forms a coherent body of knowledge or skill.

For example, a trainer in a course on sexual harassment prevention divided participants into six study groups and gave each group material on one of six legal factors that help to decide what constitutes sexual harassment:

1. Quid pro quo harassment
2. Unwelcome behavior
3. Isolated occurrences
4. Hostile environment
5. Prior romantic involvement
6. Ordinary reasonable person

After studying the material, jigsaw groups were formed and given the following six questions to discuss:

1. If a woman has tolerated repeated requests for a date by her boss, does she still have grounds for claiming sexual harassment?
2. Does there have to be a repetitive series of incidents to claim sexual harassment?
3. Does the fact that the victim suffered no mental anguish affect her claim?
4. Whose standards determine how offensive an act is—men's or women's?
5. What is the clearest violation of the law?
6. Can you allege that someone you previously dated sexually harassed you?

The trainer pointed out that all the required information to answer these questions had been acquired by someone in the jigsaw group. The participants were then instructed to share their knowledge to answer the six questions.

As exciting and productive as *jigsaw learning* is, I would still not classify it as "experiential learning." Again, it fails the test of providing direct emotional and intellectual involvement in an event that approximates or replicates one that people experience in their actual work environment. So, along with my other example, *case study*, I hope I have been clear about the boundaries that will be drawn in this handbook.

Experiential learning, as I will define it, refers to (a) the involvement of learners in concrete activities that enable them to "experience" what they are learning about and (b) the opportunity to reflect on those activities. Experiential learning can be based on both real work/life experiences (e.g., working on a current project) and structured experiences that simulate or approximate real work/life (e.g., using a flight simulator or engaging in a sexual harassment exercise, involving the abuse of distributing playing cards). Its range is enormous. It applies to content that is technical/hard (e.g., operating equipment) or non-technical/soft (e.g., selling skills). Moreover, experiential activity can be used for learning that is *cognitive* (understanding information/concepts), *behavioral* (developing skills), and *affective* (examining beliefs). For example, a wonderful way to help participants understand a highly technical process is to "act it out." Sometimes, no matter how clear an explanation is or how descriptive visual aids are, certain procedures are not understood. To help clarify the material, you might ask some participants to physically walk through the procedures (e.g., an order entry system or a manufacturing process) you are trying to explain. This can be accomplished by:

• Inviting some participants to come to the front of the room and have each physically simulate an aspect of the procedure.
• Creating large cards that name the parts of a procedure. Distribute the cards to some participants. Ask the participants with cards to arrange themselves so that the steps of the procedure are correctly sequenced.
• Developing a role play in which participants dramatize the procedure.
• Building a physical model of a process or procedure.

Acquiring skills requires more than "monkey see, monkey do." With role-playing exercises that progress from safe to highly challenging, participants can develop the confidence that enables them to employ a skill effectively in a wide variety of situations. Skill development is also enhanced by other experiential methods, such as adventure activities, creative play, and learning games. Traditional beliefs and attitudes can be shaken to the core by immersion in both realistic and metaphorical experiential activities. Some of these may take only a minute, and others encompass hours. Whatever their length, experiential activities succeed in building a level of awareness that is unparalleled, precisely because they are not just "talk," but often gut-wrenching, powerful events.

Experiential learning employs a wide gamut of methodologies, such as:

• On-the-job assignments
• Field experiences
• Action learning projects

- Creative play
- Role play
- Games
- Simulations
- Visualization
- Story telling
- Improvisation
- Adventure activities

Finally, experiential learning is not confined to a workshop. It can be experienced as part of a classroom training session, a team meeting, a coaching session, and individual and group-based e-learning.

So come and explore with me the wonderful world of experiential learning. Our guides have been chosen for a variety of reasons. Some are "veterans," having spent thirty or more years as leaders in the field. Others are "hot, new talent," who have taken the legacy of experiential learning to new heights and new arenas. All of them are passionate about experiential learning and its vital contribution to training and performance improvement.

References

Beard, C., & Wilson, J. (2002). *The power of experiential learning.* London: Kogan Page.

Dewey, J. (1938). *Experience and education.* New York: Macmillan.

Gladwell, M. (2000). *The tipping point.* New York: Little, Brown.

Kolb, D. (1983). *Experiential learning.* Paramus, NJ: Financial Times/Prentice Hall.

Silberman, M. (2006). *Training the active training way.* San Francisco, CA: Pfeiffer.

PART ONE

FOUNDATIONS OF EXPERIENTIAL LEARNING

THIS FIRST SECTION of *The Handbook of Experiential Learning* contains three chapters. Each addresses an issue that underpins the design and facilitation of effective experiential learning. The authors are thought leaders in the field of experiential learning.

Chapter 1, "Changing Attitudes and Behaviors Through Experiential Activity," examines the ultimate purpose of experiential learning. While training is often viewed as a means toward *self-awareness* and *acquisition of knowledge and skills,* its overriding goal is *change.* While no training program or intervention can ever be expected, by itself, to produce real change, casting such a vision when it is first designed and later implemented is crucial. The author argues that experiential learning activities are critical to that mission. It contains a five-step model of change and illustrates how experiential learning activities contribute to each step of the model.

Chapter 2, "Theoretical Foundations of Experiential Learning," discusses some of the fundamental cognitive processes necessary for the design and delivery of tools supporting experiential learning. One of the main points of the chapter is that the comprehension of learning content is best driven by a story framework for the to-be-learned material. The chapter ends with brief examples to showcase these ideas in action.

Chapter 3, "Dynamic Debriefing," covers several aspects of the reflection phase of experiential learning. Among the topics are the role of the facilitator in debriefing, the ways in which debriefing activities can be sequenced, and variety of debriefing tools. Central to the chapter is the notion that debriefing can be a dynamic process if it is carefully designed.

CHAPTER ONE

CHANGING ATTITUDES AND BEHAVIORS THROUGH EXPERIENTIAL ACTIVITY

Mel Silberman

Mel Silberman is the author of numerous books in the field of training and development, including *Active Training* (3rd ed.) (Pfeiffer, 2006), *PeopleSmart* (Berrett-Koehler, 2000), *Working PeopleSmart* (Berrett-Koehler, 2004), *101 Ways to Make Training Active* (2nd ed.) (Pfeiffer, 2005), and *Training the Active Training Way* (Pfeiffer, 2006). Mel is professor emeritus of adult and organizational development at Temple University and president of Active Training, a provider of seminars and publications in adult learning, training techniques, coaching, team facilitation, and interpersonal intelligence. He is a frequent presenter at conferences of the American Society for Training and Development (ASTD), the International Society of Performance Improvement (ISPI), and the North American Simulation and Gaming Association (NASAGA). His clients encompass corporate, educational, governmental, and human service organizations worldwide. Recent clients include the U.S. Senate Office of Education and Training, BMW, Linens N' Things, Consolidated Edison, Nationwide Insurance, the Federal Reserve Bank, and the Stockholm School of Economics.

Contact Information
Active Training
303 Sayre Drive
Princeton, NJ 08540
(609) 987–8157
mel@activetraining.com
www.activetraining.com

I N EVERY ORGANIZATION, there are attitudes and behaviors among leaders and employees that reduce its effectiveness. These attitudes and behaviors cluster in what I would call "arenas of change." Following are six arenas in which uncertainties, tensions, and resistance often occur:

1. Customer Service

Any organization that must attract and retain its customers needs its members to embrace a customer orientation. If customers are seen as individuals to be taken for granted or merely tolerated, those customers will become dissatisfied and go elsewhere with their business. Moreover, an indifferent stance toward customers is dangerous, even in circumstances under which customers do not have a choice as to where a need is obtained. This typically occurs in the public sector, such as with a governmental agency, a public educational institution, and so forth. Not happy with their experience, customers become less appreciative and hence less supportive of the organization.

2. Safety

Safety is a paramount concern in any organization where harmful events can happen to employees and customers. To ensure safety, procedures have to be followed that minimize danger. (A simple example is the wearing of a hard hat at a construction site.) Often, these procedures are unappealing. They may create personal discomfort, add time and stress to work assignments, and require extensive knowledge acquisition and training.

3. Teamwork

Much of an organization's work occurs through small teams. Unfortunately, collaboration does not come easily. It takes a long time for a team to become high-performing. Also, it is often frustrating to work effectively with others, and many people prefer to "do it myself." Individual styles and temperaments also interfere with teamwork. If a person is impatient or needs personal space to be effective, he or she will be a hindrance to a project team.

4. Process Improvement

In order to improve quality and efficiency, many organizations need to rethink how they do things. The rub is that most people don't like change. They are used to "business as usual," preferring the familiarity of continually doing things the way they've always been done. Furthermore, they are afraid of the risks involved in committing to what's not yet been "proven." Some hold back, and others actively resist the changes being suggested or mandated.

5. Diversity

Increasingly, the workplace has become more culturally diverse in terms of differences in gender, race, ethnicity, country of origin, special needs, age, and many other aspects. The mix can make some people uncomfortable. Some people find it difficult to understand people who act, speak, and perhaps value things differently than they do. Moreover, status issues abound. Who's in the majority? Who's in the minority? Who are the leaders? Who are the followers?

6. Role Expectations

Traditional roles of managers and employees allowed for clear expectations. One group were the leaders and the other the followers. Nowadays, employees are encouraged to be self-directing learners, to take greater initiative, and are empowered to make more decisions on their own. In turn, managers are expected to be coaches, team leaders, and facilitators, as opposed to controllers. This change in role expectations leads to confusion and resistance in many organizations. Even when the change is embraced, people are not sure how to adapt.

The Steps in Changing Attitudes and Behaviors

If you are charged with the responsibility to help promote change in the arenas just cited (or in many additional ones), you need a process that will guide your efforts. I would like to suggest a five-step process:

1. Creating Openness
2. Promoting Understanding
3. Considering New Attitudes and Behaviors
4. Experimenting
5. Obtaining Support

Creating Openness

The first challenge is to "get your foot in the door," as opposed to "getting the door slammed in your face." Recognizing that the people you are hoping to change may be resistant to your efforts, you want to be seen as open and trustworthy, without an agenda that imposes change. In these initial attempts to build receptiveness to change, the first order of business is to get people to feel open to getting their concerns "out on the table" and to validate them. It's important for people to realize that you are interested in their feelings and points of view and that you see these as real for them. That can't happen unless they feel safe enough to express themselves and you can empathize with their feelings and acknowledge the kernels of truth in what they believe. Here are some concerns that might surface if you do this.

Trying to understand someone who is difficult implies that you're sympathetic or even forgiving. When interpersonal skills training encourages participants to "seek to understand before being understood," some participants are concerned that doing so will give a person who has done something unacceptable the impression that the behavior is OK. These participants have difficulty seeing that understanding does not imply acceptance. Rather, it is an attempt to figure out the best way to deal with people instead of writing them off or being angry with them.

Some safety procedures do not really protect us. Sometimes, employees object to safety requirements, such as wearing ear plugs to avoid hearing injuries, because they may lead to other problems, such as not being able to hear a co-worker.

Customers get the idea that they can treat us any way they want. Such a conclusion is often the belief of participants in a customer-service training program in a context in which they have already experienced considerable abuse from customers.

The team concept means that you can't take any initiative without checking in with others. Often, people resist team training because they think it will rob them of personal control.

If beliefs such as those just cited are freely aired, it is now possible to examine them and perhaps find non-threatening ways to challenge the assumptions behind them. This creates some openness to considering new attitudes and behaviors. If, instead, these attitudes and behaviors are simply "urged" by the training program, they may fall on deaf ears.

Promoting Understanding

Once participants are open to examining and challenging their beliefs, they will be more willing to accept new information and make shifts in the way they see things.

For example, people previously resistant to team work may now be open to the fact that it takes a while for a team to form, storm, norm, and eventually perform. As a result, they may become more patient about the trials and tribulations of their own work teams. Or customer service trainees may now become impressed by the fact that less than 10 percent of all unhappy customers complain. They come to realize that active attempts to assist customers and obtain feedback from them is vital to an organization's ability to retain them as clients. Or participants may be made more open to seeking feedback from their boss when they become aware that such an action is often viewed favorably. Seeking feedback (but not fishing for compliments) shows that you are interested in your own development and want to take the initiative in improving your performance.

Considering New Attitudes and Behaviors

The next step is to invite participants to engage in experiences in which they see new attitudes and behaviors in action. Those experiences can be had through a variety of methods, from real-world activities to simulated ones. When well-crafted and well-debriefed, these experiences can often develop a positive motivation to try out new ways.

Typically, participation in these experiences needs to feel safe. While it is important to eventually up the challenge level to master new approaches and skills, participants tend to be more open to exploring new ones if they don't feel judged or embarrassed as they "try them on for size." They also need some time and space to get used to them. Therefore, rushing this stage often leads to resistance.

Experimenting

If the experiences in the previous step have been insightful, motivating, and confidence-building, then the work of change can really go forward. At this juncture (usually when the training is over or between sessions), people can select new activities and commit themselves to applying them back on the job. I like to suggest that this process be called "an experiment in change" instead of the more mundane term "action plan." People are more open to this back-on-the-job application if *they* view it as an experiment in which they find out how useful the new attitude or skill is to *them*. We shouldn't kid ourselves. Most people will not persist with a change unless they find that it is successful. Experimenting allows people to test their wings and find initial success to sustain themselves for further application.

Often, people leave a good training program with so much enthusiasm that they make the mistake of going for broke and then fizzle out when results don't come quickly. Therefore, it's vital to encourage participants to try on a small change first and see what happens. *Less is more.*

Obtaining Support

Changes don't last unless they are "lived." Even if people are pumped up about a change in attitude or behavior, they usually find that, while making some headway, they quickly relapse. Real change comes only by overcoming obstacles that are in the way in our daily lives.

In this last critical step, people need help in identifying their ongoing needs for support. In particular, they need help in identifying the assistance they need and how to request it and maintain it.

The Role of Experiential Activity in the Change Process

The five-step process just described usually doesn't happen through conversation alone. Participants will not air their concerns, examine their beliefs, become open to new information, consider new attitudes and behaviors, try them out and seek support to sustain them merely by convening them for group discussion. In my experience, the process gets off to the best start and is sustained by well-designed and well-placed experiential activities.

Creating Openness

In the *creating openness* stage, short games and exercises are the ticket for "getting your foot in the door." Let me illustrate with the classic team exercise: Broken Squares. Participants are placed in groups of five members. Each member is given an envelope containing between two and four shapes. The job of each individual is to form a six-inch square, a task that cannot be accomplished unless participants give each other some of their shapes. The hitch is that no one can speak during the exercise or point to any shapes he or she wants from other group members. In the ensuing minutes, many things typically occur that block the group from success. The brilliance of the exercise is that it is not simply about cooperation and sharing. Participants come face-to-face with feelings of impatience, frustration, and pessimism that mimic emotions that most people feel in team situations. Because of that fact, it's a great way to get on the table everyone's feelings about the possibilities and risks of collaboration.

Another excellent example, using squares, of an experiential starter exercise is Count the Squares. In this exercise, participants are shown a large square divided evenly into sixteen cells (themselves squares) and asked: How many squares are there?

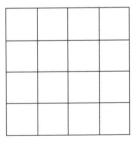

Most people respond with the answer sixteen, but a few shout out seventeen because they include both the one large square and the sixteen small squares. Eventually, participants realize that you can divide the large square into four quadrants and obtain four more "squares." Then it hits some people that you can adjust the way you find quadrants (2×2 cells) and identify five more "squares." Finally, people see that there are four "squares" containing nine cells each (3×3 cells), culminating in a count of thirty squares. This process can lead to many interesting learning points:

- There's more than meets the eye.
- Our assumptions block our view of things.
- Some people see things that others do not.
- Big problems have lots of small parts.

Such points can be related to examining feelings and beliefs on such topics as feedback, problem solving, teamwork, and more.

The opening experience can also be longer in length. Starting a cross-cultural training program, for example, with a rich simulation such as Bafa' Bafa' (developed by Garry Shirts, one of the contributors to this handbook) is a great way to prepare people being transferred abroad for the frustrations, joys, and insights that come from contact with a foreign culture. In Bafa' Bafa', participants are separated into two groups. Each group becomes a culture and is instructed in the culture's values and traditions. The two groups then exchange "ambassadors," who observe the other group and return to report on what they have learned about its culture. After consultation time, a different set of ambassadors is exchanged with the charge of interacting with the culture being visited. The game provides an excellent chance to help participants focus on what they consider normal, how they act within their own inner circle, and how they interact with strangers. They usually spend an hour in the simulation and then up to five hours discussing how stereotypes are formed and perpetuated.

Broken Squares, Count the Squares, and Bafa' Bafa' are but three of hundreds of games, simulations, and other published experiential activities available to trainers. The key is to select those that are rich in experiential learning and provide a variety of discussion opportunities for *creating openness*. (Naturally, you can create your own.)

Promoting Understanding

Most people would think that the *promoting understanding* phase would be the time for direct teaching, using primarily lecture and discussion. This might be true if the only concern were delivering key points and key information to participants. The beauty of experiential activities is how well they can be used to illuminate ideas so that their meaning is heightened. For example, imagine a trainer giving a brief lecture summarizing the problems managers face today, including low productivity, poor quality of service, high stress, and low morale. The trainer wants to point out that traditional management solutions tend to use an approach that, like the mythological Hydra, often generates two new heads for every one solved. A different approach is needed, which she calls "creating the ideal." At this point, the trainer interrupts the lecture with an exercise. She asks each participant to find a partner of approximately equal weight and strength. One of the pair is asked to hold out his or her arm horizontally and to resist the partner's attempts to bend it. Most arms are easily bent. The trainer then requests the individual to imagine his or her arm as a steel rod before the partner attempts to bend it and to sustain the vision in the process. In most pairs, arms remain straight despite increased effort from the partners. The trainer then continues: "Better results are obtained with less effort. The key is what one focuses on. In the first case, the individual tried to achieve contradictory results: keeping his or her arm straight and resisting having it bent. In the second case, he or she focused solely on the desired result." The trainer then presents four key elements that go into making a visionary approach to problem solving work.

The kind of understanding that a participant might want to promote is often more affective in nature rather than cognitive. A good illustration is any experiential activity that seeks to help participants internalize their understanding of someone else's situation. One of the best ways to "get into someone else's shoes" is to create an activity that simulates that unfamiliar person or situation. Begin by choosing a type of person or situation that you want participants to learn about. You may elect to have participants experience what it is like to be any of the following:

- In the "minority"
- In a different age group
- From a different culture
- A person with special problems or challenges
- In a demanding job

Then, create a way to simulate that person or situation. Among the ways to do this are the following:

- Have participants dress in the attire of that person or situation. Or have them handle the equipment, props, accessories, or other belongings of that person or situation or engage in a typical activity.

- Place participants in situations in which they are required to respond in the role of the character they have been given.
- Impersonate an individual and ask the participants to interview you and find out about your experiences, views, and feelings.
- Use an analogy to build a simulation. Create a scenario familiar to participants that sheds light on an unfamiliar situation. (You might, for instance, ask all participants in your class who are left-handed to portray people who are culturally different from the rest of the participants.)

An example of this is Instant Aging. This simulation is designed to sensitize participants to sensory deprivation and the normal process of aging. Participants are given eyeglasses smeared with Vaseline®, dried peas to put in their shoes, cotton for their ears, and latex gloves for their hands. Each participant is then asked to take out a pencil and paper and write down his or her name, address, telephone number, any medication currently being taken, and any known allergies. Next, the participants are told to take a walk outside the training session, first opening the door and then finding their way around. The simulation involves further directions concerning the specific details of the tasks participants are asked to perform and how they are to take turns assisting each other.

Considering New Attitudes and Behaviors

In the stage of *considering new attitudes and behaviors*, experiential activity is well neigh essential. The goal here is to introduce participants experientially to those actions you would like them to consider and, you hope, eventually adopt. A wide variety of experiential methodologies can now be utilized. Let's look at a few examples.

Games and simulations can be used to test the behavioral style and performance of participants. Playing a game at the beginning of a course allows the trainer to identify the styles and skills that already exist and those that need to be strengthened. Playing a game at the end of the course enables the trainer to assess the instructional experience. Take, for example, a simulation exercise called Desert Survival. Players are told that their plane has crashed in the desert, that their only priority is to survive, and that only certain items are available to them. In the first part of the game, players must decide how to survive individually. Then the game is replayed, with groups working toward team consensus. A trainer could include this simulation exercise at the beginning of a course on team building to assess how well teams work toward consensus. Near the end of the course, a similar exercise, such as Winter Survival, could be employed to measure progress in teamwork.

Games and simulations can also be used to create performance challenges for participants. For example, in a game called Go to Market, participants receive roles in a fictional company that is bringing a product to market and must figure out how to avoid certain management pitfalls in order to beat a competitor with a similar product to market. In another example using a supply-chain simulation, participants are put in charge of a cell phone company. They must select a model of cell phone to produce and suppliers to manufacture them, forecast demand, and react to news and events affecting the cell phone marketplace. At the end of the simulation, participants face the financial results of their decisions and a performance review by the company's board of directors.

Visualization is an interesting method to employ if you want participants to consider a new course of action without having to actually do it first. The following visualization exercise is used in a training program on Dealing with Difficult People.

1. Acknowledge that coping with especially difficult people is a challenge.
2. Invite participants to identify difficult people in their lives and pick one. Then ask them to close their eyes (or use some other focusing technique) and imagine the worst thing that this person could say to them (e.g., "You don't care").
3. Next, direct participants to bring to mind their first reaction to that statement, one that reveals how they might respond if the other person "pushed a button" or "struck a nerve." Give an example of your own to guide their thoughts.
4. Continue the imagery experience by directing participants to take a deep breath and then to imagine acknowledging what the person said, even if it was stated offensively. Suggest the response, "I can sense how angry you are." Next, direct participants to imagine asking the other person to be more specific about the complaint. Suggest the request, "Tell me more about what you want from me or what you are feeling about me." Have them imagine a positive response to their query.
5. End the imagery experience and ask participants to identify which suggestions were helpful and which they wished to question.
6. Remind participants that difficult people typically have trouble managing their own stress and tend to attack whoever is accessible. Taking their statements personally allows you to be a victim.
7. Obtain reactions to this observation.

In-basket assignments are a form of the project method in which letters, memos, phone messages, and so forth are given to the participant playing an assigned role. The participant is then given time to write actual responses to the items in her or his in-basket. This assignment below could be used in its present form as part of a time management program for managers.

For the purpose of this exercise, you are to assume the role of Pat Ladder, manager of the operations department in the J.R. Jones Company. As manager of the operations department, you report to the division head, Kelly MacDonald. The following people report to you:

- Jamie White, secretary
- Mike Crossman, facilities maintenance supervisor
- Linda Stevens, property and supplies supervisor
- Stan Powell, security supervisor
- Jay Snyder, transportation supervisor

All of them are capable people and have been in their respective jobs one year or more. The situation this exercise deals with is as follows.

Today is Monday, December 14. You have been away for several days, so you have come into your office at 8:00 A.M. (early) to catch up and get ready for the day. The normal working day begins at 8:30 A.M. Promptly at 8:30 A.M., you must leave to attend a training meeting. Therefore, you only have about thirty minutes to organize your work, and you want to get as much done as possible. You do not expect to return to your office from the meeting until 10:00 A.M. As you reach your desk at 8:00 A.M., you find items in your in-basket.

As you go through the material, take whatever action is needed, assuming that you are Pat Ladder. Use your own experience as a basis for your decisions.

Make notes to yourself or to others by writing directly on the message, letter, or memo or by attaching notes (use notepaper provided by the facilitator). Draft or write letters and memos where appropriate. Note any phone calls you plan to make, including information about when you plan to make the call and whom you plan to call. Note follow-up dates when further action is necessary. Write on the items themselves where you want them sent, such as "Follow up 12/15" or "File."

After the exercise, you will have an opportunity to compare your actions with others in the group. Remember:

- Put yourself in the position of Pat Ladder.
- Today is December 14.
- You have come in before regular working hours. There is no one else available to help or call.
- You want to get as much out of the way as possible in the thirty minutes you have to spend organizing.
- Record (make mention of) every action you make or intend to make.
- Be prepared to discuss how you handled the exercise with the group.

In-basket methodology can also be utilized in more extensive activities. A superb example is the Looking Glass Inc. simulation training created by the Center for Creative Leadership. A full description of Looking Glass is found in Chapter 18 in this handbook.

Role playing is a staple in any trainer's repertoire in the *considering new attitudes and behaviors* process. (See Chapter 11 in this handbook for an in-depth discussion of role playing as an experiential learning strategy.) It is the best-known way to help participants both experience certain feelings and practice certain skills. Let's say, for example, that your training objective is to have participants get in touch with their feelings about confronting others (something many supervisors and, indeed, people in general, avoid). You can set up a dramatic situation in which participants are required to confront someone else and then discuss the feelings generated by the role-playing experience. In addition, you can design a role-playing exercise to enable participants to practice constructive methods of confrontation.

You have many choices when designing role-playing exercises. One set of choices has to do with the *scripting* of the drama. Scripting is concerned with the development of roles and the situation in which the drama is placed. Here are six options:

1. *Improvisation.* Participants can be given a general scenario and asked to fill in the details themselves. This approach promotes spontaneity and the opportunity to gear the scenario to one's own work experience. Because the situation is not clearly outlined, however, participants may have difficulty creating details on their own.

   Example: "Let's imagine that you are at a restaurant and your order is overcooked. Let's have Mary be that customer and request that the order be redone. What if Frank is the waiter and he gives the customer a hard time? Mary, you will try to persuade the waiter to redo the order. I'd like to see you both use all the skills we've been practicing so far."

2. *Prescribed roles.* Participants can be given a well-prepared set of instructions that state the facts about the roles they are portraying and how they are to behave. This approach gives you the most control over the script, so the dramatic tension you want to create is easily obtainable. However, participants may not identify with the roles and situation you have developed or they may get lost if the scenario is too complex.

   Example: "You are an accountant for an insurance company. You have been with the company since your graduation from college three years ago. You really like the company, feel you are doing well, and are looking forward to a promotion. You like your work except for writing letters, memos, and notes on your accounting reports. You've never admitted it to anyone, but you've always had difficulty in English. Your manager has just called you in. You're afraid it might be about your writing. You'll admit your deficiency only if your manager seems genuinely interested and concerned; otherwise, you will make up excuses."

3. *Semi-prescribed roles.* Participants can be given information about the situation and the characters to be portrayed, but not told how to handle the situation. By not prescribing how characters are to behave, this approach provides greater latitude for the participants. Some of them, however, may create a scenario different from what the trainer intended.

Example: "You are a recently appointed supervisor of a support engineering group that has overall responsibility for maintaining and improving test equipment hardware and software at its repair centers. There are twenty engineers, differing widely in age and experience with the company. Each engineer is responsible for a specific list of test equipment. Until now, staff members have not been called on to work on test equipment that is not on their designated lists. This has meant that, when one of them is sick or on vacation or has a priority assignment, it is difficult for anyone else to take up the slack.

"You have decided to assemble a small team within the group to develop Support Test Equipment Protocols (STEPs) that will provide the information necessary to support the various pieces of test equipment. With these STEPs, you will be able to establish a rotation system within the group. The people you have invited to be on the team include two senior project engineers and two hardware and software technicians.

"This is the first meeting of the group. Begin the meeting."

4. *Replay of life.* Participants can portray themselves in situations they have actually faced. This approach has the advantage of bringing the most realism to the drama. However, it can be difficult to re-create the actual situation and the role play may then flounder.

Example: "I'd like each of you to think about the last time you gave a performance appraisal. Tell your role-playing partner what generally happened and reenact the situation, the first time keeping to the approach you took when you actually gave the appraisal and the second time altering your approach to include the suggestions I have demonstrated."

5. *Participant-prepared skits.* Participants can be asked to develop a role-playing vignette of their own. This approach provides them with time to create a role play and gives them a chance to rehearse before a final performance. Participants will respond especially well to this approach if they are invited to address their real-life problems and incorporate them into the skits. However, some of the spontaneity of the previous options is lost.

Example: "I'd like you and your partner to take the three management styles we've just discussed and create a skit that shows a manager using each of the styles while giving project instructions to an employee. Base your skit on your own experiences. Take about ten minutes to prepare your skits. When you're ready, let me know and we will take a look at what you've come up with."

6. *Dramatic readings.* Participants can be given a previously prepared script to act out. This approach creates the least anxiety of any of the previous options and allows the least skill practice.

   Example: "Here is a script of an exit interview. It demonstrates very effectively some of the problems and some of the solutions we've been examining. In your pairs, one will be the interviewer and the other will be the employee who is leaving the company. Read your parts aloud to get a feel for the tension and relief experienced in the situation."

Of course, a trainer has the option of combining these scripted choices. For example, participants could be asked to read a script and then act out the same drama without the script in front of them. Or they could be allowed to prepare their own scenario, followed by a trainer-prepared scenario. Mixing options in this manner helps to minimize the disadvantages of any single option.

After a role-playing exercise, remember to hold a reflective discussion or review of the role play and/or to giving performance feedback to the role players.

When using role playing as a form of skill practice, the classic way is to do a "show-and-tell" demonstration before asking participants to try it themselves. A more "active" approach is to demonstrate a skill, but with little or no explanation. Instead of telling participants what you are doing, you are asking them to observe carefully the demonstration and tell you what you did. This strategy encourages participants to be mentally alert.

Decide on a skill you want participants to learn. Ask the participants to watch you perform the skill. Just do it, with little or no explanation or commentary about what and why you are doing what you do. (Telling the participants what you are doing will lessen their mental alertness.) Give the participants a visual glimpse of the "big picture" (or the entire skill if it involves several steps). Do not expect retention. At this point, you are merely establishing readiness for learning. Then form the participants into pairs. Demonstrate the first part of the skill, with little or no explanation or commentary. *Ask pairs to discuss with each other what they observed you doing.* Obtain a volunteer to explain what you did. If the participants have difficulty following the procedure, demonstrate again. Acknowledge correct observations. Have the pairs practice with each other the first part of the skill. When it is mastered, proceed with a silent demonstration of the remaining steps, following each part with paired practice. At the end, have participants perform the entire sequence from beginning to end.

If you have the opportunity to teach one participant a skill, you can also use the "show-but-not-tell" approach, but be sure to make the participant comfortable by asking questions such as: "What did you see me do?" "What else did I do?" "Would you like me to show you again?"

Once participants can perform a skill on their own with your assistance, challenge them to redo the skill all by themselves (from beginning to end if it involves more than one step). If you have given them any learning aid that shows them what to do, ask them to put the aid away and try the skill without it.

This is an ideal time to pair up participants as "practice partners." Invite participants to demonstrate to their partners how to perform the skill in question. Using practice pairs, participants feel challenged but not threatened by having to perform under the watchful eye of the trainer or of the entire class.

You can also invite participants who can perform a skill to serve as peer tutors for participants who are still struggling. Be sure that the tutor does not seek to show off rather than assist. Remind tutors that the participants they are helping must be able to do the skill by themselves. Merely showing fellow participants what to do or correcting their performance will not get the job done.

You might also up the challenge by requiring participants to perform a skill after a period of time has intervened and the skill might be forgotten. For example, after helping participants in a business writing class to apply one grammatical rule, you might go on and help them learn several other rules. The challenge you can provide is to have them use a rule they learned a while back without any reminders from you.

Experimenting

In the *experimenting* phase, the experiential activity is no longer simulated or for practice only. It's real-time, on-the-job. As I have suggested earlier, this is the opportunity to engage participants in what I call "experiments in change." Ideal experiments in change are doing activities that the participants have already rehearsed in the prior phase and now are selected for a tryout in the real world. Here is a list of experiments of change suggestions for participants who have been part of a program called "How to Contribute to Your Team's Success."

Select one these "experiments in change" to do within the next week.

- *Involving Others:* Make a list of thing you do independently of others at work. Examine the list and identify items where it would be helpful if you involved others rather than doing things alone. Approach individuals whose expertise or assistance might benefit you and invite them to collaborate with you. Evaluate the results.

- *Promoting Team Leadership:* If you are a leader of a team, examine your leadership style. Think about how you could become a more team-oriented leader. Consider possibilities such as developing a common vision in the group, connecting staff members with each other, and asking for input on policy and procedure. Does your staff respond positively?
- *Facilitating Teamwork:* If you are a member of a group that you would like to see improve, suggest using interactive discussion formats and creative approaches to problem solving. Identify roles that you could play to help facilitate teamwork, such as heading a subcommittee, publishing group accomplishments, or even leading a meeting.
- *Observing Team Dynamics:* Take the time to notice how your team operates. Do people listen to each other? Is there equal opportunity for participation? Perhaps someone has been excluded. Perhaps someone has a good idea, but it's not expressed well. Perhaps the team is on a tangent or caught up in debate when it should be brainstorming. Based on these observations, do what you can to change these dynamics or, in the very least, share your observations with others.

Obtaining Support

In the *obtaining support* phase, there are some useful activities to help participants sustain their efforts at change. One involves having participants plan for conditions that might thwart their progress. Just as any dieter will have a hard time resisting a midnight snack, so a participant subjected to the pressures of his or her job may slip back into old ways of doing things. The most common obstacle is a lack of support from peers, supervisors, or others on the job. Another common obstacle is the lack of time to apply new skills consciously, assess how they've been used, and obtain feedback from others. In addition to offering reentry advice, a training program should build in time for participants to discuss some of the obstacles they expect to meet and ways to overcome them.

For example, a stress management trainer, concerned about the obstacles to carrying out the techniques he had taught participants, decides on an unusual strategy. Instead of giving his usual pep talk at the end of his course, he asks participants to predict the circumstances of their first moment of faltering. Using a mental imagery approach, he encouraged participants to visualize the scene in great detail. He then asked them to develop positive images of coping with the situation that they would be able to keep in their minds' eye when the predicted negative scenario began to unfold in the actual work setting.

Another activity involves self-monitoring. A well-known technique in behavior modification is to ask clients to monitor their own behaviors. For example, in a weight loss program, clients might be asked to note everything they eat, on the assumption that increased awareness will bring about greater self-control. Likewise, you could suggest to participants that they closely monitor their own behavior back on the job as a way to make training benefits last. Keeping a personal diary is one way to perform self-monitoring. The use of ready-made checklists is another approach. Whatever tools are chosen, they ideally should be tried out before the training program ends so that participants can gain comfort with the procedure and understanding of it.

In a session on time management, for example, the trainer asks the participants to brainstorm reminders to help them manage their time more effectively back on the job. Using the sentence stem "Remember to . . . ," the participants came up with the following reminders:

Remember to . . .

- Make a "to-do" list every day
- Make an appointment with myself
- Jot down notes and ideas on index cards
- Set priorities based on importance, not urgency
- Create a "to-read" file and carry it with me when I travel
- Skim books and articles quickly, looking for ideas
- Answer most letters and memos right on the item itself
- Delegate everything I possibly can to others
- Consult my list of lifetime goals once a month and review them if necessary
- Save up trivial matters for a three-hour session once a month

Participants are then asked to select the three reminders that they feel have the most relevance to them and to place them on a card to be posted in their work space.

Obtaining support efforts should include one's immediate supervisor. There are many forms in which that can take place. Here is one example used in a management development program. It involves a serious commitment on the part of the participant and others in the organization to apply what has been learned in the training program and simultaneously to benefit the organization. One of the greatest shortcomings of management development programs is the absence of any tools to measure their effectiveness. To be sure, the participants can complete an evaluation sheet that asks what they like most, least, and so on. However, such questions are not able to fully gauge the impact of training.

The only true measure of impact is the degree to which the participants retain and use the skills learned in the program. In order for this to happen, two conditions must be met:

1. The participant must work on a plan of action that spells out the specific steps for implementing change.
2. This plan is shared with the mentor and manager and supported by them.

The following ACTION PLAN is designed to assist participants in meeting these two conditions, thereby enabling both them and XYZ Company to realize a return on the investment made through participation in the program.

Many topics are covered in this module. Select a project (one of those covered or one of your own) that you plan to focus on. As you complete your ACTION PLAN, try to be as specific as possible in stating your subject. For example, if you were writing an ACTION PLAN for communication, "Written Communication" would be too broad. A more specific subject would be "Developing a Highlight Report Format for the Department."

Within the subject you have selected, state your purpose or reason for selecting it. This will be a brief description of your intent or goal. Using the example of "Developing a Highlight Report Format," the goal might look like this: "Highlight reports contain numerous details. They need to be organized so that the details appear in a logical sequence. After obtaining permission from my manager, I plan to format one of my manager's highlight reports using an eye-opener, transition 1, supporting details, transition 2, and action conclusion."

Goals are stated in broad terms; objectives are quite specific and should include measures by which your progress toward them can be determined. Objectives are the things you must achieve (deadlines, performance indexes, and so on) in order to meet your goal. Building on the same example, the objective might look like this: "To spend one day formatting a highlight report that can be used as a model for subsequent highlight reports."

To achieve your goal, you must schedule activities to move toward it. This section is your blueprint and timetable for reaching the goal. Following our example above, the activities list might look like this:

Activities	Time
1. Meet with mentor to explain my ACTION PLAN.	1. One morning next week, two hours.
2. Meet with my manager to explain my ACTION PLAN and obtain three latest highlight reports written by my manager.	2. One morning next week, two hours (after meeting with mentor).

3. Read over my manager's highlight reports.

3. Two hours following week.

4. Develop a format for organizing a highlight report.

4. Two hours same week as item 3.

5. After obtaining necessary highlight facts, data, and so on, write an actual highlight report for my manager.

5. Four hours before report is due.

As you carry out your schedule of activities, problems or barriers inevitably occur. Sometimes these can be anticipated in advance. Other times they may not. This section of the plan asks you to list and number all problems, present and potential, that you foresee as barriers to completing your activities.

Next, state how you plan to deal with each problem, numbering each solution to agree with the problem it addresses. Following the example, this section might look like this:

Problems

1. Manager may not be able to get me all the facts and data needed to complete the actual highlight report.

Solutions

1. Work directly with manager in writing highlight report.

Finally, organizations are acknowledging that follow-up coaching really helps to extend the value of training. This has been especially true in leadership training programs, where the development of key leaders is critical to the organization's future success. These individuals receive private coaching by so-called "executive" coaches who consult intensively with their clients, often focusing on those barriers that prevent them from achieving their maximum potential. Although expensive, this service can provide a strong return on investment. Other levels of the organization can benefit from coaching as well. Although not as common, group coaching is starting to be offered to personnel who are not traditionally seen as coaching clients. In small groups, participants have the opportunity for continuing practice of vital skills and for discussion of common obstacles for success. For example, after a four-day program on project management tools, participants were offered an additional four to six weeks of weekly group coaching sessions. Those who chose to attend were 95 percent more likely to use the project management tools taught in the training than those who did not attend.

Peer support groups have also proven to provide useful training follow-up. Most meet on a regular basis (e.g., monthly), often over lunch, to continue to work on course skills or issues they've encountered at work. When successful, peers support each other, from providing small suggestions on how to handle difficult situations to undertaking joint initiatives that improve the quality of their work context. For example, a support group was formed after attending a training program on meeting management. They not only shared common problems, such as how to equalize participation at meetings, but also organized a process whereby peers observed each other's meetings and provided feedback and recommendations for best practices.

Conclusion

Hopefully, a case for experiential learning as a critical aspect for supporting change has been made in this chapter. Remember the key points:

- The need for change occurs in many arenas in the workplace.
- Change is difficult.
- In order to facilitate change, look at it as a five-step process. Use that process as a framework for your planning as a facilitator of change.
- Diversify the kinds of experiential strategies you use in your design.

CHAPTER TWO

THEORETICAL FOUNDATIONS OF EXPERIENTIAL LEARNING

Stephen Fiore, David Metcalf and Rudy McDaniel

Stephen M. Fiore is an assistant professor with the University of Central Florida's Cognitive Sciences Program in the Department of Philosophy and director of the Consortium for Research in Adaptive Distributed Learning Environments at UCF's Institute for Simulation and Training and Team Performance Laboratory. He earned his Ph.D. degree in cognitive psychology from the University of Pittsburgh, Learning Research and Development Center. He maintains a multidisciplinary research interest that incorporates aspects of cognitive, social, and organizational psychology in the investigation of learning and performance in individuals and teams. He is co-editor of a recent volume on *Team Cognition* and has published in the area of learning, memory, and problem solving at the individual and the group level. Steve has helped to secure and manage nearly $4 million in research funding from organizations such as the National Science Foundation, the Transportation Security Administration, the Office of Naval Research, and the Air Force Office of Scientific Research.

David Metcalf II is an online faculty member and researcher in knowledge and learning at Walden University and the University of South Florida. He explores many leading-edge innovations related to experiential learning. Specific areas of focus include learning business strategy, performance measurement, operational excellence, outsourcing, blended learning, and mobile learning. David was formerly the chief learning technologist at RWD Technologies. He joined RWD with the sale of his NASA Kennedy Space Center laboratory spin-off company, Merrimac. Prior to spinoff, he was the lead multimedia designer at NASA KSC. He is the co-author of *Blended eLearning: Integrating Knowledge, Performance Support, and Online Learning* and recently participated as chapter author on "Operational Excellence Through Blended eLearning" for Elliott Masie's book, *Rants, Raves, and Reflections in Learning*. His newest book, *mLearning: Mobile Learning and Performance*, is now available.

Rudy McDaniel is assistant professor of digital media for the School of Film and Digital Media at the University of Central Florida. Rudy's research interests include narrative theory, video games and learning technologies, knowledge management frameworks, and XML. As a technology consultant, he has designed web-based applications for clients such as the IEEE Society and the Library of Congress. Rudy is currently director of the Partnership for Research on Synthetic Experience (PROSE) lab at UCF.

Contact Information
Stephen M. Fiore, Ph.D.
Institute for Simulation and Training
University of Central Florida
3100 Technology Parkway, Suite 140
Orlando, FL 32826
(407) 882–0298
sfiore@ist.ucf.edu

David Metcalf, Ph.D.
Faculty, Walden University, and Researcher, Institute for
Simulation and Training
University of Central Florida
(407) 882–1496
dmetcalf@ist.ucf.edu

Rudy McDaniel, Ph.D.
Assistant Professor of Digital Media
School of Film and Digital Media
University of Central Florida
Orlando, FL 32816
OTC500 Room 144
(407) 823–2488
rmcdaniel@dm.ucf.edu

IN THIS CHAPTER, we will discuss how theory and methods from cognitive and simulation sciences can be integrated with principles of narrative theory in order to produce powerful experiential learning systems. By grounding these ideas within Kolb's experiential learning cycle (Kolb, 1984), we suggest that the principled and creative use of story within simulation can scaffold thinking, thus supporting both reflective observation and abstract conceptualization. Second, we suggest that well-designed simulations that encourage active experimentation and supply concrete experience support the "doing" that is foundational to the experiential learning process.

In this chapter, we first describe a set of the core elements of experiential learning, specifically focusing on learning and transfer and the importance of context and environment to this task. We then discuss narrative theory, also from a theoretical perspective, in order to illustrate how elements of narrative can be implemented into a simulated environment. Next, we reveal how a theoretically sound integration of these factors within experiential learning supports the affective, behavioral, and cognitive elements of experience. Finally, we describe what we see as relevant examples from industry and academia. These examples illustrate how the principled and informed use of narrative, linked with simulation, has the potential to produce powerful learning outcomes.

Learning and Transfer

In this section, we discuss some of the cognitive underpinnings of the experiential learning (EL) cycle. Following Kolb (1984), we define learning as "the process whereby knowledge is created through the transformation of experience" with knowledge resulting from "the combination of grasping and transforming experience" (p. 41). We describe here some of the fundamental cognitive processes necessary for the design and delivery of simulation and training tools that support experiential learning. Our main point is that context is inextricably linked with the notion of learning and transfer.

Context and Cognition

Context has as its Latin root, *contextus*, "a joining together," which, in turn, was derived from *contexere*, "to weave together," with *com* meaning "together" and *texure*, "to weave." What must be recognized is that a particular context helps us to weave together our understanding of events in order to form a mental model of the world with which we are interacting at any given moment in time. This definition is presented not as an academic exercise, but rather to support the argument that contextual elements represent a critical factor for understanding human learning.

In particular, the definition of context illustrates why researchers must attend to context in respect to the design and/or methods developed and used for learning. Over the years, there have been a number of theoretical and methodological ideologies that have come forth in debates concerning the understanding of how context influences and interacts with learning.

The psychological sciences have a long history of producing competing methods and theories for understanding the complex phenomena associated with human learning. These can be generally classified into one of two primary approaches. On the one hand is *in vitro* research, which describes laboratory approaches that rely on tasks that can repeatedly reproduce some set of standardized conditions. On the other hand is *in vivo* research, where behavior is investigated in natural contexts in order to understand how dynamic and contextual factors influence and/or determine performance. This latter argument emerged primarily from ecological psychology (e.g., Gibson, 1966), with some researchers suggesting its roots can be traced back to Bartlett (1932) and even Dewey (1902). Nonetheless, ecological psychology is most closely associated with the writings of J.J. Gibson, who argued that human behavior must be understood in its relation to the environment and noted how significantly our environment affects our cognition. Some academics within ecological psychology use the term "radically situated" when referring to this aspect of mental behavior (e.g., Barker, 1968). Essentially, Gibson viewed humans as being inextricably linked with a larger system (the environment), and he argued that in order to adequately understand humans within this system, the environment must always be part of the analysis.

More specifically, and from a methodological perspective, Hoffman and Deffenbacher (1993) described how these ecological factors must be an essential part of psychological research if we are to truly understand humans in context. They argued that both theoretical and practical gains can be realized by simultaneously considering both ecological *and* epistemological factors associated with human learning and behavior. They described such research in human behavior in terms of *epistemological relevance* and *ecological salience*. Epistemological relevance pertains to the degree to which the experimental approach relies on concepts from existing theories, and ecological salience describes the degree to which the materials or tasks of study pertain to what is actually perceived or done in the context in which the cognition is occurring.

These debates led to the creation of fairly intense theoretical views on human behavior, one of which was the *situated cognition* approach to human behavior. For example, when writing about cognition and learning, Clancey (1991) argues the following:

> Indeed, situated cognition leads us to reject both the idea that human memory
> consists of stored representations (i.e., descriptions of how behavior or the
> world appear to an observer over time) and the idea that reality has objective

properties (Lakoff, 1987; Tyler, 1978). There is no correspondence between mental processes and the world because both our habits and what we claim to be true arise dialectically, by the interaction of mental processes and the environment. Concepts are not pre-defined feature lists stored like things in my head. I regenerate and reconstruct such representations in my acts of speaking, writing, drawing. (p. 110)

The latest incarnation of this view, found in a theory known as *embodied cognition*, dissolves any boundaries between cognition and the environmental context. From philosophy to neuroscience, the integration of embodiment and cognition is becoming increasingly recognized as a foundational issue that needs to be considered in its entirety. This notion states that:

> . . . bodiness is a combination of a physical structure (to the biological body) and an experiential structure, which corresponds to the living, moving, suffering, and enjoying body. From here we arrive at the dual acceptation of embodied cognition, which refers, on one hand, to the grounding of cognitive processes in the brain's neuroanatomical substratum, and on the other, to the derivation of cognitive processes from the organism's sensorimotor experiences." (Garbarini & Adenzato, 2004, p. 101)

What appears to be essential in these arguments is the concept of context and the claim that cognition and learning are inextricably linked to context. With this assertion in mind, we turn next to a theory of learning and transfer that empirically supports the important role that contextual processes play in cognition. We then discuss how the generalizability of this theory fits well with the complexities of modern workplaces.

Context and Transfer

The acquisition of knowledge and skills for today's complex workplace cuts across cognitive processes, ranging from perception and memory to category learning, problem solving, and decision making. Given the complexity and variety of these task environments, we briefly review a theoretical approach to learning that has evolved over the last quarter of the 20th century in order to encompass a wide range of cognition. In particular, transfer appropriate processing (TAP) can be used to support an understanding of experiential learning within a variety of different domains. This theory draws from over twenty years of research in cognitive psychology (e.g., Adams, Kasserman, Perfetto, Bransford, & Franks, 1988; Morris, Bransford, & Franks, 1977; Needham & Begg, 1991; Perfetto, Bransford, & Franks, 1983).

In its initial incarnation, TAP was used to argue against principles of levels-of-processing theory (Craik & Lockhart, 1972) and the supposed encoding strength of deeper processing (Morris, Bransford, & Franks, 1977). Some had argued that, rather than the depth of processing, "It is the qualitative nature of the task, the kind of operations carried out on the items that determines retention" (Craik & Tulving, 1975, p. 290). Original investigations of this theory focused on recognition and recall, but it has been greatly expanded on in order to account for dissociations in the types of implicit and explicit memory tasks used in response to verbal and pictorial stimuli (e.g., Roediger & Blaxton; 1987; Roediger, Weldon, & Challis 1989). More recently, the TAP theory has been used to disentangle prospective memory success/failure by focusing on the relation between the intent to perform and the task itself in which the memory requirement is embedded (Marsh, Hicks, & Hancock, 2000). Thus, TAP has been effectively used to help us understand recognition and recall memory, implicit and explicit memory tests, and prospective memory—all by exploring how a variety of contextual factors influence cognitive processing.

Transfer appropriate processing theory has additionally encompassed more complex cognitive processes. For example, within problem-solving research, TAP theory supports the notion that initial strategies influence later problem solving and that the matching of strategies during learning and test facilitates overall problem-solving effectiveness. This research has been conducted on everything from simple puzzle tasks (Adams, Kasserman, Yearwood, Perfetto, Bransford, & Franks, 1988) to more complex tasks such as learning graphics software (Caplan & Schooler, 1990). Finally, studies in using problem-based learning to train clinical reasoning for medical students have been developing a theoretical accounting of the learning process using TAP (Hmelo, 1998). More recently, TAP theory was used to account for varieties of findings in category learning. Markman and Ross (2003) suggest that "category acquisition occurs in the course of using categories for different functions. The particular information that is acquired about a category member in the context of carrying out a particular task depends on the information that is required to carry out that task successfully" (pp. 609–610). As such, TAP theory has helped researchers in more complex areas of cognition to understand how context across learning and later retrieval impacts process and performance.

Theoretical Issues of Context, TAP, and Simulations for Training

From the perspective of understanding experiential learning, what is important to recognize with TAP theory is that synchronization between processes engaged during the time of learning or acquisition of a given material and the eventual use of that material is crucial for performance across a surprising number of tasks (Roediger, Gallo, & Geraci, 2002). Contextual factors, therefore, are critical to learning and retention over and above what is typically described in the learning literature. More specifically, TAP is most cogent with respect to experiential learning in that TAP theory has consistently identified that *"recapitulating specific encoding and retrieval operations enhances performance"* (p. 325). This notion is critical to experiential learning, given that the study of learning can so often be contextually bound, yet examples of linkings between TAP theory and experiential learning have been rare.

Another important issue related to contextual learning is that the simulation and training literature does not speak about context as a disparate unit. Instead, it often refers to notions of *fidelity* in research paradigms and notes how certain components of the learning environment must match the actual environment being trained. Nonetheless, a substantial body of research suggests that only certain components of the simulation need to be faithful to the operational setting. Simulation researchers note that the use of simulations with high physical fidelity had little if any impact on the actual operational job tasks (Taylor, Lintern, Hulin, et al., 1999). Similarly, research has successfully used low fidelity PC-based simulations to train complex individual and teamwork skills (Gopher, Weil, & Bareket, 1994; Jentsch & Bowers, 1998; Taylor, Lintern, Hulin, et al., 1999). The general guidance from research in simulations is that fidelity needs to be determined by the task's behavioral and cognitive requirements such that they can support an appropriate learning environment (Salas & Burke, 2002). Thus, the concept of fidelity is similar to what we have suggested regarding context. Importantly, the research on fidelity suggests that it is the mental process to which we must be faithful, not necessarily the physical environment. Thus, ecological validity can be construed as a form of task-relevant fidelity to a cognitive process or to a particular content. In particular, *cognitive* fidelity is the term used to describe a requirement for the learning environment to faithfully reproduce the mental processes necessary for a given task (see Durlach, & Mavor, 1995; Entin, Serfaty, Elliott, & Schiflett, 2001).

In this section, we showed how context, transfer, and fidelity provide a firm foundation for an overall epistemology in experiential learning. We submit that the strong foundation of research in transfer appropriate processing is a cogent means with which to support experiential learning. In particular, TAP theory can help to address the lack of true integration of the simulation and experiential learning research communities and the equivocal nature of the findings with respect to the differing importance of physical, task, and cognitive fidelity across a variety of experiential learning studies. Specifically, TAP theory can help us to understand what aspects of fidelity are important to promote learning and transfer. To this end, the practicing community must consider how the conditions at acquisition of the knowledge match conditions at the application of that knowledge.

As TAP has shown the importance of qualitative guidance for simulation and training, we turn next to another methodology that is highly compatible with qualitative transfer between learning and operational environments. Not surprisingly, this technique is something human society is already highly dependent on for many types of learning and knowledge acquisition: storytelling.

Narrative Theory

Using the principles of narrative theory, we examine a framework of representation that is natively intuitive and familiar to anyone who has ever told a story in order to illustrate a point or to clarify an example. Narratology, a line of critical inquiry developed by literary theorists in the 1960s, attempts to study and classify narratives based on the various structural and syntactical elements of discourse found in stories (see Bal, 1997; Barthes, 1998; Genette, 1980; McQuillan 2000; Onega & Landa, 1996). In this section, we explain the fundamental properties and theories of narratology and explore the implications of such a paradigm for addressing issues in experiential learning. This overview illustrates how this paradigm may be useful for developing an improved model for experiential learning that is grounded theoretically and practically in an organizational context.

Pioneering accounts of successful learning and training using storytelling and creative implementations of the narrative form can be found in many different industries, from the World Bank and the Bank of Canada to NASA and IBM. Perhaps most effectively, researchers and practitioners in knowledge management (KM) have relied on narrative and story to capture organizational content as well as convey organizational history. According to Davenport and Prusak (1997), this approach uses information technology to maximize the *human* elements of communication while concurrently leveraging the flexibility and processing power of computers and digital networks. Such an approach allows technology to take on a more organic and flexible role within social networks and encourages the technological solutions to adapt to their users, rather than the more traditional (and unfortunate) reversal of this model.

For simplicity's sake, in our discussion of narratology we use the terms "narrative" and "story" interchangeably. Although narrative may also refer to the actual act of narrating, to the practice of telling a story, or even to the particular telling of a story using a particular medium, in this chapter we prefer to adopt a more colloquial definition in which narrative and story are equivalent semantic entities (c.f., Bal, 1997; Genette, 1980). To refer to the active task of storytelling, we use the terms "narration" or "narrating." We broadly define a story or narrative to be a series of events experienced by a central character (or protagonist) as this character struggles to overcome one or more obstacles (or antagonists) within some specific environment. In addition to the primary character serving as a protagonist, additional *actors* or *agents* exist within the narrative to bond with this central character or to provide other dramatic functions. The analysis of dramatic expression in narrative form has been the territory of literary scholars for hundreds of years and we turn next to the field of literary theory for an explanation of the fundamental nature of narrative.

Literary treatments of narrative vary according to the perspective from which they are generated. For example, a field of inquiry in literature known as structuralist semiotics attempts to break down a linguistic system into logical units known as signs. Signs, in turn, are composed of binary relationship between a *signifier,* or the sound pattern of a word, and a *signified,* or the actual concept or meaning of a word (see Sausssure, Bally, Sechehaye, & Riedlinger, 1986). To some theorists, then, a story is in fact a *signified* entity, while a narrative serves as a *signifier* for a particular story (Genette, 1980, p. 27). In this model, a single story might have multiple narratives, depending on the characteristics of the storytelling medium and the particular methods of narration (e.g., whether the story is told from the point of view of an omniscient narrator or rather from the point of view of a character in the story itself). While structuralism was later challenged by the deconstructionist movement (see Derrida, 1997) on the basis of being too rigid and reductive, the ideas it brought for the formal taxonomy of language have nonetheless proven useful in various contexts.

Russian formalists later appropriated the term *narratology* in order to reference the same type of semiotic distinction in a broader narrative context. In this paradigm, the *fabula* is the chronological construction of events in a particular story (analogous to the plot of a story), while the *sjuzhet* is the representation of these events as told through a particular medium. The *fabula* is the story; the *sjuzhet* is the telling. In this sense, one *fabula* or plot can have many different *sjuzhets,* or manifestations. Further distinctions of narrative are possible on a more general level; stories can be classified based on their medium or form, the subset of narrative techniques used in their construction, the point of view of the narrator, the type of plot structure, the sources of dramatic tension, their selection of plot devices and primary characters, and so forth.

Genette's *Narrative Discourse* (1980) is a structuralist work that attempts to formulate a systematic theory of narrative based on the characteristics of order (narrative time), duration, frequency, mood, and voice. Of particular interest in this work is Genette's tendency to represent narrative elements using what he calls "pseudo-mathematical formulas" (p. 114). For example, in his discussion of narrative frequency, Genette proposes formulas for the narration of a story that happened once (1N/1S), a repeated narration of a repeated story (nN/nS), or the repeated narration of a single story (nN/1S) (pp. 114–115). What is of some use to experiential learning theory is not necessarily the formulas themselves, but rather the general idea that narration can be algorithmically represented in a fashion suitable for finite state representation or for the application of graph or pathfinding theories. In these narrative graphs, the vertices are composed of fabula events. In this fashion, an existing narrative can be broken down into its fabula or plot event structure, and, by extension, be modeled computationally as a series of finite states. Inserting an actor or agent into the beginning state of this series then allows an audience to experience the story as that story is told through the eyes of a protagonist. Furthermore, once the plot is modeled in some fashion, perhaps using the object-oriented programming methodology (see Fiore, Johnston, & McDaniel, 2005, for an example) various sjuzhets can be generated simply by rendering or displaying the story using different types of technological mediums. These mediums may be plain text or HTML renditions of the story on a website, Flash-animated or cartoon-type versions with models of the various characters, film versions with simulated or real actors and actresses, or auditory versions of the story as read by a narrator or the protagonist.

Other literary studies of the narrative form and plot, while not always associated with the structuralist ideas of narratology, can be equally useful for thinking about how to tease apart the various elements of a given narrative or how to construct a new narrative that is compelling and worthwhile to the reader, viewer, or listener. For instance, studies of the elements of plot and drama generally arrive at a relatively small finite number of basic plots or dramatic situations (c.f. Booker, 2005; Polti, 2003). Booker (2005) speculates that there are essentially seven basic plots involved in storytelling: overcoming the monster, rags to riches, the quest, voyage and return, comedy, tragedy, and rebirth. While such a collection of plots seems alarmingly small and, at first consideration, woefully inadequate, careful analysis of successful stories generally reveals that many of these stories' authors do impressive jobs of combining plots and introducing slight variations in conventional formulas in order to maintain the interest and enthusiasm of an audience.

For example, Tolkien's *Lord of the Rings* (1967) is only one such story that contains examples of each of Booker's fundamental plot types (Booker, 2005, pp. 316–321). Frodo's journey to return the Ring of Power to the perilous land of Mordor obviously involves a quest, which is arguably the most salient of the seven plots. Frodo's company also undertakes a voyage from and return to the safety of the shire, and the narrative recounts an overcoming of several variations of monsters, the Dark Lord Sauron acting as the most heinous and powerful of these entities. The rags to riches plot is found in Sam the Hobbit's ascension to "Sam the Wise" as he transforms himself from an ordinary character at the beginning of the story to an unfailingly loyal and wise companion to Frodo by the end

(Booker, p. 318). Other instances of the remaining plots are evident throughout the story as Frodo and his band of adventurers encounter tragedy, romance, surprise, and adversity.

Other examples of narrative conformity to a small number of plots abound, regardless of the literary depth or semantic complexity of a particular story. For example, literature intended for young adults, such as the phenomenally successful Harry Potter series by J.K. Rowling or the Inheritance trilogy by Christopher Paolini, exhibits a similar pattern of normative plot structures with novel combinations and transformations of traditional fabulas. In these examples as well as in Tolkien's work, the plots that are apparent in such stories are those we expect to find in the genre of fantasy; spells, magical creatures, and evil antagonists are the types of plot devices we associate with the stories characterized as fantasy fiction. Other archetypal elements are, of course, associated with other genres of story—a reader will expect to encounter quite a different assemblage of actors and environments when picking up a science fiction novel or an existential short story.

In this section, we examined some of the fundamental ideas from narratology and considered the notion that all stories can be fashioned from a relatively small number of foundational plots. From this brief analysis, we draw what we believe to be two important conclusions related to the use of simulated narrative as a tool for experiential learning. First, we assert that it is possible to borrow from the work of structuralist theorists in order to define potential ways to represent and model information in narrative form. Second, we believe that it is not wholly implausible to formulate a small number of basic scenario plots with which to generate experiential narratives or scenarios of astonishing diversity. In other words, a series of basic plots can be used to convey the experiences involved with a wide variety of potential event sequences. The confluence of these is a potentially powerful means through which to create compelling experiential learning scenarios. In our next section, we turn briefly once again to material from the psychological sciences to help explain why it is that such predictable plot devices can hold so much appeal for us as narrative consumers and to speculate as to how new tools might be developed in order to take advantage of this narrative appeal to support sophisticated learning environments.

Linking Learning and Transfer with Narrative Theory

While the intricate details of narrative theory may be more interesting to literary theorists and critics, the notion of experiential learning is quite pertinent to the ways in which narrative information and the psychological processes involving the human experience intersect. In prior work, Fiore, Johnston, and McDaniel (2006) note the influences of narrative on cognitive, social, and affective dimensions of experience. In this section, we select key research from each of these areas and discuss examples in which these various modes of information processing are affected, influenced, or advised by the narrative form. Next, we consider some examples of narrative techniques at work in organizational learning scenarios. We conclude with a brief interdisciplinary examination of the ways in which narrative can be used as a tool for organizational or experiential learning in digitized environments.

Our first task is to return to the notion of context and environment and to examine narrative through a psychological lens. First, we turn to the cognitive implications of storytelling. Jerome Bruner (1991) is well known for identifying ten features of narrative in his article *The Narrative Construction of Reality*. He outlined each of these ten features and explained the ways in which they informed or framed our observations about the world. Among these ten features were three that are especially pertinent to our discussion thus far. Bruner defines these three features as *normativeness, genericness,* and *canonicity and breach.* Normativeness and genericness suggest that narrative's use of genre is a way of representing human experience in a predefined fashion. Bruner also notes that "[genres] are also ways of telling that predispose us to use our minds and sensibilities in particular ways" (p. 15). In other words, not only do narratives function as conduits for prior experiences that one has encountered, but they also function as active agents of shaping and reconstructing knowledge as a person experiences a story. Another of Bruner's features, canonicity and breach, is found in those especially compelling stories in which "an implicit canonical script has been breached, violated, or deviated from" in order to challenge a reader's expectations and deviate from the narrative pattern expected by a reader (p. 11). Bruner argues that it is the breach in a script that makes the story interesting in the first place; that is, a story would not necessarily be very engaging to a reader if it were only a description of the mundane activities of one's day-to-day life. Only when something out of the ordinary occurs does a story become compelling enough to tell. Bruner's ideas about narrative provide some general guidance as to why narratives are so powerful as cognitive structures and as communicative technologies.

Additional research has explored the use of narrative as a tool for learning and mental organization. Ong (1982) studied the communication patterns of primarily oral cultures and noted the reliance of such cultures on mnemonic devices such as the rhythmic or formulaic discourse patterns found in stories. In a pre-literate culture, proverbial types of expression were necessary to retain the intricate details present in the oral expressions of prior experiences and scenarios as recalled by storytellers. A long line of research also documents the importance of script-like or schematic structures in human cognition (Bartlett, 1932; Bower & Morrow, 1990; Bransford & Franks, 1971; Gagne & Glaser, 1987; Mandler, 1984; Rumelhart, 1980; Schank & Abelson, 1977; Trabasso & Sperry, 1985).

Next, we can consider the affective and social dimensions of narrative. Aside from its cognitive benefits, narrative is also touted for its ability to both elicit and communicate affective and social types of information. For instance, consider a corporation that has recently opened a new division across the country and that is attempting to gather market research based on that new location. A simple fact such as "We have recently opened a new customer service outlet in Spokane with unsuccessful results" becomes more powerful and expressive when reshaped into a brief (but complete) story such as "As assistant manager of our new service outlet in Spokane, I was recently surprised by the level of public animosity that accompanied our grand opening. Apparently, the construction process had disturbed a famous local bald eagle nest and frightened away the bird. During the first day of sales, our customers were ambivalent at best, and at worst, openly hostile." In addition to the minimalist details provided by the original piece of information, the narrative version adds agency (the assistant manager serving as the protagonist), conflict (the specific reason for the failure of the new location to garner public support), environment (a more precise setting), and emotion (the specific affective reaction of both the protagonist [surprise] and the external narrative agents in the story [public animosity, ambivalence, and hostility]). The additional contextual details present in the narrative version allow management to make a more informed decision as to how to handle the incident and how to formulate a public response.

Unfortunately, in addition to its affective use as a linking mechanism for after-the-fact types of applications, a narrative account is also that much more *personal* for the employee, both during the formation of the story and during its dissemination or distribution to groups for use or analysis. Considerations for dealing with hesitant employees should be made. Furthermore, the potentially personal elements that make their ways into stories must also be dealt with in terms of security and mechanisms for enforcing personal privacy or adequately anonymizing the narrative experiences (whether collected through interviews or more high-tech mechanisms) gathered in corporate environments. More informal narrative exchanges such as this routinely occur across the country in boardrooms or with technicians during coffee breaks (see Orr, 1996) in order to institute executive policies and to propagate expert knowledge.

Additional ideas for linking the narrative form with digital technologies can be found in literature from the computer sciences. For instance, Minsky (1985) formulated a methodology for representing a story as a generic structure, which he calls a "story-frame," wherein new instances of stories are formed by filling in generic placeholding terminals within this frame with specific instances of a time setting, a place setting, a protagonist, a central concern, and an antagonist (p. 265). Schank (1995) and his team at Yale invented the concept of a narrative script, which is "a set of expectations about what will happen next in a well-understood situation" (p. 7). Using the two techniques, it is possible to create a narrative framework in which story scripts with narrative terminals are created by an administrator in order to solicit those stories appropriate to a particular organizational event. As new stories are created, the generic placeholders are replaced with information specific to the stories being created by employees or users. A more robust definition of this narrative framework is found in McDaniel (2004), Fiore, McDaniel, and Johnston (2005), and in the second part of this chapter, in which we discuss the EDNA-E narrative knowledge management application.

From this brief interdisciplinary literature review, we can draw several tentative conclusions. First, it now seems plausible that we can model stories in simulation environments by representing them as a series of narrative events with transitions between events that indicate the progress of the primary character in the story as narration progresses. These events, when seen in their entirety, are equivalent to the fabula or the plot of the narrative. Second, we know that some research argues that there is a small subset of basic plots from which all successful (and by successful, we mean those stories that captivate a reader's attention and encourage him or her to finish the story) narratives are drawn. With this in mind, we suggest that this represents a powerful tool in which to embed contextual factors key to learning. In particular, by linking technology and narrative, we increase the possibility for transfer of learning to the operational environment. Specifically, it is possible to create a scriptable rubric for classifying stories based on their content or genre, or for specifying how new stories should be created in order to adhere to some set of carefully formulated learning objectives. Finally, we can acknowledge the inherent flexibility of narrative and perhaps agree that this flexibility may be well-suited for the cognitive interpretation of complex events in experience management.

In sum, in this section we illustrated how, in addition to its role in the normal social channels of storytelling, the narrative form is adaptable to a technological or simulated digital environment as a tool for encapsulating or soliciting stories from employees or users. While such narrative information cannot easily be condensed into a traditional data structure, it does provide a linkage mechanism for additional information, such as the affective dissatisfaction recounted in the brief narrative account above. We feel that such affective information can be extremely valuable for directing and influencing the decisions of training and simulation scenarios. Moreover, when these narrative mechanisms are coupled with technology, the possibilities for experience-based learning and institutional growth are even more impressive.

Having presented a significant degree of theorizing on narrative and the types of stories useful for experiential learning, we turn next to a description of the characteristics of stories for simulation and learning and on sample applications. We hope that many of the theoretical features and ideas we have just discussed, such as context and environment, transfer appropriate processing, and narrative theory, will become concrete through the various examples and illustrations we next provide.

Sample Applications/Examples

Organizational Narrative

From a corporate context, the notion of using story as a tool for organizational knowledge management has been well-documented in the literature (Abma, 2003; Denning, 2001, 2004; Post, 2002; Snowden, 2001; Swap, Leonard, Shields, & Abrams, 2001). Steven Denning has written two influential books that discuss the notion of using narrative as a tool for organizational learning and as a device to improve interpersonal communications. In *The Springboard,* Denning identifies three characteristics of effective storytelling for the purposes of knowledge management. The first of his characteristics is *connectedness,* the feature allowing the audience to find an opening with which to access the story and understand it on their own terms. This allows readers to relate to a story using their own backgrounds and experiences. His second characteristic is *strangeness,* which refers to the novelty or originality of a story as a result of the deviation of an audience's expectations. This fits in nicely with Bruner's notion of canonicity and breach, discussed earlier in the chapter, and verifies the idea that stories violating expectations are those types of stories that are what Bruner characterizes as being "tales worth telling" (p. 11). Denning's last characteristic of the "springboard story" is that of *comprehensibility* or of allowing an audience to connect the experiences of a story to their own lives. Again, this is in line with Bruner's ideas, in that narrative is a frame for reality in its implicit normativeness. This allows a properly crafted story to encapsulate real-world experiences and redistribute them in a way that is comprehensible in different ways by different members of an audience. Denning notes that there must be a proper balance between strangeness and comprehensibility in order for an organizational story to be effective in accomplishing its goal.

Denning's later book, *Squirrel Inc.* (2004), considers seven organizational objectives that can be accomplished using various types of stories. These objectives are to communicate complex ideas and encourage action, to communicate personal details, to communicate values, to encourage group work, to tame or neutralize gossip, to share information and knowledge, and to lead and provide visionary focus (p. 150). Several of these objectives, if not all of them, are directly relevant to the typical types of goals found in experiential learning scenarios.

Another pioneer in the field of organizational narrative is David Snowden, who worked for IBM for many years in the field of knowledge management. Upon his departure from IBM, he formed a unique research collective/consultancy called Cynefin to explore how one can leverage the integration of a number of theoretical concepts in the support of management theory and practice. Cynefin has been built around social complexity theory, simply described as that application of complexity theory to human systems (see Figure 2.1). In so doing Cynefin enables an organization to better engage in sense making by understanding the relationships among the way things are, the way we perceive our world, and the way we understand our world. In so doing we are able to recognize the complex networks that have evolved to support an organization at the intra- and inter-organizational level. Finally, the narrative form allows one to more efficiently gather and effectively interpret the data that exists in the environment (see Figure 2.2) so as to better represent the patterns of human activity (www.cynefin.net).

Cynefin is one example of how the narrative form is being used in the corporate world as part of information systems and management consulting. For analysis and searching of complex data, narrative provides context and an experiential learning form (refer to www.cynefin.net for additional detail and more recent developments).

FIGURE 2.1. CYNEFIN SENSE MAKING FRAMEWORK

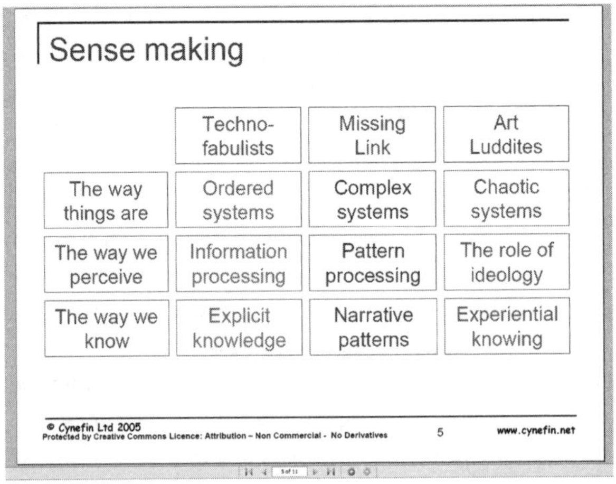

Sense making			
	Techno-fabulists	Missing Link	Art Luddites
The way things are	Ordered systems	Complex systems	Chaotic systems
The way we perceive	Information processing	Pattern processing	The role of ideology
The way we know	Explicit knowledge	Narrative patterns	Experiential knowing

© Cynefin Ltd 2005
Protected by Creative Commons Licence: Attribution – Non Commercial - No Derivatives   5   www.cynefin.net

From www.cynefin.net

FIGURE 2.2. MASS NARRATIVE: JUMPING INDICATORS

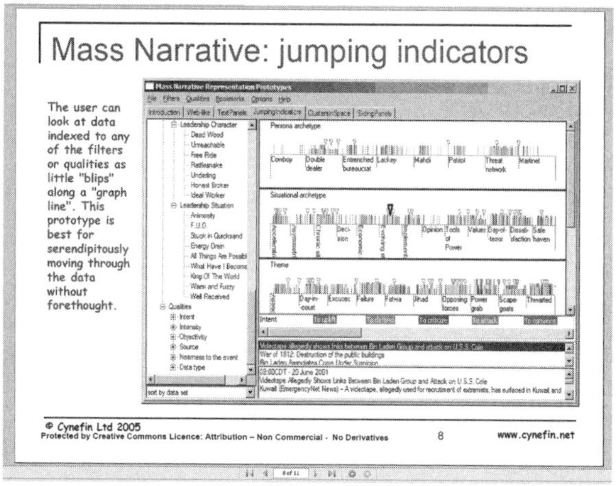

Root Learning

Another example employs visual narrative techniques and an experiential element of game play to produce a compelling training and strategy alignment activity. Many large organizations, such as Alltel, GM, Pacificare, and Scotiabank, have all presented findings related to the reaction-level results of their initiatives using Root Learning (www.rootlearning.com/www/caseStudies.asp, 2005). For example, GM initiated this activity in their attempts to foster organizational change, particularly in the area of transforming human resources. As part of a learning initiative titled *HR Skills for Success,* the overall goal was to provide an experiential context for human resources personnel to better understand the organization's need for change (www.rootlearning.com/www/caseGM.asp, 2005). Root learning worked with thousands of GM employees in the hope of more simply conveying the complex messages emerging from the organizational change environment. Their aim was to transcend cultural and language barriers by employing narrative and visual metaphor via what they have labeled the Learning Map® process. To evaluate the effectiveness of this tool, the company self-reported data suggesting that participants felt that they had obtained both a clearer understanding of the importance of organizational change and that the learning map technique was an effective tool to convey this. Participants have also reported that, in international, cross-cultural settings, the ability to visually represent a transformation story in which the organization is compared to the long-term strategic goals can build alignment among disparate parts of a large, complex organization and promote initial change management.

Text-Based Applications

While lacking in immersive technology and high-fidelity graphics, textual story-based technologies are helpful for several types of experiential learning scenarios. For one thing, their light technological footprint means that they generally run with relatively few resources and do not require expensive hardware. For another, they can be useful for revealing algorithmic procedures for representing stories in digital environments. Finally, text-based storytelling systems can collect a text-based version of an experience that can then be streamed to any number of sophisticated media outlets—one fabula, many sjuzhets.

One example of a textual narrative knowledge management application that allows for the capture of contextual and environmental information is the Event-Driven Narrative Analysis Engine (EDNA-E) application developed at the University of Central Florida (see www.textsandtech.org/~rudy/edna-e/). This prototype web-based system allows an administrative user (or story administrator) to add a series of organizational events to a database (see Figure 2.3) that becomes viewable to a group of employees or an organizational unit. Users then respond to organizational events by following scripted templates (also added by the story administrator) and are given access to the stories created by other employees. Some

FIGURE 2.3. EDNA-E ADMINISTRATIVE CONTROL PANEL

Edna-E Administration Panel

Choose An Option

- User Management Functions
- Story Management Functions
- Event Management Functions
- Organization Management Functions
- Script Management Functions
- Group Management Functions

Home   Events   Organizations   Stories   Scripts   Groups
XML   Edit XML   Config   Users   Import

You are currently in administrative mode. Return to User-Access mode degree of automatic classification and analysis is made possible by pattern matching algorithms and validation routines enforced by administrative story scripts.

Another example of a textual narrative application, which has been around for some time, is the Inform Engine that emerged from the popular Zork video games in the 1980s. Zork delivered the type of branching story game that was presented entirely in a text mode. Upon reading text such as, "It is pitch black in this room. You are liable to be eaten by a grue," an appropriate response might be "Turn on lantern." The game would pick up on the key words or phrases, such as "turn on" and "lantern," and would take you to the next branch of the story: "Ah, you escaped narrowly and get to move forward through the cellar into the tunnel." Or, if you input the wrong information for that particular narrative or situation: "We're sorry; you have been eaten by a grue."

This example may seem not to have much bearing on the current professional environment. However, understanding this branched narrative could lead to other stories that have interactive branching and some level of simulated intelligence based on textual responses. These responses could then take someone step-by-step through a procedure and lead to a rich, narrative-based experience without necessarily using rich media.

More recent examples have used the same type of engine to deliver both simple graphics and text and to process the text of those inputs, even in environments that have a very small footprint, such as personal digital assistants (PDAs) or mobile phones. The attractiveness of the small footprint and the simplified processing of information could lead to some significant ways of creating engaging experiences, with minimal media, in an easy-to-use text-based interface.

Game-Based Applications

In K-12 education, many innovative projects have started to take advantage of graphically rich, story-driven videogame technologies in order to use the technologies today's youth are already using for entertainment purposes as educational vehicles as well. *Quest Atlantis*, the *African American History Game*, and *Pax Warrior* are three such initiatives that we describe in this section.

Quest Atlantis (http://atlantis.crlt.indiana.edu/start/index.html) was developed by researchers at Indiana University's Center for Research on Learning and Technology (http://crlt.indiana.edu/). This game was designed as a means through which technology and applications from the commercial gaming industry could be combined with research on learning and motivation. It is a three-dimensional virtual world that supports multi-user game play. The goal is to immerse the players in educational tasks via quests requiring the player to travel to virtual places (see Figure 2.4). In the course of "questing," the players perform

FIGURE 2.4. QUEST SCREEN

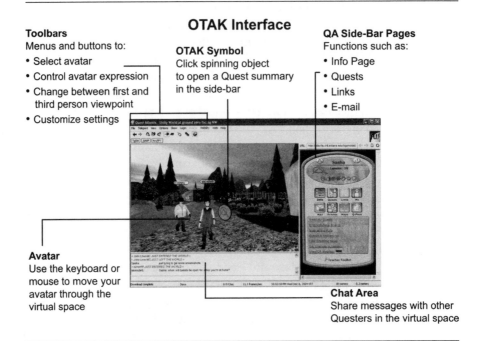

Toolbars
Menus and buttons to:
- Select avatar
- Control avatar expression
- Change between first and third person viewpoint
- Customize settings

OTAK Interface

OTAK Symbol
Click spinning object to open a Quest summary in the side-bar

QA Side-Bar Pages
Functions such as:
- Info Page
- Quests
- Links
- E-mail

Avatar
Use the keyboard or mouse to move your avatar through the virtual space

Chat Area
Share messages with other Questers in the virtual space

a variety of educational activities through which they interact with both real and virtual players. Importantly, the Quest community has shown how the game is able to connect "Quests" to local academic standards. For example, quests can be designed so that they require students to engage in activities that are socially and academically meaningful by traveling to virtual villages. These include quests ranging from researching other cultures to conducing environmental studies with embedded tasks such as calculating frequency distributions and developing action plans. Quest Atlantis builds on the Vygotskian notion of play in young children, viewing the game as a context for learning. "Play can be thought of as a scaffolding activity that expands the children's [zone of proximal development], engaging them in issues and debates that are not addressed directly through participation in society or even through the normal curriculum of schools (Barab & Jackson, 2006).

The African-American History Game (http://mundyhr.com/game.htm) was created by the University of Central Florida's Institute for Simulation and Training (www.ist.ucf.edu) in collaboration with UCF's School of Film and Digital Media (www.dm.ucf.edu), the Partnership for Research on Synthetic Experience (PROSE) lab, and Carol Mundy's organization, African-American History Education and Culture (http://mundyhr.com). This project involved developing a story-driven learning game for research in teaching children about African-American culture and history. The goal was to create a compelling introduction to the Underground Railroad (see Figure 2.5) using existing commercial off-the-shelf technology for role-playing computer games to stimulate interest and understanding of events of historical significance while introducing the public to the Mundy Collection, a vast selection of artifacts associated with African-American history (Fiore, McDaniel, Greenwood-Ericksen, Scielzo, Sanchez, Cannon-Bowers, & Mundy, 2005). This effort demonstrates how interdisciplinary research that combines story lines, learning objectives, and candidate artifacts from local cultural collections can support research and development in the production of compelling story-driven games. Such partnerships allow the research community to work with those in the humanities to scaffold experiential interactions that allow children to learn about history via navigating a virtual world where they interact with historic artifacts, objects, and characters (Fiore, McDaniel, Greenwood-Ericksen, Scielzo, & Mundy, 2006). This particular game was developed using a modification of the popular Neverwinter Nights video game.

A final example that allows for complex decision making and a compelling interactive narrative engine is Pax Warrior. This is described as technology that builds on the notion of "interactive documentary" (www.paxwarrior.com/home/index.php). The developers suggest that this capability can easily incorporate

FIGURE 2.5. AFRICAN-AMERICAN HISTORY GAME

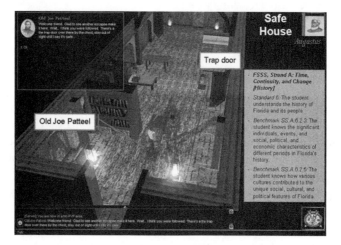

FIGURE 2.6. SCREEN FROM PAX WARRIOR

collaborative learning and simulation to support decision making. This can then be used to build an engaging game that aids in teaching topics such as history and social studies as well as current events. For example, Pax Warrior has created a module based on the political and civil unrest in Rwanda. (See Figure 2.6.) In this module, the player takes on the role of a commander from the United Nations and experiences the decision making necessary to solve such a complex scenario. Pax Warrior is just one example of the compelling nature of interactive narrative as an example of experiential learning in action.

Conclusion

The first half of this chapter was heavily weighted in theory and gave few examples of both the types of stories useful for experiential learning and the practical applications of narrative and simulation technologies. Hence, the latter half was fully focused on the characteristics of good stories for simulation and learning and on sample applications. We hope that many of the theoretical features and ideas we discussed earlier in the chapter, such as context and environment, transfer appropriate processing, and narrative theory, were made concrete through the various examples and illustrations we have provided.

While we have suggested that a digital storytelling model can be quite useful for certain types of experiential learning applications, a cautionary note is necessary. We began our discussion of narratology by writing about the lack of human-oriented solutions to problems involving the manipulation of information or knowledge assets. While a narrative framework built on simulation technology does address the socio-cognitive and emotive nature of communication during the gathering of the stories, the actual *presentation* of this data to an audience is still a purely technological process. (The audience's *interpretation* of the data is another matter entirely.)

As a final caveat, we assert that the benefits in audience immersion and captivation that are more likely to be present during something equivalent to an oral storytelling session may in fact not be present to the same extent in a virtual session. In this instance, a user is simply reading a story from a computer terminal or directing a virtual avatar through a simulated environment to advance a scenario's story line. Also, in conjunction with simulation technology and narrative, interactive performance may extract even more impressive results from experiential learning tasks, especially given the added contextual influence of body language, vocal inflection, and so forth. Further investigation is needed to determine the efficacy of virtual storytelling systems as experiential learning tools in comparison to live presentations of stories, in which the sound of the storyteller's voice and the ambient cues from the environment are also present. Research from other fields with heavy narratological foci, such as folkloristics (Georges & Jones, 1995), is also worthy of examination as a potential source of useful information for linking narrative to experiential learning tools and technologies. In short, only via true interdisciplinary research, with researchers and scholars from the learning sciences and the humanities working together, can we realize how to construct experiential learning environments. Via the principled integration of context, story lines, and learning objectives, experiential learning has the potential to substantially improve learning.

References

Abma, T. A. (2003). Learning by telling: Storytelling workshops as an organizational learning intervention. *Management Learning, 34*(2), 221–240.

Adams, L. T., Kasserman, J. E., Yearwood, A. A., Perfetto, G. A., Bransford, J. D., & Franks, J. J. (1988). Memory access: The effects of fact-oriented versus problem-oriented acquisition. *Memory and Cognition, 16*(2), 167–175.

Bal, M. (1997). *Narratology: Introduction to the theory of narrative* (2nd ed.). Toronto: University of Toronto Press.

Barab, S., & Jackson, C. (2006). From Plato's Republic to Quest Atlantis: The role of the philosopher-king. *THEN: Journal of Technology, Humanities, Education and Narrative*. Retrieved March 9, 2006, from http://thenjournal.org/commentary/95/.

Barker, R. G. (1968). *Ecological psychology.* Palo Alto, CA: Stanford University Press.

Barthes, R. (1988). Introduction to the structural analysis of narratives (R. Howard, Trans.). In *The semiotic challenge* (pp. 95–135). New York: Hill and Wang.

Bartlett, F. C. (1932). *Remembering-A study in experimental and social psychology.* Cambridge: Cambridge University Press.

Booker, C. (2005). *The seven basic plots: Why we tell stories.* London: Continuum International Publishing Group.

Bower, G. H., & Morrow, D. G. (1990). Mental models in narrative comprehension. *Science, 247,* 44–48.

Bransford, J. D., & Franks, J. J. (1971). The abstraction of linguistic ideas. *Cognitive Psychology, 2,* 331–350.

Bruner, J. (1991). The narrative construction of reality. *Critical Inquiry, 18,* 1–21.

Caplan, L. J., & Schooler, C. (1990). Problem solving by reference to rules or previous episodes: The effects of organized training, analogical models, and subsequent complexity of experience. *Memory and Cognition, 18*(2), 215–227.

Clancey, W. J. (1991). Situated cognition: Stepping out of representational flatland. *AI Communications—The European Journal on Artificial Intelligence, 4*(2/3), 109–112.

Craik, F.I.M., & Lockhart, R. S. (1972). Levels of processing: A framework for memory research. *Journal of Verbal Learning and Verbal Behavior, 11,* 671–684.

Craik, F.I.M., & Tulving, E. (1975). Depth of processing and the retention of words in episodic memory. *Journal of Experimental Psychology: General, 104,* 268–294.

Davenport, T. H., & Prusak, L. (1997). *Information ecology: Mastering the information and knowledge environment.* New York: Oxford University Press.

Denning, S. (2001). *The springboard.* Woburn, MA: Butterworth-Heinemann.

Denning, S. (2004). *Squirrel Inc: A fable of leadership through storytelling.* Hoboken, NJ: John Wiley & Sons.

Derrida, J. (1997). *Of grammatology* (1st American ed.). Baltimore, MD: Johns Hopkins University Press.

Dewey, J. (1902). *The child and the curriculum.* Chicago: University of Chicago Press.

Durlach, N. I., & Mavor, A. (Eds.). (1995). *Virtual reality: Scientific and technological challenges.* Washington, DC: National Academy of Science Press.

Entin, E. B., Serfaty, D., Elliott, L. R., & Schiflett, S. G. (2001). DMT-Rnet: An internet-based infrastructure for distributed multidisciplinary investigations of C2 performance. *Proceedings of the 6th International Command and Control Research and Technology Symposium.* June 19–21, 2001, Annapolis, Maryland.

Fiore, S. M., & McDaniel, R. (2006). Building bridges: Using the narrative form to better connect humans and human-systems. *THEN: Journal of Technology, Humanities, Education and Narrative.* Retrieved March 9, 2006, from http://thenjournal.org/commentary/95/.

Fiore, S. M., McDaniel, R., Greenwood-Ericksen, A., Scielzo, S., Sanchez, A., Cannon-Bowers, J. A., & Mundy, C. (2005). Mundy learning game prototype. Presentation to the Metro Orlando Urban League. December 2004, Orlando, Florida.

Fiore, S. M., McDaniel, R., Greenwood-Ericksen, A., Scielzo, S., & Mundy, C. (2006). The Carol Mundy game. Presentation to the Annual Meeting of the Florida Folklore Society, Crealde School of Art. March 2006, Winter Park, Florida.

Fiore, S. M., Johnston, J., & McDaniel, R. (2005). Applying the narrative form and XML metadata to debriefing simulation-based exercises. *Proceedings of the 49th Annual Meeting of the Human Factors and Ergonomics Society.* Santa Monica, California.

Gagne, R., & Glaser, R. (1987). Foundations in learning research. In R. Gagne (Ed.), *Instructional technology: foundations.* Hillsdale, NJ: Lawrence Erlbaum.

Garbarini, F., & Adenzato, M. (2004). At the root of embodied cognition: Cognitive science meets neurophysiology. *Brain and Cognition, 56,* 100–106.

Genette, G. (1980). *Narrative discourse* (J. E. Lewin, Trans.). Ithaca, NY: Cornell UP.

Georges, R. A., & Jones, M. O. (1995). *Folkloristics: An introduction.* Bloomington, IN: Indiana University Press.

Gibson, J. J. (1966). *The ecological approach to visual perception.* Boston, MA: Houghton Mifflin.

Gopher, D., Weil, M., & Bareket, T. (1994). Transfer of skill from a computer game trainer to flight. *Human Factors, 36,* 387–405.

Hmelo, C. E. (1998). Problem-based learning: Effects on the early acquisition of cognitive skills in medicine. *Journal of the Learning Sciences, 7,* 173–208.

Hoffman, R. R., & Deffenbacher, K. A. (1993). An analysis of the relations of basic and applied science. *Ecological Psychology, 5,* 315–352.

Jahn, M. (2004). Foundational issues in teaching cognitive narratology. *European Journal of English Studies, 8*(1), 105–127.

Jentsch, F., & Bowers, C.A., (1998). Evidence for the validity of PC-based simulations in studying aircrew coordination. *International Journal of Aviation Psychology, 8,* 243–260.

Kolb, D. A. (1984). *Experiential learning: Experience as the source of learning and development.* Englewood Cliffs, NJ: Prentice-Hall.

Lakoff, G. (1987). *Women, fire, and dangerous things: What categories reveal about the mind.* Chicago: University of Chicago Press.

Mandler, J. (1984). Stories, scripts, and scenes: Aspects of schema theory. Hillsdale, NJ: Lawrence Erlbaum.

Markman, A. B., & Ross, B. H. (2003). Category use and category learning. *Psychological Bulletin, 129*(4), 592–613.

Marsh, R. L., Hicks, J. L., & Hancock, T. W. (2000). On the interaction of ongoing cognitive activity and the nature of an event-based intention. *Applied Cognitive Psychology, 14,* S29–S41.

McDaniel, R. (2004). *A software-based knowledge management system using narrative texts.* Unpublished doctoral dissertation. Orlando, FL: University of Central Florida.

McQuillan, M. (Ed.). (2000). *The narrative reader.* London: Routledge.

Minsky, M. (1985). *The society of mind.* New York: Simon & Schuster.

Morris, C. D., Bransford, J. D., & Franks, J. J. (1977). Levels of processing versus transfer-appropriate processing. *Journal of Verbal Learning and Verbal Behavior, 16,* 519–533.

Needham, D. R., & Begg, I. M. (1991). Problem-oriented training promotes spontaneous analogical transfer: Memory-oriented training promotes memory for training. *Memory and Cognition, 19*(6), 543–557.

Onega, S., & Landa, J.A.G. (Eds.). (1996). *Narratology: An introduction.* London: Longman.

Ong, W. J. (1982). *Orality & literacy: The technologizing of the word.* London: Routledge.

Orr, J. E. (1996). *Talking about machines: An ethnography of a modern job.* Ithaca, NY: ILR Press.

Perfetto, G. A., Bransford, J. D., & Franks, J. J. (1983). Constraints on access in a problem-solving context. *Memory & Cognition, 11,* 24–31.

Polti, G. (2003). *The thirty-six dramatic situations* (L. Ray, Trans.). Boston, MA: Kessinger Publishing.

Post, T. (2002). The impact of storytelling on NASA and Edutech. *KM Review, 5*(1), 26–29.

Roediger, H. L., Gallo, D. A., & Geraci, L. (2002). Processing approaches to cognition: The impetus from the levels-of-processing framework. *Memory, 10,* 319–332.

Roediger, H. L., & Blaxton, T. A. (1987). Effects of varying modality, surface features, and retention interval on priming in word-fragment completion. *Memory & Cognition, 15,* 379–388.

Roediger, H. L., Weldon, M. S., & Challis, B. H. (1989). Explaining dissociations between implicit and explicit measures of retention: A processing account. In H. L. Roediger & F.I.M. Craik (Eds.), *Varieties of memory and consciousness: Essays in honor of Endel Tulving* (pp. 3–41). Hillsdale, NJ: Lawrence Erlbaum.

Rumelhart, D. E. (1980). Schemata: The building blocks of cognition. In R. J. Spiro, B. Bruce, & W. F. Brewer (Eds.), *Theoretical issues in reading and comprehension.* Hillsdale, NJ: Lawrence Erlbaum.

Salas, E., & Burke, S. (2002). *Quality and Safety in Health Care, 11,* 119–120.

Saussure, F. D., Bally, C., Sechehaye, A., & Riedlinger, A. (1986). *Course in general linguistics.* LaSalle, IL: Open Court.

Schank, R. C. (1995). *Tell me a story: Narrative and intelligence.* Evanston, IL: Northwestern University Press.

Schank, R. C., & Abelson, R. P. (1977). *Scripts, plans, goals, and understanding: An inquiry into human knowledge structures.* Hillsdale, NJ: Lawrence Erlbaum.

Snowden, D. (2001). Narrative patterns: The perils and possibilities of using story in organizations. *Knowledge Management, 4*(10).

Swap, W., Leonard, D., Shields, M., & Abrams, L. (2001). Using mentoring and storytelling to transfer knowledge in the workplace. *Journal of Management Information Systems, 18*(1), 95–114.

Taylor, H. L., Lintern, G., Hulin, C. L., et al. (1999). Transfer of training effectiveness of a personal computer aviation training device. *International Journal of Aviation Psychology, 9,* 319–335.

Tolkien, J.R.R. (1967). *The lord of the rings* (2nd ed.). Boston, MA: Houghton Mifflin.

Trabasso, T., & Sperry, L. L. (1985). Causal relatedness and importance of story events. *Journal of Memory and Language, 24,* 595–611.

Tyler, S. (1978). *The said and the unsaid: Mind, meaning, and culture.* New York: Academic Press.

◆ ◆ ◆

Acknowledgments

Writing this paper was partially supported by Grant Number SBE0350345 from the National Science Foundation and by Office of Naval Research Grant N000140610118 to the first author. The opinions expressed in this paper are those of the authors only and do not necessarily represent the official position of the University of Central Florida, the National Science Foundation, or the Office of Naval Research. Correspondence regarding this paper should be sent to Stephen M. Fiore, sfiore@ist.ucf.edu.

CHAPTER THREE

DYNAMIC DEBRIEFING

Roger Greenaway

Roger Greenaway writes extensively on the subject of active learning, especially about how to engage participants actively during debriefings. His books include *More Than Activities* (Save the Children, 1990) and *Playback: A Guide to Reviewing Activities* (Duke of Edinburgh's Award, 1993). He is a regular contributor to *Training and Learning,* the monthly publication of the Institute of Training and Occupational Learning. He also contributes articles to Fenman's resource manual: Train the Trainer. His articles include "How Transfer Happens" (Organization Development Topical Papers, Brathay, 2002) and "Active Reviewing" (Bulletin, Group Relations Training Association, 1983), as well as many articles that are published as part of Roger's own web-based *Guide to Reviewing Activities.* Roger has presented at conferences and provided trainer training throughout Europe and in South Africa, China, Hong Kong, Canada, and the United States. His typical clients are training organizations or training departments of larger organizations who want to enliven the whole learning process—including reflection and transfer.

Contact Information
Reviewing Skills Training
9 Drummond Place Lane
Stirling
Scotland, FK8 2JF
+44 1786 450968
roger@reviewing.co.uk
http://reviewing.co.uk

DEBRIEFING IS IMPORTANT. Many writers say so. But few writers explain why debriefing is important or what it involves. A recent survey of journal articles found that: "most writers, while emphasizing the importance of debriefing for a game or exercise, do not fully describe the debriefing process, or explain why it is important—it is simply assumed to be important" (Markulis & Strang, 2003). An international survey of "exemplary practices" in the field of experiential training and development had even less to say about debriefing—just these two words: "Debrief appropriately" (Bronson et al., 1999). Sound advice, but short on detail!

This chapter is intended to raise your sights higher than debriefing "appropriately": it aims to help you debrief effectively, inspirationally, and dynamically. The chapter begins with the basics about debriefing and its facilitation before introducing various models of debriefing. This is followed by "the experience of debriefing" and why this perspective matters when debriefing experience. A section about sequencing in debriefing is followed by descriptions of dynamic debriefing methods—showing how the theory can be applied in practice.

What Is "Debriefing"?

Debriefing* is the facilitation of learning from experience. Debriefing can be used to assist learning from almost any experience. The experience might happen at work, in the community, or as part of an education or training program. Most of the examples in this chapter refer to the debriefing of training exercises, but they can be readily applied or adapted to other situations. The various roles in which people may want to help others learn from experience include parenting, coaching, mentoring, supervising, managing, instructing, counseling, teaching,

*In the military, "debriefing" refers to the control of information. It refers either to interrogations for obtaining information or to exit interviews for keeping information secret. The term "psychological debriefing" also has a military origin. It is a controversial method for the treatment of people suffering from post-traumatic stress disorder. (The controversy is about whether reliving traumatic experiences helps or hinders recovery.) The kind of "debriefing" that is the focus of this chapter (using experience as a source of learning and development) has a very different purpose to any of its military uses. In a curious twist of terminology, when the U.S. Army wants to generate learning, they refer to the process as an "after action review" rather than as a "debriefing." The military may have brought the term "debriefing" into common usage, but its current meaning in the broader field of experiential learning owes very little to the military connection. During the evolution of our abilities to help each other learn from experience, we have failed to coin a term that accurately describes one of the most human gifts that we possess. The term "debriefing," with all its misleading connotations, will do for now.

training, and facilitating. Debriefing skills and methods can be useful in all such roles, but the emphasis of this chapter is on debriefing in group settings.

What Is "Dynamic Debriefing"?

Sometimes, a lively discussion can bring a sense of action to the debriefing: "Without the sense of action to the debrief, it is often a lifeless, futile exercise. . . . The experience can come alive in the debrief. The experience can be relived. The discussion is not a static, safe, merely cognitive exercise. It has feeling, anger, frustration, accomplishment and fun" (Schoel, Prouty, & Radcliffe, 1988, p. 166). But dynamic debriefing is more than a lively group discussion. When a debriefing is truly dynamic, each person is fully engaged in the learning process and has some influence over its direction. The experience being processed is probably being relived and communicated through visual aids, movable media, and physical action as well as through words. Of course, the spoken word can be very engaging, but by placing a variety of tools for communication and learning in the hands of participants, the facilitator increases the chances that everyone (not just the most reflective and articulate) can participate in a full and meaningful way.

Dynamic debriefing aims to engage the whole person as an aware, active, and self-directed participant in the process of learning from experience. This involves learners in expressing, examining, and exploring their experiences in ways that enable them to learn, grow, develop, and make changes in their lives. "Dynamic" primarily refers to the nature and degree of the learner's involvement in the learning process, while "debriefing" primarily refers to what the facilitator is doing to enhance the quality of the learning process. The first list below shows what can be achieved through effective debriefing. The second list shows how a more dynamic approach can produce even better results.

Through *effective* debriefing you can . . .

- Add value to what is already happening
- Increase awareness of other perspectives
- Develop communication and learning skills
- Help learners clarify, achieve, and even surpass their objectives
- Use success or failure as a source of learning and development
- Make benefits tangible and generate useful data for evaluation
- Improve prospects for the effective transfer of learning
- Show that you care about what people experience and value what they have to say, and that you are interested in the progress of each individual's learning and development

Through *dynamic* debriefing you can . . .

- Reduce the gap between talk and action
- Provide more ways to communicate, learn, and develop
- Engage everyone fully by involving all learning style preferences
- Give better access to intuitive and tacit knowledge
- Stimulate more powerful learning experiences
- Generate more effective learning from experience
- Pay more attention to the experience of learning
- Allow more realistic testing of future plans
- Increase the range of strategies for the effective transfer of learning.

The Role of the Facilitator

Most experiential learning theory is clear about what learners do after their "experience": they reflect, interpret, and experiment. But experiential learning theory is less clear about what role (if any) facilitators should play in this process. The principles, strategies, and tactics of facilitation cannot be deduced from experiential learning theory alone: We also need a theory of facilitation. And preferably one that goes beyond the slogan that we should change from being the "sage on the stage" to become the "guide on the side"—because "guiding" is only one kind of facilitation.

John Heron, founder and director of the Human Potential Research Project, University of Surrey, provides a model of facilitation that sits well with the principles of experiential learning theory. It helps facilitators decide whether key decisions about facilitation should be made with or without consulting the group, or whether they should be left to the group to decide. Heron outlines potential problems with each of these three modes of decision making (hierarchical. cooperative, and autonomous), and he explains why it is important to move between them:

> Too much hierarchical control, and participants become passive and dependent or hostile and resistant. They wane in self-direction, which is the core of all learning. Too much cooperative guidance may degenerate into a subtle kind of nurturing oppression, and may deny the group the benefits of totally autonomous learning. Too much autonomy for participants and laissez-faire on your part, and they may wallow in ignorance, misconception, and chaos. (Heron, 1999, p. 9)

Heron applies these three modes of decision making to each of these six dimensions of facilitator style: *planning, meaning, confronting, feeling, structuring,* and *valuing*. As an example of how this works, here is some further detail about the "meaning" dimension. When in hierarchical mode in the meaning dimension, Heron writes: "You make sense of what is going on for the group. You give meaning to events and illuminate them; you are the source of understanding what is going on." In the cooperative mode: "You invite group members to participate with you in the generation of understanding. You prompt them to give their own meaning to what is happening in the group, then add your view, as one idea among others, and collaborate in making sense." In the autonomous mode, writes Heron: "You choose to delegate interpretation, feedback, and review to the group. Making sense of what is going on is autonomous, entirely self-generated within the group" (Heron, 1999, p. 16).

An awareness of Heron's model discourages the facilitator from settling down in a single favorite position for too long because the model shows that there are clear disadvantages with this kind of consistency. A facilitator who makes deliberate moves among these three modes of decision making also frees up learners to be more mobile and responsible in how they exercise and share power. Such mobility helps to make debriefing and learning more dynamic, versatile, and effective.

Models of Debriefing

If the purpose of debriefing is to facilitate learning from experience, it follows that a complete model of debriefing would need to integrate experiential learning theory with facilitation theory. Just as there are different kinds of experiential learning, so there are different kinds of facilitation. This creates many potential combinations for producing a theory of debriefing! John Heron (above) is one of the few writers who combine both kinds of theory. Below is a list of what I would consider to be the minimum requirements for a complete model of debriefing. Against each requirement, I have suggested models that have the potential for fulfilling that requirement—if known.

A complete model of debriefing would include:

1. *A model for sequencing questions to create a suitable flow and direction to a learning conversation.* There are so many sequencing models to choose from (mostly presented as cycles) that these are discussed later in a separate section on "sequencing in debriefing."
2. *A model for keeping all learners engaged when debriefing in a group.* The pattern "1–2–All" is a good way to start a debriefing (or a new stage within a debriefing). "1" = solo thinking time or writing time or making a brief personal statement; "2" = talking in pairs; "All" = whole group discussion.

This kind of preparation helps to generate higher levels of involvement and a higher quality of group discussion. At any time, you can reverse the process by using "All–2–1." The same or different pairs talk together, and each individual makes a note of his or her learning or of the next step to take. If appropriate, a session can end back in the whole group, with each individual invited to speak. "1–2–All–2–1" can be used with most question sequences, because it is about patterns of interaction rather than about the content of what is said.

3. *A model that captures the rhythm of learning and change.* John Dewey used the analogy of armies moving and resting; George Kelly wrote about tight and loose construing; Kurt Lewin used the terms freezing and unfreezing; for David Kolb it was convergent and divergent thinking; for Terry Borton it was about switching between analytic and contemplative modes. Borton recommends that questions based on his "What? So What? Now What?" cycle are asked "in two quite different manners. The first is the analytic mode . . . hard-driving, pointed, sharp, logical, tough, and rigorous. But [writes Borton] it is difficult for people to change if they are put under much pressure, so we also employ a contemplative mode, a more relaxed approach which avoids picking at one's self and allows alternatives to suggest themselves through free association and metaphor" (Borton, 1970, p. 89). These various to and fro motions are like the rhythm of pistons driving a wheel: over-dependence on one piston could bring learning to a grinding halt. The alternation of activity and debriefing provides a large, slow, two-stroke rhythm; there is also scope within debriefing to facilitate these to and fro rhythms of learning and change.

4. *A model for focused questioning.* The debriefing funnel uses a succession of filters that focus in at every stage (Priest & Gass, 1997, p. 196). The six filters are *review, recall and remember, affect and effect, summation, application,* and *commitment.* Priest and Gass describe it as an expansion of Borton's three questions: What? So What? Now What? The image of the funnel and its filters clearly aligns the model with Borton's analytic mode but provides little encouragement for divergent or contemplative thinking as part of the debriefing process. A more complete model might include an inverted funnel to prompt lateral or creative thinking or to promote a helicopter view. The authors do encourage adaptation of this model and encourage readers not to be bound by a single view of debriefing as the only way to guide reflection. Thiagi's advice on preparing questions for debriefing follows a similar pattern—moving from open to probing questions within each of his six stages: How do you feel? What happened? What did you learn? How does it relate? What if? What next? (Thiagarajan & Thiagarajan, 1999, pp. 37–47).

5. *A model that keeps in touch with learners' motivations.* "Ripples on a Pond" (Race, 2003) emphasizes the driving force that is missing from other learning models.

Professor Phil Race has developed his model based on questions he has asked to "tens of thousands of people," from schoolchildren to training managers. He places "wanting to learn" (or, as a second best "needing to learn") at the center of his ripples model. The ripples lead outward through doing, making sense, feedback, training, and understanding. Race says you should also ripple inwards and keep revisiting the central "wanting to learn." As an example, the right kind of feedback (at the third ripple) adds to people's desire to learn. The outer ripples will disappear if there is no energy at the center. Race points out that, unlike cyclical models of learning, all factors in his model are involved at the same time. This is why he writes: "Any model based on a cycle won't do." If following a cycle too rigidly, the learning process becomes fragmented and loses touch with the whole as well as losing touch with the heart: "wanting to learn."

6. *A model that recognizes the importance of what learners experience during the debriefing.* Race (above) underlines the importance of learners wanting to learn, but this sixth "requirement" goes further by recognizing that the quality of the experience during the debriefing also has a significant impact on learners' motivations. It can also have a significant impact on their learning and development: both the experience being debriefed and the experience of the debrief are potential sources of learning and development. These possibilities are explored further in the next section about the experience of debriefing.

7. *A model that helps to keep the learning process moving.* Perhaps "spinning plates" is an apt metaphor here. It illustrates how a facilitator needs to pay attention to many different factors when debriefing in a group—and especially to the plate that is most likely to fall next. The plate most likely to fall next may well be the "wanting to learn" plate (as in Race's model), but it could be any plate that has escaped recent attention—and this keeps changing (Greenaway, 2004).

8. *A model about working with whole persons throughout the debriefing.* This is partly about how models are readily misinterpreted. As soon as a model can be used as a sequence, it is—whatever its author might say. Borton writes of his "Sensing, Transforming, Acting" model: "The model's three divisions are arbitrary, for the processes do not function in a simple 1–2–3 fashion, but are interwoven in a dynamic fashion" (Borton, 1970, p. 78). After describing all the factors in his "Ripples in a Pond" learning model, Race writes: "All these factors are involved at once" (Race, 2003). It is difficult (although not impossible) to represent dynamic, simultaneous, or interweaving processes in a model. Unfortunately, anything that looks like a sequence or a cycle is likely to be applied as a one-thing-at-a-time linear process—even when this is not the author's intention. Many debriefing models are designed to be about working with whole persons, but are interpreted and applied in ways that fragment the integrated process intended by its originator. Borton warned "Do not dissect to disintegration,"

but many users of his What? So What? Now What? model do not know of the author's warnings nor of his advice about using the model.

9. *A model that discourages a routine approach to a dynamic phenomenon.* A primary function of a model is to provide a useful simplification of complex realities. Is it possible to create a model that simplifies while also staying in touch with the complex reality that it models? In my own model of the debriefing cycle (Greenaway, 2002), I use the four playing card suits (diamonds, hearts, clubs, and spades), with each suit representing a stage of a learning cycle (facts, feelings, findings, and futures). A joker (representing freedom) is at the center of the cycle as a reminder that reality is more complex. Unlike other cards, the joker has no preordained meaning—it is a wild card that has an infinity of possible uses and it can be played at any time. On its own, the joker would have little power, but when it is ever-present as an option within a cycle (for the facilitator or participants), the joker tends to bring about whatever is needed. The joker makes it easy to customize or even abandon the model. This in-built flexibility helps to ensure that debriefing is both "appropriate" and "dynamic." As a wild card, the joker refuses any label, but is often seen wearing the blue hat (process overview) of Edward de Bono's "Six Thinking Hats" model (de Bono, 1985). However, a multicolored rainbow hat would better suit the image and function of the joker (Greenaway, 2004).

A complete model of debriefing would include all of the above (and more). But once a model gets too big and cumbersome, it loses its value as a practical model, even though it may have the virtue of being more complete. Perhaps every model should include a wild-card joker as a reminder that a model is only a guide and that good practice arises from using models intelligently.

The Experience of Debriefing

The experience of debriefing is as important as the debriefing of experience. What participants experience during the debriefing will influence their whole attitude toward learning from experience, both in the present and in the future. These are some of the "experiential" factors that the facilitator needs to keep in touch with during the debriefing process.

Balancing Positive and Negative Experiences

People learn from success as well as from mistakes. Reliving positive experiences can be a very powerful way of harnessing the energy and insights found in the experience. In fact, much debriefing in experiential learning deliberately encourages people to draw strength, learning, and inspiration from positive experiences. Because people learn from both positive and negative experiences, we should encourage and support both kinds of learning. When learning comes from a negative experience, people want to take the learning but leave the experience behind; when learning comes from a positive experience, people want to carry forward both the learning and the experience. In both cases, it is helpful if the learning process itself is enjoyable, vivid, and memorable, no matter what the nature of the experience from which the learning was generated. Otherwise there is a risk that the original experience sticks in the mind, but what was learned from it during the debriefing evaporates.

Creating a Climate for Learning

Some participants may feel most at home and even "in flow" during training exercises. They relish each new challenge and enjoy putting their skills to the test; they like being in a highly motivated team and (if successful) they savor their accomplishment as they "high five" each other at the end. Other participants may feel more at home in the debriefing, where (typically) the pace slows down, each person is listened to, misunderstandings and conflicts are resolved, the "important" stuff happens, and the point of it all becomes clear: learning is identified and recorded and is even put into a plan. Some participants may feel a bit peripheral and uncomfortable during the training exercise, whereas others may feel peripheral and uncomfortable during the debriefing. This matters. The quality of the experience matters both in the training exercise and in the debriefing. Arguably, the quality of the experience matters even more in the debriefing—because debriefing should always be happening in a highly supportive learning climate in which it is safe to speak out and take risks. A favorable learning climate is not only better at generating learning, but it also helps to make learning satisfying and enjoyable. It is an extra bonus if participants' desire to learn is rekindled.

Improving the Climate for Learning

The facilitator should be able to provide optimal conditions for learning for each participant. The wise facilitator will not jump to a learning styles theory as "the" explanation of why some participants are not optimally engaged in the learning process. "Learning style" is only one of many possible explanations—and the wise facilitator will already know the importance of ensuring that debriefings result in full engagement of all learning styles, no matter what the profile of people's learning style preferences might be. The most straightforward advice is to ask each learner what is helping or hindering his or her learning or what would improve the learning environment for him or her. Then take action to improve it (Krupp, 1985).

Creating a Climate for All Learning Styles

If a participant says he is not comfortable sitting and talking because he sees himself as a "hands-on" learner who has to do things, you can always offer him something practical to do within the debriefing. For example, you could ask the participant to tell the story of his team's development by making a series of patterns with pebbles (with each pebble representing a team member). You can sidestep the issue of whether people who see themselves as "hands-on" learners really do need to touch things in order to learn, because you are looking for a means of engaging the person in reflective learning. If the person believes he has to touch and do things in order to learn, feed that belief with a suitable task that requires both action and reflection. The example with the pebbles above is not a special technique reserved for people who like to be active: it is a useful method for getting any team to communicate about their development as a team.

Using All Minds

Debriefing is primarily the province of the rational mind. However, there are many theories that give a broader picture of the mind's abilities, so it also makes sense to harness all (or most) of these within the debriefing process. If we have seven or eight intelligences (Gardner, 1993), including emotional intelligence (Goleman, 1995), a left brain and a right brain (Sperry, 1980), an experiential mind and a rational mind (Epstein, 1989), and a multitude of learning styles (for which there are over one hundred theories!), then it makes sense to use debriefing methods that also tap into some of these other mental abilities.

One view of experiential learning is that a complete learning cycle does draw in all learning styles, so if participants are patient enough they will be alert and motivated during at least one part of the cycle—when it happens to come around. What does this view mean for those who come alive in the activity and fail to achieve any meaningful involvement during the debriefing? Some facilitators may hope that the buzz from the activity may keep a buzz going during debriefing, but how much better it would be if the debriefing session itself were a source of buzz— rather than being heavily biased toward only one or two learning styles.

Engaging the Experiential Mind and the Rational Mind

We do not have on-off switches for experiencing. We do not stop experiencing when the debriefing begins. Similarly, we do not stop thinking and reflecting while taking part in a training exercise. In fact, training exercises are usually designed to be so challenging that as participants we summon up all that we can from prior experience of similar situations to help us contribute in a useful way to achieving the task. The ways in which we take part will also be influenced by recent experiences with this group and by any learning that we have gained so far from working and learning together. In fact, there may not be very much difference between the learning processes taking place during a training exercise (i.e., drawing on past experience) and the learning processes taking place during the debriefing (i.e., drawing on past experience!).

Experience-based learning (especially when it is also adventure-based) creates experiences that can be enriching, intensive, confusing, or complex. If the quality of the experience is to have maximum impact for learning, then it must be matched by debriefing methods that are capable of dealing with the depth, essence, and richness of the original experience. If the debriefing methods offered are merely discussion-based, then the less-discussible aspects of experience will remain untapped and unharnessed. Important sources of power, energy, and insight will remain neglected and underused. In the methods section of this chapter, you will find some practical ways of generating a range of experiences within a debriefing session—thus allowing all (or most) minds, including the experiential mind, to be active and alert.

Sequencing in Debriefing

Several sequences have already been described in the preceding text (Borton, 1970; Greenaway, 2002; Priest & Gass, 1999; Thiagarajan & Thiagarajan, 1999), so they will not be repeated here. This section is an exploration of principles and issues associated with sequencing within a debriefing.

Finding a Starting Point

You can start a debriefing with the experience and let issues or topics emerge, or you can start by using a topic as a lens through which to select and view an experience. If starting a debriefing with the story (or stories) of what happened, you can use techniques such as *action replay* (described later) that rerun the experience, pausing to investigate key moments. There is no law of debriefing that says you should give equal attention to everything that happened or that you should give equal time to each stage of a learning sequence. It is in everyone's interest that you focus on what matters most, even if this is not apparent until the debriefing is under way. At other times, a debriefing will start with a question that leads people to draw on whichever experiences best answer the question. This might, for example, be a search for teamwork highs or lows in the exercise just completed, or in a recent period at work. Or you can simply ask the group to list issues, questions, or topics they wish to explore. You can then introduce debriefing methods that will help them to explore their inquiries in ways that take them back into the experience. Wherever they begin, they are probably entering a learning cycle that, strictly speaking, has no start or finish point.

The Role of Debriefing in Experiential Learning

Experiential learning is often presented in the form of a cycle in which an experience is followed by a sequence of different processes until the next experience, after which the sequence is repeated until the next experience, and so it continues. Debriefing can assist any part of the learning sequence that comes after the experience—from sharing feelings to transfer planning. With so many potential directions to take, a poorly sequenced debriefing can become dissatisfying and chaotic.

Poorly sequenced debriefings can result in:

- Clichéd conversations with no questioning or learning
- Meandering discussion going wherever the most dominant people happen to take it
- Paralysis by analysis, with learning stagnating at the investigation stage
- Post-mortems, producing a distorted negative bias that drains energy
- Jumping to false conclusions by missing out on significant stages
- Future planning that is not well-grounded in what was learned from experience
- Chaos and conflict, with people being out of sequence with each other (while one person is talking about the future, another is still "in the exercise," another is speaking her mind, another is excited about a personal insight, and so on)

Sequencing is not the only answer to the above problems, but having an understanding of sequencing can certainly help identify the problem and indicate solutions worth trying.

There Is No Best Sequence for Debriefing

There is no single correct or best sequence to follow. There are many different theories, each promoting a particular sequence, and there is no standard "best practice" that can be routinely applied to all opportunities for experiential learning. Facilitators should be familiar with a variety of useful debriefing sequences, as well as having a variety of debriefing tools that enable learners to fully engage with any sequence that is adopted.

Decisions About Sequencing

- What should be included in the sequence?
- In what order should these items be included?
- What should be the pace of the sequence?
- Should the sequence be followed once or several times during the debriefing?
- How strictly should the sequencing be adhered to?
- How dynamic should the process be?
- Who should make these decisions (and how is this decision made)?

What Should Be Included in a Sequence?

It may not be realistic to include all of the features listed below every time, but over a series of debriefings, it would usually be important to include all of these aspects:

- Clarification and/or negotiation about the process and purpose of the debriefing (which changes from one to the next)
- Past, future, and present perspectives
- Plus, minus, and interesting perspectives (suitably balanced)
- Individual and group perspectives (both "I" and "we" statements)
- Feedback to everyone and to individuals ("you" statements)
- Opportunities for all learning style preferences to be included and engaged (both for the sake of inclusiveness and to extend everyone's learning skills)
- Support and challenge in a spirit of inquiry
- Opportunities for connection and transfer to the wider world
- A debrief of the debriefing! (so that everyone can contribute to improving the experience and quality of the debriefing session)

Begin at the Very Beginning?

Beware of assuming that a debriefing begins at the start of the "official" session. Some important informal or independent reflection may have already taken place. For example, if participants have already spent time independently on stage 1 and stage 2 (of your particular sequence), they may be ready to dive into stage 3 at the start of your debriefing session. Also, the more that participants get into the habit of debriefing, the greater the chances that they will be doing debriefing (formally or informally) during the training exercises. So even if you start your debriefing immediately after a training exercise, you may discover that the learning process is already well under way. The best starting point is not always stage 1. It is always worth checking where people are in the process—and there can be wide variation in any group.

Whose Agenda? Whose Cycle? Whose Pace?

One decision you need to make is whether the whole debriefing is to be structured as an agenda (possibly equivalent to one tour of a learning cycle), or whether the goal (or goals) would be better achieved by participants making several journeys round a learning cycle. A related issue is whether each participant is traveling around his or her own unique learning cycle—and if so, does each one travel at his or her own pace or in unison with others? If working with a group, your answer to the above questions will necessarily be a compromise. This is because experiential learning theory is about how individual learners learn, rather than about how facilitators work with learning groups. But there are clever ways of making this compromise. If you keep the whole group together all of the time, it is practical and convenient if everyone moves at the same time at the same pace. But if you include individual and paired work, this gives more opportunity for individuals to move at their own pace, and the group session can be used for finding out where each person has progressed. In this approach, debriefing happens in ones and twos and the whole group is used for sharing information, rather than for moving around the cycle. The "clever" compromise is to move between the two approaches. Many debriefing methods described later in this chapter have this compromise built in.

How Important Is the Original Experience When Debriefing?

The more stages there are in a sequence, the more layers of separation there can be from the original experience. For example, Wight (1991) describes an eight-stage experiential learning cycle, with from three to five topics per stage. That moment of action and experiencing is receding into the distance as each new stage adds at least one more filter. This distancing can be beneficial. But even if it is beneficial, the chances are that a multistage debrief does not feel "experiential" when the original experience is no longer central to the debriefing. This does not necessarily mean that it is better to keep referring back to the experience at every stage of a debriefing cycle, because it is usually also important for each new stage to refer back to the previous stage of the sequence. This is yet another situation in which the facilitator needs to play things both ways. In this case, the facilitator needs to work with what's coming out from previous stages, as well as refer back to the original experience. There are many debriefing methods that help to achieve this balance by bringing the experience into the debriefing, for example, through video replay, reenactment, or creating a storyboard, map, or lists that provide a visual record of the experience. If the switch from "experiencing" to "debriefing" is too sudden and abrupt, there is a risk that the learning will be poorly grounded and detached from the experience. The challenge is to maintain some interplay between experience and reflection throughout the debriefing, unless it was your intention to use the experience simply as an energizer to precede a discussion, rather than as a significant source of learning and development.

Follow a Sequence or Just Move Together in Any Order?

There is at least one interesting midway position between following a predetermined sequence and free-flow. You can avoid the potential chaos of free-flow by at least ensuring that everyone is on the same page at the same time—whatever the order in which the pages are being visited. A good example of this solution comes from Edward de Bono, who realized that there can be a lot of wasted energy in free-flowing meetings that become chaotic and argumentative. He introduced his "Six Thinking Hats" model to help people conduct meetings in a more orderly and effective way (de Bono, 1985). Six Thinking Hats does not require people to follow any particular sequence, but it does require that when a particular colored hat is showing people may only contribute according to the rule associated with that color. For example, when the yellow (sunshine) color is showing, only positive comments are allowed. There are also hats for critical views (black), creative thinking (green), facts and figures (white), feelings and intuition (red), and a blue hat for commenting on the thinking process itself. Of course, some free-flowing meetings can be highly effective, so a facilitator needs the judgment to know when free-flow is best, when a structure is best, and which structure is best. In other words, the facilitator always needs a blue hat, which allows him to clarify, when necessary, what kinds of contribution are most welcome at any particular point.

Dynamic Debriefing Methods

The six dynamic debriefing methods described below show how the principles described and discussed in earlier sections of this chapter can be enacted in practical ways: *Action Replay* highlights key moments and brings them alive in ways that enable focused questioning and new insights; *Objective Line* shows how much people can learn from experience at the start of a new journey; *Metaphor Map* generates a customized debriefing tool on which personal or team journeys can be traced and learned from; *Missing Person* draws attention to what is missing in a team by breathing life into what was once an energy-draining listing process; *Horseshoe* turns a scaling exercise into animated discussion; and *Turntable* helps people understand other points of view by going there and trying them out. These methods demonstrate how physical, creative, and intuitive movement can facilitate the process of learning from experience.

Action Replay

Recommended uses: Action Replay is best suited to the debriefing of exercises in which there is plenty of action involving the whole group. If the "action" was repetitive, it may be too difficult for participants to synchronize their replay. Games that involve getting the whole group from A to B are often well-suited to Action Replay. Games in which there is little movement (such as mental puzzles or board games) are less suitable.

Resources: dummy microphone and dummy remote control (real or improvised)

Action Replay is a classic example of dynamic debriefing, as well as being a challenging team exercise in its own right. Action Replay involves reenacting an activity as if a video of the activity is being replayed. Just as on TV, the action is played back to examine an incident more closely or to replay an event worth celebrating. In the age of TV and video, Action Replay is readily understood and needs little explanation.

Compared to video work, Action Replay is much quicker to set up, edit, and replay (no technical problems!); it is more convenient and versatile—it can be used almost anywhere; it keeps involvement and energy high; it is an exercise in memory, creativity, and teamwork; it brings out humor and honesty; it provides opportunities for leadership, interviewing, and commentating; and it can be used as a search technique to find incidents or issues to debrief more thoroughly.

Variation: A dummy microphone adds extra purpose (and interest) to the replay. Any group member (actor or audience) can pick up the dummy microphone to interview someone involved in the action. They can ask questions from any point of the learning cycle:

- To clarify what was happening
- To give people a chance to express their feelings (especially if unknown to others)
- To analyze the situation (Why were you doing that? How did that happen?)
- To look to the future (How could you build on what worked well? What could you take from this experience into the workplace?)

Variation: Introduce a dummy remote control before the replay starts. You (or participants) can pre-select which moments to replay by requesting "Selected

Highlights" or you can just ask for the whole activity to be replayed. While taking part in (or viewing) a replay, anyone can ask for the remote to slow down to replay a particular moment or to see it again. Remind people about useful buttons on the remote and warn that you may invent some new buttons that no one has ever heard of before. Once you have demonstrated the possibilities of using the remote control, participants can take it in turns to direct the action. The dummy controls are not only fun to play with, but they also provide opportunities for some very focused and controlled debriefing. Action Replay is also readily adapted for rehearsing future scenarios. This is strictly "pre-play," rather than "replay," but why send people back to their seats as soon as you start discussing the future?

Objective Line

Recommended use: for preparing for a journey toward a goal by reflecting on experience.

Resources: A 5-meter rope for each pair. Paper and marker pens, if using written goals.

Demonstrate with a partner. Lay a 5-meter rope on the ground. The near end represents the starting point on a journey toward a goal and the far end represents the goal (for the program or for the transfer of learning). Your partner places an object or picture or word representing the goal at the far end of the rope, describes it, and returns to the starting point at the near end.

This is your skeleton script: "I don't think you are at the very start of this journey, so let's check. . . . Take a few steps forward and turn around to face your starting point. What have you already done that will help you on this journey? . . . What knowledge, skills, resources, experience, motivation, values, support, and so on do you already have that will help you on this journey?"

This is your side of a dialogue, so pause for responses! "So where do you think you really are on this journey? Further forward? A bit further back?" Allow your partner to move to the place he or she chooses. (Following a good dialogue, moving toward the goal is typical, but moving closer to the start is also OK.) "Now face your goal and tell us what the next step of your journey will be. Now face your starting point. What has helped you on your journey so far that might also be useful in the next step of your journey? What other factors (internal or external) might help you on this next step?"

Explain that this is the essence of the technique: facing forward to talk about your goal or about the next step toward it, and then turning backward to review the skills, resources, and so forth that you already have that will help you with the next part of your journey. This exercise does not involve walking into an imagined future;

it is about recognizing helpful factors in the past and present that are real and available. It includes accessing relevant experiences and drawing confidence, energy, and learning from them precisely when these assets and strengths are needed. It is just-in-time learning! This process helps people to approach their goals more wisely and confidently. It also develops the habit and skill of just-in-time learning.

After your demonstration and explanation, pairs work together with one rope per pair, taking turns in the different roles. Much the same process can be used later in the program with pairs returning to their ropes and standing at a point that represents their current progress toward (or beyond) their goals. Their conversations follow a similar pattern to the original exercise.

Metaphor Maps

Recommended use: for individuals or groups to map their world and use their maps to help them reflect on individual or team experiences.

Resources: flip-chart paper and colored markers

Participants create metaphor maps that represent the kind of places they visit, avoid, or seek in their working day. Map-making can be a group or individual exercise. Places might include: Field of Dreams, Stormy Seas, Safe Haven, Mountains of Work, Pool of Relaxation, Stretch Zone, Swampland, Play Area, Road to Nowhere, Stream of Ideas, Point of No Return, Terra Incognita, Short Cut, Black Hole, Magic Spot, Site of Antiquity, Stadium of Light, Great Wall, Greener Grass, Fountain of Knowledge, Bridge Under Construction, and so on.

Warning: People generally seem to be full of ideas for unpleasant and frightening places to put on a map, so be sure to ask people to check that their maps are reasonably balanced and include places they like to visit and want to visit. It is meant to be a map of their own territory—so it should include places that are familiar as well as a few strange ones.

Map-making is itself a reflective exercise. Once a map is created, it can be used as a more focused debriefing tool. Participants tell their stories about an experience while tracing their journey across their map with a finger. The listener prompts as necessary to help the person tell his or her story using the map: "Did you visit any of these places?" "Where did you spend most time?" "Can you trace the journey you took?" "Do you need to create new places on the map?" After the story is told (or during its telling), the listener asks questions that help the storyteller to consider alternative or preferred routes on the map and how they could succeed in making these journeys. Metaphor Map is a tool that can be readily combined with most debriefing sequences.

Variations: With more resources and imagination, Metaphor Map can be scaled up to room size or field size. These larger versions allow people to walk around their maps with facilitative partners. The floor-size map is a good scale for demonstrating the method.

Missing Person

Recommended use: for helping a group to assess its strengths, needs, and priorities. This exercise achieves the same results as when a group discusses its strengths and weaknesses, but in a more powerful and memorable way.

Resources: flip-chart paper and colored markers

Inform the group that their task is to create a new person to join their group. Ask participants to think creatively about the kind of person they would like this to be. The person will probably share some of the characteristics already in the group (e.g., sense of humor, good looks, friendly, enthusiastic) and may also represent some characteristics that are missing (e.g., timekeeping, leadership, telling decent jokes). Suggest they start by giving the person a name and some interests before thinking about his or her strengths and weaknesses, as this provides a fun and intuitive way into the process. Creating a missing person is an activity that typically takes a group through a full debriefing sequence—without much or any prompting. The new character represents the skills, roles, and qualities that the team has so far lacked and now aspire to. Some groups so like their missing person that you will find that they later call out the person's name when they need help or keep the person on display for inspiration.

Warning: Take care with how the image of the "missing person" is treated. Do not put the team's mascot in the trash! As in all creative work, the creators should dispose of their own work in their own way and when they are ready to do so.

Horseshoe

Recommended use: for exposing and discussing different views

Resources: One long rope (or other marker) in the shape of a horseshoe. The rope should be about twice as long as the length of the group when standing shoulder to shoulder.

This debriefing method is a variation of a scaling technique that goes under many names, including "spectrum," "lineup," "positions," and "silent statements." The main difference is that the "horseshoe" is a curved line. In this method, you simply define the two ends of the spectrum and ask everyone to stand at a point on the line that represents his or her point of view. The benefit of the horseshoe shape is that everyone is more likely to be in eye contact with each other—which makes facilitating whole group discussion much easier.

Example: One end represents "We worked well as a team during that exercise"; the other end represents "We did not work well as a team during that exercise." Everyone chooses a point on the line and then talks to one or two neighbors (who are likely to have a similar point of view). Ask everyone to notice where individuals are standing as well as the overall pattern of distribution. Ask "Any surprises? Any comments? Any questions?" Given a natural tendency to focus on the two extremes, ensure that attention is also paid to other positions. Encourage participants to move as and when their views change and invite them to explain why they are moving. You can also ask stationary participants why they are not moving. Facilitate discussion for as long as it is productive.

Variation: Choose different points in time. For example: "How would you each have rated this team before the exercise started?" "What was the quality of teamwork like up to the end of the initial planning?" "What is your personal prediction for the quality of teamwork in the next exercise?"

Horseshoe is a classic example of the "1–2–All" sequence described earlier in this chapter: "1" is the "silent statement" when choosing a point on the line; "2" is the conversation with a neighbor; "All" is the facilitated discussion. Whenever you feel tempted to ask for a show of hands during a debriefing, try Horseshoe instead. It is more accurate because it allows a scaled response. It is also more participatory and more fun.

Turntable

Recommended use: to allow participants to see and experience two or more sides of an issue

Resources: Two semicircles of chairs facing each other

The simplest form of a Turntable discussion is to set up two teams facing each other in a semicircle. This is how I would brief a Turntable discussion about teamwork: "When you are sitting in this semicircle you have a positive view about your performance and progress as a team; but when you are sitting in the opposite seats, you may only express negative views about (for example) performance problems and slow progress as a team. So that you don't get stuck in one position, and to give you the chance of achieving a balanced view, you will be spending roughly equal time on both sides of the argument. In this exercise, you may find yourselves saying things you don't really believe. That's OK. You are allowed to adopt an attitude that is not your own, but you should not make up untrue facts to support your argument, and you should generally promote your own side's view, rather than seeking to undermine the other side's view. Every minute or so, I will stand up as a signal for you to move two places to your left."

Variation: To assist with the transfer of learning near the end of a training program, have one semicircle of pessimistic seats (for expressing pessimistic views about being able to transfer their learning) arranged opposite a semicircle of optimistic seats.

Warning: Rearrange the furniture (and participants) to mark the end of Turntable—otherwise people can get "stuck" in their last positions, which is not where you want to end an exercise about helping people to appreciate other points of view!

Other variations: The ideal group size for Turntable is ten—for a "five-a-side" discussion. For a group of twenty, you can create two groups of ten to operate independently or have an outer circle of "listening chairs" included in the rotation. A better way of including more numbers is if you discuss a topic in which a third view is worth exploring. If fact, three- and four-way discussions are generally of a higher quality than two-way discussions. A third side can bring in lateral thinking to unlock the confrontation, and a fourth side can be an opportunity for practicing facilitation skills. If there are mobility problems in a group, you can pass around colored hats, signs, or ropes, with each color representing a different side. But moving around in a circle has more impact. Moving always has more impact! Minds move when bodies move.

References

Borton, T. (1970). *Reach, touch, and teach: Student concerns and process education.* New York: McGraw-Hill.

Bronson, J., et al. (1999, March 18). *The definition, ethics, and exemplary practices (DEEP) of experiential training and development (ETD)* (Version 6.2). DEEP Task Force: www.etdalliance.com.

De Bono, E. (1985). *Six thinking hats.* Toronto: Key Porter Books.

Dewey, J. (1938). *Experience and education.* New York: Collier Books.

Epstein, S. (1989). Values from the perspective of cognitive-experiential self-theory. In N. Eisenberg, J. Reykowski, & E. Staub (Eds.), *Social and moral values* (pp. 3–22). Hillsdale, NJ: Lawrence Erlbaum.

Gardner, H. (1993). *Frames of mind: The theory of multiple intelligences.* New York: Basic Books.

Golman, D. (1995). *Emotional intelligence.* New York: Bantam Books.

Greenaway, R. (2002). The art of reviewing. *Journal of the Institute of Training and Occupational Learning, 3*(1), pp. 47–53.

Greenaway, R. (2004). *Playing the joker: Old traditions and new trends.* Buckinghamshire, UK: The European Institute of Outdoor Adventure Education and Experiential Learning.

Heron, J. (1999). *The complete facilitator's handbook.* London: Kogan Page.

Kelly, G. A. (1955). *The psychology of personal constructs.* New York: Norton.

Kolb, D. A. (1984). *Experiential learning: Experience as the source of learning and development.* Englewood Cliffs, NJ: Prentice Hall.

Krupp, J.-A. (1985). Hey world, adults are people too! A holistic view of adult learners. *The International Journal of Higher Education, 2*(1), 25–32.

Markulis, P. M., & Strang, D. R. (2003). A brief on debriefing: What it is and what it isn't. *Development in Business Simulation and Experiential Learning, 30,* 177–184.

Priest, S., & Gass, M. (1997). *Effective leadership in adventure programming.* Champaign, IL: Human Kinetics.

Race, P. (2003). Ripples on a pond: A model of learning. *Train the Trainer, 1.* Cambridgeshire, UK: Fenman Publishing.

Schoel, J., Prouty, R., & Radcliffe, P. (1988). *Islands of healing: A guide to adventure-based counseling.* Hamilton, MA: Project Adventure, Inc.

Sperry, R. W. (1980). Mind-brain interaction: Mentalism, yes; dualism, no. *Neuroscience, 5,* 195–206.

Thiagarajan, S., & Thiagarajan, R. (1999). *Facilitator's toolkit.* Bloomington, IN: Workshops by Thiagi.

Wight, A. (1991). In R. R. Harris & R. F. Moran (1991), *Managing cultural differences* (3rd ed.) (pp. 249–250). Houston, TX: Gulf.

PART TWO

EXPERIENTIAL LEARNING METHODOLOGIES

THIS SECOND SECTION of *The Handbook of Experiential Learning* contains ten chapters. Each one focuses on a single, major experiential learning strategy in common use today. The authors are known for their special expertise in the methodology they write about.

Chapter 4 highlights what ingredients make for successful *experiential simulations*. The focus here is on experiences that represent, but not replicate, sensitive issues such as cross-cultural understanding, team responsibility, and the use of power.

Chapter 5 examines the use of *action learning*, a popular method in which participants work together to resolve their own real problems in real time with the aid of a coach.

Chapter 6 takes on a versatile, fun method called *"junkyard sports."* Participants learn valuable lessons as they create and test creative ways to play sporting events such as golf or basketball.

Chapter 7 overviews the vast world of *learning games* and gives advice on how to employ them as anchors in a hands-on, participant-centered training event.

Chapter 8 discusses how to engage learners in *computer-based simulations* in which they develop and practice vital skills by their involvement in realistic decision-making problems.

Chapter 9 shows how the many elements of *improvisation* (spontaneous dramatic play) contribute to the practice of experiential training and how specific improv exercises are used in a variety of training contexts.

Chapter 10 involves us in the world of *adventure learning*, where participants are given challenging physical tasks in the outdoors, such as mountain climbing, and take away everyday learnings.

Chapter 11 emphasizes ways to make *role playing* effective so that participants have solid skill practice and feedback. Consideration is given to how to make role playing natural rather than artificial.

Chapter 12 looks at the place of *storytelling* in experiential learning, including its use by both facilitators and participants.

Chapter 13 penetrates the use of *reflective practice*, a core technique to help people inquire about and learn from their own real-world attempts to master skills and improve their performance.

CHAPTER FOUR

EXPERIENTIAL SIMULATIONS

Ten Secrets for Creating Training Success

Garry Shirts

Garry Shirts is president of Simulation Training Systems Inc. of San Diego, California. He has more than forty years of experience developing programs for businesses and educational institutions. He served as a faculty member of the Western Behavioral Sciences Institute School of Strategic Studies in La Jolla, California. He also taught the art of simulation design at the University of California, San Diego, and at Oregon State University. He is the designer of several popular simulations, including BaFa' BaFa', StarPower, The Power of Leadership, and "What Is No?," as well as numerous customized simulations and experiential training programs for corporations. Garry was recently awarded the Ifill-Raymond lifetime achievement award and the "Legend" award by the North American Simulation and Gaming Association.

Contact Information

Garry Shirts
Simulation Training Systems
11760 J Sorrento Valley Road
San Diego, CA 92121
(858) 755–0272

garry@stsintl.com
www.stsintl.com

A N EXPERIENTIAL SIMULATION can be a wonderful training method. But it's easy to create one that is not as effective as it could be. Here are some suggestions for improving your chances of being successful.

One of the most satisfying experiences in training or education, no matter what the subject, is the so-called "Aha!" moment, that instant when sudden, spontaneous insight cuts through the tangle of loose ends in a learner's mind to reveal a memorable truth.

Having spent nearly forty years designing experiential simulations, I believe simulations are the most likely teaching method to create those "Aha!" moments. In a simulation called "StarPower," the moment occurs when participants, who might be police officers or corporate managers, unexpectedly realize that the only way to keep power over others is not to use it. In "BaFa' BaFa'," the moment comes when participants suddenly grasp the idea that good intentions can actually worsen cultural misunderstandings. In a team-building simulation called "Pumping the Colors," it happens when participants abruptly comprehend that the rules a team operates under are actually the team's responsibility.

When combined with other unique strengths of simulations—their ability to simplify systems, to demonstrate other people's perspectives, to develop "battlefront" skills in safety, and to solve problems from the inside out—these eye-opening moments can endow participants with a vivid, often deeply personal understanding of even the most abstract training concepts.

Simulations, however, are widely misunderstood. The most experienced trainers, called on to design a simulation, often create a workaday version of the board game "Monopoly." These are sometimes successful as play, but rarely effective as training.

Here are ten secrets for creating successful training simulations. They represent lessons learned from my own hard-fought struggles to understand the elusive, often perverse human dynamics at work in simulation training. Taken in sequence, they can supply relatively safe passage through the tricky terrain of simulation design.

1. Don't Confuse Replication with Simulation

The temptation in designing a simulation is to make a small-scale replica of some full-blown reality. It seems logical that the closer the simulation comes to reality, the more valid and memorable the experience will be. If you're designing a flight simulator for airline pilots, this may be so. But in "soft skills" training, the opposite is usually true. The job of the designer is to look past the details to the essence of reality.

Two Navy projects taught me that lesson. A sailor on shore leave in Athens, after buying a memento in a bazaar, discovered a shipmate had bought the same memento from the same merchant for a lot less money. Unaware of the Greek custom of bargaining, the sailor returned to the bazaar and flattened the hapless merchant.

The Navy asked me to devise a simulation that would teach sailors to respect—and expect—unfamiliar customs and relationships in foreign cultures. Since the Greek culture was only one of many the sailors would encounter, my associates and I created a simulation that postulated two abstract cultures defined in broad strokes: One was patriarchal and relationship-driven, the other individualistic and task-oriented. In neither culture did we attempt to simulate language, religion, or attitudes toward time, work, leisure, or whatever.

Participants were divided into two groups. Each learned the rules of its own culture. Then representatives from one culture had to visit the other and attempt to function. Despite my initial fears that the simulation might be too abstract, it was an immediate hit. By concentrating on the essence of the cross-cultural experience rather than the details, the simulation had a powerful "aha" effect on many of the participants. "Bafa Bafa" has since been used extensively by thousands of schools, corporations, and government agencies.

The next effort was an abysmal failure because we got caught in the replication trap. The Navy asked us to design a simulation to help newly arrived American sailors learn to live in Japan. One objective was to show participants how complex a foreign culture can appear when you don't understand the language, so we replicated the Japanese experience in considerable detail. We set the exercise in a model of a Japanese railroad station and hired Japanese-speaking housewives to staff shops and ticket windows. The sailors were to face a series of real-life quandaries: asking directions, ordering train tickets, buying gifts, and so forth.

When the simulation got under way, however, all this authenticity quickly buried our good intentions. The participants were lost in detail. We had exaggerated the problem and overwhelmed the point of it all. The simulation collapsed of its own weight.

2. Choose the Right Subject to Simulate

Some subjects lend themselves better to simulation training than others. I don't claim to have discovered any ironclad rules to determine likely subjects, but I believe a topic is more apt to be suitable for simulation if it embodies at least one of the following characteristics:

- *Seeing the world through other people's eyes.* A pharmaceutical company wanted a training program that would awaken its complacent marketing department to the competition threatening its principal product line. We designed a simulation that divided the marketing staff into five competing teams, one represented our client company and the others its principal competitors. Each team designed an aggressive marketing plan to increase its "company's" share of the threatened product's market segment. The unqualified success of the competitor's marketing plans revealed just how vulnerable the client company's product was. The marketing staff was shocked into action.

- *Performing tasks simultaneously.* Traditional training methods teach skills in a linear fashion, one by one. In the real world, skills are often needed in clumps: A manager may find herself simultaneously negotiating with a vendor, listening to a customer complaint, and planning the response to a memo from her boss. A simulation can create an environment in which she learns to do all three, and more, at once.

- *Performing under pressure.* Some people are skillful negotiators, excellent listeners, clear direction-givers—but only when they don't have to perform under pressure. Simulations can create environments full of genuine but nonthreatening pressure, affording such people opportunities to practice their skills under duress.

- *Developing systems thinking.* Many people find it difficult to grasp the concept of how systems operate. They know the parts of a system are related, but they resist understanding the relationships because they think they are impossibly complicated. A simulation can put people inside a system. As part of the system, they see first-hand how change to one component affects the others.

- *Recognizing cognitive dissonance.* People often hold contradictory attitudes or beliefs without being aware of the contradiction. This is known as cognitive dissonance. For instance, if a manager sincerely believes he is nonsexist yet behaves in a sexist manner, chances are he suffers from cognitive dissonance. Many of the "Aha!" moments created in simulations come when such a person suddenly realizes that he or she has been living a contradiction.

3. Develop a Design Plan

In preparing to design a simulation, you must make two key planning decisions. First, will you design it alone or use a design team? Second, will you employ a structured creative process or fly by the seat of your pants?

Whether you go it alone or put together a team, you need to fill the following roles: principal designer, who has first-hand knowledge of training simulations (and, for a team, the commitment to lead); subject-matter expert, who has a thorough understanding of the subject to be simulated; administrator, who sets and maintains the design schedule, oversees acquisition or production of materials, and schedules alpha and beta tests (more on these later); and client or representative, who provides a reality check as the project develops (in an oversight capacity only).

While some feel the most productive creative process is no explicit process at all, I believe a simple but well-defined creative program can counteract the pressures that often cause designers to settle for second-rate ideas. I have tried most of the creative techniques espoused by experts, and I've found that their best advice can be distilled into three suggestions:

1. *Avoid premature closure of ideas.* Don't stop searching for ideas after the first workable one appears. Often the best idea comes second, third . . . or tenth. Think of ideas as stepping stones to other ideas rather than as destinations in themselves.
2. *Get outside a problem and look at it from different angles.* For example, try approaching a problem in a marketing simulation from the point of view of a customer, a salesperson, a distributor, a person who has never seen the product before, someone who doesn't speak English—you get the idea.
3. *Give your subconscious a chance to work on the problem.* The solution to an especially intransigent problem will often pop into your head when you least expect it— on the freeway, in the shower, at the beach. Give it the opportunity.

4. Design the Simulation So That Participants Take Responsibility for Their Actions

Most simulations are divided into two sections, the simulation proper and a session analyzing the results. Conscious learning occurs primarily during the analysis session. Learning is sidetracked, however, whenever participants disavow responsibility for their behavior during the simulation. If they can claim they did what they did only because the simulation suggested or encouraged that action, their motivation to learn from the experience evaporates.

When you design your simulation, watch out for these guaranteed responsibility avoiders:

- *Pretending.* If the rules even imply that participants should "pretend" to be someone or do something, then at the end of the simulation they will exclaim, "That's how I thought such a person would act!" When you allow participants to become actors playing roles, you compromise their stake in the outcome. Instead of telling someone to act like the president of a company, for example, assign him the authority and responsibilities of the president. Design all "roles" in a simulation so that participants must be themselves.

- *Using competition for its own sake.* Employing competition between participants to increase interest in a simulation can, and often does, backfire. Participants can then justify all kinds of inappropriate behavior in their quest to win. If competition is not a factor in the real-world situation you are simulating, leave it out. Even if it is a factor, it is often a mistake to increase the reward for winning by offering non-simulation prizes, such as bottles of wine to the winners, money from a pot collected from the participants, and so forth. If the simulation of a competitive situation is designed well, the inherent competitiveness of most participants will create enough competition to motivate energetic participation. Sweetening the pot with extra-simulation rewards often creates such an intense environment for the participants that it is difficult for them to learn from the experience. Unless your goal is to show how competition and the desire for winning can distort their decision-making ability and cause them to abandon long-held values, the competition should be kept in perspective.
- *Giving inappropriate importance to chance.* Stymied simulation designers often fall back on the trusty old device of a deck of cards, with outcome-altering directions like, "The company is being sued" or "The workers are on strike." Such cards invite participants to escape responsibility later by insisting, "We made the right decisions, we were just unlucky." Limit chance to events that actually occur randomly in the real world.

There are other common mistakes designers often make when they first begin designing a simulation. Being aware of them can help you avoid them.

- *Emphasizing fun at the sacrifice of learning.* Many people use the words "simulation," "simulation games," and "games" interchangeably. I did at the beginning of my career, but now I try to call what I do simulations that fall in the general category of experiential learning. I do not refer to them as games, even though they are game-like for the following reasons:
  - The word "game" evokes feelings and expectations that I think make it difficult to design effective simulations.
  - As soon as you say "game," many people think of winning and competing to win. Many simulations do involve competition, but not always. As I mentioned earlier, when competition is involved, it is important to manage the competitive elements of the simulation so that the competition doesn't overwhelm the learnings.
  - Games often create an expectation of fun and frivolity. I believe participants must be fully engaged for maximum learning. Being fully engaged is not the same as having fun. Most of the time it is also fun to participate in a simulation, but not always. I feel I learned more from participating in Harold

Guetzkow's Inter-Nation Simulation (INS) and William Gamson's Simulation of Society (Simsoc) simulation than I did from all of my teachers during my graduate school years. I became incredibly involved. I still replay some of the experiences from those two simulations in my head. They were challenging, thought-provoking, and frustrating experiences. The Inter-Nation Simulation lasted for two days; Simsoc lasted for two days. "Fun" would *not* be one of the words I would use to describe the experience, but they completely changed the way I think about what's going on in the world. When having fun is one of the criteria used by designers to create a simulation, I think it greatly limits the design options.

- *Dumbing down the experience.* I believe shorter simulations are better than longer; simpler is better than complicated; learning something is better than learning nothing; capturing the essence is better than replicating every detail—providing you can figure out what to do to make them shorter and simpler *and still meet your learning goals.* Young people who play computer games spend hours figuring out the rules and trying different strategies. Reality, even the essence of reality, is often a challenging, complex task requiring difficult choices. If we remove the difficult parts from the simulation, we risk missing an opportunity to teach extremely important ideas, concepts, and values.

- *Underestimating the time and energy to build commitment.* It's quite easy to create that first level of commitment: "Come and join in this activity; you'll learn something and have fun." But to get people seriously invested in the outcome sometimes requires time and effort from the participants before they reach this level of commitment. Experiments have shown that ducklings will imprint on a moving block of wood. The more effort they expend following the block of wood, the stronger the imprinting bond. This principle holds true for many simulations: the more effort the participant must put into finding a solution, the more likely the lessons will be longlasting. Just as a movie or a play requires time for the audience to identify with the characters before they are faced with a crisis, time is often required in a simulation for participants to become familiar with the other participants, the resources they must allocate, and the payoffs that each type of decision is likely to yield.

This also applies to the debriefing. I understand the need for a person trying to sell an experiential learning session to their corporate bosses to say "This simulation teaches these seven things." In Pumping the Colors, we help them understand and use seven tools to help them build more effective teams. We've developed learning points for our other simulations as well. The good news is that these learning points help us be clear about what we're trying to accomplish. The bad news is that focusing on these learning points, if not done correctly, may rob the participants of a more important learning, how to learn from experience. The temptation is to do the work for them . . . to say, "Here's what the simulation is about and here's what you should have learned," instead of requiring them to identify the learnings and how they apply in the real world. Surprisingly, the participants often learn concepts, ideas, and principles that are unique to them. In fact, these are often the most important learnings of the experience. To help them reflect on the experience often means that the first analysis is superficial. If we believe that is all the participants are capable of, then we'll stop there. But most students are capable of much more. In other words, we should not dumb down the simulation, and we shouldn't dumb down the debriefing.

5. Use Symbols and Metaphors to Deal with Emotionally Charged Ideas

Occasionally, a simulation focuses on an emotionally charged issue that threatens to overpower the learning experience. For example, in the early Seventies a teachers' association asked me to design a simulation to teach campus conflict resolution. My scenario proposed that a trivial misunderstanding between a white and black student has escalated into a riot. I tested it with a group of college professors from a state university. They were divided into four groups—a black militant group, a white right-wing group, a moderate black group, and a moderate white group—and were given the task of resolving the conflict.

Seconds after our first test began, the black militant group (all white, middle-class males) leapt onto a table and began shouting obscenities. The right-wing group responded with threats of violence. The moderate groups attempted to mediate but were buried in the verbal mayhem. After an hour, we stopped the simulation and discussed the experience. The professors loved it. I hated it. I felt that, instead of responding honestly, the participants had merely stepped into stereotypical roles—the opposite of my mandate. I canceled further tests and went back to the drawing board.

I realized that by incorporating such emotionally charged and politically correct themes as "black," "white," and "race riot," I had made it difficult for them to respond genuinely. In hiding behind stereotypes, they were taking advantage of a convenient escape hatch. This made it impossible to get at the essence of racism: power or the lack thereof.

I changed the name of the simulation from "The Race Game" to "Starpower." Instead of blacks and whites, I named the groups Circles, Squares, and Triangles, and gave the Squares power over the other groups. At the next test,

I worried that participants would not identify with such abstract groups, thus weakening the simulation's emotional impact. I stopped worrying when I noticed a Triangle questioning a Square's right to order him around. The Square drew himself up. "You want to know why I can tell you what to do?" he growled, shoving his badge in the Triangle's face. "Because I'm a Square, that's why!"

6. Don't Play Games with Participants

When we first tested "StarPower," we instructed the facilitator to secretly increase the probability of the top group, the Squares, becoming even more powerful and rich. I was trying to make the point that the rich get richer. This tactic served our purpose well—until it was revealed during the analysis session. The participants were so angry to discover the deception that their fury overpowered all discussion.

We changed the rules, but only slightly. We told the facilitator to explain at the start that whichever group did best in the early going would gain an advantage in later stages. We still stacked the odds, but without secrecy. It worked. The participants, no longer feeling manipulated, now accepted the concept "the rich get richer" without complaint.

Another kind of game playing can backfire by trivializing the whole experience. I refer to the use of cute proper names, like the "Yell and Holler Telephone Company" or "Caught in the Act Security Services." No matter how clever such names seem to designers at the time of creation, they undermine the authority and effectiveness of the simulation by signaling participants not to take it seriously.

7. Use Non-Participants to Add Realism

Non-participants, people who have no stake in the outcome of the simulation, can add an exciting, even crucial, sense of realism.

In "Pumping the Colors," a team-building simulation, participants build a water transfer system that is tested near the end of the simulation by a non-participant "customer." The team has to provide this untutored stranger with written instructions that enable him or her to operate the complicated apparatus. The presence of this outsider in the equation forces participants to consider the system's simplicity of use and elegance of design at every stage of development.

In another simulation, one designed to train sales managers, ten workers are hired from a temporary agency for the day. The participants must interview them, select some as sales staff, train them to sell a product, organize them into efficient departments, and coach them to success. The use of strangers adds real-world authenticity to the training experience.

Non-participant participants are not suitable in every simulation (neither is real-world authenticity, as we've seen). But when they are, they can bring it alive.

8. Develop an Appropriate Performance Assessment Model

Because of a perceived superiority of mathematics-based scoring systems in training, simulation designers often attempt to develop quantitative models for assessing participant performance. These may be appropriate for quantitative simulations—those dealing with financial or other formulaic disciplines—but for most qualitative simulations they are not.

By "qualitative," I mean simulations that teach human-centered subjects such as ethics or teamwork or cultural diversity. Mathematical analogs are usually too limited and inflexible to account for their myriad variables—or too complicated to produce meaningful results. Also, participants often figure out quantitative models and skew the results.

In the marketing simulation we designed for the pharmaceutical company, we considered using a quantitative model to score the competing marketing plans. But then we realized that measuring every relevant aspect of the plans numerically would require a list of variables as long and about as informative as a telephone book. Instead, we used a panel of actual marketing experts to evaluate the plans and assign each plan a share of the market. This not only produced a realistic outcome, but it offered participants an opportunity to challenge, and better understand, the results and, more important, the reasoning that the judges used to make their determination.

9. Alpha Test Your Simulation in Low-Risk Circumstances

Both alpha and beta testing are critical to the development of even simple simulations, but confusing them can be disastrous. A beta test is a real test—a shakedown—of an anticipated final product, always occurring after the design is at least provisionally set. Alpha testing often happens so early in the design process that it might more properly be termed a design technique.

The purpose of an alpha test is to evaluate the basic assumptions of the simulation, its overall structure, and the logic of its progression. You should expect problems to surface and be prepared to reinvent the whole simulation if necessary.

Never include anyone in an alpha test who has an investment in the success of the simulation. No matter how forcefully you insist that this is only a preliminary test and that nobody should get excited if he sees problems, anybody with a stake in the outcome will panic the minute something goes wrong. And something will go wrong.

Do yourself a favor and stage alpha tests with people who love you.

10. Set Your Own Standards for Success

When you spell out the purpose and goals of your simulation at the beginning of the design process, you are defining standards by which to judge its ultimate success. Don't lose sight of those standards as your project nears completion.

By the time you get to beta testing, you may find your simulation seeming to take on a new and unfamiliar personality. This is often due to the cumulative feedback of participants who take part in the tests. Participants often overvalue (or undervalue) the participative aspect of simulations; they are, after all, used to sitting passively through lectures. Or they can become so emotionally involved in the simulation that they exaggerate the result, giving you a false positive assessment of what they've actually learned.

Don't get me wrong. You must listen and learn from participant reactions, good, bad, or indifferent. And you must be prepared to modify the simulation when necessary. But you can't let yourself be seduced by enthusiasm or destroyed by criticisms. The success of the simulation depends on your ability to maintain objectivity.

As you test and modify, you will watch your simulation come closer and closer to accomplishing its purpose. At some point—if you are like me—you will have a surprising but memorable "Aha!" moment of your own. That's when you'll know it's done or that it's not going to work.

CHAPTER FIVE

ACTION LEARNING

Resolving Real Problems in Real Time

Michael Marquardt

Michael J. Marquardt is professor of human resource development and program director of Overseas Programs at George Washington University. Mike also serves as president of the World Institute for Action Learning. He is the author of eighteen books and over ninety professional articles in the fields of leadership, learning, globalization, and organizational change, including *Optimizing the Power of Action Learning* and *Action Learning in Action*. Over one million copies of his publications have been sold in nearly a dozen languages worldwide. Mike's achievements and leadership have been recognized though numerous awards, including the International Practitioner of the Year Award from the American Society for Training and Development. He has held a number of senior management, training, and marketing positions with organizations such as Grolier, American Society for Training and Development, Association Management Inc., Overseas Education Fund, TradeTec, and U.S. Office of Personnel Management. Mike has trained more than 95,000 managers in nearly one hundred countries since beginning his international experience in Spain in 1969.

Contact Information
1688 Moorings Drive
Reston, VA 20190
(703) 437–0260
mjmq@aol.com

ACTION LEARNING IS A POWERFUL experiential learning methodology that builds leaders, teams and organizations. Since Reg Revans first introduced action learning in the coal mines of Wales and England in the 1940s, there have been multiple variations of action learning. However, all forms of action learning share the elements of real people resolving and taking action on real problems in real time and learning while doing. The basic requirements for action learning include an important and urgent problem, a diverse group of four to eight people, a reflective inquiry process, implemented action, a commitment to learning, and the presence of an action learning coach.

Theoretical Foundations

Action learning is built on a wide array of (a) educational, (b) psychological, (c) sociological, and (d) management science theories that interlace and buttress the relatively simple elements of action learning.

- *Education*—Action learning capitalizes on the theories, principles, and practices of education, namely the behavioral, cognitive, humanist, social learning, and constructivist schools of thought. Unlike most development programs, which tend to favor one approach or another to learning, action learning bridges these schools and builds from their best ideas and practices.
- *Psychology*—Action learning utilizes key aspects of individual, group, social, and organizational psychology, including classic theories of Jung, Skinner, Rogers, and Mead.
- *Sociology*—Action learning taps into the principles of the field of sociology, and the benefits gained by having diversity of members with different organizational rank, ages, gender, education, and experience allows action learning to be so powerful.
- *Management science*—Action learning incorporates the leadership principles and theories espoused by theorists and world-renown authors such as Collins, Drucker, Peters, Goleman, and Sashkin. It integrates theories of organizational change and complex adaptive systems, as well as the major management principles developed by Maslow, McGregor, and McClelland.
- *Biology, physics, economics, political science*—Action learning builds on brain theory, quantum physics, chaos theory, supply and demand, power, and numerous other principles of these divergent disciplines.

History of Action Learning

Reg Revans, acknowledged worldwide as the father and founder of action learning, developed the principles of action learning during the mid-twentieth century. Action learning first began to stimulate interest in corporate and academic circles with the publication of Revans' *Developing Effective Managers* in 1971. Quickly, many organizations, universities, and training institutes around the world began to use action learning in the 1980s. The International Management Center Association began in 1984 with Reg Revans as president and offered degrees using action learning. Mike Pedler edited *Action Learning in Practice* in 1983, 1991, and 1997. It contained articles written by the top practitioners of action learning. The first Congress on Action Learning was held in London in 1995 with participants from around the world. Global Action Learning Forums are held annually.

Numerous articles and books on action learning began appearing in the 1990s and early 2000. Institutes began to emerge, such as the Swedish Management Institute, Revans Institute of Action Learning, and World Institute for Action Learning. Action learning is now used in elementary and secondary school systems, at universities in nearly thirty countries, and in thousands of corporations worldwide. The Academy of HRD and the International Institute of Performance Instruction (ISPI) have devoted journal issues to action learning. In 2004, a new journal that focused solely on action learning, *Action Learning Research and Practice*, was introduced. It is fair to say that action learning has become the fastest-growing leadership training methodology, as well as the most effective approach for solving organizations' most complex and pressing problems.

Guiding Principles of Action Learning

Action learning is a process that involves a small group working on real problems, taking action, and learning as individuals, a team, and an organization while doing so. Action learning has six components:

1. A Problem (Project, Challenge, Opportunity, Issue, or Task)

Action learning centers around a problem, project, challenge, issue, or task of high importance to an individual, team, and/or organization. It should provide an opportunity for the group to generate learning opportunities, to build knowledge, and to develop individual, team, and organizational skills. Groups may focus on a single problem of the organization or multiple problems introduced by individual group members.

2. An Action Learning Group or Team

The core entity in action learning is the action learning group (also called a set or team). The group is ideally composed of four to eight individuals who examine an organizational problem that has no easily identifiable solution. The group should have diversity of background and experience so as to acquire various perspectives and to encourage fresh viewpoints. Depending on the action learning problem, groups may be volunteers or be appointed, may be from various functions or departments, may include individuals from other organizations or professions, and may involve suppliers as well as customers.

3. A Process That Emphasizes Insightful Questioning and Reflective Listening

Action learning emphasizes questions and reflection above statements and opinions. By focusing on the right questions rather than the right answers, action learning focuses on what one does not know as well as on what one does know. Action learning tackles problems through a process of first asking questions to clarify the exact nature of the problem, reflecting and identifying possible solutions, and only then taking action. The focus is on questions, since great solutions are contained within the seeds of great questions. Questions build group dialogue and cohesiveness, generate innovative and systems thinking, and enhance learning results.

4. Taking Action on the Problem

Action learning requires the group be able to take action on the problem it is working. Members of the action learning group must have the power to take action themselves or be assured that their recommendations will be implemented, barring any significant change in the environment or the group's obvious lack of essential information. If the group only makes recommendations, it loses its energy, creativity, and commitment. There is no real meaningful or practical learning until action is taken and reflected on. One is never sure an idea or plan will be effective until it has been implemented. Action enhances learning because it provides a basis and anchor for the critical dimension of reflection. The "action" of action learning begins with taking steps to reframe the problem and determining the goal, and only then determining strategies and taking action.

5. A Commitment to Learning

Solving an organizational problem provides immediate, short-term benefits to the company. The greater, longer-term, multiplier benefit is the learning gained by each group member, as well as the group as a whole, and how those learnings are applied on a systems-wide basis throughout the organization. Thus, the learning that occurs in action learning has greater value strategically for the organization than the immediate tactical advantage of early problem correction. Accordingly, action learning places as much emphasis on the learning and development of individuals and the team as it does on the solving of problems. The smarter the group becomes, the quicker and better will be the quality of its decision making and action taking.

6. An Action Learning Coach

Coaching is necessary for the group to focus on the important aspects of the process (i.e., the learning) as well as the urgent (resolving the problem). The action learning coach helps the team members reflect both on what they are learning and on how they are solving problems. Through a series of questions, the coach enables group members to reflect on how they listen, how they may have reframed the problem, how they give each other feedback, how they are planning and working, and what assumptions may be shaping their beliefs and actions. The learning coach also helps the team focus on what they are achieving, what they are finding difficult, what processes they are employing, and the implications of these processes. The coaching role may be rotated among members of the group or a person may be assigned to that role throughout the group's existence.

Two Group Norms/Ground Rules

The need to balance chaos and order explains why action learning, with its great flexibility and search for innovation, needs clarity and stability. Since the power of action learning is based on two key behaviors—reflective inquiry and continuous learning—establishing the following two ground rules help assure that these fundamental tenets of action learning are practiced successfully.

1. Statements Should Be Made Only in Response to Questions

Since questions provide so many benefits, this action learning ground rule assists all the group members to make the important transition from advocacy to inquiry. This ground rule does not prohibit the use of statements; as a matter of fact, there may still be more statements than questions during the action learning meetings, since every question asked may generate one or more responses to that question from each of the other members of the group, or as many as five to ten statements per questions.

However, by requiring people to think "questions first," the entire dynamics of the group is transformed. The natural impulse to make statements and judgments changes to one of listening and reflecting. Once the problem or task has been introduced to the group, the members must first ask questions to clarify the problem before jumping into solving the problem. In action learning, we recognize that there is almost a direct correlation between the number and quality of questions and the eventual final quality of the actions and learnings. Balancing the number of questions and the number of statements leads to dialogue. Dialogue is a proper balance between advocating and inquiring.

2. The Action Learning Coach Has Power to Intervene

The action learning coach focuses all of his energy and attention on helping the group learn. The coach is not involved in working on the problem. He looks for opportunities to enhance the learning of the group so that its ability to solve the problem and develop innovative action strategies is increased. The well-known axiom of how the "urgent drowns out the important" (also called the "tyranny of the urgent") underscores the necessity of assuring that the important will not be forgotten or neglected. Accordingly, if power is not provided to the person who is focusing on the learning, the urgency of the problem will always win out over the importance of the learning. To assure that learning is maximized for the group, the action learning coach must have the power to intervene whenever she believes there is an opportunity for the group to learn, to improve on what it is not going well, and to continue behaviors that are conducive to solving the problem.

This ground rule requires that, when the action learning coach decides to intervene, the group will temporarily stop working on the problem, listen to the questions of the action learning coach (she only asks questions), and respond to those questions. And only when the learning coach indicates to the group that she has finished her questions should the group resume problem solving. It is vital that the action learning coach be careful and economical in the timing and time taken in her interventions. She should be cognizant of the fact that the group members will be subconsciously continuing to work on the problem during her intervention and, when returning to the problem, will be rejuvenated and more creative than before the intervention.

The action learning coach also controls the ending of a session, and thus lets the group know in advance when the problem solving will end at that session. She then uses the last ten minutes or so to capture the learnings of that session and how these learnings might be applied as individuals, a team, and to the organization.

Multiple-Problem and Single-Problem Groups

Action learning groups may be formed for the purpose of handling either a single problem or several problems. In the *single-problem* group, the group members focus all of their energies on solving that problem. In this type of action learning, both the membership and the problem are determined by the organization. The primary purpose of the group is to solve the problem proposed to them by the organization. The group may disband after handling just one problem, or may continue for a longer, indefinite period of time and work on a series of challenges submitted to them by the organization. Membership in the action learning group is determined by the organization, based on the type of problem and the aims of the programs. For example, if the organization is seeking to create networks across certain business units, members from those units will be appointed. If the development of high-potential leaders is the goal, then such leaders will be placed in these action learning programs. If the issue is more focused, then participants may be selected according to their interests, experience, and/or knowledge. In some in-company action learning programs, individuals may be allowed to volunteer, but the organization reserves the right to confirm or not confirm the final composition of an action learning group.

In *multiple-problem* sets (also referred to as open-group or "classic" action learning), each individual member brings his or her problem/task/project to the group for fellow members to help solve. The members self-select to join the group and support and assist each other on the problems that they bring. During each action learning session, each member is allocated time for the group to work on his or her problem. Thus, a six-member group that meets for three hours would devote approximately thirty minutes to each person's problem. In open-group action learning, the members may meet on a monthly basis for a few months or a few years. Open-group action learning is usually voluntary and has more limited funding. Thus the groups often meet on their own time and rotate the coaching role among themselves. Over a period of time, new members may join as older members withdraw. The members are usually from a variety of organizations, as well as independent consultants and people who are no longer in the workplace.

The Stages of Action Learning

There are many different forms of action learning. Action learning groups may meet for one or several times over a few days or over several months, may handle one or many problems, may meet for short periods or long periods.

However, action learning generally operates along the following stages and procedures:

Formation of group—The group may be volunteers or appointed and may be working on single organizational problem or each other's individual problems. The group will have a predetermined amount of time and sessions or may determine these aspects at the first meeting.

Checklist for Group Formation

- Will membership be by choice or by appointment?
- What will be the size of the action learning group?
- Will members from outside the organization be included?
- Will the groups operate full-time or part-time?
- How often will the groups meet?
- Are the most appropriate people in the group?
- Are the members clearly oriented to the principles of action learning?
- Are they aware of how action learning is different from task forces and other problem-solving groups?
- Is the role of the action learning coach clear and accepted?
- Are there any specific organizational or individual learning goals?
- Will we be using single- and/or multiple-problem groups?
- Have set members agreed to processes and norms relative to air space, asking questions, and reflection?
- Is there agreement on ground rules relative to confidentiality, starting and stopping on time, being supportive, and taking action between meetings?
- Have they agreed on future dates for set meetings and committed to attending them regularly?
- Do we have access to the necessary outside resources and knowledge?
- Is there a sense of ownership and responsibility for the problem?
- Have they identified a place convenient for participants?
- Is the group clear as to its sponsor and champion?

Selection and presentation of problem or task to group—The problem (or problems, if a multi-problem group) is briefly presented to the group. Members ask questions to gather more information about the problem or task.

Checklist for Selection of Problem/Project for Action Learning Groups

- Who will choose the problems/projects—the organization or individual managers or the group members?
- Who will be presenting the problem?

- Do the problems meet criteria for action learning problems?
  - Are the problems feasible and manageable?
  - Are they urgent and important
  - Do they provide opportunities for learning and development
- Is there a timeframe for completing the project?
- Do the problems or program need to be discussed with top leadership?
- Do managers and participants understand the time involved in working on these problems?
- Are they true problems, or does management already have a solution?
- Does the organization have restrictions on possible strategies?
- Will groups work on single or multiple problems?

Reframing the problem—After a series of questions, the group, with the guidance of the action learning coach, will reach clarity and a consensus as to the most critical and important problem that the group should work on and establish the crux of the problem, which may differ from the original presenting problem.

Checklist for Reframing Problems

- What is the quality of problems (framing)?
- What type of problem is it—technical or adaptive?
- Have we identified the real problem versus the presenting problem?
- Are our goals specific, measurable, feasible, and beneficial to the organization?
- Are we asking fresh questions and taking risks?
- Have the obstacles been identified?
- What is our level of commitment to solving the problem?

Determining goals—Once the key problem or issue has been identified, the group searches for the goal, the achievement of which would solve the reframed problem for the long term with positive rather than negative consequences for the individual, team, or organization.

Checklist for Determining Goals

- Are we committed to innovative, high-quality goals rather than quick solutions?
- Have we examined and tapped where the power, passion, and knowledge reside?
- Are the best-leveraged solutions chosen?

Developing action strategies—Much of the time and energy of the group will be spent on identifying and pilot-testing possible action strategies. Like the preceding stages of action learning, strategies are developed via the reflective inquiry and dialogue mode.

Checklist for Developing Strategies of Action

- Have outside resources and links that may be needed been identified?
- Are action plans specific and part of each meeting?
- Have the actions to be taken been clearly identified at each meeting, including the responsible person(s) and the specific dates?
- Are strategic actions recorded and then reviewed at the next meeting?
- Have learnings from our actions been achieved?
- Have we considered the impact of our strategies?
- How can we pilot-test the strategies?
- What have we learned from the pilot-testing?
- What communications between the top management, sponsors, and group have occurred during the life of the action learning group?
- Will we be sharing our learnings as well as our recommendations?
- Are the strategies for the actions clear, systems-oriented, and time-based?

Taking action—Between action learning sessions, the group as a whole as well as individual members collect information, identity status of support, and implement the strategies developed and agreed to by the group.

Checklist for Taking Action

- Will the group have the authority to implement their recommendations?
- Will proposed solutions first need to be presented to higher management for implementation? If so, to whom will the group present its recommendations?
- How will the group's recommendations be handled and implemented?
- Who will be implementing the strategies?
- Are there likely to be difficulties in implementation?
- Were problems resolved and actions taken?
- How effective were the actions taken?
- Is there sufficient support from top management?
- Is there follow-up to the action learning actions?

Capturing learnings—Throughout and at any point during the session, the action learning coach may intervene to ask the group members questions that will enable them to reflect on their performance and to find ways to improve their performance as a group.

Checklist for the Learnings of the Action Learning Group

- Have the learnings been applied throughout the organization?
- What is the quality of individual development and learning? Of team development and learning?
- Are the greater, long-term benefits and leveraging of learning valued?
- Is there commitment to team and individual learnings?
- Has there been a review of the learning?
- Has a systematic analysis of the learning been applied to other parts of the organization?
- What were the major benefits to the members of the action learning program?
- Have verbal or written reports been prepared for clients, managers, and others interested?
- How can future action learning programs in the company be improved?
- What is planned for follow-up?

An Action Learning Case Example

A large energy company needed to develop a new work schedule that assured that the facilities were covered twenty-four hours a day. The present system was one that sapped the earnings, energy, and morale of the workers and often left the company unable to meet demands of customers. Management's imposition of a six-day-a-week schedule was a burden to the workers and their families, especially since many of the workers needed to drive more than two hours a day to the remote mines. Frustration and anger abounded on all sides, and everyone saw the problem in a different way. The situation demanded action.

A diverse group of eight people was brought together to work on this problem over a two-day period. Management indicated that it was looking for a new solution. After the group received a brief introduction to the six components of action learning, the group began diagnosing the problem and soon saw the problem not only as a stimulus/opportunity to design and take effective action but also as a way to learn how to work better as a team and become more competent leaders. The action learning group consisted of a wide variety of individuals—technicians from different work sites of the company, a senior administrator, and a manager from another industry. The eight members included employees new to the company as well as older, experienced workers. Some were actually experiencing the problem, while others needed to understand why it was a problem. There was pressure to solve this problem and high hopes placed on performance improvement. Management indicated that the group could indeed come up with the solutions, and that everyone's ideas were needed. If the group could ask good questions and learn from one another, the problem could be solved.

Initially, the questions came rather hesitantly and reluctantly. Many wanted to use statements and push for their solutions. Occasionally, the action learning coach asked them to turn their statements into questions and to listen and reflect before answering. Everyone became involved; oftentimes the younger, inexperienced members had better questions and became more confident and received more support. Gradually, the group came to realize that the issue was as much a feeling that employees had no say in the changes as it was of the difficulty of finding a solution that met the needs of workers, customers, and management. The members quickly moved from focusing on individual solutions to seeking what would be best for the organization.

Following a systematic examination of numerous issues, potential impacts of actions, and likelihood of success, the group developed three possible solutions that were submitted to employees at the affected sites as well as to top management. The alternatives were tested as well as refined. Four weeks later, the plants shifted to new schedules that resulted in improved morale among workers, higher satisfaction for customers, and better earnings stability—a measurable performance benefit for management.

The members of the group were advised that this activity was both a problem-solving as well as a learning program. If the group could learn and share together, they would reach a truly innovative solution. Also, they were expected to learn about themselves as leaders and professionals and to identify learnings that could be applied to their particular worksites and to the organization as a whole. The climate and expectations were established to increase learning and performance: they should seek to learn from each other and be aware of the presuppositions and filters that hindered or helped their learning. Consequently, everyone could and did become concerned with helping each other learn and develop.

Throughout the sessions, a person served as a learning coach who focused on helping the group reflect on learning. His very presence alerted everyone that time and effort would be spent in learning, that he would be assisting them to seek creative "breakthrough" thinking and strategies, and that he encouraged everyone to learn from one another. The coach would be a model by only asking positive, supportive questions so as to help members understand and improve the work of the group and to apply learnings throughout the organization.

Applications of Action Learning

Action learning is used to accomplish the following five objectives: (1) solve problems, (2) develop leaders, (3) build teams, (4) create learning organizations, and (5) increase individuals' professional skills.

1. Problem Solving

Action learning begins and builds around solving problems—the more complex and the more urgent, the better-suited is action learning. The dynamic interactive process used in action learning allows the group to see problems in new ways and to gain fresh perspectives on how to resolve them. Questioning from multiple perspectives creates solid systems thinking in which the group sees the whole rather than parts, relationships rather than linear cause-effect patterns, underlying structures rather than events, and profiles of changes rather than snapshots. The action learning process enables the group to look for underlying causes and leveraged actions rather than symptoms and short-term solutions. Action learning examines both macro and micro views so as to discover when and how to best implement the proposed actions. As a result of its fresh approach to problem solving, action learning generates "breakthrough" insights, solutions, and effective strategies.

2. Leadership Development

Most leadership development programs, whether corporate or academic, have been ineffective and expensive. The weaknesses of traditional leadership development program are caused by a number of factors, most notably: (a) teachers rather than practitioners are the purveyors of knowledge; (b) a separation exists between the learning and action; (c) very little learning is transferred to the workplace; (d) the business environment is changing so fast that the knowledge gained from the programs is too slow and inadequate; and (e) the absence of reflective thinking in the education process. Typical executive development programs provide little of the social and interpersonal aspects of the organizations and tend to focus on tactical rather than strategic leadership.

Action learning differs from normal leadership training in that its "primary objective" is to ask appropriate questions in conditions of risk, rather than to find answers that have already been precisely defined by others—and that do not allow for ambiguous responses because the examiners have all the approved answers. Action learning does not isolate any dimension from the context in which managers work; rather it develops the whole leader for the whole organization. What leaders learn and how they learn cannot be dissociated from one another, for how one learns necessarily influences what one learns.

Traditional leadership programs that use case studies are like learning how to steer a boat by looking out the stern. Examining what happened yesterday will not drive change or make a company competitive. Today, success factors keep changing, and no company can stay on top by doing what it used to do. In action learning, we have the opportunity to grow as leaders because we are reflecting on what is urgent and important to us when our assumptions are challenged. Action learning provides managers the opportunity to take appropriate levels of responsibility in discovering how to develop themselves.

3. Building Teams

Action learning teams are extremely cohesive and high-performing; they become more effective every time they meet because the action learning process focuses on how, individually and collectively, teams can become smarter and faster. A "teamthink and teamlearn" capability steadily emerges. The group shares clear responsibility and accountability on real problems, causing a need for deliberative team unity and success. The process of ongoing questioning and shared learning builds powerful caring and cohesion among the members. Developing consensus around problems and goals develops clearness of task, strong communications, collaboration, and commitment, during which powerful team synergy and learning emerge.

4. Creating Learning Organizations

A learning organization is constructed around four primary subsystems: (a) increased learning skills and capacities; (b) a transformed organizational culture and structure; (c) involvement of the entire business chain in the learning process; and (d) enhanced capability to manage knowledge. Members of action learning groups transfer their experiences and new capabilities to their organizations in a number of ways.

First, action learning groups themselves are mini-learning organizations and model perfectly what a learning organization is and how it should operate. Action learning groups seek to learn continuously from all their actions and interactions. They adapt quickly to external and internal environmental changes. Learning and knowledge are continuously captured and transferred to other parts of the organization that could benefit from these experiences. Individuals who participate in action learning groups appreciate the tremendous benefit of questions and reflection in helping them to continuously improve when they return to their respective jobs. They are better learners as well as better leaders. As the action learning members resume their day-to-day activities, their new mindsets and skills gradually impact the entire organization, resulting in a culture more likely to continuously learn, reward learning, and connect learning to all business activities.

5. Individual Professional Growth and Development

Participants in action learning achieve learning at three different levels: (a) understanding something intellectually, (b) applying some newly acquired skill, and (c) experiencing and thereby undergoing an inner development that touches on beliefs and attitudes and leads to personal development. Action learning is particularly effective at this third level because it provides the opportunity for internal dissonance, while the problem and/or action may provide the external trigger. In action learning, we become more aware of our blind spots and weaknesses as well as our strengths, and we receive the feedback and help that we have requested.

Action learning generates tremendous personal, intellectual, psychological, and social growth. Action learning participants experience "breakthrough learning" when they became aware of the need to reach beyond their conscious beliefs and to challenge their assumptions about their present worldviews. This readiness to change and grow is a prerequisite for development. Some of the specific skills and abilities developed for those participating in action learning include:

- Critical reflection skills, which are key to *transformative* learning for the individual
- Inquiry and questioning abilities, through which the individual can do more than just advocate and push personal opinions
- Systems thinking so that individuals begin to see things in a less linear, less accurate fashion
- Ability to adapt and change
- Active listening skills and greater self-awareness
- Empathy, the capacity to connect with others, which is one of the most valuable relationship skills developed in action learning
- Problem-solving and strategy-selection skills
- Presentation and facilitation skills

Action learning has also been utilized as a highly valuable tool for examining and advancing one's personal career. For example, job seekers have effectively used action learning to help them better understand themselves, their career goals, their strengths, and the best resources for locating and landing a job.

The following case demonstrates how all five objectives can be applied.

An international financial firm decided to use action learning as the methodology for handling a critical organizational challenge, as well as for developing their high-potential leaders, building teams, changing the work culture, and improving key individual skills. Six managers from different departments were chosen to be members of the action learning group. Prior to the commencement of the action learning, they were asked to identify the specific leadership competencies that they sought to improve during their participation in the action learning sessions. The challenge assigned to the six managers was to develop a global strategy for the manufacturing division of the company and report their recommendations to the executive council within three months. The firm decided to utilize an external action learning coach to work with the group. The action learning group met one day a week for three months, during which time the goals were clearly established, strategies developed and pilot-tested, and actions recommended. At the end of each session, the action learning coach assisted the group members in reflecting on the application and development of the competencies they had chosen to develop. During each session, learnings and knowledge that could be applied to the team and to the financial firm were also targeted. At the end of the three months, the group presented to the executive council its recommendations as well as its individual, team, and organizational learnings. The executive council, following some questions and minor modifications, accepted the proposed strategies and assigned the team the responsibility for coordinating and implementing the proposed strategies and action plan.

Emerging Trends

Action learning has quickly emerged as one of the most popular and powerful methodologies in organizations to develop leaders and teams, create learning organizations, and enhance professional competencies, as well as solve their most difficult problems. Action learning programs have become instrumental in creating thousands of new products and services, saving billions of dollars, reducing production and delivery times, expanding the customer base, improving service quality, and positively changing organizational cultures. A growing number of universities (George Washington, Virginia Commonwealth, Colombia, Texas, Georgia State, Minnesota, Harvard, Oxford, Helsinki) include action learning courses in their MBA and/or human resource development (HRD) programs. Elementary and secondary schools in the United States, Europe, and Asia now use action learning for staff development and teaching purposes. More and more organizations are developing action learning coaches to coordinate these programs.

References

Argyris, C. (1982). *Reasoning, learning and action.* San Francisco, CA: Jossey-Bass.

Boshyk, Y. (Ed.). (2002). *Action learning worldwide: Experiences of leadership and organization development.* New York: Palgrave Macmillan.

Boshyk, Y. (Ed.). (2000). *Business-driven action learning.* New York: Palgrave Macmillan.

Butterfield, S., Gold, K., & Willis, V. (1998). Creating a systematic framework for the transfer of learning from an action learning experience. *Academy of HRD Proceedings,* pp. 490–496.

Dilworth, L. (1998). Action learning in a nutshell. *Performance Improvement Quarterly, 11*(1), 28–43.

Dilworth, L., & Willis, V. (2003). *Action learning: Images and pathways.* Malabar, Fl: Krieger Publishing.

Dotlich, D., & Noel, J. (1998). *Action learning.* San Francisco, CA: Jossey-Bass.

Inglis, S. (1994). *Making the most of action learning.* Brookfield, VT: Gower Publishing.

Marquardt, M. (1999). *Action learning in action.* Palo Alto, CA: Davies-Black.

Marquardt, M. (2000). Action learning and leadership. *The Learning Organization, 7*(5), 233–240.

Marquardt, M. (2004). *Optimizing the power of action learning.* Palo Alto, CA: Davies-Black.

Marsick, V., & O'Neil, J. (1999). The many faces of action learning. *Management Learning, 30*(2), 159–177.

McGill, I., & Beaty, L. (1995). *Action learning.* London: Kogan Page.

McNulty, N., & Canty, G. (1995). Proof of the pudding. *Journal of Management Development, 14*(1), 53–66.

Mezirow, J. (1991). *Transformative dimensions of adult learning.* San Francisco, CA: Jossey-Bass.

Mumford, A. (1995). Managers developing others through action learning. *Industrial and Commercial Training, 27*(3), 19–27.

Pedler, M. (Ed.). (1983, 1991, 1997). *Action learning in practice.* Aldershot, UK: Gower Publishing.

Pfeffer. K., & Fong, C. (2002). The end of business schools: Less success than meet the eye. *Academy of Management Learning and Education, 1*(1), 78–95.

Raelin, J. A. (1997). Action learning and action science: Are they different? *Organizational Dynamics,* pp. 21–33.

Revans, R. (1938). *Memorandum to the Essex Education Committee.* Unpublished.

Revans, R. (1980). *Action learning: New techniques for management.* London: Blond & Briggs.

Revans, R. (1983). *The ABC of action learning.* London: Chartwell-Brett.

Waddill, D., & Marquardt, M. (2004). Action learning and the schools of adult learning. *Human Resource Development Review, 2*(4).

Weinstein, K. (1995). *Action learning: A journey in discovery and development.* London: HarperCollins.

York, L., O'Neil, J., & Marsick, V. (Eds.). (1999). *Action learning: Successful strategies for individual, team and organizational development.* San Francisco, CA: Berrett-Koehler.

CHAPTER SIX

JUNKYARD SPORTS

Learning Through Creative Play

Bernie DeKoven

Bernie DeKoven's lifelong belief that things can be made more fun led him to develop and implement new ways of playing, new games for groups of all ages and sizes, from singles, couples, and families to schools, communities, and cities, and, most recently, to the publication of his book on junkyard sports. His *Interplay Curriculum*, a comprehensive program in self-esteem and social skills based on over one thousand children's games, was used in classrooms and playgrounds throughout the city of Philadelphia. For the Philadelphia Bicentennial, he designed and orchestrated Playday on the Parkway, a community games event involving hundreds of thousands of celebrants. He established The Games Preserve, a retreat center in Eastern Pennsylvania where teachers, therapists, and recreators could conduct in-depth investigations of games and play. In his book, *The Well-Played Game,* he voiced a philosophy of "healthy competition" that formed the core teachings of the New Games Foundation. He became co-director of the foundation and has developed internationally successful programs in facilitating collaborative games, community events, and business meetings.

Bernie has designed award-winning games with Ideal Toy Company, Children's Television Workshop, CBS Software, and Mattel Toys and has recently published a game through Gamewright. He is currently an adjunct professor at the Multimedia Division of the USC School of Cinema-Television. Bernie is a lifetime member of The Association for the Study of Play.

Contact Information

223 Avenue G
Redondo Beach, CA 90277
(310) 792-7227
bernie@junkyardsports.com
www.junkyardsports.com

THERE WAS A TIME WHEN you wanted to play baseball with the kids in the neighborhood, and the only obstacles were no one had a ball or a bat, you had to play in the front yard, your cousins and uncle wanted to play, too. So you made do. You used a piece of PVC pipe for a bat and made a ball out of duct tape, had your big cousin play pitcher, and, when your uncle was up to bat, your little cousin played runner.

And then you played some serious ball. Well, as serious as you could make it. But not so serious that anybody might get hurt, or not get a chance to play, or was treated unfairly. And if something happened that wasn't actually covered by the rules (like the ball going into the street), you'd make more rules.

Playing like that—playing hard, playing fair, with nobody getting hurt—you were all, ultimately, on one team, making things up as you were going along, designing and redesigning baseball so that everyone could play, as I said, hard, fair, with nobody hurt.

You were also playing with the environment, transforming it, as a matter of fact, into a baseball field that would exist only as long as you were playing in it— creating your tools of play out of found objects that you could whisk away when supper was ready.

A junkyard sports event involves people, junk, and environment. The combination and composition of each creates the challenge and frames the learning. Playing junkyard sports, you tend to become totally engaged: mentally, physically, socially. You have to think as hard as you play, keep your connection to and awareness of the place, the people you're playing with, the way the game is being played.

The Elements of a Junkyard Sport

The sport. Take all the sports that everyone knows how to play. Take a few of your favorite parts. Now make a new sport.

The junk. Given a good collection of junk, it's possible to recreate the needed equipment for almost any sport, from playing equipment to cheer leaders' outfits and trophies, too.

Given a not-so-good collection, the team has to work together to figure out what to use and what to use it for. Plastic grocery bags, socks, cardboard boxes, bowling balls, and sledge hammers.

The people. With a nigh-unto-unmeasurable goal of "total involvement," or at least "each-according-to-his-own involvement," team members again have to work together, intellectually and sensitively, toward inviting involvement from all members—by changing the mix so that you're playing with young and old, for example, or blind and deaf, or disabled.

The environment. Each environment offers its own challenges and its own advantages. The more successfully the team is able to incorporate the environment into the game, the more successful everybody will be.

The method. The group is divided into teams—any fun, relatively random method will do (favorite ice cream flavors, odd or even birth years, clothing color . . .).

You have a garbage bag full of junk for each team—junk being stuff that's too good to throw away, but not really worth keeping. If possible, it's junk from their own business: recycled paper and water bottles, cartons and packing, pieces of this and that.

Teams are then asked to come up with a new way to play a chosen sport (whatever sport you choose), using as much of the junk as they need, as well as play-worthy properties of the environment they're playing in and the people they're playing with. Give them approximately fifteen minutes. (This time limit is important. The key is to make participants feel exactly as much pressure as they need to keep from getting into long-winded discussions about the relevance of different alternatives and the sheer significance of it all.)

Then, participants on each team play each other's games.

That's about all there is to it, really. But what you get in return is a shared, rich, and often profound experience that combines collaboration and competition, creativity and physicality, sensitivity, and adaptability.

Since people have worked together to create their own sports variation, you get collaboration and teamwork.

Since sports are competitive to begin with, you get people wanting to win, above all else. So you get engagement, commitment, complete involvement.

Since the sports they play are made-up, and the equipment made out of junk, you get a kind of self-trivializing exercise that defeats any attempt at making winning or losing more significant than the fun people were able to create for each other.

Since real success can be measured, not in terms of individual or team score, but rather only in terms of the games they've crafted together, you get an experience that embraces competition and cooperation, performance and creativity.

Such a rich play experience can lead to an even richer learning experience about individual and collective behavior, about the dynamics of cooperation and competition, about the uses of resources and responsiveness to individual differences, about success and failure, and more.

Two Examples of Junkyard Sports

Junkyard Golf

The event consists of two different phases. In the first, participants divide into teams of three or more, each team trying to figure out how to use its collection of junk, along with any other junk-like materials in the environment, to create a fun, challenging golf hole. In the second, players invite each other, members of the organization, or community, to test and refine (play) their completed golf course.

Warning: just about any attempt to keep score or par or decide which hole to play next in any meaningful way is pretty much doomed. Creating a hole that is inviting and fun and makes use of everything—that's just one challenge. And it's hard enough. Playing other people's courses and actually managing to get the ball in—given whatever they use for a club and whatever else they use for a ball and wherever they put the hole—is often little short of miraculous.

Gathering Junk At the beginning, give each team pretty much the same collection of junk. Things will change later as each team discovers how to incorporate other junk, but it's most fun if people get to show off their ingenuity by all starting the same. You'll want one collection of junk for every team. And a team can be anywhere from two to twelve players.

Here's the start of a typical junkyard golf junk collection—as I said, it's only a start. Who knows what other junk is right in the area, just waiting to be made into something golfish?

Golf clubs: brooms, empty plastic 2-liter bottles, PVC pipe, hoseballs, rolled-up newspaper or blueprint paper, plastic water bottles or soda bottles or milk bottles or jugs.

Golf balls: aluminum foil balls, sock balls, Ping-Pong balls, plastic bag balls, tissue paper balls, Play-Doh balls.

Tees: plastic bottle tops, soda cans, paper cups, breast pumps

Holes: trash cans, paper bags, paper or plastic cups, cardboard boxes, coffee cans, shoes.

Ramps and bumpers: pizza boxes, paper plates, bike chains, more newspaper, belts, telephone books, computer monitors, keyboards.

Greens and roughs: floors, tabletops, carpets, wood floors, grass, cement, sand, newsprint, cardboard, paper, bubblewrap.

You could think of junkyard golf junk gathering as a kind of art, which is why it falls to you, the junkyard golf pro, to collect and sort the stuff ahead of time.

Building the Course. As the holes are developed and the course laid out, your job, as the golf pro, is to coach each team of hole-makers on how to use everything in their junk pile, and anything else they can find, to create their own golf hole and golf equipment. You make yourself generally available to assist in any aspect of the design of the hole and the golf-like equipment so that teams can design it basically any old way they want.

There doesn't even have to be a golf club.

For example, how about the panty hose sling? Not a golf club, definitely. Yet inarguably fulfilling the golf club function. Even though you have to have two other people to hold the ends of the panty hose—and they have to release the pantyhose at the same time you release the ball—something ball-like gets launched towards the hole.

The ball can be thrown or kicked as well as, of course, hit with a golf-like club or water bottle, or perhaps a shoe. It can be very small or even basketball-size. The tee, it turns out, can be almost anything with a mouth—a bottle, a jar lid, even the business end of a discarded breast pump. Holes can even have human components. For example, some people are exceptionally good at being windmills.

Testing After building the course, teams test their holes and even invite others and help test them. This tends to be great fun and can easily be confused with already playing.

Try to keep the testing time to a joysome minimum so that the people these holes are purportedly being designed for can play, too.

The Tournament. Basically, players get to play any hole in any order, pretty much as often as they want to. Hole-makers who are not actually part of the holes can assist players and, should the spirit so move them, continue to make last-minute adjustments to everything. Par is set by the players. Keeping score is optional.

If it gets crowded and more than a couple players are waiting, have them play together. After the first player shoots, the next player continues from where the ball stopped. Continue taking turns until the ball finally reaches the target. If playing for a score, all players have the same number of strokes counted against them.

Re-recycling. You pretty much really want the event to conclude with some kind of collective collecting of all the junk. Hopefully, all the junk you used is of the kind that your city happens to recycle in the same container—cardboard, paper, plastic, socks.

Junkyard Basketball

The "challenge." Play a game of basketball in the hallway using bubblewrap and plastic grocery bags.

The Competition

- Three teams of seven people each
- Fifteen minutes to make and play test sport
- Thirty minutes to play everyone else's sports

Baggyball: An Example. A bubblebag is made of a plastic grocery bag wrapped around a chunk of bubble wrap. Note, if you will, that there is no tape being

used to keep everything together. Note again how the cunning use of the bag handles stretched over the bubblewrap-containing bag makes possible the construction of a tight and durable ball cover. Yes, the ball could be rounder. However, after several hours of deft experimentation, it became clear that bubblewrap resists being made into a round ball. And as the bubble wrap goes, so goes the bubblebag.

Enough about the bubblebag, except, perhaps, to note how wonderfully hit-uppable it is—different than a balloon or beach ball. Light, yet hefty. Clearly not round. Possessing properties. One could imagine oneself hitting the ball up in the air repeatedly, as if one were engaging in a sort of anti-dribble, bouncing up, where one would normally bounce down. This is, it turns out, almost all the inspiration required to lead one inexorably toward the new, and profoundly playworthy sport of Baggyball.

Here you see an image of a bubbleball adjacent to a plastic shopping bag. Note the relative size. It is somewhat central to the playability of the game that the bag is larger than the bubbleball. Two such bags and one bubbleball make up all the equipment you need to play Baggyball.

Baggyball, you see, is played very much like basketball, except for the following distinctions:

1. One dribbles up instead of down.
2. The baskets are bags that are held by players, who position themselves anywhere they want throughout the court (because it's too boring to pretend to be an immobile basket, and it makes the game a lot more fun and strategically

complex if the baskets can run around). This makes the basket actually a member of your team—and a key member, at that.

3. The game can be played anywhere, on sand or grass, or even a basketball court.

Generalizing Junkyard Sports for All Experiential Designers*

Junkyard sports, as you have read, is a unique and exciting way to engage learners in a variety of ways—like any good experiential learning model. This section is designed to help you think beyond the specifics of individual sports. In other words, to find ways to modify, adapt, and create your own specific solutions and sports.

About the Game

You have read about junkyard golf and basketball. Just as there are many other sports beyond these (e.g., bowling), your junkyard sports repertoire can be unlimited.

Rather than focusing on a game, think about the junkyard framework first. Start your design by thinking about your task or instructional need. Identify and list the key factors or criteria related to your instructional need. Read your list and look for mental or metaphorical connections to a "real" game.

Taking these two steps will help you find the best game for your instructional situation. This will allow you to take advantage of the junkyard framework and make connections between the game you create and the context or content you are teaching.

Once you have identified a game, think about the components of that game, and begin to apply the junkyard concepts to it. Use the examples here as a guide, but be creative!

About the Junk

Finding and collecting the junk needed to run any junkyard sport can seem a bit daunting and quite unusual. Here are several things to take into consideration when selecting and collecting your junk.

---

*I wish to thank Kevin Eikenberry for writing this and the next section. See Kevin's piece (Chapter 15) on experiential learning in team training for more of his wisdom.

- *You can do it, you really can.* Be creative—search your house in your office. Ask your friends and neighbors for help. Everyone likes to get rid of junk. And while they may not understand your reasons, they will be happy to help.
- *Get the group to do it.* Have an office cleanup and use those items as a part of the collection. Or have each participant bring three items of random junk as part of his or her entry to the event. If you will be using existing work-group server teams within the event, you can even consider having each team collect and bring their own junk. Just make sure you don't tell them what the junk will be used for—you'll want to keep that to yourself until the event.
- *Same junk / different junk.* Depending on your instructional goals for your sporting event, you may find it appropriate to collect the same junk for each team. Don't limit yourself to this, however! In many cases, creating one great big pile of beautiful junk that all teams can scavenge from and share will add an additional component that will be instructionally valuable to your design.

Times to Use Junkyard Sports

While there are many concepts or skills that junkyard sports might help you engage people in learning, there are some situations and content for which junk couldn't be put to better use.

- *Long events.* If you are designing a retreat over a weekend or several days with a group that you want to really bond, junkyard sports can be a great option, regardless of your content. It can be used as an opening event or as a session designed to break up or change up the overall flow of the retreat.
- *Ongoing events.* If you bring groups together, consistently over a long period of time, consider junkyard sports. It will serve as a surprise—different from your normal process people have come to expect—and can reinvigorate the group's attitude and enthusiasm for the overall learning process.
- *Gatherings.* If you are bringing people together from different divisions or geography, junkyard sports can be a great way to invite engagement and networking, and at the same time provide a platform to reach instructional goals.
- *Thinking about change.* The structure and experience of junkyard sports is perfect for any situation in which groups are experiencing or preparing to experience change. Junkyard sports give people a safe way to play, and yet think about the concepts of change and examine the rules that are challenged by whatever changes are put into practice.

Other Factors to Consider

As you design your junkyard sports event, there are several factors to consider. Make sure to take these things into account.

- *Team size.* Some sports will be more conducive for larger teams, others for smaller teams. Think about your overall instructional process and what clues that might give you regarding the size of teams you want. Perhaps you want to have natural work groups work together, or perhaps you want to randomly split up the teams. Regardless, desired team size is an important consideration when selecting and designing your sport.
- *Physical space.* Make sure you will have the right size, shape, and amount of space you'll need for the game you are designing. This is a factor that must be considered from the very beginning, in order for your event to have the greatest possible success.
- *People's limitations.* Beware of any physical or other limitations people might have and take that into account in your design. Doing this is the thoughtful thing to do, but also ensures the greatest success for all participants.

Specific Debriefing Suggestions

While the content that you could use junkyard sports to teach is limited only by your imagination, there seem to be some truly natural "fits" for this instructional approach. Below are some suggested debriefing questions to use for these specific content areas.

As with any experiential approach, the debriefing of the exercise is the most critical component in creating the desired learning for all participants. The lists of debriefing questions below follow a natural learning progression. Consider reading each list, even if you plan to use junkyard sports for a different instructional purpose, as they will help you develop those you need for your specific situation.

Creativity

- What were you thinking throughout the exercise?
- What did you observe in yourself and others?
- What were the most creative acts you saw throughout the game? (If your sport included both the design and playing components, you can ask questions about each phase.)

- What surprised you?
- What was the most fun about this exercise? Why?
- What did you see as your strength (or your team's strength) during the game?
- If you were going to play this game again, what would you do differently?
- What about this exercise reminded you of your own life/work situation?
- What lessons about creativity can you take from this exercise?
- How will you remember and apply these lessons in real life?

Teams and Teamwork

- What were you thinking throughout the exercise?
- How did your team form?
- Did a leader or leaders emerge? If so, how?
- What styles or approaches did the leader(s) use?
- Were they successful?
- What kind of planning did your team do? How successful was it?
- How would you characterize your team's effectiveness?
- How did you feel throughout the exercise?
- In what ways was your team most successful?
- What surprised you?
- What was the most fun about this exercise? Why?
- If you were going to play this game again, what would you do differently?
- What about this exercise reminded you of your own life/work situation?
- What lessons about teams and teamwork can you take from this exercise?
- How will you remember and apply these lessons in real life?

Understanding and Leading Change

- What were you thinking throughout the exercise?
- How comfortable were you with the instructions and the process?
- What did you observe in others?
- How did you feel?
- What kind of planning did your team do? How successful was it?
- How does planning relate to successful change efforts?
- What surprised you?
- What was the most fun about this exercise? Why? How does that relate to change?

- If you were going to play this game again, what would you do differently?
- What about this exercise reminded you of your own life/work situation?
- What lessons about change—both for yourself and others—can you take from this exercise?
- How will you remember and apply these lessons in real life?

CHAPTER SEVEN

LEARNING GAMES

Hands-On Participant-Centered Activities

Lorraine Ukens

Lorraine Ukens is owner of Team-ing With Success, an improvement performance consultancy specializing in team building and experiential learning. She is the author of numerous training books and games, including *Getting Together, Working Together, All Together Now, Energize Your Audience, The New Encyclopedia of Group Activities, Adventure in the Amazon, Stranded in the Himalayas, Arctic Expedition, Lost in the Cradle of Gold, Trouble on the Inca Trail, Pump Them Up, Common Currency: The Cooperative-Competition Game, SkillBuilders: 50 Customer Service Activities,* and *101 Ways to Improve Customer Service.* She was the editor and contributing author for *What Smart Trainers Know.* Lorraine served as an adjunct professor for Towson University in Maryland before her recent move to central Florida.

Contact Information
Team-ing with Success
25252 Quail Croft Place
Leesburg, FL 34748
(352) 365–0378
ukens@team-ing.com
www.team-ing.com

THERE'S NO DENYING that learning games are a mainstream approach for conducting training sessions these days. Our early experiences as children start us on the road to learning through play. Play is an essential part of our development, and as adults, we incorporate our early learning to create a manageable version of the real world where we can practice behaviors and improve on our mistakes. A game-based activity will be interesting to adults if it provides a challenge and, therefore, an opportunity to overcome an obstacle with real feelings of success and real learning, even if the situation is a virtual one.

Hands-on, participant-centered games can be used as an innovative and enjoyable part of any learning experience. They stimulate discussion and help illustrate, emphasize, or summarize a point in a very effective way. Because of their flexible nature, such activities meet a variety of learning styles and can be applied to a wide range of situations. They work with any subject matter, any segment of the workforce, and any length training session; however, they must be used thoughtfully and be relevant to the overall learning situation. They are not meant to be used merely because we want participants to have fun during the learning process, but as a means to an end. Facilitators must remember that they are using tools for instruction and keep focusing on the results they want to achieve.

Selecting Appropriate Activities

There are a number of different types of games and activities that can meet similar needs, and you should examine how and when each is best used in terms of process, content, and audience. With literally thousands of published activities from which to choose, selecting ones that are appropriate to your specific needs can be a daunting task. Before you can begin to sift through the mountain of possibilities, it is good to become familiar with the various types of experiential games available. Then you can arm yourself with a set of considerations that will help you refine your search so that you can choose the best activity to suit your specific needs.

Training Games

For any given learning objective, there are endless possibilities for structured activities differing in complexity and in the demands made of the participants. Experiential games can use many different formats besides asking participants to literally play a "game," whether it is a board game, a recreational game, a pen-and-pencil game, or a computer game. They also can require such actions as solving problems and puzzles, analyzing information, making self-disclosure statements, creative expressions in art or song, playing roles, competing in physical challenges, or critiquing case studies and videos. The list is limited only by the imagination!

In general, a game has four critical features: (1) obstacles that prevent the achievement of a goal (*conflict*), (2) rules that deal with different aspects of play (*control*), (3) a special condition that indicates how the game ends (*closure*), and (4) some built-in "inefficiencies" that allow for a degree of variability in play (*contrivance*). A training game involves a fifth characteristic of *competency*, which refers to the objective of improving the players' level of competency in particular areas (Thiagarajan, 2003).

Simulations. One very powerful type of experiential game is the simulation, which adds an additional feature to those listed above. In essence, a simulation is a contrived situation that contains enough reality to induce a real-world response by those participating in the event. The simulated environment requires the participant to "play" a structured role, which produces certain actions and behaviors that are compared to real-life situations. It is this direct connection between game elements and real-world events (*correspondence*) that distinguishes the simulation from other types of training games.

Simulation games are extremely useful tools for examining process-oriented issues, such as team building, leadership, communication, and decision making, because they focus on social or interpersonal skills and group dynamics. They examine the flow of behaviors in a group, where the emphasis is as much on how things happen as it is on the final outcome of the simulated event. As such, simulations are useful to assess skill levels, encourage trying new skills, illustrate the relationship between person and actions, and test decision making.

Process simulations provide the context of a plausible but imaginary situation in which group members are free to learn real lessons about how their behavior affects others. These activities focus on interactions among people and the ways that one's beliefs, assumptions, goals, and actions may be hindered or assisted in interactions with others. The primary concern of such simulations is for participants to experience some of the dynamic social processes that are part of the fabric of organized social groups. Because the simulation allows them to share a common experience, all group members participate as equals. Working through this type of learning activity can provide a team with immediate feedback on how well its members perform. In this sense, simulation games are ideal assessment tools to help determine possible areas of concern that might require additional interventions.

The diversity game *An Alien Among Us* (Powers, 1999) is a good example of a process simulation activity. It can be used for introducing general intercultural awareness, for exploring reasons for cross-cultural differences, or for surfacing individuals' bias or prejudice. Small groups of participants are asked to select the best international candidates for a hypothetical interplanetary mission. Making the selections reveals stereotypes and attitudes of the participants because they are given only partial information about each candidate. A system of having to pay for additional information heightens decision-making discussions. Participants commonly reexamine their thinking and discover that a supposed limitation of an individual need not be considered a liability. The game is designed to be flexible so that facilitators can substitute real-life situations for the interplanetary mission.

Survival-based consensus-decision-making activities constitute one type of process simulation that I often use in my team building and leadership development sessions because they equally explore the concepts of synergy and consensus decision making. By ensuring that all group members have the same level of knowledge about the prescribed situation, they must set objectives, analyze alternative strategies, evaluate the ideas, and choose a solution that best meets the objective. Participants generally enjoy these activities because they offer a free-flowing learning environment that can draw in the vast majority of people. The group members like the "brain work" associated with the simulations—the opportunities to apply logic, knowledge, and even educated guesses to a process of finding workable solutions.

There are typically two varieties of consensus survival simulations: priority-setting ones, where participants rank-order a list of available items necessary for survival in a particular environment, and decision-making simulations, in which participants are presented with specific situational dilemmas that require the selection of the best choice of action from among several options. An example of a priority-setting simulation is *Adventure in the Amazon* (Ukens, 1998), in which fifteen items must be ranked in order of priority for survival after a plane crashes in the jungle. For the decision-making variety, *Trouble on the Inca Trail* (Ukens, 2005) requires participants to make choices on the best actions to take in twelve survival situations within three types of geographical regions in Peru.

Simulations can be used to teach content as well. Originally used in war games for training officers and soldiers, this strategy is currently used in business games for teaching complex concepts. Content simulations have been found to be extremely effective for response training in disaster relief efforts, and organizations such as the American Red Cross and the Peace Corps often use this type of simulation to prepare workers and volunteers for the rigors of their work.

Another example of a content simulation is *Lost in Cyberspace* (Richter & Willett, 2002), developed for Wharton's MBA orientation retreat. The exercise was framed in terms of current business survival and set out to teach some content about the best practices of global virtual teams. The simulation scenario involves trying to win an e-commerce project and thereby prioritizing a mix of technology, information, and team or human factors. It employs the method of individual ranking, followed by team ranking (based on group consensus), and finally reveals the target rankings, which in turn provides the scoring for the individual and team decisions. In the debriefing session, process dynamics (especially how decisions were made by each group) is discussed, but the content is emphasized so that participants learn aspects of global virtual team best practices.

Role Plays. Role plays are similar to simulations, but they differ in the degree to which the participant controls the simulated environment and the amount of decision making that occurs. A simulation specifies the parameters in which the individual can make a decision, whereas the way in which a role play flows is less defined. Traditionally, soft skills taught in the classroom are practiced using role plays. This type of activity may sometimes have limited value because the participants often role play with others who have limited or no experience with the actual skills being taught. In addition, participants may feel like they are being "put on the spot" when they perform the role plays. One way to strengthen the merits of a role play is to allow the participants to design the scenarios themselves based on actual experiences from the workplace. Another way is to have the role plays occur in groups of three to four, where two of the group members role play and the others act as observers. The member roles can be rotated until all the participants have a chance to present an individual situation and play the lead role.

Selection Guidelines

Experiential games can be used for a variety of reasons. They can act as ice-breakers to have participants get acquainted, mix together, or form groups; as energizers to help invigorate and increase attention levels; as a way to transition from one content area to another; or as a group challenge to promote team building. A single extended activity can be used as the main training event, or a series of shorter games can be strung together to encompass a complete training session.

Generally, published activities are written with a specific set of directions for the facilitator to follow. At the same time, experiential games are extremely flexible in terms of group size, time, materials, and even content application. This offers the additional opportunity to vary conditions to meet the specific needs of any group. However, when choosing a game, the facilitator should keep in mind that it must fit within the context of the whole instructional process.

Before you begin the process of selection, an assessment should be made to determine your overall training goals and the audience's experience level, especially in terms of their readiness to take risks and to experiment. After this has been accomplished, the facilitator can use the following considerations to help select and design training games that are both relevant and effective for the intended learning outcomes:

- How relevant is the activity in helping the audience learn skills and concepts that are applicable to the workplace?
- How obvious is the connection between the actions and the mastery of skills and knowledge?
- How involved are the participants during the flow of the activity?
- How challenging are the tasks to be accomplished?
- What content and/or process modifications can be made to the activity?
- What materials and advance preparations need to be made?
- How rigid are the time constraints for the session?
- How clear and concise are the instructions?
- How cost-effective is the game in relation to the training outcomes?

Another issue that might be considered is the amount of competition that should be included in the experiential game. Competition often gives training games their vitality, and they help prepare participants for challenges in the real world. Competitive activities may be designed to challenge the physical or mental capabilities of individuals or teams. When the competition exists among teams rather than individuals, the activity provides a way for group members to work together to do their best. For increased competition, look for a game that rewards effective performance. To emphasize cooperation, select an activity that reduces the element of conflict among the individual participants and increases the challenge between the participants and external constraints, such as time or resources.

Always determine a training game's appropriateness to the characteristics of the audience, the content you wish to cover, and the interaction process you would like to observe. When selecting an activity, it is generally better to err on the side of conservative risk taking rather than take the chance that participants could feel manipulated or vulnerable. Remember, the best way to test the effectiveness of a training game or simulation is to play it!

Designing Your Own Game

Even with the endless choices available from books, magazines, Internet websites, and colleagues, there may be times when you would like to, or must, design your own activity. For example, you might be faced with a situation in which you want to teach information that is specific to your industry or organization or you have content-heavy programs or sessions that teach lots of disparate information. Or you might have the desire to act on your own curiosity in developing a new and different game. You can choose to modify an existing activity in order to present it in a different format that better suits your needs; you might borrow basic structures from non-instructional games and activities; or you can start from scratch.

Novice designers might want to start with brief icebreakers, energizers, and closing activities to become comfortable with the design process. I have found that popular games like dominoes, cards, and *Bingo,* as well as children's games, such as hopscotch and jumping rope, can be used as a basic structure for creating new activities. An opening activity based on a scavenger hunt or treasure map can be very stimulating for the audience and creates a heightened sense of group cohesion that can continue throughout the training session. I have developed quite a few games based on variations of the game of poker to examine problem-solving and decision-making skills, and they always seem to capture the attention of the participants.

Off-the-shelf board games are readily available training tools that can be used for your specific needs simply by adding appropriate debriefing questions. Some examples of games that I have used regularly include *Master Mind*® for logical problem solving, *Break the Safe*® for teamwork, and *Taboo*® for communication skills. *Bop It*® is another game that I used during a customer service training session for hotel employees. Four or five participants were asked to line up, and the first person was handed the game unit. The object was for each person to complete the required instructions and to pass the unit to the next person when told. If any one person failed to complete the instructions correctly, the process needed to begin again. A discussion followed on the importance of each person performing well so that the complete process was successful.

In addition, question-and-answer competitions can be designed for a powerful review option or for teaching new material. To reduce the amount of time it takes to create this type of activity, you can have one group of participants create a set of questions/answers that will be used with other groups. Another approach is to create a classification card game by printing pieces of information (such as facts, concepts, technical terms, definitions, principles, examples, quotations, and questions) on cards. Players are required to use instructional content to classify and sequence the information cards by following procedures borrowed from traditional playing card games.

The well-known *Jeopardy* format is often used to test participants on their knowledge. A simple game board can be constructed from poster board with columnar headings covering content areas from a course. Post-it® Notes can be prepared with answers written on the back (sticky) side and a point or dollar amount on the front. These notes are then placed in the appropriate columns for individuals or teams to select and answer in the form of a question.

Even Hollywood movies can provide a great "case" for review. Movies like *The Bridge on the River Kwai, Twelve O'Clock High,* and *Gandhi* have been used to present a basis for studying leadership. Ratings would be made, as individuals and then in teams, on leadership characteristics as portrayed by the two leaders in the movie, then measured against targeted ratings based on an objective (as much as possible) reading of the movie. In each case, the leadership characteristics would be tailored to the wording of the leadership competencies of the organization undertaking the training. In this way, it is almost like evaluating how well (or badly) the leader would work out if he were leading your organization.

Frame games are excellent sources for creating activities that examine specific content. They use templates for the instant creation of training games by replacing one set of information with another one (Thiagarajan, 2003). An example of this format was applied to customer service training in the activity "Hot Topics" (Ukens, 1998). I used an image of the sun with twelve points to designate twelve terms: technology, fast, training, team, perception, communication, perception, telephone, accurate, distance, sales, and quality. The terms represent attributes that will be linked to determine associations relating to the challenge of providing quality service. Participants select cards that show a two-number combination that corresponds to the attributes, which will be the basis for discussion. The basic framework for the activity also could be used for a discussion on communication by replacing the terms with twelve new ones pertinent to various aspects of the topic: listening, feedback, timely, open, limited, procedures, tasks, participation, leadership, decisions, shared, and informal. In addition, you can cover the same terms using a simple grid matrix or some common arrangement such as compass points, hours on a clock, or a different twelve-point illustration.

Another option is to modify part of the basic structure of an established game to create a new one that better meets your personal learning requirements. This can involve a more complex design process, but it may result in a highly effective experiential game. If you take this approach, it is a good idea to pilot-test the game with a group. Based on the feedback from the participants and your own observations, you may need to make some revisions before you have your final product.

In my own early experiences facilitating team-building sessions, I discovered that very few people were aware of the beneficial nature of competition within a collaborative environment. I wanted to create a game to explore the issue of cooperative competition, while still using a structure that was flexible enough to meet a variety of other team-building concerns. I realized that an important issue I would face during development was the need to devise limited resources to create a heightened sense of competition, while utilizing a process that would require teams to collaborate with one another. I stumbled upon a "parlor game" called *Haggle* that I thought would help build the basics for a potential simulation game.

The objective of *Haggle* is for each player to accumulate the most valuable collection of cards possible. The value of a collection of cards is determined by a predetermined set of rules; however, these rules are not told to the players. At the start of the game, each player receives a secret, random collection of cards, plus one or more slips, each showing one of the valuation rules. Thus, different players will have different sets of knowledge about the rules. Players may trade cards or information about the rules on any terms they choose. Before the end of the game, the final card collection must be handed in for scoring, and the player with the highest score wins.

I used the basic concept behind this game to design a process simulation called *Common Currency* (Ukens, 1996). A defined scenario was developed to help build a simulated "user-friendly" atmosphere and a sense of teamness. Color coins of varying values were added, and twelve pieces of information providing clues to their valuation were created. The coins were to be distributed in random order to teams so that there would be an unequal distribution, and a duplicate set of information cards was incorporated to create the risk of bargaining for information that was already known. In an attempt to gain the most valuable coin set, participants needed to cooperate within their own teams as well as negotiate with other groups for information and coins. The process resulted in a debriefing session that included the topics of teamwork, strategic planning, leadership, communication, conflict resolution, negotiation, goal setting, resource sharing, problem solving, and decision making.

No matter how you approach the design of your own activity, you should consider the following factors: learning objectives, approximate duration, recommended group size, materials, preparation needed, room setup, step-by-step directions on how to run the activity, and appropriate debriefing questions. The processing questions should cover all three basic stages of the learning cycle: what was experienced, what insights were gained, and what will be done with this information. Effective, stimulating questions are open-ended and encourage participation to facilitate individual reflection and practical application of the learning.

Facilitating the Learning

The process of experiential learning happens through the guidance of a group facilitator, and how this leader performs that role influences learning outcomes. During a training session, the facilitator's role is to carry out the process of the activity so that there is movement in the direction of learning.

The first thing a facilitator must remember is that adult learners have strong feelings about learning situations in general. This fact influences three very important issues when facilitating a training session that uses experiential games:

1. Adult learners have a high degree of pride and may fear a loss of respect as well as reputation.
2. Adult learners have established values, attitudes, and tendencies that result in set habits and strong tastes that affect their personal learning process and the way in which an activity flows.
3. Adult learners have a good deal of first-hand experience, so they bring along a wealth of ideas to contribute.

In response to these points, the facilitator must use experiential activities thoughtfully and sensitively to help alleviate many of the fears that adults associate with the learning process and allow for a comfortable environment of discovery. Facilitators must be attuned to audience preferences and experiences so that they create a suitable and safe environment in which the participants can perform. Finally, it is the job of the facilitator to tap into the reactions and ideas of the participants, guiding them in making connections between the outcomes of the activity and the real world.

Learning Environment

The facilitation process begins with the creation of the actual learning environment, from setting the mood to modeling acceptable behaviors. Selecting a theme for the overall training session can help participants immerse themselves emotionally in the overall experiential learning process.

When I present a workshop using my *Adventure in the Amazon* (Ukens, 1998) simulation, I set a jungle theme. I dress in khaki attire, complete with a regulation pith helmet, place a few stuffed parrots strategically about the room, and play jungle sounds in the background. Animal cutouts are placed on each table and, as participants enter, they are given corresponding animal-shaped erasers that help them form teams. Team leaders are chosen and each is given a straw pith helmet. After the debriefing session for the simulation, I run the activity *What You Herd* (Ukens, 2004) that has the participants use animal cookies to select one breed of animal to collect. This closing event builds on the simulation by requiring the members of each team to interact and negotiate with other teams, as well as explore the need for flexibility in goals and planning strategies.

The facilitator should prepare the group so that members know why they are there and what is to be accomplished by explaining the purpose of the session and setting the tone. Showing enthusiasm and interest shows that you believe in what you are doing. Individuals should be listened to and recognized, objectivity must be supported, and the learning environment should provide a safe place to be.

Participants also need to be encouraged to participate fully while respecting the rights of others. You can begin using experiential games right from the beginning with an activity that develops group norms for participation in the training session. This can be anything from developing and posting team-discussed session guidelines in an opening activity to using a preset number of poker chips to guarantee equality in individual participation during the debriefing session, as seen in the activity "Chip In" (Ukens, 2004).

It is critical that the leader stay in control without assuming an authoritarian position—keep the group on track and moving forward. Unless an activity calls for the facilitator to take an active role, participants should be allowed to experience the event on their own. They should be allowed the freedom to make mistakes, because this is in itself an excellent way to examine the situation and learn from its outcomes. The leader must provide clear directions, but should intervene only on questions of procedure and only to give as much detail as necessary to answer inquiries without influencing the results.

Debriefing Process

The debriefing is the critical point at which to make connections with the real world, and it must be interactive. The facilitator leads participants to insights by discussing, reflecting, and questioning what was experienced. Unless an experiential game is used strictly to teach new information through a tournament or question-and-answer format, a debriefing session should occur.

The facilitator must emphasize the instructional message so that participants take the training seriously. The learning outcome of a game often depends on how well the facilitator is able to lead the debriefing discussion. Therefore, the facilitator should feel confident with the information, both in terms of the content and the process of the activity, so that he or she can guide the discussion with appropriate questions and respond appropriately if the discussion yields outcomes that are not necessarily anticipated.

In general, the debriefing discussion should cover the actual results of the activity (outcome) as well as the process aspects of the learning event. The process dimension examines the dynamics that occurred in reaching these final results. Participants should be encouraged to reflect on *how* and *why* the outcomes occurred while examining the underlying group roles that played a part in determining the final results. Task-oriented processes involve those aspects that contribute to task accomplishment and include such aspects as planning, goal setting, problem solving, decision making, creativity, and risk taking. Relationship-oriented processes explore the working relationships within a group, including such things as group cohesiveness, collaboration, trust, conflict management, and negotiation.

Rather than telling them the learning points, an effective facilitator guides the participants into realizing what occurred during the activity. During the debriefing discussion, the facilitator should encourage expression of feelings from the participants. This is important because individual feelings influence how much change in behavior will be considered, how much effort will be expended, and whether energy goes toward action or toward defensiveness. A successful learning event is one in which the participant leaves with at least one powerful and useful insight. This process of forced reflection and subsequent internalization of the possible learning points makes experiential games worth the time, energy, and money expended by both the individual and the organization.

There are a variety of ways to process information during a debriefing session. Some of these options include:

- Individual reporting;
- Small group discussions and reports;
- Large group question-and-answer format;
- Surveys and polling, using show of hands, flip-chart tallying, and so forth;
- Public opinion polls, obtaining as many different answers to each question as possible;
- One-on-one participant interviews and reports;
- Panel or round-table discussions; or
- Whips (quick, free-association go-arounds).

Published training games provide a set of debriefing questions that are recommended for processing the activity in terms of the proposed content applications. The facilitator should concentrate on those questions that are relevant to the main topic of the session, providing additional ones as necessary. A multi-stage feedback approach is recommended, with each stage identified by a specific question. The debriefing questions should examine three key areas: What happened, why it happened, and how it applies to the real world.

Although the facilitator may have a specific objective for introducing an activity, participants may get something else out of the experience that goes beyond the expected. The facilitator must be prepared to "go with the flow" of the debriefing session and guide the process without judgment. Therefore, participant feedback will help determine the actual direction and composition of the debriefing period. This is especially true when "mistakes" are experienced during the actual event that lead to new insights. For example, a group might be asked to devise a structure and build it, but then ultimately it collapses. Although a specific question is not included for this occurrence, a discussion can develop as to why the structure did not last: Was it poor design, ineffective use of materials, unresolved conflict in the group, limited participation by individuals, or was it something else?

A sufficient amount of time should be devoted to the debriefing session, since it is the part of the session that is absolutely essential for learning to occur. The more elegant the design of the simulation, the longer the debriefing will run compared to the actual activity. It is also important to remember that, although the facilitator may have a specific intention in mind for the activity, participants may get something else out of the experience that goes beyond this initial objective. Therefore, be flexible enough in estimating the time needed for your debriefing session to allow for unexpected observations.

Using goal-setting and action-planning activities at the end of a learning session can help participants transfer the skills from the classroom to the real world. In addition, a written action plan generally strengthens a participant's commitment to behavior change. These action plans can range from a simple listing of the steps that individual participants will take in the immediate future to a structured exercise whose outcome is a detailed plan of action for a team to accomplish in a specified timeframe. A team-planning activity that combines elements of content review with motivation for change is illustrated through *Transfer Vehicle* (Pike & Solem, 1997). The team draws a vehicle to represent the transfer of learning, identifying the group's vision (where they are going), the people involved, the baggage (what they are taking along), the motivation (fuel), and exhaust (what is being left behind).

Summary

Hands-on, active learning experiences help keep participants active, alert, and productive. Experiential games stimulate discussion and learning; and they help illustrate, emphasize, or summarize concepts in a very effective way. The flexible structure of these activities helps meet a variety of learning styles and can be applied to a wide range of topics. As learning becomes enjoyable, people develop the desire to comprehend even more. The actual learning occurs when a person engages in the activity, looks back on it critically, abstracts some useful insight, and then puts the result to work through a change in behavior or planned applications in real-life situations. To make the right choices, facilitators should keep in mind the balance of their needs with their selection of training games. They must consider such factors as the intended learning outcomes, audience characteristics, the issue of transferring the learning, learning environment, cost, and effectiveness of the exercise under given circumstances. Remember, the actual activity is merely the vehicle for learning. It is the processing of the information in terms of applying it to the real world that makes an experiential game worth the time and effort.

References

Pike, R. W., & Solem, L. (1997). *50 creative training closers.* San Francisco, CA: Pfeiffer.

Powers, R. B. (1999). *An alien among us: A diversity game.* Boston, MA: Intercultural Press.

Richter, A., & Willett, C. (2002). *Lost in cyberspace.* San Francisco, CA: Pfeiffer.

Thiagarajan, S. (2003). *Design your own games and activities: Thiagi's templates for performance improvement.* San Francisco, CA: Pfeiffer.

Ukens, L. L. (1996). *Common currency: The cooperative-competition game.* King of Prussia, PA: HRDQ Press.

Ukens, L. L. (1998). *Skillbuilders: 50 customer service activities.* King of Prussia, PA: HRDQ Press.

Ukens, L. L. (2004). *The new encyclopedia of group activities.* San Francisco, CA: Pfeiffer.

Ukens, L. L. (2005). *Trouble on the Inca Trail.* San Francisco, CA: Pfeiffer.

CHAPTER EIGHT

COMPUTER-BASED SIMULATIONS

Principles of Engagement

Clark Quinn

Clark N. Quinn has been leading educational system design for since the late Seventies, working with business, education, government, and the not-for-profit sectors to develop innovative applications that meet real needs. Currently working through Quinnovation, he previously headed research and development efforts for Knowledge Universe Interactive Studio. Before that he held executive positions at Open Net and Access CMC, two Australian initiatives in Internet-based multimedia and education. Clark has held positions at the University of New South Wales, the University of Pittsburgh's Learning Research and Development Center, and San Diego State University's Center for Research in Mathematics and Science Education. Clark earned a Ph.D. in cognitive psychology from the University of California, San Diego, after working for DesignWare, an early educational software company. He has developed mobile learning, performance support, and intelligent learning systems, as well as conducted strategic learning design. Among other things, he has been responsible for the design of award-winning online content, educational computer games, and websites. His book on designing e-learning games, *Engaging Learning, Designing e-Learning Simulation Games* (Pfeiffer), came out in 2005.

Contact Information
Quinnovation
(925) 200–0881
clark@quinnovation.com
www.quinnovation.com

AT THE END OF THE DAY, it's not about learning. No, it's about doing. Doing something new, something valuable. Learning is a means to an end. So we need to consider the end before we consider the means.

There are lots of outcomes we might care about. We might care about new knowledge that lets us adapt what we're doing to new understanding. We might care about new skills, which let us do new things. We might care about new attitudes or values that help us understand what we should be doing.

Each of these has its own mechanisms. For new knowledge, often we can suffice with a job aid that brings that knowledge to the point of need. If it needs to be memorized, there are well-known mechanisms for that. For attitudes, the best-received wisdom I've found (and this is an interesting area for exploration) is that learners must make their own views explicit, be exposed to other views, explore the tradeoffs, and then commit to the new values, before receiving support in acting in accordance with those values.

If the focus of our learning efforts is skills, however, we need practice opportunities. Ideally, these are real world, for fastest transfer, but many times costs of various sorts prevent this, so we engage with *simulations* of the real practice. And when we do this, there are some principles that suggest how to do it optimally. And that's what we're going to talk about here, designing simulation experiences that work best.

Note that the discussion is assuming, to some extent, that this is about designing *technology-mediated* learning practice, or e-learning. The principles, I maintain, are of far broader applicability, but this will be written from the point of view of designing interactions, and abstraction to the broader principles will be an exercise left for the reader.

So what's known about effective learning practice?

Effective Learning Practice

The cognitive principles of designing effective learning practice are well known. We know that minimizing the distance between the practice context and the application context is important, and the broader the application context, the broader the practice contexts we need. We know that we need to strip away some of the details and provide *scaffolding* (support during performance, such as simplified tasks or where some of the steps are performed for the learner) that is gradually removed as the learner becomes more proficient. We need to ensure that the learning focuses on relevant differences and doesn't incorporate meaningless or well-known components.

A list of elements of effective practice, derived from a variety of learning theories, isolates the following repeated elements:

- *Contextualized:* the experience is in a context.
- *Clear goal:* the learner has, or discovers, a clear goal.
- *Appropriate challenge:* the challenge is within the learner's range *with assistance.*
- *Anchored:* the task is a real application of the skills.
- *Relevant:* the learner cares about the task.
- *Exploratory:* there are different options to try.
- *Active manipulation:* the learner must commit to a choice.
- *Appropriate feedback:* the learner receives feedback that ultimately ties his or her individual performance back to the concept.
- *Attention-getting:* the learner's attention is maintained throughout the experience.

These are the important cognitive components of designing effective learning practice experiences. However, we need more. What other elements might contribute to simulation experiences that are not just effective, but meaningful, even engaging?

Engaging Experience Elements

One of the elements that is almost completely missing (with the notable exception of Keller's ARCS model, 1983) from traditional instructional design is the emotional component of learning. Keller recognized that elements of the learner's *attention,* the *relevance* of the material, the learner's *confidence,* and the ultimate *satisfaction* of the learning experience contribute to the success of learning. Here I'm taking a slightly different cut that still addresses these elements. Technically, in cognitive science, we tease the non-cognitive components of learning into affective and conative categories. *Affective* has to do with who you are as an individual learner, which in learning typically means *learning styles*. *Conative* has to do with your intentional and volitional stance toward the learning, and essentially means your motivation to learn and your comfort with the learning experience.

These emotional elements are important. Do learners learn best when they're unmotivated and anxious? Of course not, yet much of instructional design and e-learning has ignored that element. So we are beginning to see emphasis on *motivating* examples in an introduction, and not just a presentation of what will be learned; of writing the objectives to be achieved in terms of the learner's goals, not the designer's; of making the contexts of the examples and practice of interest to the learner; and providing support for maintaining engagement throughout the learning process, as well as providing emotional closure in the wrap-up of the learning process. This is in addition to the traditional cognitive enhancements, including multiple representations of the concept, guided reflection linking performance back to the concept, and supporting maintenance of the learning beyond the learning experience.

Here we are focusing on practice, so we need to explore the elements that make emotionally meaningful experiences. To address the emotional side of motivation, we will want to create an *engaging* experience. I use engagement as the term to characterize an experience that is enjoyable, that makes us want more, that we might even be willing to pay for. What makes such an experience? Where do we look?

Note that the emphasis here is on active engagement. Movies and theatres, although we draw on their lessons, engage imagination but do not require learner actions or choices. We are still experimenting with interactive experiences, notably the computer game industry. However, we know we need learners to make choices, to commit themselves between alternatives, to create learning. Just viewing information is not enough, unless and until they've created a specific need for that information through some task they're trying to accomplish and can get it wrong. In learning (versus, say, performance support) we need to create that task, hence the need for interactive experiences.

There are a number of different sources of information about experiences. Formally, psychology has looked at the experience of the "flow" state, being "in the zone." Researchers in computer interface design have looked across game design, theatre (film and stage), and even stage magic. My own explorations have included stories, myths, and even ritual.

Just as there are emergent elements that arise across learning theories, so too are there elements that arise across characterizations of meaningful and engaging simulation experiences:

- *Thematic coherence:* an integrating world is created for the actions of the player.
- *Clear goal:* the player is given or discovers a goal to achieve.

- *Balanced challenge:* the challenge is just within the player's capability.
- *Relevance—action to domain:* the actions the player takes affect the story in meaningful ways.
- *Relevance—problem to player:* the player cares about the story and the goal.
- *Choices of action:* there are a variety of (or at least the perception of) possible actions the player can choose to take.
- *Direct manipulation:* the player acts directly in the world.
- *Coupling:* the world reacts in ways coherent with the player's actions.
- *Novel information/events:* there are unexpected occurrences in the world.

These elements contribute to an engaging experience.

Synergy

There is a perfect alignment between the elements of effective learning and engaging entertainment experiences (see Table 8.1).

Our intuitions have told us that learning should be engaging, and we have research about the effectiveness. Now we know why. This synergy says why our learning experiences should be engaging to be most effective. We will integrate (and expand) these two lists and create one unique set of terms to guide our design process.

- *Theme:* an integrating world to serve as context for the learning
- *Goal:* a clear goal to achieve
- *Challenge:* the right level of difficulty in achieving the goal
- *Action/domain link:* the learner's actions must meaningfully affect the learner's ability to achieve the goal in the world

TABLE 8.1. LEARNING/ENGAGEMENT ELEMENT ALIGNMENT

Learning Elements	Engagement Elements
Contextualized	Thematic coherence
Clear goal	Clear goal
Appropriate challenge	Balanced challenge
Anchored	Relevance: action to domain
Relevant	Relevance: problem to learner
Exploratory	Choices of action
Active manipulation	Direct manipulation
Appropriate feedback	Coupling
Attention-getting	Novel information/events

- *Problem/learner link:* the goal and world need to be of interest to the learner
- *Active:* the learner will have to make choices and explore the entailments of the world
- *Direct:* the learner must act directly in the world
- *Feedback:* the world must react to the learner's actions
- *Affect:* the world will address the learner's emotional engagement through novelty and humor

We now know learning *should be* hard fun. *Can* we make it so?

Engaged Learning in Simulations

What are we really talking about here? What characterizes the types of learning experiences we want to develop in simulations? To answer that question, let's take a step up and consider the larger context in which this happens. As mentioned, it's about simulating real experience. Real experience, of course, brings the biggest direct transfer of learning to similar experiences. The value of simulated practice is in providing practice before any real application until sufficient skill is developed to prevent costly mistakes. We do not want to risk lives, for instance.

There are other benefits to simulated learning, however. We can strip away unnecessary details and focus on underlying abstractions. This can help support far transfer. When we talk about education versus training, we're talking about far transfer to all applicable situations, not just those seen in the learning situation. We may alter the timing of important elements so that they come more often than normal to give concentrated practice, or slower than normal to give a chance to learn the necessary skills and gradually acquire the ability to handle them faster.

Regardless of whether our decisions to simulate are for safety or educational purposes, once we decide a simulation of an experience is necessary, we want to ensure our design optimizes to achieve the learning outcome.

At this point, I'd like to make a point about terminology. I've called the goal a simulation of an experience. Technically, a simulation is just a model. It can be just a one shot "start and let it run," like modeling a chemical reaction, or it might be something you can twist the dials on. However, I want to differentiate between a model and the case in which you put a simulation in a particular initial state and ask the learner to achieve a final state. I want to call that latter case, often wrapped in a story, a *scenario.* If you tune the scenario until you get an experience of engagement (and the foregoing should have convinced you that you should), then I believe it qualifies as a game.

As I mentioned, I'm talking about digital experiences, but again the principles hold true for interpersonal experiences also. Some interactive learning tactics work to process information more effectively. Here we're going beyond, not just to learn new concepts, but to apply knowledge to solve problems and make decisions like the ones we want to be able to solve after the learning experience. Ideally, this practice motivates the search for the necessary knowledge, rather than having to dress up "drill and practice."

One of the things I've learned since I laid out the elements above, and an associated design process (Quinn, 2005), is that a useful guide to take that theoretical stance into a workable tool is to characterize the learning situation in terms of a repetition of a core structure of decisions, setting, misconceptions, and consequences (see Figure 8.1).

The key is focusing on the decisions that learners can make *after* the learning intervention. Starting with a setting, the learner is thrust into a situation that requires a decision. By focusing on what learners can *do* differently afterward, particularly the tough decisions that they need to make, we're ensuring that our learning objectives are high enough. They may need knowledge as well (cf., Van Merrienboer, 1997), but that's both a well-known problem and also the source of much of our misguided emphasis. Subject-matter experts (SMEs) will tell you that learners need to know this, and that, and this other thing, but what you want is the learner to be able to make new decisions correctly,

FIGURE 8.1. SCENARIO CORE STRUCTURE.

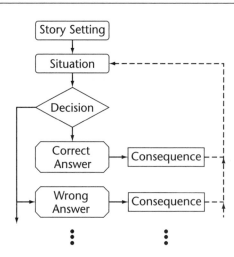

perhaps based on that knowledge. Much of our education focuses on knowledge, and not on the ability to use it to solve problems. That leads to what is known in cognitive science as "inert knowledge," knowledge we can systematically demonstrate we know, and yet do not access in appropriate situations for use.

These decisions tend to travel in packs; we see a series of them in play across a situation or task. So, in the sales process, for instance, the ideal might be that we want our learners to gather information before contacting a client and then just establish the relationship and verify information before discussing product. What we need to do is establish a setting that contextualizes the decisions, putting them in a thematic world that provides a rationale to make those decisions. This world will include a context and a goal. These have to meet the dual constraints of being a real application of the knowledge (that is, making the decisions affects the outcome of the story toward achieving the goal), and being a setting and goal of interest to the population of learners.

The right answer, of course, is necessary, but how about the wrong answers? Here's where we bring in a robust phenomenon in complex performance: learners don't tend to make random errors in attempting to solve a problem. Instead, there are reliable patterns of incorrect performance. These patterns come from learners bringing in different models or frameworks (ones useful elsewhere but inappropriate here) about how to perform in this situation. Quite simply, we generally operate in the world on the basis of our understanding of the world, constituted as models. We bring these into new situations and try to find a match. When wrong, we don't tend to simply toss away the incorrect model and ask for a new one, we have a habit of "patching" the existing model. In general, this is a good survival strategy, but it makes it difficult to adopt a new model.

The good news about these misconceptions is that they make the perfect alternative to the right answer. Written well, these misconceptions are good distractors such that we get the necessary level of challenge, and when that choice is made we have a clear opportunity to address the misconception. So we should try to identify all existing (or in the case of new information, anticipated) misconceptions accompanying each decision.

Once we have the correct answer as well as the misconceptions, we need to know what happens in all cases; we need to capture the *consequences* of each decision. This lets us know what happens next, to play out the story. Particularly, in the case of making mistakes: is it terminal, can you get another chance, or where do you end up? This information is used to structure the flow of the learning experience to let the experience play out in the form of a story. The consequences will create a new situation to be dealt with.

The Systematic Design of Simulated Experiences

There's a fundamental perspective necessary in delivering this sort of learning experience. It's far too frequent that designers think they create content; the necessary perspective instead is that we are *designing experiences*. We need to consider the flow of the learner's emotions and attempt to achieve a particular outcome. The goal should be a wry recognition of the need for the learning, as well as a slightly anxious eagerness to begin. The anxiety should dissipate, but a curiosity should replace it. There might be some initial frustration mixed with some exciting discoveries as well. The pattern should shift to growing confidence and excitement, culminating in the experience of success that is wrapped into a feeling of closure. How do we systematically design *experiences*?

Design

A generic process of design consists of analysis of the situation, specification of a potential solution, implementation of that solution, and evaluation of the success. That model certainly contains the necessary elements, but needs to be augmented with the reality that, at least when dealing with a material as complex as the human mind, we will need to iterate and approach a final design, not merely make one pass through the process. Thus, we will develop interim representations and test them in increasing fidelity with increasingly close approximations to our final audience, cycling until we achieve our design goals (see Figure 8.2).

FIGURE 8.2. DESIGN CYCLE.

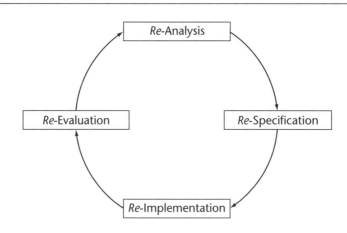

We need to keep in mind the emotional component as well as the cognitive. We will need to understand the emotional components of our audience, and we will need to consider addressing motivation and anxiety as well as independent learning styles. Years ago I took a multicultural learning workshop, and after they surveyed different cultural approaches to learning, what I was left with as the take-home message was that the best learning approach works for all learning styles, but you may have to support them into this form of learning. Similarly, it has been argued that there is a new generation of learners who can't (or won't) learn any other way. I suggest that the proposed new learning approach is simply the best for all learners, regardless of generation, learning style, and so on. We may provide different story lines for different generations, certainly for different audiences, but the underlying approach of presenting challenging decisions in a meaningful story line will remain a constant, as it works for the "wetware" we all share.

So what does an engaged learning design process look like? I believe that a new design process would not be able to be adopted in many organizations, since it's too hard to totally redesign a process. Fortunately, the core elements of design remain the same, and we augment them to accommodate our richer picture.

Analysis

Our analysis phase must gather some additional information. First, we have to ensure that our objectives are capable of being stated at the level of decisions. From experience, it's often work to get the SMEs to talk in terms of cognitive skills, at a high-enough taxonomic level of description. We can still use the traditional Mager style of objective (Mager, 1975), where we stipulate context, objective measure of performance, and criteria, but we need to ensure that we're talking about knowledge application, not recitation, so using the concept of decisions has proved useful in this regard. As indicated above, we will need to capture as well the misconceptions and consequences, as well as settings in which the decisions occur.

The second area of new information we need is about the audience. Traditionally, we started with what they needed to know at the end and then identified where the audience starts from, and that gave us the parameters around our learning design. We still need this information (with the caveat above about ensuring high-level objectives), but we need more. We now need to understand the audience's interests and motivations—who the learners are as people. We will want to find ways to characterize them that differentiate them from other audiences. In past projects, I have found differences between engineers and nurses, and even between different types of nurses. These characteristics suggest that story lines for one audience will not work for others. I have found it useful to talk to the SMEs and ask them why they like this work. At a level below the "making the world a better place," which motivates essentially all of us, there're unique characteristics to the task that appeal to the individuals who've self-selected this role.

The outcome of the analysis process should include not only the necessary decisions and attendant information and audience knowledge and characteristics, but also criteria that would indicate a successful solution. The answer to the question of "when do we stop iterating" should not be when we've run out of time and money, but instead when we've achieved the metrics we set as success criteria (practically, you may change your criteria as your development process reveals unforeseen limitations, but you should do it consciously, not through expediency). These metrics will now include not only the usability and learning outcome metrics, but also an aesthetic evaluation. As engagement is, at the end, largely a subjective experience (there *are* physiological indicators, but you probably don't want to go there). A subjective rating will be sufficient, but decide *a priori* what an acceptable rating is. In some cases it might well be commercial success, where people will actually pay money for the experience. In more cases, however, it will likely be preference over other forms of learning. There should, however, be metrics set explicitly.

Specification

Once you have done the analysis, you move into the specification process. Here we design a solution that integrates the necessary decisions into a story setting that is interesting for the audience. This is the creative part, where you draw on your knowledge of popular culture (you now have license, nay, a mandate, to read novels, watch films, play games, etc.—it's *research*) to specify the world that will host the action and command interest.

In some cases it will make sense to have the setting be very close to the actual performance context, and in others we may choose to make the context fantastic. For instance, if we want near transfer, we will want to make the context very realistic. In a game we did to help kids learn to survive on their own, the player wandered around a simulated town. We stripped away unnecessary details to focus on the key skill of persistence and the knowledge of the various options available. In other cases, such as far transfer to all applicable situations in which the number of application or performance contexts is more than we can cover in the game, we may want a setting that is quite different from any application, and then we explicitly support abstraction and transfer, either within the learning environment or afterward as part of the overall learning experience. We did so in a game about project management (for non-project managers) where we set it in space, a science fiction setting (that appealed to the audience of engineers and played to the strengths of the production team). It was close in some respects to the tasks that the engineers normally performed, but different enough to find ways to remove unnecessary detail and focus on the underlying concept.

We can save ourselves some work if we tap into familiar genres of settings. Familiar story categories can tap into western, medieval, science fiction, and other such settings. Similarly, for games there are particular types, such as strategy (allocating resources), role playing (exploring and interacting), adventure (exploration and problem solving), first-person shooter (movement and first-person perspective), and others. Choosing the right genre of game, mapped onto an appropriate setting, simplifies the understanding for the learner and gives a variety of tricks to draw from. Also, some of the game genres provide tools to customize the underlying game engine implicit in particular versions, such as the Unreal engine for first-person shooters. Beware, however, of prematurely converging on an engine for its appeal; if you adapt the decisions to the engine, instead of the other way around, or add extrinsic tasks (I'm reminded of a medical scenario set in a hospital where you had to operate an elevator, completely irrelevant), you are violating the principles of designing learning games. Ensure that the decisions drive the design process.

A key tool in specifying a game is exaggeration. This means enhancing the story line, and the importance of events, to create more excitement and associated motivation. Use topical events, as long as they won't be dated throughout the shelf life of the learning. If you're working on a patient, make it the ambassador involved in a critical negotiation, or if you're calculating a budget, make it the anti-terrorist department. In the real world, the pressures of life will make most tasks feel critical, and you want to enhance the learning experience to similarly embrace a sense of urgency and importance. This isn't the only way you want to tap into their personal goals (saving the planet, helping people, etc.), but it's one important item in your tool chest. It's a careful balance, of course. SMEs will often err on the side of conservatism ("such unnecessary drama about intrinsically *important* stuff"), and your audience will have a tolerance level that can be exceeded, but push the envelope a wee bit beyond the comfort zone and my experience has been that the audience is appreciative.

In later iterations, the task of tuning becomes important. You typically won't get the best experience on your first pass. You'll have some parameters that need adjustment, and you'll want to test and tune those settings (recall the software engineering comment earlier). A revered game designer once said that 90 percent of the work in a game is tuning the experience. Many times we won't be working to achieve commercial significance, but we will want an experience that at least achieves our engagement metrics set in the analysis phase. To do that tuning, we'll need a working prototype.

Implementation

In iterative development, there are two approaches: you either develop a full implementation and refine it (*evolutionary* prototyping) or you use different implementations at different stages and refine the design before committing the effort to a full implementation (*revolutionary* prototyping). In reality, many people use a mixed strategy. For instance, a storyboard capturing all the major screens or screen types (a useful tool) can serve as an interim prototype to mentally simulate the experience and to refine it before committing to a digital implementation. I recommend matching the implementation of the design to the stage of development—low-tech early, then more fully realized later on.

There are different forms of final implementation, as well. At it's simplest, we can (and should) wrap engagement around even a single decision (essentially, a multiple-choice question). We can also have a fixed sequence of connections, commonly known as a *branching* scenario. In this case, your decision at any point always leads you to the same next place. As a result, you have limited replay, but can get a lot of the value of the engagement for a relatively low production cost (the design cost is only marginally lower; the extra effort to specify the contextual nature of the decision in rules is not that much more than the initial amount of effort to extract the necessary information and specify misconceptions and consequences). The next stage is to have an "engine," a model of the world in terms of variables and states, and a set of rules that determine the next decision based on the current state of the model and the learner's decision. This latter is, I believe, the richest and most effective experience, but it has an extra production cost in terms of the necessary skills to develop it. In addition to the media, you need significantly more programming time. Whichever approach you take, you'll develop a working prototype to test.

Evaluation

The evaluation is only one step more than the normal evaluation phase. The questions you need to address at any iteration will likely include establishing usability before addressing the learning outcomes (in that order), and both need to occur before assessing the engagement. When all three goals have been hit, you're ready to release and move to a maintenance phase.

The evaluation methods you use, I recommend, should include alternations between *expert review* and *user testing*. In learning technology applications, you need two types of expert review, one on the subject matter and another on the learning interactions. Here you might also want an expert on engagement. The benefit of expert review is that the experts can often identify major known problems and provide recommendations for solutions. User testing finds unexpected problems. Using one exclusively isn't as effective as using both. Note that your users should progress as well as the level of prototype. Testing on yourself or the development team gets rid of coarse bugs; testing on easy-to-acquire users who aren't part of the development process (someone two cubicles over or a secretary) will refine some of the problems; and only use your typically difficult-to-acquire users when you're ready. Of course, if you have a ready source of victims, that is, learners (e.g., you're in a school or have a readily accessible and rotating crew of learners), you should use them as often as possible.

The cycle of testing and refining the solution, asking ever more detailed questions about the ultimate design, including the parameters around the interactions, increasing the level of sophistication of the prototype, and cycling through expert testing and user testing, until you achieve your (potentially revised) metrics, is the process that leads to a successful solution.

There are several extensions to this concept that are worth noting. We've already mentioned that the principles should hold for other than technology-mediated experiences. We also want to consider hybrids, address assessment, multi-learner simulations, and more.

One of the roles technology can play is not only independent "anywhere/anywhen" learning, but augmenting face-to-face learning. Typical "blended learning" wraps e-learning before (and potentially after) face-to-face sessions to get content presentation out of the way and not take that valuable (and often expensive) interpersonal interaction. However, beyond using technology to mediate face-to-face sessions, we can go further. Tools can be introduced into a live simulation that represents the ones they'd see in the performance context, and they can be developed to support the overall simulation. We can also use technology in the face-to-face sessions as a collaboration and data-processing tool, so that learners can work together to solve problems, and submit them to advance a simulation that's being run live.

Which brings up the issue of using technology to support multi-learner simulations, whether live or completely technology-mediated. The same principles apply as for independent learning design, where you focus on the decisions and misconceptions, but you also have to consider whether you are going to have different roles for the learners (much as in other face-to-face simulations or experiential learning activities). In the technology-mediated sessions, you have to decide whether a human serving as moderator/scenario-master can and will interpret the outcomes and make up the consequences (potentially easier if there are ways the person can quickly communicate the outcomes back to the learners) or whether these need to be programmed with rules. In the latter case, the modeling may be more complex. Again, the same design principles hold, but the interactions between the different roles must be an additional consideration.

As with any practice activity, the question of assessment comes up. It surprised me to find out that many people seem to think that scenarios are a formative assessment and that a separate summative assessment may be necessary. However, any practice activity is inherently a performance opportunity and can serve as an assessment opportunity. In fact, the very contextualized practice, the close simulation of the actual performance situations, makes it a rich assessment tool, particularly compared to most knowledge-assessments typically used (e.g., a test). At the least, a portfolio of scenario performance coupled with a knowledge test is a richer indicator of learning than just the knowledge test.

If a separate summative assessment is needed, a couple of options present themselves. For far transfer, a separate scenario with a vastly different context would be a good assessment. In the case of a branching scenario, not engine-driven, creating such for both near and far transfer is feasible. One of the issues can be whether all learners have faced the same situation. In the case of an engine-driven scenario, creating a special path to be pursued under certain circumstances can be arranged, or ensuring that the engine drives a certain sequence of decisions regardless of how the decisions are populated with data to make unique situations can also be delivered. Even adaptive testing can be developed, where the engine changes the situations to identify what the learner does and does not know. However, if the goal is to ensure the learner can perform, not to assess how much he or she can perform (and I suggest this in many cases should be the goal), then having the learner eventually succeed at the scenario should be sufficient assessment.

Programming the underlying engine (or even developing a robust branching implementation) brings up the topic of the team to successfully develop such an implementation. While tools exist that allow an individual to create a full scenario (they can even be developed in PowerPoint or hard-coded HTML, and there are tools that are specialized for the task of branching scenarios at least), ideally a team with the correct combination of skills exists or is assembled. Success in creating compelling engagement requires delicately balancing all the elements, including the visual design, the prose, and the underlying implementation, as well as additions such as audio, video, and so forth. At a minimum, the skill set needs to include the ID design, the prose writing, the graphic design, the project management, and the implementation. While you might have (or be) the polymath who can handle it all, that's not the way to bet. My recommendation is to get the talent necessary, and then manage the process to get a successful design that will withstand the audience's scrutiny.

Conclusion

If we're really concerned with creating effective new skills through computer-based simulated practice, then we need that practice to be as effective as possible, to respect the time of our learners and to best achieve our goals. Examining the alignment of principles of engagement and education gives us the tools we need to optimize the learning experience.

Learning with Scenarios

Scenarios are only part of the overall learning process. We need to ensure that we have suitably addressed the additional components that complement the learning practice. These include the introduction, concepts, examples, and summary.

The traditional way is to provide all these elements (except the summary) first. However, there are alternatives. Problem-based learning suggests that we provide learners with the problem as a motivator to access relevant concepts and examples. We could have the introduction to the scenario actually precede the formal introduction to the course, as well (not expecting that the learners complete the scenario before accessing content introduction, concept, etc.). Or we can have small scenarios that precede the formal content.

Note that we don't have to have concepts and examples separate from the scenario, as there are many ways to embed the materials into the scenario. We might have a library in an organizational setting for a scenario in which the learner can access concept material. We can have characters in the scenario who tell you stories about their experiences that serve as examples.

The feedback and summary are important as well. The feedback should connect their actions to the concepts, *within* the story. Particularly for wrong answers, some characters' reactions or some outcome of an action in the world should provide feedback that indicates how the learner's action violated the model.

Once they've terminated the scenario, correctly or not, you can then provide an external voice providing feedback, but first provide emotional and action closure on the scenario experience. You can (and to the extent that what they're practicing is not direct transfer but requires some abstraction, you should) also add reflection questions. Two possible roles for such questions are to ask them what the underlying principles guiding the experience were (asking them to restate the concept model), and to ask them how this would play out in a setting familiar to them (asking them to generalize and transfer mentally). Such reflection is a powerful tool to help the learner transfer more readily to all applicable situations.

When to Use Scenarios

When are scenarios relevant? As mentioned above, they're not necessary to automate knowledge, and their role in attitudinal change may be limited to helping learners become aware of their own attitudes and then to practice behavior in alignment with the new set of values. The latter two situations can be considered as cognitive skill practice, which is the main role of scenarios.

There are strong reasons to focus intently on cognitive skills. Knowledge acquisition is a fairly well-known process, and I'm afraid we over-apply such solutions, rather than focusing on the things that will make a real difference. Our difficulties typically are not knowledge acquisition. However, using knowledge to

The Handbook of Experiential Learning

make decisions through scenarios helps motivate the knowledge acquisition. Also, typically the intervention that will make a big difference in performance has to do with skill acquisition, not knowledge acquisition.

So then the question becomes when we can use fixed path scenarios, such as branching scenarios, and when we have to move to rule-driven behavior. As mentioned, there are marginal costs to get the more flexible interaction. The benefits of rule-driven include almost infinite replay, through unpredictability. We can also get adaptive performance. Thus, when lots of practice is important, so is a rule-driven experience. Such situations include when it's very expensive to get it wrong or when it's difficult to get the behavior change (such as when it's deeply ingrained, contrary to some well-established models, or requires more effort). Having lots of potential users also makes it more reasonable to shoot for the better experience and the bigger performance impact. Still, the fixed link approach, particularly when several are used to create different contexts and make the task more difficult, is a very feasible alternative.

The Transformation Economy

In essence, what we're talking about is creating experiences that transform what people can do. Gilmore (2003) has argued that the global economy has transitioned from a "goods" economy, through a "services" economy, to an "experience" economy (where we pay for experiences, such as themed travel). He argues that the next change will be to a "transformation" economy, where we pay for experiences that transform us. I suggest that the approach outlined here is the way to systematically develop a transformation to a desired end. We are creating experiences that transform individual skill sets, and this is a goal that is not only useful, but may be quite valuable going forward.

References

Gilmore, J. H. (2003, Fall). Frontiers of the experience economy. *Batten Briefings*.
Keller, J. (1983). Motivational design of instruction. In Reigeluth, C. (Ed.), *Instructional-design theories and models: An overview of their current status*. Hillsdale, NJ: Lawrence Erlbaum.
Mager, R. (1975). *Preparing instructional objectives* (2nd ed.). Belmont, CA: Lake Publishing.
Quinn, C. (2005). *Engaging learning: Designing e-learning simulation games*. San Francisco, CA: Pfeiffer.
Van Merriënboer, J.J.G. (1997). *Training complex cognitive skills: A four-component instructional design model for technical training*. Englewood Cliffs, NJ: Educational Technology Publications.

CHAPTER NINE

IMPROV

Its Contribution to the Art of Experiential Training

Kat Koppett

Kat Koppett is a consultant, trainer, and author, specializing in creativity and communication skills. Founder of The StoryNet, Kat is the co-director of The Thiagi Playhouse. Her book, *Training to Imagine: Practical Improvisational Theatre Techniques to Enhance Creativity, Teamwork, Leadership, and Learning,* was published by Stylus Publishing in 2001 and is currently in its third printing. Kat has designed and delivered training for Oracle, Kaiser-Permanente, Cadence Design Systems, Roche Molecular Systems, Price-Waterhouse Coopers, the University of San Francisco, and Microsoft, among others. Kat holds a B.F.A. in drama from New York University and an M.A. in organizational psychology from Columbia University. She was instrumental in creating the corporate training wing of Freestyle Repertory Theatre in New York and the corporate division of BATS Improv, one of the premiere improvisational theater companies on the West Coast. A member of the National Speakers' Association, Kat has presented for the American Society for Training and Development (ASTD), the North American Simulation and Gaming Association (NASAGA), Influent, International Society for Performance Improvement (ISPI), the Rotary Club, and the Young Presidents' Organization. She is a founding member of the Applied Improv Network.

Contact Information

The Thiagi Group
20 Iroquois Trail
Slingerland, NY 12159
(518) 847–9882
kat@thiagi.com
www.thiagi.com

TURN ON YOUR TELEVISION and you might just run into "Who's Line Is It, Anyway?" or "Curb Your Enthusiasm" or any number of other improvised programs. A few years ago, television producers cringed at the idea of producing a show with no script, in which they had no foreknowledge of what would happen. Now, improv is flourishing around the world. From Japan to Finland to the United States, improv can be found, not just on television, but in theatres in virtually every community. If you are familiar with their work, you know that improvisers make up scenes, songs, stories, sometimes entire plays, with no rehearsal or pre-planning. It is a high-wire performance without a net. Entertaining, you might think, but what does that have to do with experiential training?

A decade or so ago, as improvisational theater neared its tipping point, a few rogue trainers and business leaders thought they saw some applications of improv techniques to their world. They figured, "Hey, improvisers have to perform on-the-spot, collaboratively, under pressure, with immediate results. So do we. Perhaps there are some practices we can appropriate for our purposes." Most people, of course, did not think like this. They thought, "Improv? Well, it may be 'fun,' but this is the real world. Our work is serious and important. We would never waste our time and money on fluffy, touchy-feely drivel." Improvisers wondered, too, even as they started developing workshops for corporations. Was there really value for organizations in practicing the skills of improv, or was teaching improv workshops to business professionals merely a momentary diversion for the participants and a way for starving actors to pay the rent?

These days the landscape looks different on both sides. Improv has become a recognized and respected technique for enhancing creativity, communication, and teamwork within many leading-edge organizations. And a new breed of improviser has emerged: one trained in facilitation and instructional design and savvy about the needs and culture of business clients. Like many things that have gone from being wacky, out-of-the-box initiatives to being mainstream practices, the value of improv in training now seems straightforward and intuitively obvious to many.

As the world moves faster and becomes more global, there is less time to plan and more need for collaboration. So business people are turning to improv for help. Trainers, especially, are learning to tap into the improv world for process and content inspiration. Many of the current experiential training games have their origin in the world of improv. But improv has more to offer than just fun activities to break up the monotony of lectures. Improvisers have developed specific approaches and exercises to hone their creativity and collaboration "muscles." These techniques help hone the skills of both trainers and their participants.

Trainers ARE performers. Sivasailam Thiagarajan (Thiagi), the great guru of training games, says that he believes there is no better preparation for becoming a trainer than acting. Trainers must have excellent presentation skills, as well as the flexibility to sense a group's needs and respond in the moment. Improv can help trainers develop these skills. Next, as creativity and communication—teamwork, coaching, leadership, idea generation—skills continue to be increasingly in demand, trainers can tap the world of improv for content-related exercises. Improv exercises can be wonderful "jolts"—introducing individuals to new ways of thinking as well as wonderful workout routines for exercising the muscles of creativity and teamwork. Finally, many improv techniques and games are templates that can be used to enhance learning, regardless of the specific content. Improv activities have been used in training on topics as varied as product training, new-hire orientations, technical training, and diversity workshops. To summarize, improv can be used by trainers:

- To develop the presentation, design, and coaching skills of the trainer;
- To enhance the creativity and communication skills of participants; and
- To increase the effective delivery of virtually any course content.

Let us start by taking a closer look at some of the improv principles that can help trainers and the people they train. Then, we will explore some specific activities and their place in workplace training.

The Principles

Build Trust

The greater the risk, the greater the necessity for instilling trust. Improvisers risk humiliation in front of hundreds of people each time they perform a show. Business professionals may have even more at stake. Imagine, the financial well-being of their organization, the livelihood of their colleagues, their professional and personal success, sometimes even people's lives, depend on how they perform every day. Therefore, if organizations wish people to be innovative and collaborative, to take risks and try new things, they must be highly skilled at creating an environment that is supportive of that risk taking. As trainers, we are, by definition, asking people to try something new, do things at which they are not already expert, so having a safe and encouraging environment becomes all the more important. Improvisers have developed ways to consciously build such a culture and to build strong, trusting relationships.

First, improvisers simply value the process of getting to know their colleagues in a deep and relatively intimate way. This is not to say that it is necessary to share early childhood trauma or one's most embarrassing moments in order to strengthen teamwork. Surprisingly, innocuous information can be as useful as deep, dark secrets. It is the act of sharing, as well as the content, that builds the team. In business, we tend to err on the side of separating our personal and professional lives. What improvisers understand, however, is that there is no such thing as separating work and life. Improvisers know that it is their life experiences that inspire their professional creativity, enhance their awareness and understanding of others' needs, and create the underpinning of their ambitions and values. Improvisers use themselves fully. They have nothing else. Business professionals are recognizing the same imperative to "show up."

In addition, getting to know one's colleagues is becoming an increasing difficult and important step at work. It used to be that the "Golden Rule"— "Do unto others as you would have others do unto you"—was good enough. Now, in our ever more diverse communities, we are realizing that we need to go further. Now the rule is "Do unto others as they would be done unto." We can no longer assume that our preferences coincide with our colleagues'. The more we reveal about ourselves, the more others can support us. The more we seek to understand about others, the more we can assist them. And there may be good reasons to do so. But what improvisers realize is that, by really understanding their partners, they can offer help and inspiration, meeting needs that might otherwise have gone unmet.

The second trust-building rule of improv is "Make your partner look good." It is what we do with our shared knowledge of each other that makes the difference. "Make your partner look good" means concentrating on your partner rather than on yourself, and taking responsibility for both of you. "If your partner drops the ball," we say, "it is your responsibility, not his." The concept of accountability gets bandied about these days. Ironically, the conversation often consists of admonitions directed at others, as in "YOU should be more accountable." Thinking always of making your partner look good is a way to separate true accountability from thinly disguised blame.

Trainers can apply these rules in overt and subtle ways from the moment they begin to design their sessions. They can learn to establish credibility and instill trust both by revealing parts of themselves and by soliciting information from their participants. By using trust-building activities (most trainers have some in their back pockets), as well as simply asking questions about participants' individual experiences and objectives, trainers can both create an overall environment conducive to learning and target the specific needs of individuals. Then, when participants do take the risk to try something new or reveal a sensitive issue, trainers can work to "make them look good" by rewarding the risk itself and building on the ideas offered. Which brings us to the next important improv concept.

Be Spontaneous

From a very early age, most of us are taught to censor ourselves. Good thing, really. Without the ability to control our impulses, make judgments, and choose when and if to act, we would be crippled. We could not learn to read, eat with utensils, or shed our diapers. Civilization itself is a set of agreed-on limits we place on our uncensored actions. However, there is a price. We spend so much time exercising our judgment muscles that our creativity muscles can atrophy.

In improv, there is no time to evaluate. By definition, improvisation is creating in the moment, without the ability to revise. Improvisers practice getting out of their own way so that they can recognize and utilize their innovative ideas. What is especially interesting about unleashing one's impulses is that it is often the ideas that seem the most dangerous or the most obvious—the ones that our rational mind would have us censor—that yield the greatest fruit. What many people label wit or cleverness in improvisation is simply a willingness to say whatever comes to mind. Spontaneity is the fuel of creativity. And creativity is at the heart of problem solving and innovation. Craig Harrison, a sales consultant and trainer in California, says, "So often we are bound by rules and regulations, restrictions and proscriptions. Sometimes, we're so bogged down we can't respond to the issue at hand." The best trainers pay attention, not to their prescribed agendas, but to what is happening in the room. They trust their instincts and go with the flow. They solve personal and practical problems as they arise, rather than sticking to a predetermined method or structure. And they encourage their participants to do the same.

The improv exercise *Soundball* is a simple way of raising awareness about how much we censor and of working out our spontaneity muscle. In *Soundball*, the participants stand in a circle and throw an imaginary ball back and forth. Each time a participant tosses the ball, she makes a sound. Her partner, the person to whom she has thrown the ball, repeats the sound as he catches it. There are no rules about what kind of sound to make, no parameters around what sounds are acceptable or prohibited. Anything goes.

Initially, learners can express discomfort playing *Soundball*. It is sort of silly to throw an imaginary ball around, and looking foolish rates as one of the top taboos in many business cultures. But there is more to their uneasiness. Regardless of the lack of skill required or of any rules of right and wrong, people find all sorts of ways to evaluate their input and feel not only foolish, but incompetent. They worry that their sounds were wrong: "It was too soft." "It had too many consonants." "It was too similar to the sound I made the first time." "It wasn't interesting." They admit to planning sounds ahead of time and trying to store them up. They share moments of panic when they could think of no sound at all.

   Soundball is one activity that highlights the arbitrary nature of our judgments. Usually, when we evaluate a product or an idea, we feel we have substantial reasons for doing so. We would love to say "yes" and follow our impulses, but they are wrong! The idea is just bad! *Soundball* illustrates how capricious our internal judge can be. At this point, most people know intellectually the value of brainstorming, generating a quantity of ideas without evaluation. But in practice, this kind of non-evaluative idea generation can be difficult to achieve. To increase spontaneity and support it in others, improvisers practice:

- *Being silly.* Creativity is, by definition, a departure from the status quo. As a trainer, encourage participants to share whatever thoughts they have. Tell them they may preface a suggestion with "I know this sounds crazy, but . . ." if that makes them feel less responsible for it.
- *Being obvious.* Sometimes we reject ideas because we believe they are not creative enough. When you articulate the obvious, either you are voicing something that everyone is thinking, but no one else has the courage to say, or you are contributing something that seems very obvious to you, no one else has thought of. Both have value. In addition, by simply naming something you notice, you may uncover an important need or objection. Facial expressions and body posture tell us a lot. Follow your impulses when you think you see a clue. Support participants in a workshop to do the same.
- *Celebrating failure.* In order to create, we must take risks. In order to take risks, we must be willing to fail. Bad ideas may spur great ones. Have teams generate ideas collaboratively, and award a prize for the worst one. Improvisers talk about "mistakes as gifts." One of the most famous examples of accepting a mistake as a gift is the invention of Post-it Notes. If the chemist at 3M had said, "Huh, well this glue doesn't stick very well. Better ditch that. And I'd better hide my failure to boot," we would not have that beloved little tool that has become such a staple of our professional lives.

Accept and Amplify

When we practice being spontaneous, we learn to accept our own ideas. It is equally important to accept others' ideas. The "yes, and . . ." rule is the foundational one in improv. We build trust by accepting others' "offers," and then, using our spontaneous responses, we build on those offers to create something. An offer is an improv term that refers to anything, ANYTHING that the other person says or does. It can be a word, a gesture, an attitude, a request. Anything. Our job as improvisers is to recognize the offers and use them.

Let's look at the "yes" part: organizations lose speed and opportunities because ideas are rejected without really being explored. This happens for a variety of reasons. New ideas may mean more work; others might get more credit; the idea feels risky; and someone thinks he has a "better" idea of his own. However, every time we say "no" to an idea instead of "yes," an opportunity is lost. That does not mean, of course, that evaluation is not useful. Or that we should commit to every idea. When we depend on our judgment muscles exclusively, though, we throw the baby out with the bath water, the electricity out with the light bulb.

Keith Johnstone, an improv guru and the author of *Impro*, says, "There are people who prefer to say 'Yes,' and there are people who prefer to say 'No.' Those who say 'Yes' are rewarded by the adventures they have. Those who say 'No' are rewarded by the safety they attain." Often it may be that simple. Saying 'no' feels safer. Less to do. Less to think about. Less to risk. But when organizations begin to recognize the price of saying "no," perhaps the equation is not so neat.

The "and" part goes like this. Not only must I, the improviser, accept an offer, but I must build on it. I must contribute. I must make an offer of my own in response to my partner's. It is this process that harnesses the power of collaboration. Everyone offers and accepts. Each team member is responsible for both contributing to and supporting the group's activity. Remember our "make your partner look good" rule? "Yes, and . . ." incorporates the two rules above—build trust and be spontaneous. It says that whatever you offer, I will hear, accept, and build with. What a powerful and unusual collaborative approach.

There is a simple exercise that improv trainers use to illustrate the power of saying "yes, and . . . " instead of "yes, but. . . ." It is played in two rounds. In the first, five volunteers are asked to plan a company picnic or holiday party. After the first suggestion is made, each successive idea must begin with the words "Yes, but . . ." It usually goes something like this:

"Let's have the party on a cruise ship."

"Yes, but . . . people could get seasick."

"Yes, but . . . we could hand out Dramamine."

"Yes, but . . . some people don't like to take pills."

"Yes, but . . . that's their problem."

"Yes, but . . . we want to have a nice party."

"Yes, but . . . we're never going to please everyone."

"Yes, but . . . we could at least have a party that won't make everyone sick."

"Yes, but . . . I'm feeling kind of sick now."

Entertaining, perhaps, but not much of a party. If the exercise does not conclude in an argument, it tends to degenerate into lots of discouraged and silent participants staring at each other and the facilitator, devoid of ideas. Everyone is relieved to sit down.

Now comes round 2. Five more volunteers are invited to complete the same task—planning a company party—with one variation. This time, instead of starting their sentences with "Yes, but . . ." they begin each offer with our words, "yes, AND. . . ." With the adjustment, the dialogue progresses in this fashion:

"Let's have the party on a cruise ship."

"Yes, and . . . we could have a dance band."

"Yes, and . . . a giant buffet."

"Yes, and . . . lots of drinks.

"Yes, and . . . a kereoke machine."

"Yes, and . . . we can have juice for the teetotalers."

"Yes, and . . . cookies."

"Yes!"

"Yes, and . . . clowns."

"Yes!"

This time, the participants report feeling happy, enthusiastic, and relaxed. Observers agree that this sounds like a much more enjoyable party to attend, even if it is a little wacky. Everyone understands that saying, "yes, but . . ." is just a cagey way of saying, "no." Nothing that comes before it counts. Whereas saying, "yes, and . . ." allows the team members to accept and build on others' offers.

Trainers must practice "yes, and-ing" as much as they teach it. The more of a knowledge expert we become, the easier it can be to fall into the trap of shutting participants down, delivering our material and our ideas in our way, without really hearing and building on the participants' offers. By seeking to find the value in every comment, every objection, facilitators can enhance the value of their courses and the probability that individuals will integrate and apply their learning.

Tell Stories

As the art of improvisational theatre matures, improvisers and audiences are gravitating toward more narrative forms. A diet of nothing but wacky gags just does not satisfy after a while. Similarly, organizations are rediscovering the power of story to help them align behind a vision, create a culture, or sell a product. Most organizational leaders now realize that presenting graphs and numbers will not motivate their people. What will inspire them is a compelling story that weaves that information together. People love stories. Jerome Bruner says, "Story *is* meaning." The way we make sense of the world is by linking little bits of data together into a connected whole. Stories deepen learning, enhance retention of information, and give us a context for all of our daily choices and activities. As trainers, when we support the deliberate telling and creating of stories, we support learning. (See Chapter 12 in this handbook for more details on storytelling as an experiential methodology.)

Ultimately, storytelling is an innate human ability. One can, though, hone specific storytelling skills. Improvisers work on both creating a solid narrative structure and on adding rich, engaging details. And just to add a degree of difficulty, improvisers often tell their stories collaboratively. These collaborative storytelling activities can be mined by trainers to introduce or review virtually any topic or to teach communication and collaboration skills.

Perform

Something even more fundamental underlies this whole endeavor. Improvisers perform. They learn to play different characters, show different facets of themselves, and act in different ways, depending on the needs of a scene. They learn to stretch their repertoire of behaviors, and they develop a facility with changing their bodies, voices, and attitudes to best effect.

At first, the idea of playing a role—giving a performance—in our real, everyday lives may seem uncomfortable. We are supposed to be "authentic." We see ourselves as individuals with specific ways of thinking and responding that are inviolate. We take comfort in instruments like the Myers-Briggs or DiSC that tell us who we are and how we predictably respond. But, in fact, we play roles all the time. Consciously or unconsciously, we change our demeanor, our language, our responses, depending on our immediate objectives, who we are interacting with, and where we are. Improv can help us become more aware of the choices we make and expand our capacity to perform effectively. As trainers, of course, we are also giving formal presentations/performances regularly. And, increasingly in corporate America, our clients are too. The act of improvising strengthens our performance muscles and allows us to increase our effectiveness as trainers, and as humans.

The Application

Some improv activities have become familiar to trainers who may not even know their origins. And some exercises from the improv world may not seem much like performance games. There are, after all, thousands of games improvisers use to hone their skills and ingrain the above principles. Below you will find a mere smattering of some of the most popular and unique improv activities and how they can be applied. Of course, many of the following activities can be used in more than one way.

Icebreakers

Performers and athletes warm up before their events. Good trainers know that learners must be warmed up, as well. In a training session, "icebreakers" serve to relax the participants, creative a safe and welcoming environment, and set some ground rules of participation. Here are a couple of improv activities that have become popular icebreakers.

Colleague Commercials: In pairs, participants interview each other and then present a commercial for their colleague to the rest of the group. This activity has a number of strengths to recommend it. First, the participants get to connect with someone else in the room in a deeper and more complete way than if they were merely listening to everyone say a sentence or two. A bond develops between the pairs, which can help people feel more at home. Second, because each person is introducing another, and doing it in the form of a commercial no less, he or she is free to—nay, required to—brazenly highlight his or her partner's best, most impressive, and interesting characteristics, something that has a very different flavor if one did it for oneself. (And most participants would not.) Finally, the performance aspect of this simple activity sets the bar for participation high, while still focusing the learners on their colleagues, rather than on themselves. After performing a commercial, most other activities will seem easy and tame.

Stats: Stats is another getting-to-know-each-other activity. The participants sit in chairs in a circle, with one chairless person standing in the center. The person in the middle shouts out a fact about himself, and everyone to whom that fact also applies must get up and find a new chair. The game creates an environment in which the participants themselves control what they reveal about themselves and decide what they wish to learn about others. In addition, the exercise is designed so that it is not the most aggressive or most vocal people who are in control. In fact, it may turn out that the more retiring team members find themselves in the center of the circle more. This enables those who might not otherwise have a voice to lead the discussion. Stats also allows self-revelation in a low-pressure, light-hearted atmosphere, where it might not feel so loaded. Doctors in a patient-physician communication skills course, for example, were shocked during this activity to find how many of their colleagues struggled with the same senses of insecurity and being overwhelmed that they themselves felt. Admitting such "weaknesses" was such a taboo that the doctors had never shared their experiences.

Needs Assessment

The playfulness and lightheartedness of improv, with its demands that participants dare to be spontaneous and risk sharing themselves, make improv a nice tool for exploring the current state and uncovering needs, without blame or pressure. Stats, described above, can be used for the purpose of uncovering group needs. By asking the group to focus their sharing on a specific topic area, the trainer can get a sense of what resonates with more or fewer participants and what knowledge and attitudes exist in the room. Some other needs assessment improv games include:

Experts: An improvised version of a simple talk show format, in which one participant plays the host and another a guest "expert." As a needs analysis game, it can be fun to have the expert be from the future, discussing both the current state and what happened later. The activity can be framed to focus on either the individual or the organization. If it is the collective that is the focus, have other participants ask questions and debrief after the activity to capture others' reactions and thoughts. The idea with this activity is not for the expert to get things right. It is to start a conversation. In fact, with especially serious groups, it can help not only to have the expert from the future, but to give him or her a specialty that takes away from literal analysis, such as art historian or archeologist.

Color/Advance: Story sharing is also a wonderful way to start a workshop and learn more about the participants. This activity is a guided storytelling activity that allows both the teller and receiver to delve more deeply into a story and understand it in a richer way. It goes like this: The participants are divided into pairs. Partner A is asked to tell a story. When using *Color/Advance* as a needs analysis, the story should be true. The facilitator can prompt, "Share a time (dealing with the topic) when you felt either extremely successful or really frustrated and ineffective." Partner B acts as a guide/editor/director. Whenever the guide hears something that he wants to know more about, he says, "Color the. . . ." The storyteller then describes, in as much detail as possible, that element of the story. When the director is satisfied with the details, she says "advance," and the storyteller continues with whatever happens next. For example:

Storyteller: Last year I had two partners who were both assigning me more work than humanly possible.

Guide: Color: more work than humanly possible.

Storyteller: One kept giving me assignments the day before they were due to the client. There was no way I could produce a complete, polished result in the amount of time he gave me, especially when there was necessary research involved. The other simply gave me a workload that should have been divided among three people.

Guide: Advance.

Storyteller: Well, I decided I should talk to them about it, because I didn't think I could live up to my own or their standards this way. What a disaster. . . .

The stories can be debriefed as a group, or individuals can make notes afterward to inform their work. Another variation has one pair telling a story in front of the room. This works as a conversation starter, as well.

The difference between an improv activity, like "Color/Advance," and simply sharing stories lies in the interaction between the teller and the director. Because there is shared control of the story, the partners are collaborating in the moment to find what is most compelling. Often the teller will report remembering details and finding meaning that had eluded him or her to this point, even if he or she has told the story before. "Color/Advance" also develops creativity and communication skills, of course.

Creativity

A well-known improv teacher once said, "If you can't think of anything to say, you are censoring what you thought of." As evidenced by the principles above, improvisers believe that the secret of being "creative" lies in simply getting out of your own way, daring to be silly, or boring, or obvious, and trusting your impulses. This frame differs from some creativity tests that equate originality of thought or number of ideas with creativity. Improvisers will tell you it is the getting-out-of-the-way part, not the coming-up-with-ideas part. "Sound Ball," described above, is an example of an activity that helps bypass those nasty little censors and lets ideas bubble forth unimpeded.

Picture/Math: Another activity designed to undermine the inner gatekeeper is "Picture/Math." Participants work in groups of three. The person in the middle is on the "hot seat." The participant on the right asks the person to describe pictures in an imaginary photo album. The third participant intersperses simple math problems for the participant on the "hot seat" to solve at the same time. The rational mind, then, is kept busy, leaving the generative, visual mind free to create. Most people, after this experience, realize that creating is really the easy part. And a good portion of being creative is feeling that you are so.

What Would _____ Do? All that said, a part of being creative does lie in the ability to think "outside the box"—or at least with fresh eyes. "What Would _____ Do?" is a game in which groups of participants are given a famous person. Their task is to brainstorm strategies to deal with a difficult issue as if they were that person. What would Oprah do? The U.S. President? Homer Simpson? Exploring the situation through someone else's eyes allows the participants to offer silly or stupid ideas without feeling their egos are at risk. And the new lens may uncover some unique and viable ideas.

Teamwork and Collaboration

The fly in the ointment for improvisers, and for many professionals in today's organizations, is that not only must they create, but they must create collaboratively. This is where the idea of accepting and building on offers becomes so valuable. Teaching the skill of "yes, and-ing"—accepting and adding—can transform a group's ability to create together.

Yes, and Stories: Once the concept of "yes, and" is introduced, virtually any improv game can be employed to exercise the accepting offers muscle. A favorite used by improv trainers is "Yes, and Stories" because it allows the participants and trainer to examine the offers and how they are accepted in minute detail. Very simply, the participants create a story one sentence at a time. Each sentence, after the initial one, starts with the words "Yes, and. . . ." The point is not to tell the most interesting or original story. The goal is to really receive, accept, and build with the offers being made. This simple exercise reveals how difficult it can be to co-create—sharing control and responsibility—and how easy it is to get seduced by your own ideas, your assumptions, and unspoken agendas.

Conversation Weave: Once teams notice their tendencies and the difficulty of really hearing and receiving offers, they can work their muscles in these areas. In Conversation Weave, three or four volunteers get up in front of the group. Each has an individual conversation with an imaginary friend. They take turns speaking (although not in any predetermined order), each saying a few sentences at a time. The stories should be unrelated, for example, calling home to wish Mom a happy birthday, going on a job interview, disciplining a child, but the participants begin to weave words and details from the other stories into their own as the exercise progresses. In addition to providing entertainment, the activity works the participants' listening and awareness muscles, and it highlights how we are influenced by events and attitudes around us.

Presentation Skills

Whether in an official presentation skills class or in a more general leadership, team building, or communication context, trainers increasingly turn to improv and the theater to teach participants about how to give a compelling performance. "Influencing skills," "charismatic leadership," "media savvy"— the buzz words go on and on. Simply put, organizations are recognizing the importance of the "how," not simply the "what" of a message. Any performance game or role play that gives a participant an opportunity to stretch in new ways can help participants recognize that they have more behavioral choices than they might have thought.

Status Games: Improvisers have a few favorites that trainers have borrowed. An especially compelling way that improvisers are teaching individuals to expand their performance ranges is by exploring "status" behaviors. Status is defined, for our purposes, as power relationships. Status is dynamic, changing with circumstance, and can only exist when measured in relation to something else. Keith Johnstone, the creator of Theatresports™, recognized that status can be understood not as something we *are*, but as something we *do*. We confer or accept status through our behaviors, and it is those interactions that determine who is perceived as holding the power.

Status is not the same as official title or rank. In studying power, social science researchers have investigated different sources of power. They have then divided them into two classes, positional and personal. We make a mistake if we assume the two always go hand-in-hand. The work of actors and improvisers can help us play with our personal status, regardless of our positional power.

How can the concept of status help us communicate better?

- Our awareness of status can help us navigate situations with appropriate behavior.
- Equalizing status facilitates open communication.
- Raising our own status gives us more authority and can increase trust.
- Raising others' status communicates empathy and can increase trust.

Playing with status also highlights the power of nonverbal behaviors to change the sense of a message. In an exercise adapted from Johnstone's book, *Impro*, participants are given a short script of neutral dialogue and asked to play it over and over with different status relationships. The huge effect of a roll of the eyes or a giggle is stunning. Often, I will use a job-interview setting for the short scene written by the participants. It might look something like this:

A: Good morning.
B: Good morning.
A: Have a seat.
B: Thank you.
A: I have looked over your resume.
B: Yes?
A: I see you worked at Global Inc.
B: Yes. For a number of years.
A: Very impressive.
B: Thanks.

Often, participants assume that the interviewer will have high status by default. All the actor playing the role must do, however, is sound impressed and eager to please, and the interviewee's status rises. Conversely, even a line like "very impressive" can seem cutting when said with a dismissive tone.

Because it is so fundamental to our social structures, our sensitivity to status is highly honed. "Status Cards" plays with status behaviors. Participants are given a playing card that they put on their foreheads without looking at the face. The card signifies their status, and the group treats each member accordingly. When they are asked to line up in order of status, based on how they were treated, most groups have over 90 percent accuracy, and many individuals can guess their cards exactly.

Both within the arena of status dynamics, and generally, when individuals recognize life as a performance and think in terms of choosing how to "play the scene," they expand their options and are often more successful in navigating life challenges. As Performance of a Lifetime, an executive education firm in New York City specializing in the use of theatre and improv techniques in business settings, says, they become "better performers on the job."

Review and Close

In the theatre, everyone knows that how you begin and how you end are much more important than what comes in between. Trainers know the same thing. A number of improv activities can be used to review the material, increase retention, and close a session with energy. Many of the activities already listed here can be modified for use as closers, such as Color/Advance, Expert Interviews, or Stats. In addition, trainers have enjoyed the following.

Elimination Lists: Four or five participants stand in front of the group. The facilitator assigns or elicits a category. She then points to someone and that person names something that falls into that category. If a player makes a mistake, he or she is eliminated and another person takes the spot. There are three types of mistakes: pausing too long before saying something; saying something that doesn't fit into the category; or saying something that has already been said. For example, if you were training a group on product knowledge, the topic could be "products we make that are under $500." Or the topic might be "words to use to diffuse a conflict" or "characteristics of a high-performance team." The topic could even be as broad as "things you learned today." The game flows quickly, mistakes are inevitable and without real consequences, and participants are reminded of the course content, as well as having the opportunity to share their knowledge and thoughts.

Story Seeds: When looking for an activity that is a little more thoughtful and less manic, trainers have been drawn to Story Seeds. The facilitator or group members come up with four neutral sentences. Then, individually or in small groups, participants create stories encompassing those sentences, adding characters, details, or connections. In a communication skills course, for example, the sentences might be something like: "Carol walked into the partner's office with sweaty palms." "He tossed the papers on the desk." "A cell phone rang." "With all of her new skills in play, Carol left triumphant." The participants, then, incorporate the day's learning to reach the happy ending and employ their own skills virtually in the process.

Summary

As we see, the job of a professional improviser and the job of an effective human being are really the same. Create a supportive environment, build and respond to the offers around you, connect with others by getting to know them, share your own stories, and tailor your behavior to fit the scene. And because improvisers consciously practice these skills and create activities that support them, we, as trainers, can employ their techniques. Not only can we pass them along to others, but we can practice them ourselves and enhance performance, in all senses of the word.

For more on this topic, here are a few of my personal favorite resources. The list is, of course, by no means exhaustive. And remember that improv, like training, is an art. The best way to learn about it is to do it. If you wish to play, there is almost certainly an improv company near you.

Books

Impro by Keith Johnstone

Improv Wisdom by Patricia Ryan Madsen

Tales for Trainers by Margaret Parkin

Training to Imagine by Kat Koppett

Organizations

The Applied Improv Network, www.appliedimprov.net

BATS Improv, www.batsimprov.org

Creative Advantage, www.creativeadvantage.com

Performance of a Lifetime, www.performanceofalifetime.com

The StoryNet, www.thestorynet.com

The Thiagi Group, www.thiagi.com

References

Allred, K. (1996). *Class notes, negotiation*. New York: Columbia University.

Armstrong, A. (1992). *Managing by storying around: A new method of leadership*. New York: Doubleday.

Campbell, J. (1973). *A hero with a thousand faces*. Cambridge, MA: Bollingen Series/Princeton University Press.

Chekhov, M. (1953). *To the actor: On the technique of acting*. New York: Harper and Row.

French, J.R.P., & Raven, B. H. (1959). The basis of social power. In D. Cartwright (Ed.), *Studies in social power*. Ann Arbor, MI: Institute for Social Research.

Halpern, C., Close, D., & Johnson, K. (1994). *Truth in comedy: The manual of improvisation*. Colorado Springs, CO: Meriwether Publishing.

Johnstone, K. (1979). *Impro: Improvisation and the theatre*. New York: Theatre Arts Books.

Parkin, M. (1998). *Tales for trainers: Using stories and metaphors to facilitate learning*. London: Kogan Page.

Schank, R. C. (1990). *Tell me a story*. Evanston, IL: Northwestern University Press.

Spolin, V. (1983). *Improvisation for the theater*. Evanston, IL: Northwestern University Press.

Vogler, C. (1998). *The writer's journey: Mythic structure for writers*. Studio City, CA: Michael Wiese Productions.

CHAPTER TEN

ADVENTURE LEARNING

Choose the Right Peak

Mark Lord

Mark Lord is a principal of Synergy Learning Systems, based in Santa Cruz, California. As a trainer and consultant in leadership and adventure learning with over eighteen years' experience, he works in North America, Europe, and Asia and consults and is lead faculty on dozens of team and leadership development programs every year. He also conducts executive development programs in wilderness settings across the world. Mark's clients include Autodesk, Cisco Systems, eBay, Genentech, Google, Societe Generale, Stanford University, UBS, and Turner Construction. He has also authored several recognized guidebooks on mountain biking and backcountry skiing.

Contact Information
Synergy Learning Systems, Inc.
P.O. Box 3939
Santa Cruz, CA 95063
(831) 460–4444
mark@synergyls.com
www.synergylearningsystems.com

THE VIEW WAS GLORIOUS. We could see across the straits to the hazy landform of North Africa. The group's spirits were high as members congratulated one another and shook hands in their success in ascending the rugged limestone peak in southern Spain. Little did they know that their congratulatory spirits would soon be dampened. "How's everyone feeling right now?" I asked, not certain how to break the news to them that they had misread their map. "Great," "We nailed it," "This wasn't so difficult" were the responses. I proceeded carefully: "If I told you that you were on the wrong peak, would you feel the same?" "Of course not, why?" "What are you talking about?" I couldn't stall any longer. "This is the wrong peak, team. Your peak is about two miles over there," I said, pointing to a massif to the north. The wind whistling in our ears was the only sound for what felt like endless minutes as the group grasped their mistake, dumbfounded. "Damn, I knew it . . . ," a quieter member finally grumbled, breaking the silence.

It was the crucible moment for this group of executives, the culmination of a six-day leadership program. They were a large multinational hardware and software company whose success was unparalleled in the Eighties and early Nineties. But their market share was slipping and their CEO was worried that they were losing their edge and had become too comfortable. "I want something beyond the ordinary, something that will test their leadership and stretch them. I want to instill a more global focus, something that will require them to rise to new capabilities. And I don't want them to just sit and talk about it; I want them to have to do it."

We were contacted because of the ropes courses that we had provided for one of their vice presidents when she was with another company. She remembered that we "did that adventure stuff" and that we could also provide the organizational context and follow-up that she knew would be needed. The program we designed had two days of traditional leadership content—360-degree assessment, communication modules, group development theory. But the final four days were off the map. After a day of rock climbing, we then headed into the backcountry, where the group chose and set up their base camp, were taught map and compass skills, cooked their own meals, and planned their summit bid. We defined the summit. They had to find it and figure out the route.

We made certain that each program had good global representation from Europe, Latin America, Asia, and North America. After an alpha test conducted in the Sierra Nevada of California, we went on to conduct them in the mountains of New Zealand, France, Arizona, and now Grazelema, Spain. Spain was my favorite location; the backcountry near Pico de Orizaba was perfect. Not too high, only about 3,000 meters, but the terrain was wickedly deceiving. A peak that appeared to be only a short easy walk up suddenly became epic in its ascent because of one-hundred-foot deep limestone chasms that blocked the route, trails that suddenly vanished across into the brush, and prickly thorn bushes that seriously complicated cross-country travel. Add in maps that were nearly worthless because of their insistence in trails that didn't exist or refusal to show trails that did made for the perfect leadership challenge.

What Adventure Learning Is

Adventure learning can be defined as a specific subset of experiential programming wherein the outcome of the experience is uncertain and often includes real and perceived risk or hazard (physical, mental, and/or emotional). Success is not guaranteed and requires a group or individual to apply skill in resolving the outcome. Direct participation is critical, while still balancing individual "challenge by choice" criteria.

But what does climbing mountains have to do with developing leadership in organizations in the 21st century? Everything and nothing. As I often explain to my clients, it's not the task, it's the process. Learning can best occur when it requires a new approach, a different mindset. The wise Zen monk Suzuki said, "In the mind of a beginner, all things are possible. But in the mind of an expert, only a few."

Thriving in today's organizations requires an ability to deal with incredible complexity . . . rapid pace, change, technology, global competition, time pressures with ambiguous information, shifting market share, limited resources, and doing more with less. We know that top-down driven leadership is limited in its capabilities and that the strength of an organization is in its ability to create solutions that have many people's input, commitment, and diversity of thinking. One person cannot possibly have all of the answers, and managers and executives are expected to do more with less.

Action, risk, uncertainty, challenge. These are all of the key ingredients in a successful adventure learning program. Without them, it can still be a learning program, but not an *adventure* learning program. Adventure brings the sense of stretching oneself, of being uncomfortable, of new and unfamiliar terrain. This is adventure learning's strength, its sweet spot.

If adventure and challenge is the approach, then the outdoors is the vehicle— the stimulus that is experienced by the learners. For the purpose of this discussion, I differentiate an outdoor adventure program from a program that can be conducted either indoors or outdoors. In fact, conducting the activity indoors causes a significant portion of the program's "unknown" to be lost—the elements of wind, rain, snow, heat, cold, sun, darkness, and light. When all is moved into an indoor location, the essence of the program is lost. Likewise, we can play monopoly outdoors, but it's hardly an adventure activity. I prefer to think of it being differentiated by the notion of a certain amount of adventure being included in the experience. Yes, a ropes course can be conducted inside a gym with platforms constructed on the walls and with trapezes and ladders suspended from the ceiling. And participants will experience the rush and excitement in much the same way as with an outdoor experience. Indoor climbing gyms have become popular, but what's missing is a certain unknown—weather and environment play a significant role. It acts as a metaphor for numerous learnings—changing business climate and markets, competitors, customer demand, and so forth. You can control the response and your plan, but you cannot control the market.

The outdoors is the perfect classroom for learning about decision making, collaboration, goal setting, navigating ambiguity, and fortitude. I'll explore some methods to apply adventure learning to work groups and share some stories that I've gained over the years in the coming paragraphs. But first, I want to share some history and attempt to explain its evolution to increase understanding and what makes it work.

The Origins of Adventure Learning

Confusion certainly exists on the exact origin of adventure learning. The military has used obstacle courses for training troops since the early Greeks, although the focus was primarily on fitness and physical strength and obviously less on team building. Likewise, the use of belay and safety systems on such courses was limited or often non-existent. If you survived it, you were in. If not, the selection process was obvious and feedback immediate by way of severe injury or death. Not the best method for corporate training, however.

Adventure learning programs still had far to go before they could be used by non-military organizations. George Hébert has been cited as one of the originators of what bears the most resemblance to today's ropes course. A French naval officer in the early 1900s, Hébert developed his own method of physical education, apparatus, and principles to train in what he called the "natural method," which included the development of physical, moral, and "virile" qualities in an outdoor environment. By drawing from his naval background, Hébert patterned some of his obstacles on ones found on the decks of ships. "Hébertism" grew during and between the World Wars, becoming the standard for physical education training for the French military. Many ropes courses and challenge course programs in French Canada and Europe are still known as Hébertism courses today.

Consider another early pioneer who contributed much to this field of adventure learning. Kurt Hahn, founder of Outward Bound, significantly, if not single-handedly, influenced this approach. Hahn's belief was that individuals who wish to succeed in the world must balance book knowledge with physical skills such as running, jumping, and throwing, as well as learning to live in the outdoors through an expedition.

Hahn, with British shipping baron Sir Lawrence Holt, embarked on a joint effort to teach young British sailors the vital survival skills necessary during World War II. The curriculum was based mainly on Hahn's belief that character development was just as important as academic achievement, and the new school became the wellspring of experiential learning in the post-war period. Hahn found that people who were put in challenging, adventurous, outdoor situations gained confidence, redefined their own perceptions of their personal possibilities, demonstrated deeper compassion, and developed a spirit of camaraderie with their peers. Sounds like qualities a manager would trade some of his or her stock options for to reside on the team.

Outward Bound is known for having brought adventure learning forward in the world, but its approach of "let the mountains speak for themselves" has been debated by many, including some Outward Bound instructors. The belief is that a facilitator should not debrief the experience by asking a series of questions that helps the group and/or individuals draw conclusions to develop specific learnings. Instead, each individual should reach his or her own conclusions.

Project Adventure is credited with having significantly popularized ropes courses in the Seventies and Eighties, with many other organizations developing and sophisticating the field today. Today, ropes courses are still in demand. They continue to be an effective and impactful learning experience that builds teamwork and creates strong bonds.

What Makes Adventure Learning Work

I've explained why adventure learning is compelling and shed some light on its origins. But what exactly happens in an effective program?

When I first began working with groups in the outdoors over twenty-five years ago, leading individuals into the backcountry with the specific task in mind to teach technical skills (how to ascend a scree slope, the best place to camp in a storm, how to descend a steep icy slope on skis with a 30-pound pack on your back), I gave little attention to the group dynamics that played out. One group successfully navigating the backcountry, while another mired in hopeless power struggles was the luck of the draw. I knew little about group process and leadership skills.

Taking groups into backcountry was an incredibly rich experience that individuals never forgot. A few nights together in adverse, foul weather conditions could bring out the best in people and bond them for a lifetime or create unbelievable tension and disrespect. I noticed that the person you met in the lodge or parking lot before taking off for the backcountry bore little resemblance to the individual I got to know when the going got tough. However, I had not a clue how to develop the learning potential of the experience.

In the spirit of "let the mountains speak for themselves," I let the experience speak for itself. When lack of agreement came up between individuals, I found ways to diffuse the tension or let them work it out themselves, but, with time, I discovered that the tension was grist for the learning mill—that the stress that was created by adverse conditions, bad weather, and difficult tasks was exactly what groups often needed to coalesce and successfully navigate the challenges they faced. When groups were effective in the areas of communication, strategy, and leadership, they had the strongest bonds and the most capability.

Thankfully, most providers, not only myself but most Outward Bounders, no longer "let the mountains speak for themselves." In fact, its not unusual to find the reverse to be true. Many adventure providers now utilize technical staff who focus solely on the "hard skills," leaving the "soft" skills to those with extensive training and experience in human and group dynamics.

What helped me change the most was Bruce Tuckman, who back in the Sixties and Seventies studied numerous groups and developed an impressive and now very well-known group development model of *Forming, Storming, Norming,* and *Performing.* All groups go through the stages organically; but not all groups go through the stages smoothly or efficiently. Each stage was either positively or negatively affected by the previous stage's completion. New group member? Back to forming. Likewise for a new task or new process. I observed how quickly groups would fall into dissention or poor performance due to incomplete forming or ineffective storming.

The groups that spent a bit more time assessing resources, increasing familiarity, initially defining the goals and roles—all forming tasks—were usually significantly more likely to achieve satisfying results. Likewise, groups that were encouraged to explore alternative methods and solutions, despite whatever the deemed leader thought, were often more successful in their outcomes. By holding Tuckman's model—beautiful in its simplicity and yet complex in its power—in my mind, I was able to unlock the mystery of why some teams worked and others failed, despite the technical skill resident in the individuals.

With this basic but powerful knowledge, I began to create more powerful learning opportunities for groups. The activities were nearly bottomless springs in their potential to find strengths and development areas for groups.

It remains the case that what makes adventure learning so powerful is that the experiences are visceral and involve some degree of physicality. They're memorable because they tap into the imagination and are certainly not business as usual. But they're only as good as the facilitation that is conducted during or immediately after the program. Without expert observations and inquiry, the program will stay in the realm of recreational and not cross the threshold of a learning program.

And this is a tricky process. I've observed many skilled and seasoned trainers and consultants fall flat on effectiveness for lack of understanding the basic structuring of facilitation. Let's look at processing the adventure experience.

Processing an Adventure Learning Experience

As I've noted, the experience is only a small part of well-conceived outdoor learning programs. So what exactly is an effective process to process the process? Borrowed from many sources, I use a processing model with three steps: *analysis, identification/generalization,* and *application.*

Let's apply this model to an actual group with whom I recently worked.

They are a group of ten engineers from a construction management organization. Its members are culturally diverse. There are six males and four females. The group faces a very important, although difficult, project that is just under way. To be successful, they need to build strong bonds, define operating agreements, and create an ability to effectively coach and support one another through the project ahead of them.

I decide to take them on a one-day "trek," traveling a couple of miles, gathering information, and navigating a series of challenges and tasks in order to reach an "island" destination on which they are "stranded." Once there, they must send a signal to be "rescued" from the "island." The challenges are a blend of physical and mental problems that must be solved; they must define the problem, generate solutions, and converge on the best solution. Strategy, effective communication, styles of leadership, and group development are all applied in addition to a fun although challenging opportunity to build relationships with their colleagues.

In their journey, the group encounters a "river" that must be crossed. There are short lengths of lumber that will allow the group to span bridges between concrete blocks or "stones." In addition, the group must also build a scale or measuring device that enables them to accurately weigh multiple "food" containers (one is "contaminated" and is a different weight than the others and must be accurately defined). They have sixty minutes to accomplish both of these tasks. With numerous setbacks and struggling leadership, the group successfully crosses the river and, with less than thirty seconds remaining, accurately defines which is the bad container. I gather the group together to talk about the experience.

The first phase of the debriefing is the analysis or "what" of the experience. The facilitator asks an individual or individuals to explain what occurred during the experience. I frequently ask someone to briefly tell the story of what just occurred so that someone who may not have been present could understand—conciseness is key, but also avoiding judgment or attributions. "Abby directed the group to place the beams on the blocks to allow the group to cross the river" is very different from "Abby was controlling the group because she wants to be the leader." "There were several attempts at spans between stones that wouldn't work, and we nearly lost the beams in the river." "While several of us were working out the pathway, Maria and Ling were solving the container problem."

Next is the identification/generalization or "so what" phase of the discussion, in which meaning is assigned to the actions taken. This phase can be tricky for the facilitator. It's where differences of opinion between individuals or negative meanings based on someone's action can arise. If Abby was directing the group in building the bridges with little input from others, the group may feel too tightly controlled and have little support for her as a leader. All may be fine if she's successful, but observe the blame and anger that occur if she has made a bad decision. I typically encourage members to talk about the impact of someone's behavior when tension arises. "When Abby was directing the group, I felt little buy-in/ownership on her solution because I wasn't part of the decision-making process." Defining negative and positive behavioral impact is critical for a group to understand and will go far in defining important agreements when building guidelines for how the group wants to work together.

The final step of the debriefing is the application or "now what" phase. The group has defined the actions, identified or given meaning to them, and now should talk about how to apply what they've learned both to the next activity or problem that must be solved and, most importantly, should begin to build understanding of what will be applied to real-world situations. In this case, how the group will decide what to do more of, what they do well as a group, and what to do less of that constrains them.

Continuing with our example, a key learning for the group may be: "Buy-in is critical for complex tasks; it's imperative for those leading tasks in the project to solicit input from others or be explicit that, due to time issues, they are going to be directing the actions." Or "When there are multiple phases in the project, it's important to divide labor so that each specialize in tasks but also stay connected with updates and 'big picture' thinking." The facilitator can keep note of key learnings that the group has defined for later when the group talks about action plans. The learnings here aren't always earth-shaking; sometimes recommitments and reminders are all that are needed. This allows the group to experience and build agreements in a non-defensive, well-facilitated environment that is just different enough from their typical task to allow for new behaviors. Likewise, the group has built positive memories and a sense of "can do" or momentum for the upcoming project.

Although contextual and dependent on skill of the facilitator, attention span of the group, desired outcomes, and so forth, I generally consider a minimum of two parts experience to a maximum of one part debriefing. I rarely run dry on what to debrief, but I do believe that most participants' attention span runs thin after more than an hour and a half debriefing an experience. Certainly, creating a work plan or defining operating agreements based on learnings gained from an adventure experience will take much longer than an hour and half to forge, but the actual discussion time should probably rarely exceed this magic number. Be kind to your participants and leave them at least slightly desirous to keep talking about the experience back in the office. Positive memories create strong bonds that will see groups through difficult times.

I now want to explore some other specific methodologies in applying adventure learning.

Blending Adventure Learning with Other Activities

Often trainers and providers want to provide more engaging programs, but still want to employ more traditional teaching methods. Many have found that outdoor adventure learning complements other training approaches and can be imbedded into programs. Following are some examples.

Lend Lease, an Australian headquartered leading property management firm with offices in forty-two countries and over nine thousand employees, offers its employees *Springboard,* a leadership program beyond the ordinary. *Springboard*'s primary objective is to assist participants in developing skills to find that place where people are most alive and vibrant and operating at upper levels of performance.

Natalie Braid, manager of *Springboard,* explains that she decided to revamp the program four years ago from its traditional strictly classroom approach to include a more experiential adventure component. This four-day program runs multiple times every year, with approximately fifty cross-cultural, cross-functional participants in each group. It blends learning approaches—half the time is spent in classroom lectures and discussions, with the other half of the time spent out-of-doors participating in a learning journey. Every program includes a high ropes course experience and multiple low initiatives that are based on an expedition story line. Teams can gain or lose "calories" depending on their ability to succeed in the activities. Activities are complex and blend some physical tasks with challenging problems that must be solved with limited resources and time.

Paul Kessler, a partner with the Syncretics Group, works with executives, focusing on leadership and change. Although this isn't unique, what is quite different is his approach. He studies groups who are "at their edge," extreme cases of human behavior in challenging conditions (two of the better known are the 1914 trans-Antarctic expedition led by Sir Ernest Shackleton and the *AFR Midnight Rambler*, overall winner of the grueling 1998 Sydney-Hobart sailing race). Kessler has found that a certain essence of leadership or teamwork behavior is distilled from these cases.

Syncretics has participants study these extreme survival stories and integrate experiential activities into their programs to reinforce the concepts and help people internalize the lessons. They have found that using experiential activities complements their use of story and metaphor and has many benefits for the participants. Hearing about the epic and harrowing experiences of others, blended with adventure activities and skillful facilitation, enables participants to begin to develop newfound strengths and capabilities in meeting their own challenges.

Making a Difference on the Individual Level

Adventure learning is certainly a powerful group experience that helps to build strong, effective bonds. Another useful application is for the individual. Here is a case in point.

Susan is a consultant in a professional services firm. Although she is successful, she hasn't been seen as one of the leaders in the firm. She tended to play it safe and never worked as an innovator of the services. Her firm decided to reward the team for their hard work with a day of team building on the high-challenge course. The day had gone fairly well, if not predictably. Individuals played within their typical roles, partners in the limelight, associates following behind, support staff on the ground, belaying everyone else. With only an hour left, the group was resolute in its desire to stay with tradition, despite my nudges and observations. I was looking for the "hook" that would help to shift the group from business as usual into deeper insights and possibilities.

Susan was waiting her turn for the zipline, a 400-foot wild slide on a cable, suspended 70 feet between enormous redwood trees. She climbed the first few rungs up the ladder, but then signaled her desire to descend. "I can't do this," she said quietly. "This is way harder than I thought." Not wanting to push her, I also knew she had the capability if she wanted to go. I reminded her of the following model I had shared with them earlier:

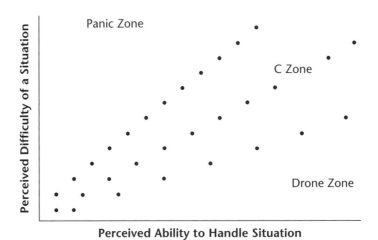

Note: Each performance zone encompasses a different type of behavior.

In the C Zone, stress is positive because it is controlled. In both the Panic and Drone Zones, stress is negative due to lack of control. (See Table 10.1.)

TABLE 10.1. ZONES MODEL

Panic Zone	C Zone	Drone Zone
Too much challenge	Balance of challenge and	Not enough challenge
Not enough mastery	mastery	Too much mastery
Overcommitted	Committed	Uncommitted
Overconfident	Confident	Underconfident
Out of Control	In Control	Overcontrolled
Nervous	Calm	Lethargic
Scattered	Focused	Sluggish
Hyper	Energized	Bored
I HAVE to	Can do	Don't chance it

Developed by Mihaly Csikszentmihalyi

"Where do you see yourself right now?" I asked. "Deep in the panic zone," she confided. "And when you're back here on the belay team, then where?" "Deep in the drone zone," she confided, rolling her eyes. "Can you see the dichotomy? You're playing at extremes. Try to challenge yourself, and you jump in over your head, then back out and go to your overly comfortable place and fall asleep because you're not engaged or learning new skills." I reminded her of the tools available—looking for resources to help her, asking for coaching and support in the task.

Ultimately, Susan went off the zipline. She was ecstatic, much as I would have expected, and she received lots of congratulatory praise from her colleagues. But I was more interested in the long-term effect. Several months later, I met with her team for follow-up. After the session, she sought me out: "I have to tell you that zipline has become an icon in my life. I won't say that it's completely changed my life, but it's a beginning. I now have a mentor here. I've contracted with one of the partners to have her coach me. We often use the zipline as a metaphor. When I start feeling either in the drone or panic zone, she reminds me of my choices. It's made a difference in the decisions I make and the projects I take on."

The Future of Adventure Learning

Adventure learning will stay as a valid offering to learning organizations if it remains relevant and fresh. Most practitioners thought that ropes courses would last only as long as the 20th century, with little room in the 21st for something so "last millennium." Yet, they continue to be built and well utilized, solely because it still offers a unique perspective for clients, and practitioners continue to find new ways to use and facilitate them. Wilderness will always offer the unknown, challenge, risk. But what about other offerings?

Many practitioners are utilizing technology in their adventure programs. Web-enabled cell phones, handheld computers, and global positioning systems provide an interesting addition to programs often utilized for search functions. This also allows for increased sophistication and complexity in the design.

Media is also showing promise. Peak Teams—a cutting-edge company in Australia—has developed an unparalleled concept that applies DVD technology and decision-tree processes in a virtual expedition. "We provide behavioral simulations that test individual and team performance under pressure and stress," says founder Shane Toohey. With his partner, Ian Schubach, they provide high mountain climbing and African safari adventures. Through edgy, realistic footage shot on location, participants are presented with real-life climbing choices . . . a fierce storm has descended, so do we bivouac or descend? Further choices are presented (one of the expedition members has severe altitude sickness, so do we send him down by himself or split the party up?). Numerous problems are presented, just as on an actual expedition. Although I'm not a fan of "virtual" programs, this one promises to bring the adventure experience to those who cannot access the real thing.

Conclusion

So what about our group that had climbed the wrong peak? I had to carefully maneuver with the group to ensure good learnings and not come across as an egotistical facilitator.

"We've got lots to talk about, people, particularly what went wrong. My guess is it's going to be difficult to look at what worked well. And we've got plenty of time to think and talk about it on our descent back to base camp before nightfall. No, you didn't make the right summit. But better to not have achieved the goal here than back at the workplace. So I'd like you to think about your process, and later tonight and tomorrow we'll discuss how to apply these learnings back to work. First though, let's get off this peak."

The descent was quiet as the group reflected. Their error created a somber mood. By the time we got back to base camp, the mood had improved and they were able to joke a bit about it. Like most groups, they did a fine job of defining their errors: "Too much group think," "We narrowed our options too soon before checking all of the data," "We did a poor job of listening to all members, only the loudest ones were heard," "We didn't check our assumptions," "We were seeking confirming data and missed the cues."

But it was critical that they realize their strengths—not to stroke their egos or give false praise, but instead to ensure that they didn't lose the lesson, although they had lost the peak. I wanted the group to understand that their steadfast resolve, cohesiveness, and enthusiasm were qualities that will serve them well. Better to summit something big than to have disintegrated from infighting and indecision.

When I met with the group several months later on a follow-up meeting, they all wore sweatshirts with *Escoge la Cumbre Correcta* (Choose the Right Peak) embroidered just above their company name. One member stood up as they presented me with my own sweatshirt and said, "I think I can speak for the group in saying this lesson has been etched into our everyday thinking!"

CHAPTER ELEVEN

ROLE PLAY

Principles to Increase Effectiveness

Les Lauber

Les Lauber has been a training and development practitioner for nearly a dozen years in various private and public sector organizations. He currently works at the Kansas Department of Transportation as the organization development system project manager. Known for content-rich, highly interactive sessions, Les has made presentations across the United States and in Canada to various corporate audiences and conferences, including the North American Simulation and Gaming Association (NASAGA) and the Annual Conference of the Certified Public Manager Academy (AACPM). Les focuses his training efforts in management skills, leadership skills, and train-the-trainer seminars.

Contact Information
1512 W. 9th Street, #4
Lawrence, KS 66044
(785) 296–2754
lauber@ksdot.org

OTHER THAN STRAIGHT LECTURE, perhaps trainers and trainees malign role play more than any other learning method. Thousands of pages have been written on the use, misuse, benefits, and drawbacks of role play in both academic and practical writings. Many trainers insist that it be written in to nearly every soft-skills training, and we then cover it up with vague terms like "skills practice" or "demonstrations." With thought and planning, though, this can be an especially powerful tool in the trainer's toolkit, both for practicing skills and affecting learners' attitudes about the subject being learned. This chapter briefly explores these uses of role play, then offers nine principles to consider when developing role plays. After each principle, I offer a brief example of that principle from my practice in facilitating role playing. The last part of this chapter includes a brief synopsis of different approaches to role play.

Role Play Reflects Reality

Consider how Alan Klein defined role play in 1956: "reality practice." Of the three areas we concern ourselves with in training and development—knowledge, skills, and attitudes—role play doesn't work so well with knowledge. That's not to say it doesn't work at all for developing learners' knowledge of a topic. Other methods, covered elsewhere in this book, simply work better. The reason is easily understood. Learners develop skills in communication, approaches to conflict, managing meetings, and the like, with practice and feedback. Role play provides just that kind of practice and can provide effective feedback, as well. Learners' attitudes change as they gain new insights about how reality works. These new insights allow them to sensitize themselves to others' ideas, sensibilities, feelings, and values. Ethics training, which necessarily delves into areas of values, usually concerns itself with what happens in the affective domain and provides rich opportunities for role play.

I think of role play as a form of simulation. The key to simulation is that it approximates reality in some way. NASA's high-end space shuttle flight simulators represent the highest end of accuracy or have "high fidelity to reality." On the opposite end are activities that have something "stand in" for whatever is being simulated. The famous time management example of putting rocks into a jar with sand in it is one such low-fidelity simulation. The rocks represent priorities, which must be placed in the jar before the low-priority items, which the sand represents. The rocks and sand are what Sivasailam "Thiagi" Thiagarajan calls "metaphorical simulations": low-fidelity activities in which one thing—rocks and sand in this case—represents another. One use of these metaphorical simulations is to simulate events or situations that may be too painful or too sensitive to be directly represented in a simulated scenario.

FIGURE 11.1. SIMULATION CONTINUUM

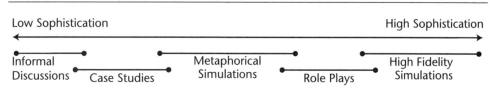

There seems to be a "simulations continuum" of educational and training activities. As shown in Figure 11.1, this continuum runs from the least sophisticated methods (informal discussions of a situation over coffee, perhaps) to the most sophisticated (that NASA flight simulator). Various case studies, role plays, and simulations—metaphorical or literal—fit somewhere in between.

The overlap in the figure is intentional. Informal discussions can turn themselves into case studies, flight simulators certainly require an element of role play, and so on. Trying to define the overlap out of the continuum is counterproductive.

Principles for Effective Role Play

Too many trainers simply throw together a role play. Writing a scenario and populating it with characters is not always sufficient to create effective learning opportunities. When they fail to observe some simple principles, trainers inadvertently frustrate their learners. The learners often react poorly to the activity out of this frustration. This sequence can reinforce any previous ideas the trainer held about the inadequacies of role play.

The following principles can dramatically increase the opportunity for role play success. When developing a role play, check it against these principles to enhance its effectiveness. Each principle is followed by examples of how I use it when I facilitate role plays.

1. Attach the Role Play to a Learning Objective

Although this principle seems obvious on the surface, too many trainers ignore it. (I've spoken to some who even put role plays into sessions because they enjoy putting their learners on the spot. These trainers manipulate their "learning objectives" to create uncomfortable role plays because they enjoy the power they feel over their learners. It often occurs that a successful role play will have the effect of making a learner uncomfortable, but that should nearly always be an effect and not the activity's goal.) Each role play, like any other activity, should have a direct relation to the point of the training program. If it doesn't, it is not appropriate and should not be used.

For example: In my class on behavioral event interviewing, one of the learning objectives is to focus an interviewee's general answers to specific, historical examples. By role playing an interview, learners have a close-to-life experience in which they ask a question and must judge whether it is a specific answer, then probe deeper if it is not. I have seen other trainers use fill-in-the-blank worksheets for this, but simulating a real-life interview with a real person is a better choice here.

In an advanced supervision class, I set an objective that learners would "Respond to inappropriate behaviors by subordinates." The content I developed for this objective dealt directly with the reason so many supervisors do not respond to inappropriate behavior: they are uncomfortable confronting it and question their abilities to manage the conversation. My approach was to give an example of some behavior that would both have an emotional impact on the learners and some shock value—the employee was insubordinate, or insulted the learners' family, or was a close friend of the family—and force the learning into the affective domain. The use of vulgar language combined with the intensely personal nature of the offending behavior had the effect intended. The learners were forced to deal with the attitudes they held regarding what was appropriate or inappropriate for the workplace. Simultaneously, they had to practice good conflict management skills. They learned that, even though they were uncomfortable responding to behaviors in highly emotional situations, they could do it.

2. Define the Experience You Want Learners to Have

One of my greatest learning experiences about planning role plays came from a training session I attended on meeting facilitation. The trainer explained that an agenda is really only half the preparation for a good meeting, but is where most facilitators end. In truly effective meetings, the facilitator also goes in with a plan for what the meeting participants should experience. Because role playing is about the experience of practicing a skill or encountering a situation, the advice is equally applicable here. By approximating the experiences of others, the learner can become sensitized to others' feelings and reactions. The behavioral change this inspires is much greater and much longer-lasting than can be achieved through lecture or many other activities.

For example: One of the learning points in my class on behavior event interviewing is that silence on the interviewee's end often means he or she is trying to remember a specific example. Each manager taking this class plays the part of an interviewee to experience what it is like to be asked a question and have to think of a specific example for an answer. That experience sensitizes them to how difficult it can be on the interviewee's end of the question. That one ten-minute experience does more to encourage them to allow their interviewees thinking time than any other activity, discussion, or lecture that could be used.

In a class on communication techniques for a team of librarians, I chose a role play around why this library didn't have a particular book available for a specific patron. Before the role play, I asked the librarians to write on 3-by-5 cards common responses a patron to their library might hear. Then I turned the tables on the learners. I played the part of a librarian and asked them to play the parts of their customers. As they would try to engage me in my role and ask for information, I would use one of the responses from the prepared cards. As the role play went on, they realized that it sounded like I was using jargon to avoid responding to their questions. They also noticed during the debriefing that my answers seemed pat, almost rehearsed, and that I just used whatever was on my card (whatever "came to mind") without really thinking whether it fit this customer's situation. The ensuing conversation about how to make a personal connection with the patron became the centerpiece of the entire session.

3. Make the Roles as Natural as Possible

When practicing a new skill, the learners are working hard enough remembering the steps they are learning or adjusting to the other role players' behaviors. Asking them to adopt a role they have no experience in, or a personality that is unlike themselves, creates a kind of mental disconnect. It shifts their focus from the learning to the new personality or role, and it increases their stress. When they adopt roles with which they are already comfortable instead, their mental energy frees up to focus on those steps or reacting to others' behaviors.

For example: In the Kansas Civil Service, employees have certain due process rights during the disciplinary process. While interviewing supervisors and managers to prepare for a class on constructive discipline, I learned that this due process seemed mysterious to many of them. To reduce the mystery, I designed a role play around an appeal of a disciplinary action. Three learners were involved as the disciplining manager, the disciplined employee, and the employee's witness. I invited members of the office that oversaw the disciplinary process to participate as the appeal committee chair and legal counsel for the manager and the employee. The rest of the class participated as committee members who heard evidence, asked questions, deliberated on the facts they heard, and came to a decision. The activity illuminated the employees' due process, as I had hoped, and the role of the supervisor in discipline. The committee deliberation element of the role play also made a profound impact on the learners' attitudes toward the disciplinary process. By participating in a mock committee, they realized that insufficient documentation and failure to seek out good advice can leave an appeal committee to make its own conclusions. One of the learners remarked that she now understood how difficult it was for a reviewer to determine whether a supervisory action was fair when the supervisor was too complacent about following the process.

In behavioral event interviewing, I used to hand out sample resumes and job applications. The individual taking the interviewee's role often found it difficult to find specific answers to the interview questions that fit the applications. Repeated coaching to "draw from your own experiences" did not help. However, asking participants to bring their own resumes and portray themselves did. Now, the learners really do draw from their own experiences. It's still stressful, but now they are stressed about coming up with answers from their own experience, rather than playing an assigned role. And, as I mentioned in Principle 2, that's the stress I want them to experience.

4. Build Situations, Not Roles

Often, you need learners to represent a role they don't or wouldn't often fill in real life. Look for plausible ways to put them into that situation as themselves. Build a situation in which they have to represent the role you need them to play. Learners are often resistant to playing a role that "isn't who I am." Placing them into a situation that allows them to be who they are can reduce that source of resistance. This is especially effective when creating role plays for learning objectives in the affective domain. The key here is to give the learners a place to start where they can ground on their existing knowledge or experience.

For example: In my train-the-trainer session on effective role plays, our immediate activity after the icebreaker is a role play. This role play's purpose is to explore different attitudes people hold about this activity type. Each role player is given an assignment sheet, *not* a role. The learners' assignments come as e-mails or memos that ask them to represent their boss in a meeting on whether role play should be used in the company training department. The assignment includes an explanation of their boss's beliefs and position. In one case, the boss makes a threat to raise the issue to a corporate director if he doesn't get his way. It's always fascinating to watch this role play unfold, since some individuals truly adopt their assigned positions, but others shift the blame up. All points of view are represented, though, and no one has to play a role with which he or she disagrees—they simply have to represent their boss. And most people have existing experience with situations like that.

My role play on the disciplinary review committee made similar use of this principle. The committee members were themselves, bringing their own approaches, experiences, and thoughts to the deliberation process. The entire process was much more real to them than to the three who portrayed the manager, employee, and witness. Because the committee member-learners were not encumbered with taking on another persona, they experienced the role play as themselves. The frustrations they had with the lack of supervisory documentation, the sense they had that the employee's witness didn't know what he was talking about—all of these were reactions the learners were having and could not discount as "my character's reaction." During the debriefing, we discovered that they walked into the situation wanting to side with the supervisor. After all, they were supervisors themselves. This case was the supervisor's to lose. Through the debriefing, the learners came to realize that, by failing to follow their employer's process, they shoot themselves in the foot. Again, I could have presented the course content in any number of ways, but the role-play experience did more to shape their feeling of a need to learn and follow the process than any other approach I might have chosen.

5. Create an Observation Checklist

Checklist items are different for skills practicing role plays than for sensitizing role plays. When a role play is to provide practice for building skills, the observers should be given a checklist of the skills they should be watching for. When it provides an experience for sensitizing learners to learning objectives in the affective domain, the checklist should guide the observers in what behaviors and reactions to watch for. A good number of items on an observers' checklist is probably five-to-eight. Fewer than five and the richness of role-play experiences is not likely to be exploited; more than eight and the level of observation and detail of feedback to learners is likely to be unfocused and overwhelming. Include plenty of space for notes. Also, share the checklist with everyone before the role play begins. Something about knowing what the observer will provide feedback on creates a subtle form of peer pressure that encourages all but the most die-hard resistant participants to take the role play seriously.

For example: In behavioral event interviewing, the observers' checklist includes specific items such as "What did the interviewer do to create a comfortable interview environment?" and "How did the interviewer handle generic answers to specific questions?" From this, the interviewer can be given specific feedback on the interview.

A similar but more general checklist directs observer feedback in my train-the-trainer session on role play. Since this role play focuses on perceptions and attitudes surrounding role play, this checklist contains more items from the affective domain. Examples are "What feelings appear to be present in the individual(s) you are observing?" and "What feelings did this individual seem to evoke in others at the table?" I don't mind making inferences about the behaviors in this role play. As we discuss during the first debriefing, people naturally make these inferences. Only by bringing them into the open and discussing what the inferences are and why others make them can we understand the impacts our behaviors have on other people—and on their attitudes. The observers and interviewees suggest alternative phrases or actions that will help the interviewer hone his or her skills. As you will see with our discussion of the next principle, each observer is assigned to a single role player. This helps focus, and also helps provide specific feedback.

6. Everyone Has a Role

In addition to learners feeling "on the spot" when they have to role play in front of others, those who don't have roles may lose interest in what is happening at the front of the room. Both of these situations can be easily addressed by making sure everyone has a clearly understood role. Not every role will be a playing role, but each role must add to the experience and the learning objectives. In the simplest role plays, one person is the individual practicing a new skill or experiencing a new situation, and the other is providing someone to practice or experience with. The most complex role plays involve multiple people undertaking multiple activities. Anything in between is fair game.

For example: I adjust the size of the "role-play meeting" in my train-the-trainer session. No more than one-half the class ever participates in the meeting. The other half of the class is assigned to observe a specific individual. This technique provides several benefits. First, the role player is freed up to simply be "in the moment" of the meeting because someone else is worried about tracking what is going on. Second, since everyone is being observed, the odds of any significant but subtle event going unnoticed are greatly diminished. Finally, and most importantly, those individuals who are not part of the role play itself still have the role of the observer to carry out. I review the checklist and brief the observers on my expectations while the role players are reviewing their documents and thinking about how to represent their bosses in the meeting. I stress the contribution this group will make during the debriefing discussion. After the meeting breaks up, the participants have small group debriefings with their observers before I facilitate a large group discussion.

In contrast, the behavioral event interviewing role play is a simple triad approach in which one individual interviews another while an observer watches with the checklist. Each learner takes each role once. For my sensitizing objective, each learner experiences being on the firing line of a behavioral event interview. For the practicing objective, each learner must practice using the interviewing skills. Neither in the train-the-trainer nor the interviewing role play does anyone "just watch."

7. Give Every Role Motivation

The best villains in literature, film, and other storytelling arts are not really bad people. They are people who are motivated by something that conflicts with the hero's motivation. This gives the characters dimension that makes them both interesting and believable. The same should be done with characters in role play. Assigning someone to role play an employee who is constantly late to work can be counterproductive in a couple of ways. First, it leaves the learner to fall back on reasons that may not be very real. Second, the learner may allow the role to fall into a two-dimensional caricature. Instead, give the learner some motivation that will create the problem behavior desired in the role. As a result, the role is humanized, with real issues and a level of complexity.

For example: When I train teams on meeting management, we role play a meeting. Rather than assign learners a disruptive behavior when they portray meeting participants, I will give one or two a card with something that motivates the disruptive behavior I desire the team to learn to deal with. I have a number of these written up, printed on card stock, and separated into individual cards that I can draw and hand out at random. On one is written: "You have a headache today, and are finding it hard to track." On another: "Just before the meeting, you received a phone call that your best friend from school was in an accident and is going into emergency surgery." The point is to go beyond the behavior into the underlying reason for the behavior, and give them a reason to behave in a way that will disrupt the meeting.

Role play is particularly effective in training managers and supervisors to deal with unacceptable performance. The persons playing the performers, however, usually need to know why their performance has been suffering. Letting them "wing it" nearly always leads to exaggerated conditions, reactions, and excuses. Providing them with reasons such as dealing with family pressures, insufficient resources, and the like improves the approximation of reality. A bonus often occurs here for me. I find that the individuals most often promoted to supervisor and above tend to have very good performance records, and are therefore often skeptical that any reason for a performance issue is a "good" reason. By giving the employees' roles legitimate reasons for the performance problems, the supervisors taking on those roles often must deal with that skepticism. Many supervisors over the years have told me that this role-playing experience made them more conscious of how they were coming across to employees with performance problems.

8. Role Play, Debrief, Repeat

The effectiveness of many skills-building role plays is diminished when learners participate, are given feedback by their observers, and then the trainer moves on to the next topic or activity. The best time to provide feedback is immediately after the skill being practiced is performed, and most role plays do that very well. However, seldom is time devoted to re-performing and incorporating that feedback. Simply repeating the role play allows the learners to change gears and fix mistakes. This step strongly reinforces the skills being trained and increases the chances that they will be transferred to the workplace. This can work as well for trainers using role play for its sensitizing purpose. A careful role play debriefing can surface assumptions or attitudes the learners hold and the results of those attitudes or assumptions on their interactions with others. Spend time exploring feelings the characters (separate from the role players) likely experienced, whether those feelings are typical of individuals in the role-played scenario or not, and why the participants believe this is or is not so. Once this process is complete, a second role play can be used to explore how approaching the situation with different assumptions or attitudes can change the results. The second debriefing shows dramatic gains each time. The learners, seeing the improvements, gain confidence and buy into what they have been learning. Again, this is a very powerful learning approach.

For example: In my role play train-the-trainer, the chief debriefing point is not about which points of view about role play are right and which are wrong. Instead, it is about the reactions that learners have to role play, the beliefs they hold, and how those beliefs and reactions play out. After a short interim in which each meeting participant debriefs with his or her observer(s), we hold group discussion about what happened in the meeting. Then the participants retake their seats at the meeting table and resume their meeting. The second role play always shows more sensitivity to all sides of the issue, a greater willingness to listen to concerns and explore them, and a genuine attempt to find common ground. I could lecture or assign readings about each of these things, but this approach gives my learners an experience they wouldn't have through those means. Even the observers walk away with a sense that they participated. In just under an hour, the learners have explored multiple perspectives on role playing as a learning activity, investigated reactions, and tested different ways to deal with those reactions.

I once consulted on a role-play design for training emergency personnel how to evacuate persons with mobility problems from dangerous situations. We designed the package with this play-debrief-repeat approach. The emergency personnel received training on the transfer process. The process was reasonably complex, beginning with the learner asking specific questions of the person being transferred and choosing correct responses to the person's answers. Each learner then demonstrated that process in a role play that was videotaped using a professional actress. The debriefing included the learner, the actress, and the trainer discussing the process and reviewing the recording together. This allowed the trainer to provide specific feedback and the learner to practice and correct improper technique. After debriefing the role play, the learner and actress repeated the role play so the learner could immediately apply the correct techniques. One of the learners later reported that, as a consequence of receiving feedback on asking the individual to be evacuated whether he or she could walk, he did that in a real-life situation. It turned out the real person who really needed to evacuate could walk, and did. Before the role-play training scenario, the learner said he would have assumed she could not and simply carried her out, which may have aggravated her impairment.

9. Approximate Work Settings

One means to successful transfer of behavior is to make the practice scenario look, feel, and sound like the workplace. A role play does not need to be placed in an actual cloth-walled cubicle to be effective, but attention to minor details can send the message to learners that this is relevant. A CD with sound effects from an office place might be one such detail. Seating arrangements, using "real" forms or papers, or inviting guests to play themselves, when appropriate, can all lend a sense of legitimacy and help the learners get closer to that feeling of the real work setting.

For example: Ideally, the emergency personnel role play should have occurred in the appropriate room of a house. The training actually occurred in a conference room of a training facility. The trainer did several things to approximate the situation the workers would face as closely as possible. First, she rearranged the room to reduce its familiarity to the learners. Second, she obtained real-life equipment that would be used by the persons with the represented mobility impairments and the emergency workers and placed them in appropriate places around the room. Third, she obtained a hospital-style bed for the actress to lie in and situated it near a window, much as it would be in a home. Finally, she arranged other chairs around it to create a reasonable facsimile of a home bedroom. The illusion for the learners wasn't perfect, but it was close enough to ease transfer of learning to their real work environments.

I seat learners in the behavioral interview class in such a way that the interviewee and interviewer are across a table from each other. When they sit in an open triangle, it feels less formal, less like an interview. Placing a table be-tween them creates a subtle but important sense that "this feels right." That feel-ing that the situation is right is often all that is needed to make the learning transferable.

Role-Play Variations

The nine principles discussed here can be applied to any approach to role play. The two most common approaches to role play are the "fishbowl" and the "round robin" techniques. A number of variations can be applied to either.

Fishbowl

This is the standard role play in which several individuals engage in the role play and the others watch. This is what most people think of when they say, "I hate role playing." Some techniques exist that may make it less nervewracking for the players who feel they are performing for an audience.

Stage-as-simulator: The area in which the role play will occur can be set up to resemble the learners' real-world workplace as closely as possible. The more the area in which the learners role play feels like their natural work area, the more likely they are to tune out the observers.

Rotating players: Allow others to "tag in" and replace the players when they get stuck. Often, by promising that no one will need to be on the "hot seat" for more than two or three minutes, everyone will be willing to take a turn. Trainers using this technique can draw from a rich resource of actions that worked particularly well.

Scripts: Providing a written script to the role players takes the pressure off—now if they do something wrong, it's because the script called for it. This approach is reminiscent of reader's theater.

Professional actors: Some organizations hire professionals to act out a scripted scene for the observers to watch. The professionals can then accept feedback from the observers and re-play portions of the scene, utilizing that feedback.

Trainer-takes-lead: Mel Silberman (2006) suggests a technique in which the trainer becomes the role player who is demonstrating the skills or attitudes to be learned. Participants can play any other necessary parts. The trainer stops frequently throughout the interaction and asks for coaching from the observers.

Triple-role-playing: Another recommendation Silberman (2006) makes is to select four learners for two parts. The first learner assumes the first role—a supervisor delivering a performance review, for example—and the others leave the room. They return one at a time, and the supervisor practices the task (delivering the review). Because each learner portraying the employee reacts differently, the supervisor must adapt the skills being practiced to that learner's reaction. This approach can also be rich for debriefing.

Role-play coaches: Thiagarajan (2003) suggests that each role player have a coach with whom he or she can discuss the scenario before the role play. During the activity, the coach can provide prompts to help the role player.

Immediate feedback: To increase the activity of the observers in a fishbowl role play, they can be provided with simple prompts for communicating when they see behaviors they agree are appropriate or believe are inappropriate. Silberman (2006) recommends raising hands, whistling, snapping, or clapping as possible prompts.

Round-Robin

This is the other major role play approach that is used. The learners are divided into pairs, trios, quads, etc., and each group conducts a simultaneous role play. At the end of the role play, players switch roles and the role play (or a similar one) is reenacted. The sequence is followed until each learner has taken each role. This method has benefits of involving each person at each step, and learners perform for only the several people in their groups. Many of the same general variations can be applied to this format, as well, including stage-as-simulator, scripts, professional actors, triple role playing, coaches, and immediate feedback.

Improving Feedback to Role Players

The essential elements of providing feedback are the same for role play as for coaching, performance management, or any other leadership role in which one engages. The feedback should be specific to the learners and what occurred within the role play, rather than general to the scenario or the learners' roles in their workplace. Involve the learners in the discussion early—they are the first ones to answer the questions: "What improvements can be made next time?" and "What really went well this time?" This allows them to self-identify their own needs for improvement, and the rest of the discussion can focus on helping the learners achieve that improvement. Finally, frame the feedback as actively and positively as possible. Discussing what the learners can do promotes the learners being active. Telling the learner what to stop doing limits the learners' ability to be active and encourages passivity.

Mel Silberman (2006) identifies six different types of feedback, each of which is represented in the preceding examples.

Trainer Observation

Understand that the more credibility the trainer carries with the group, the more important this type of feedback becomes. The importance of allowing the learner to maintain dignity and self-esteem while receiving feedback is always important. This importance grows geometrically with the trainer's credibility, however. While providing feedback, the effective trainer provides the constructive feedback necessary for improvement, consciously works from the assumption the learner was trying to do the right thing, even when subconsciously skeptical of that assumption, and acknowledges both the learner's intent and attempts. It is easier to build on skills and approaches that exist than to start from scratch. Thus, effective trainers find what was right in a role play as existing skill structures on which the learners can build.

The scenario with the emergency personnel provides an example of this. The trainer was a subject-matter expert with a graduate degree. Her credibility was extremely high to the entry-level personnel with whom she was working. Her feedback was specific, she was clear about her desire to help the learners in their mission to help others, and she always found elements of their performance that were worthy of her sincere praise.

Designated Observers

As noted earlier, this technique provides every person a task to perform during the role play. This technique is also particularly powerful for the purpose of deconstructing a role play into its most basic elements. A checklist of behaviors and reactions derived from the learning objectives provides the observers enough structure to make informed decisions about the elements to provide feedback. Examples of excellent, appropriate, and inappropriate behaviors can be particularly effective when role playing soft skills such as communicating or reviewing performance.

The interviewing seminar includes a checklist of about eight items. Open-ended questions comprise this particular checklist. The use of open-ended questions encourages interaction and discussion between the interviewer and the observer. For example, one question is "What did the interviewer do to establish rapport at the opening of the interview?" Another question is "What did the interviewer do to encourage the applicant to provide specific examples?" Although the checklist could ask observers to check off specific items they see, the open-ended questions force the observer to make notes that improve the quality of the conversation. The checklist is always shared with the interviewer while he or she is preparing for the interview, which encourages the practice of the specific behaviors being trained.

Subgroup Discussion and Feedback

When two to four observers sit down and hold a short discussion with the role player, the role player can check assumptions about what was happening. A strong benefit of this approach is the diversity of interpretation of what was happening, when appropriate, or the consensus of observers.

During the train-the-trainer role play, the role players meet with their observers for a short conversation. The learners' instructions are to begin with the role player sharing his or her perception of the role play. The observers then share their own perceptions, and they discuss discrepancies between the two. Within a ten-minute discussion, a large number of assumptions about role play surface among all the small groups, which can then be brought out and discussed in the large group debriefing without placing any one individual under a spotlight.

Open Audience Discussion

This approach to feedback works well when actors are invited to the training session to conduct the role play and model the behaviors to be learned and all learners observe. It can also work well when using the stage-front or fishbowl approach. Again, checklists provide structure for the feedback, and the comments should be focused rather than general. When using this feedback approach in situations in which the roles are played by learners instead of actors, many trainers find success in requiring that any constructive feedback be preceded or immediately followed by positive feedback that reinforces something that went well. It is good to remember that in these scenarios, those learners volunteering to role play in front of their peers have taken quite a bit of risk, which should be acknowledged.

A form of open audience discussion was used in the disciplinary action committee role play. Although the learners each played a committee member, the feedback process was one of describing for themselves what worked, what did not, and how they would need to approach a similar situation to be prepared for an employee to appeal an action. I opened the discussion with the question, "Specifically, what did the supervisor do in this process that was convincing to you?" Then we discussed: "What did the employee do that you found convincing?" From there we proceeded to items that undermined first the employee's, then the supervisor's positions, and finally to the role and interaction with the committee chair and the attorneys.

Benchmark Comparison

A script of a near-perfect or idealized situation can be an alternative to the checklist approach I suggested earlier. Most behavior modeling approaches to training have examples along these lines. Designing such a script for a scenario the learners will role play, then distributing the script after the role play, can allow the learners to discuss with each other how closely they matched the script. They essentially provide themselves their own feedback as they describe how their performance differed from the script.

The trainer working with the emergency personnel had an abbreviated script for what she expected to happen in the scenarios being trained. She went through that script with the learners after their initial role play, which had been videotaped. The learners had an opportunity to ask questions about why one approach was better than the other or to challenge those areas they thought were inconsistent with their department's policies. Each discussion point enriched their learning.

Video Feedback

This particular tool also contains rich opportunities for enhancing learning. On the other hand, camera fright can be a real concern. Silberman (2006) recommends lightening the mood to relax the learners, allowing them enough preparation time, and leaving the room during taping if it will help. He also suggests taking notes—a suggestion I strongly second—during the role play, regarding ways the learners can improve as well as those areas in which the learners are doing well, and not interrupting the role play during taping for feedback or correction. He points out that allowing the learners to review the tape uninterrupted lets them self-critique. Combining this technique with a checklist and/or a small discussion group can also enrich the learning.

Returning again to the emergency personnel training scenario, the use of the video allowed the learners to review their own performance. When the learners compared the video against their notes and the prepared script, their errors became obvious to them. In each situation, a second role play showed dramatic improvements over the first. In most cases, the second role play nearly perfectly mimicked the script.

Ending the Role Play

As with any activity, the role play is not truly over until a debriefing has occurred. Trainers should be especially careful in debriefing role plays that evoke strong reactions, either by design or through the activity's natural flow. The debriefing should begin with exploring those reactions. Appropriate questions cover what reactions were exhibited, to what degree the reactions were consistent with what one might expect in such a situation, and what other reactions one might encounter in the scenario just role played. The discussion then naturally turns to one of what happened in the role play that triggered the reactions and how the reactions could be different if the behaviors in the role play changed. If training soft skills, ask a few questions about how the role play would have differed without the utilization of the skills the learners are acquiring. Be sure to ask learners what they would do differently if given another chance.

A second role play, in which the participants can implement the feedback they receive, is always a good idea. Again, it is worth every second it takes. The improvement in skill applications is noticeable. The learners generally show increased respect for the other role players' sensibilities. It gives them a chance to practice applying the feedback they received immediately.

Conclusion

Trainers who use role play effectively can create intensely meaningful learning experiences for their trainees. The keys are to be respectful of the learners—to use the activity because it is appropriate, not because we can—and to find ways to allow them to focus on the action and not on the fact that this is a role play. Using the nine principles in this chapter can guide you in doing just that. The suggestions in this chapter really only begin the steps of making role play more relevant and effective. By using imagination and creativity, trainers can adapt the variations and principles here into new and innovative approaches that go beyond the ideas on these pages.

References

Klein, A. F. (1956). *Role playing in leadership training and group problem solving.* New York: Association Press.

Silberman, M. (2006). *Active training* (3rd ed.). San Francisco, CA: Pfeiffer.

Thiagarajan, S. (2003). *Design your own games and activities: Thiagi's templates for performance improvement.* San Francisco, CA: Pfeiffer.

CHAPTER TWELVE

STORYTELLING

Its Role in Experiential Learning

Terrence Gargiulo

Terrence L. Gargiulo is an author, international speaker, organization development consultant, and group process facilitator, specializing in the use of stories. He is a recipient of *Inc.* magazine's Marketing Master Award. Some of his past and present clients include GM, DTE Energy, Dreyer's Ice Cream, UNUM, the U.S. Coast Guard, Boston University, Raytheon, City of Lowell, Arthur D. Little, KANA Communications, Merck-Medco, Coca-Cola, Harvard Business School, and Cambridge Savings Bank. Terrence's books include: *Making Stories: A Practical Guide for Organizational Leaders and Human Resource Specialists*, *The Strategic Use of Stories in Organizational Communication and Learning*, *On Cloud Nine: Weathering Many Generations in the Workplace*, *Stories at Work: Using Stories to Improve Communications and Relationships*, *Building Business Acumen for Trainers: Skills to Empower the Training Function*, and *Once Upon a Time: Using Story-Based Activities to Develop Breakthrough Communication Skills*.

Terrence is a frequent speaker at international and national conferences. including the American Society for Training and Development (ASTD), International Society for Performance Improvement (ISPI), Academy of Management, and the Association of Business Communications. He is also a field editor for ASTD. Terrence and his father's opera *Tryillias* was accepted for a nomination for the 2004 Pulitzer prize in music.

Contact Information

MAKINGSTORIES.net
121 Las Brisas Drive
Monterey, CA 93940
(781) 894–4381
terrence@makingstories.net
www.makingstories.net

STORIES ARE ALL AROUND US. They are so pervasive in all our forms of communication and learning that it's easy to take them for granted. This chapter examines the role stories play in experiential learning. The link between stories and experiences is established to explain the relationship between stories and behavior. Nine functions of stories are discussed to identify the unique experiential learning effects of stories. Next, nine ground rules for working with stories are outlined, complete with tips and techniques. Among these is a summary of nine ways to use stories to promote experiential learning. Eliciting stories during any participant collaboration activity is shown to be the fastest and easiest way to leverage the power of stories. Developed from research with Fortune 500 leaders, nine essential competencies for facilitators and groups working with stories are shared. The chapter ends with instructions for conducting an experiential activity with stories and a case study to illustrate how it works.

The Link Between Stories and Experience

At any moment during a learning event, stories can offer a wealth of opportunities for inciting insights in others. Stories are a powerful tool for experiential learning because they have the power to move participants safely away from their comfort zones and help them to encounter something totally new. In this way, stories act as transporters. They are low-tech virtual reality simulators capable of fabricating vast intricate worlds of discovery. Every time a story is told, listeners enter the realm of the imagination.

The imagination is a sacred learning place that touches our hearts, emotions, and minds. Stories activate our imaginations. Stories offer us the opportunity to

FIGURE 12.1. THE PATH OF STORIES

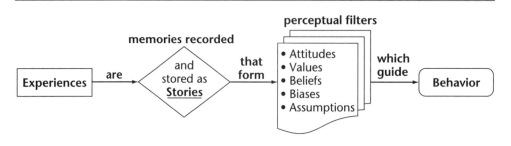

scrutinize our operating models of the world. Through stories, we realize we do not have to be a slave to the perceptual filters we have constructed over time. We build these models of the world from our experiences, which are stored as stories. Our behaviors are often unconsciously guided by these perceptual filters. (See Figure 12.1.) Stories are theaters of imagination where people can play with characters and plots to fashion new possibilities for themselves. As we become more conscious of how our experiences have built our set of perceptual filters, we gain more control of our behaviors.

Our experiences are stored in the containers of stories. The act of remembering a story enables us to assemble parts of ourselves for greater introspection. Stories are vehicles for experiential learning because they allow us to tap into the wealth and variety of personal experiences and share it collectively with a group.

Stories require active listening. This is the most essential aspect of stories. It is easy to get caught up in telling stories. It's what we are the most familiar with. But telling stories just scratches the surface of why they are such effective learning tools. By its nature, learning is both a solitary and a communal phenomenon. No one can *give* us learning. We have to work with whatever is offered to us and turn it into something we own. Whether it be a concept, an idea, a practice, or an insight, we must use our faculties to take active possession of it. In this way, learning is solitary. However, we cannot learn in a void. We require interaction. Like molecules of water heated and bouncing off one another to create steam, our learning is accelerated by the knowledge and experiences of others.

The quickest way to share experiences is through stories. When we use stories to stimulate experiential learning, people gain the benefit of a network full of nodes rich in experiences. Our learning is driven by the correspondences between our experiences and the experiences of others. Even if the relationship between your experience and mine is not a direct one, we are still given an opportunity to reflect. Stories trigger associations, and it is through these associations and our reflecting on them that we are invited to learn in a deep, lasting, and fundamental way.

The Nine Functions of Stories

Whenever anyone asks me for a definition of stories, I steer clear of giving one. Stories can mean lots of different things to different people. There is a whole discipline devoted to just the study of narrative. In order to leverage stories for experiential learning, I do not think it is important to nail down a definitive definition. It is more useful to examine how stories function and how these functions are conducive to facilitating experiential learning. From my research and work with stories, I have found the nine functions of stories shown in Table 12.1.

TABLE 12.1. THE NINE FUNCTIONS OF STORIES

Stories are used to:	Stories have the following effects:
1. Empower a speaker	Entertain
2. Create an environment	Create trust and openness
3. Bind and bond individuals	Elicit stories from others
4. Engage our minds in active listening	Listen actively in order to: *Understand context and perspective* *Identify the root cause of a problem* *Uncover resistance and hidden agendas*
5. Negotiate differences	Hold diverse points of view Shift perspectives in order to: *See each other* *Experience empathy* *Enter new frames of reference* Become aware of operating biases and values
6. Encode information	Create a working metaphor to illuminate an opinion, rationale, vision, or decision
7. Act as tools for thinking	Establish connections between different ideas and concepts to support an opinion or decision
8. Serve as weapons	
9. Bring about healing	Think outside the box to generate creative solutions and breakthroughs

These nine functions are essential aspects of leading any learning experience. On the surface, we use stories to warm up a group, entertain them, and/or create an environment. When you tell a story to a group, think in terms of how it will help you set the stage and model the ground rules you wish to follow for a learning event. As a general rule of thumb, if we are a little vulnerable, circumspect, or reflective, and if we don't take ourselves too seriously, our intentions will spread through the group and positively affect its behaviors. People will also form better bonds with one another. Each story told exposes more points of connections between people.

Steer away from using stories to encode information. Stories that encode predigested messages such as allegories offer the weakest form of learning. This is only one function of stories. Although it is probably one of the most familiar functions, it is the least useful one for creating compelling experiential dialogues that can catapult learners to new insights. Experiential learning requires us to help people suspend their habitual ways of thinking to make room for new perspectives. Empathy can be a wonderful byproduct of stories.

When people listen actively to one another, they enter the world of another person. Our understanding of another person's story is gained by working with bits and pieces of our own stories to find common connections between the story being shared and our own experiences. While we are dependent on our experiences to construct meaning out of what another person shares with us, we are less likely to fixate narrowly on evaluating his or her story in terms of our world view. Like dreams that can present contradictory elements yet still be real (e.g., swimming and flying at the same time, or a figure that appears in the dream is two people at the same time), stories invite us to work with conflicting things. When we actively listen to someone's story, we are not as emotionally invested in our point of view. Differences become opportunities. Since experiential learning bridges the gap between people's current knowledge and desired learning, stories facilitate leaps of imagination that might never be realized by other modes of instruction.

Stories are wonderful tools for thinking. You can place people vicariously into a story and use it to work through new ideas and solutions. For example, if you were leading a discussion on leadership, you might ask the group to explore how the story and characters of *The Wizard of Oz* offer insights into the nature of leadership. As long as people know the story, they will jump right into it and use it as template for abstract thinking. The energy this creates in a group is contagious. The story mode of discussion will touch every kind of thinking and communication style in the room. Creative types will love coming up with zany connections between *The Wizard of Oz* and leadership, while more analytical types of people will enjoy exploring the details and nuances of the connections being found.

As you become more aware of how the nine functions of stories operate, you will get better at naturally incorporating them into learning solutions. I no longer think about it. Sharing stories and eliciting people's stories is what I do every time I am leading a dialogue with a group.

Nine Ground Rules for Working with Stories

To be effective at working with stories in learning environments, there are some important ground rules to follow:

1. Be Able to Expand or Collapse a Story

Stories can vary in length. Stories can be as short as a sentence or two. In fact, I have been in situations in which a single word becomes associated with a story already known by the group or that has emerged from my time with them. For example, consider the phrase, "The emperor has no clothes." If a group of learners were wrestling with a theme of mass denial, the reference to the classic Hans Christian Andersen story of an emperor who is wearing no clothes but which people are afraid to point out could bring quick clarity to learners.

As a facilitator, it is your job to decide what the right amount of detail for a story is. If you are using a story as an energizer or to give the group a chance to catch its breath, lavishing a story with rich detail may be a wonderful way of massaging people's tired brains and emotions. On the other hand, if you are stringing together a complex set of interconnections between ideas in a discussion and key learnings, your story will be more succinct. The composition of the group also factors into your decision of how much detail to include. This necessitates that you be able to reconstitute a story with either less or more detail, depending on your analysis of the group and its needs.

Even if you are not the one telling a story, it is your job as a facilitator to guide participants to share their stories with the appropriate amount of detail. This is done by acting as a good model and anticipating the tendencies of individuals and, if necessary, giving them some constraints before they launch into their telling.

2. Incorporate Material Relevant to the Group into Stories

Good storytellers know how to customize a story to a group. Think back to when you were a kid and your teacher personalized a story by using your name or one of your favorite things as a detail in the story. Didn't you feel engaged and exciting to become an integral part of the story? Was your imagination stimulated?

The same is true for adult learners. We love to see ourselves in the situations being painted by a compelling story. Our techniques for incorporating relevant material into stories with adult learners can be as simple as weaving in a personal fact to richer ones such as referencing other people's personal stories. As you become more adept at this, you will find yourself naturally weaving in all sorts of artifacts from the group's process or history. In this way, stories cease to be stale, because they offer tellers a way to stay invigorated. The very act of weaving in new material with the story will create opportunities for the teller to uncover new nooks and crannies of meaning.

3. Be Willing to Be Vulnerable with a Group

Stories are not for the faint of heart. Stories open the space between us and others. They are a scared tool for deeper reflection and insight. We have to let go of our need to control the thoughts, reflections, and learning processes of others. In their truest sense, stories are not a behavioral tool for hitting the right button in others to produce a desired, predictable outcome. The experiential nature of story demands vulnerability. Are we willing to learn in front of others? Can we remove the artificial boundaries that we erect in learning environments to protect our authority? Stories broaden our awareness before they focus it. Imagine an hour glass. The top of the glass is wide. The sand drops down through a narrow crack before it falls into a wide basin below. Stories are similar in this respect. As we explore the interconnections between our stories and their relationship to other people's experiences, the learning environment might feel scattered and chaotic. People might ask, "Where is this going?" Inevitably, you will ask yourself the same question. Until suddenly the story drops through the narrow hole of analytical discourse and opens into a new vista of insight and meaning. The story has been a catalyst for learning and is a new buoy for anchoring future ones. None of this is possible if we do not make ourselves vulnerable with a group. Sharing a personal story is a wonderful way of softening a group and modeling the openness stories require to work their magic.

4. Be Authentic

Whether we are conscious of doing it or not, we are constantly evaluating the authenticity of others. Whenever we detect even a hint of falseness or any other form of selfishness or negative intentions in someone, we shut the person out. Any hope of building a bridge constructed with mutual active listening is completely destroyed, and most of the time there is very little chance of rebuilding it once we lose the trust of others. You might share an experience or two as a means of enforcing credibility with a group. However, avoid telling stories for self-aggrandizement. It never achieves the kind of longlasting impacts of reflective, experiential learning that stories are perfectly suited for.

5. Make Sure There Is Congruence Between Your Stories and Your Behavior

We lessen the potential of our personal stories when our actions and stories do not correspond with one another. No one is asking you to be perfect. When leading a group, we often need to accentuate ideals. If there is a blatant contradiction between stories we tell and how we act, we will ruin the climate of trust, openness, and reflection we have created by working with stories.

Sharing a story with a group is a perfect opportunity to model how to work with stories in a reflective manner. Offer people a chance to react to your story. Be open to hear what others see in your story. If it triggers a story for someone else, make time to hear the story and explore the relationship between the stories. It's not to say that you should never have a premeditated reason for sharing a story, but realize that any such intentions should only be used to jump-start a process of discovery. Experiential learning invites the unexpected. The unknown epiphanies and how they happen are an essential part of the magic of stories.

6. Elicit More Stories Than You Tell

The shortest distance between two people is a story. One of the chief reasons to tell a story is to elicit them. Stories act as triggers. We want to draw stories out of people. As the number of personal experiences shared increases, so does the quality and quantity of experiential learning. Even if someone does not share his or her story out loud, our story will set off a series of internal reflective events. People scan their index of personal experiences to find ones that match or resonate with the ones we tell them. It is not always a direct one to one correspondence. In other words, the stories we elicit in others will not always have an easy to see relationship to our own. We are after connections.

Experiential learning occurs when we have impregnated the environment with possibilities. Our stories catalyze the Petri dish of learning. We are experimenting with growing new insights. Stories are used to help us stumble along old, distant, dried-up tributaries until learning flows into an ocean of new consciousness, joined with the diversity of other people's knowledge and experiences. Think more in terms of drawing out people's experiences and relating these to the discussion at hand, rather than telling premeditated or orchestrated stories. Of course, you may find yourself sharing a story at a specific point during a learning event or when certain themes emerge, but experiential learning is not a public speaking event that is a rehearsed show.

7. Be Open, Respectful, and Nonjudgmental of the Stories People Share

Treat all stories with respect. When someone shares a story, he or she has given us a part of him- or herself. Handle it accordingly. The fragile pieces of our identity rest in our narratives. Never feel entitled to know anyone's story. People will share what they want, when they are ready, and in a manner that does not violate their sense of themselves. However, you will be surprised at how willing and eager people are to exit the precarious myth of their separateness and embrace the sense of belonging granted by tying their experiences to those of others in a tapestry of shared consciousness.

The most vivid pictures we own are the stories in our hearts. Stories support a lattice of human experience. Each new story acts as a tendril tying us to the past, making the present significant and giving shape to the future. Stories by their nature are a microcosm of who and how we are, so be sure you're always respectful and nonjudgmental. We can never fully understand the mysteries of someone else's journey. Stories have no need to compete with one another, and stories exist to coexist with each other. Act as an unbiased, self-aware, gracious curator, and stories will usher in a cornucopia of delights and wisdom.

8. Connect Stories to One Another

Treat each story as a building block that can be pieced together with another one to generate greater understanding. Stories left in isolation are like cold statues in abandoned temples erected as grand testimonies of heroic accomplishments, but devoid of depth and significance. I developed a group facilitation technique called Story Collaging™ for helping groups see the connections between stories. It is a brainstorming technique that allows groups to discover relationships among their personal stories, the stories of others, and the group's discussions. (More information on the technique can be found in the book *Stories at Work: Using Stories to Improve Communication and Build Relationships.*) Leave no stone unturned. As members of a group create a shared history, lots and lots of stories will naturally emerge. Your job is to remember these stories and constantly look for how they relate to one another. You are also tasked with inciting others in the group to do the same thing.

Stories are reflection in motion. One story leads to another and before you know it, you have a mosaic of experiences crisscrossing with one another. Stories are like the tiny pieces of glass in a stained glass window. Every time the sun shines through, new colors and shades of meaning emerge. Story listeners function like the sun in our image of a stained glass window. This is one of the most exciting things I do as a facilitator. I never know what will surface. The stronger the connections between the stories and the greater the number of connections between them directly correlates with the quality of learning.

9. Build In More Room for Story Sharing When Designing Learning

Time to retire heavily scripted courses. Facilitating experiential learning with stories is not for the faint of heart. It requires guts, courage, authenticity, and an ability to think on your feet. Here's the secret: once you become accustomed to being in less control and collaborating with a group, the richer and more significant the learning will be. We must be willing to surrender a certain amount of our positional power to be effective. Chuck Hodell, in his book *ISD from the Ground Up*, makes this point in a subtle way by saying, "The better the training goes, the less chance there is that anyone will appreciate the effort that went into it." If you make stories a core part of your experiential learning strategy in an event, you will be wiped out. As we discussed earlier in the chapter, stories require active listening, and this make them exhausting as well as exhilarating. Stories are the most effective when used as a tool to facilitate participant collaboration.

Even very technical topics or regulatory forms of learning can benefit from building in time for knowledge sharing through stories. Of course, topics that are softer in nature require lots of time and space for stories. As we have become more and more harried in our daily lives, we have lost the art of conversation. Good conversations are full of stories. When we design learning, less will always be more. I use other forms of instruction to give people variety and a break from the intense, reflective nature of dialogue through stories. Group dialogue saturated with stories needs to be at the heart of experiential learning. Even when we create event-driven experiences for people in learning, we are in essence giving them new stories to reflect on. In this way, stories are effective because they help us enact our intentions and thoughts versus announce them. More traditional forms of instructional design are focused on instructing and telling us what we need to know. Stories always lead by offering examples and an endless playground for our imaginations to unearth new treasures.

Nine Ideas for How to Use Stories to Promote Experiential Learning

1. Answer People's Questions with a Story

Are people asking similar questions? Questions are good. It means people are thinking. Now your job as a facilitator is to transport people into a reflective space. Telling a story or finding someone in the group to share one will enrich the discussion. Normally, when we have a question we seek to alleviate the uncertainty caused by it. We want an answer. This, however, is not always in our best interest. As the great romantic poet Rainer Maria Rilke wrote in a letter to a young man, "Learn to love the questions." Answering a question with a story encourages people to sit and mull them over in new ways. Stories encourage self-discovery and community discovery. The questions become building blocks. Each question acts as a new thread to be woven into an intricate tapestry of knowledge and wisdom. When you use a story, be sure to get people to draw parallels between the story told and the questions they are asking. If people become stuck, offer some analysis and insights.

2. Elicit Stories from the Group

Are there common themes to the comments people are making? Comments made during group discussions tend to cluster around themes. Rather than just collecting bullets on flip charts, elicit stories from the group and use them as organizing devices. Ask people to be specific and give examples. They will end up sharing personal experiences in the form of stories. These are your gateway to great insights. Synthesize people's experiences to make new points and to reinforce previous ones. Stories are great tools when you have lots of complex information. You can manipulate stories to encode and decode information far more efficiently than you can other forms of information. Eliciting stories during group discussion will help you tie people's comments together in a meaningful way that they are likely to remember.

3. Use a Metaphor or Analogy

Do people need an idea or concept to be illustrated? Help people to visualize the idea or concept you are trying to explain by applying a metaphor or analogy from another domain. When we draw an example from an area people are familiar with, it establishes a linkage of learning to the new information we are introducing. These analogies and metaphors acting as stories allow us to drop people into mental simulators that fabricate new constructs. After you provide one, ask people to think of another one. This solidifies the concept for them and gives them confidence. It also allows you to make sure they have grasped the concept.

4. Tell a Story to Change the Group's Energy

What is the group's energy? There are natural ebbs and flows. A story can stimulate and revitalize a group. Likewise, stories can help a group relax and become centered. Stories are wonderful tools for creating an environment. Be sure to develop a large repertoire of stories. These do not have to be long in order to be effective nor do they have to be told by you. Your main challenge as a facilitator is to begin to become cognizant of subtle shifts in the group. It is your job to maintain the most optimal environment. Use stories to redirect people and adjust the group's energy.

5. Tell a Story with Your Voice and Body Language

What are people saying with their body language? When you tell a story, match the tone and body language of individuals in the group. People will become more aware of what they are saying through their bodies and begin to modify their body language. As they do so, there will be subtle shifts in their perceptions and emotions.

6. Validate and Transform Emotions with a Story

Are there underlying emotions? Tell a story in a non-didactic and non-patronizing way that mirrors the emotions you sense in the group. This validates unspoken emotions and allows people to move past them. Once negative feelings are acknowledged, they can be examined safely through the story—and even transformed into more positive ones. Stories are multisensory vehicles of communication. We can use them to mirror what we observe in the group. For example, if a group is feeling vulnerable after a discussion or workshop, share a story that you know will resonate with those feelings of vulnerability. Be careful, this can be dangerous territory. As with any technique, we must be mindful not to abuse it. When we mirror, people check our intentions. If gaining power and control of people is your motivation, stay clear of these techniques. Authenticity and genuine care for people's well-being should be at the forefront of our minds.

7. Tell a Story to Change People's Perspectives

Has the group become stuck? Stories can be used as tools to encourage thinking. A group becomes stuck when it is unable to imagine other possibilities. The psychologist James Hillman talks about getting stuck in our habits of thought and behavior. These are the places we frequent and habituate. When we become locked into one story, the best way to escape its gravitational pull is to introduce another one that moves our imagination in a new way. Stories can be rich sources of irony and paradox. These, in turn, challenge a group's current thinking and can lead them in new directions.

8. Use People's Stories to Build Role Plays on the Fly

Are people sharing similar types of experiences? As people share their experiences, others may respond with similar stories of their own. These stories can be revisited to examine alternative behaviors by turning them into role plays. Ask people for permission to use their stories as role plays for the group. Elicit as many details about the situation or person to help re-create the story as a role play in the most compelling fashion possible. This helps everyone to enter the story and work with it as a virtual simulator. It also gives the teller an opportunity to dive deeper into past experience and, by doing so, gain new insights. Listeners will also have an opportunity to scan their experiences for corresponding elements. The assignment of roles in the role play can be done in a variety of ways, depending on the situation and the nature of the role play. Use your judgment. When in doubt, you can always ask the teller to play him- or herself in the role play, and you can take on one of the key roles if there is more than one. One of the more challenging aspects of turning stories into role plays is knowing when to freeze the role play to point out learning, obtain suggestions from the group, or allow the group to process what is occurring. In general, thirty seconds of role play can yield up to fifteen minutes of group processing. Some examples of the types of discussion you can lead following a role play include asking people to analyze how their own stories would have been different if they adopted any of the strategies identified by the group and what people will try differently when they find themselves in a similar situation.

9. Use a Joke or Tangent

Has the group become too analytical? Jokes are a great tool for getting people to be less analytical. Jokes are like little epiphanies. A joke is funny because the punch line is unexpected. It hits us as a surprise. Telling a joke or leaving the subject at hand to go off on a tangent will help a group become less analytical and more creative.

Nine Essential Competencies for Facilitators Working with Stories

The more I worked with stories, the more I realized there must be some core competencies to being an effective communicator, learner, and thinker with stories. After conducting some research with Fortune 500 leaders, I developed a competency map (see Figure 12.2) that consists of three rings and nine competencies (see *The Strategic Use of Stories in Organizational Communication and Learning*, M.E. Sharpe, 2005).

FIGURE 12.2. COMPETENCY MAP

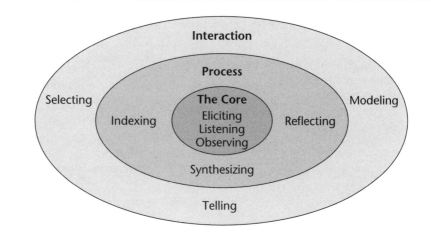

Here is a breakdown of the competency map. There are three rings and nine competencies, which are described further in Table 12.2.

Three Rings

1. The Core
2. Process
3. Interaction

Nine Competencies

1. Selecting
2. Telling
3. Modeling
4. Indexing
5. Synthesizing
6. Reflecting
7. Eliciting
8. Listening
9. Observing

The rings represent three levels of personal story competencies related to communicating and learning. Each ring consists of three competencies. The outermost ring, Interaction, characterizes the competencies we use to engage with

TABLE 12.2. BREAKDOWN OF THE COMPETENCY MAP

Ring	Competency	Description
Interaction *Describes how we use stories to connect with others and communicate*	Modeling	Being aware of one's actions and using them to create lasting impressions in the eyes of others. Employing a variety of analogical techniques to bring an idea or concept alive.
	Telling	Relaying a story with authenticity that paints a vivid, engaging picture for listeners.
	Selecting	Picking a story that is appropriate to the situation at hand and that clearly communicates concepts, ideas, or feelings.
Process *Describes how we work with experiences to transform them into meaningful and reusable stories*	Indexing	Developing a flexible, vast, mental schema for retrieval of experiences, and knowledge.
	Synthesizing	Finding patterns in new experiences and creating connections between them and old ones.
	Reflecting	Reviewing experiences with circumspection and extracting knowledge from them.
The Core *Describes how we open ourselves to be aware and sensitive to stories*	Eliciting	Asking questions and finding ways to pull stories from others.
	Listening	Absorbing stories and invoking the imagination to enter them in a fundamental and deep way.
	Observing	Practicing mindfulness to become aware of the stories implicit in others' words and actions.

the external world. Many people mistakenly assume that using stories well requires little besides knowing what stories to select and being good at telling them. Although these are useful competencies, they are superficial compared to the others. We can communicate more by eliciting stories than by telling them. Consequently, a greater value is given to the competencies found in the Core than in the interaction ones found in the outmost ring of our map. Also in the outermost ring is the competency of modeling.

There are two levels to the competency of modeling. The first level describes how our actions model our beliefs, attitudes, and values. Through our actions, we create stories. People are far more likely to remember our actions than our words. Whether they do it consciously or unconsciously, people observe our actions and look for incongruence between our words and behaviors. We have the ability to create stories by being mindful of how our actions impact the people around us. Memorable actions become part of other people's stories. Furthermore, our actions have the potential to cause others to reflect. Purposeful actions leave their mark on the environment and travel quickly in personal channels of communication and reach non-specific targets otherwise beyond our range. The second level to the modeling competency is our ability to create compelling representations of the concepts we try to communicate to others. Developing a facility with analogies, metaphors, word pictures, and visuals are a few of the subcomponents of this competency.

The second ring of the map is the Process ring. It is characterized by all of the internal things that we do in our minds when we are conscious of our stories and the stories around us. It is hard to discuss the three competencies in this ring in any causal order, because these internal processes of indexing, synthesizing, and reflecting happen most of the time in parallel. The reflection competency is the discipline we develop in stopping to notice our stories. To paraphrase a Greek philosopher, "An unexamined story is not worth having." While we gather new insights from our own stories, a highly developed capacity for reflection makes us more mindful of others. We are less likely to react to people. Reflection gives us a chance to behave proactively and continually revise our perceptual filters.

The second competency in the Process ring is synthesizing. By reflecting on our stories, we begin to find connections with other stories and other domains of knowledge. Through synthesis we discover relationships between previously unrelated experiences, ideas, concepts, and knowledge. We take the new pieces of information and transform them into insights. The link between learning and stories is found in this competency. Roger Schank at the Institute of Learning at Northwestern University was one of the first to point this out. Schank argues that the ability to find a story in one domain and apply it by analogy to another is the hallmark of intelligence. Being effective at doing this requires all three competencies of reflecting, synthesizing, and indexing.

The last competency in the Process ring is indexing. Our experiences recorded as stories in our memories do not fit into neat categories. Every experience can be indexed, re-indexed, and cross-indexed in a variety of ways. This is further complicated by the fact that each of us develops our own indexing schemes. You and I will not use the same keys to codify our experiences and the learning or knowledge that results from them. Developing a rich index enables us to quickly see the applicability of our stories in different situations. We can uncover patterns of relevance and encounter greater resonance between others' experiences and our own by deliberately maintaining a diverse index.

The third ring of the map is the Core. It contains the central competencies that are at the heart of using stories effectively to be a better communicator and learner. All the competencies found in the other rings build off of the central ones of eliciting, listening, and observing. Listening is the common thread to the three competencies found in the Core; for example, being able to elicit stories demands sensitivity and attentiveness to the stories around oneself. Drawing stories out of others requires astute observation skills. We discover what questions to ask or what stories to tell in order to stimulate the storytelling of others by watching for cues in their words and actions. We must also be equally aware of our own thought processes. Listening ties them all together and involves more than hearing. As we gather information, listening engages our imaginations. What we hear is fused with our experiences. The new information co-mingles with the old to become relevant and immediate; otherwise, it is dead on arrival.

These nine competencies represent the communication and learning competencies one needs to develop in order to be an effective facilitator of experiential learning with stories. (For more ideas on how to develop these competencies, see *The Strategic Use of Stories in Organizational Communication Learning.* The whole last section of the book has a collection of self-development exercises for developing these competencies.) These competencies go beyond the facilitator. From my experience, groups with well-developed story competencies are very effective communicators, learners, and thinkers.

Sample Experiential Activity with Stories

Here is a sample experiential activity with stories.

The Magic Three

Directions

1. Give this as an overnight assignment during a multi-day workshop or retreat.
2. Tell participants to think of three personal stories that have some relationship between them.
3. Ask participants to share their stories with the group the next day.

Variations

- Vary the number of stories (however, it should be two at a minimum and under most circumstances not more than five).
- Have participants work on the assignment during the workshop.
- Tell stories during a working lunch.

- Change the type of stories you ask participants to think about and tell (e.g., from personal to work). Depending on the nature of the workshop and the composition of your group, you can be very specific in the parameters you set.
- Limit the number of participants in the exercise.
- Spread out the number of people who share their stories across multiple days.
- Break participants into smaller groups and have people share their stories within the smaller groups. Ask the groups to select one of their members' stories and have a member of the group other than the owner of the story retell it to the group at large.
- Invite one of the participants to facilitate the group debriefing.
- Ask everyone to anonymously write down three major things that struck them about the stories (do this before any group debriefing). Provide the feedback to the story owner.
- Add a visual component to the exercise. Instruct participants to create a collage or some other kind of visual to document their stories.
- Encourage listeners to share any of their stories that have been triggered by tellers' stories.

Debriefing

The good news: this is *almost always* an easy exercise to debrief given the richness of the experience for the teller and the group listening to him or her. The exercise runs itself. Your main job is to give people ample time to react to the story. When a teller is finished, it is a good idea to allow some silence in the room. Start the debriefing process with the teller. Ask, "How did that feel?" Alternatively, if the person hasn't done so already, ask him or her to explain how he or she came up with the three stories. If it was an emotionally charged set of stories, feel free to ask a few follow-on questions about one or more of the stories. However, be prepared to redirect the group if one or more people become too engrossed in the details of a story or pursue tangential lines of questioning. Some of this sort of thing is okay, but can quickly take a group off track.

Next, if it hasn't started happening naturally already, ask the group to provide feedback, impressions, and reactions to the teller. Some people may even feel compelled to spontaneously share stories of their own. Query the teller and then the group to reflect on the relationship between the stories and discuss insights that have emerged from them.

Tips

- Be purposefully vague in your instructions. This is one of those times when less is more. Some participants may struggle with the directions. Encourage them to grapple with the ambiguity. Out of the ambiguity comes the reflective soul-searching that is necessary. Be aware that detailed-oriented people may become slightly frustrated by your lack of clear and precise directions. That's okay. Apologize to them and explain that it will make more sense to them after the exercise. Realize that you may need to be the brunt of their temporary aggravation. At this point, there is no need to relieve it. It would only alleviate your feelings, but not help the participant. Afterward, point out that the success of the exercise is contingent on participants finding a path through their experiences. I'll sometimes joke and say, "In the words of Hamlet, 'I must be cruel to be kind.'"

- Emphasize that stories need to have some sort of thread or connection between them. Encourage them to look for non-linear connections. That is to say, the stories they select that have a relationship to each other can be from very different times and parts of their lives.
- Do not provide an example in advance of any participant's stories. After one or more participants share their three stories, you may feel free to share yours. The purpose in doing so is to generate greater trust, intimacy, and authenticity with the group. Your stories as a facilitator of the group may also be a good tool for defusing any intense or difficult dynamics that arise in the group as a result of someone else's stories.
- Never judge the stories or anyone's response/reaction to them.
- Allow there to be some silence after a participant shares his or her stories.
- Insist that people come to the front of the room to tell their stories. Unless someone is completely emotionally or physically incapable of being in front of the room, it is an essential part of the exercise. People overcome their inhibitions about public speaking when they tell stories.
- Confiscate notes from the participant sharing his or her stories. Despite whatever inclination the person may have, he or she will not need notes, and using them will prevent him or her from reliving the story.
- Tie the outcomes of the exercise to the major themes, lessons, and insights of the workshop.
- Limit the number of tellers if you are pressed for time. People listening learn from the exercise sometimes as much if not more than tellers do.

Objectives/Applications

1. Provide a structured activity to guide people through an experience of reflection.
2. Practice authentic communication.
3. Create a connection with listeners.

Outcomes to Emphasize

- How did the teller's communication style change when he or she was telling a story? How were you impacted as listener? People who find it difficult to speak in front of a group will experience a real connection with their audience. Likewise, listeners will describe the teller as engaging, and the stories as rich or stimulating. This is the result of the teller reliving an experience.
- What's the connection between the stories? How and why did these three stories become associated with one another? Before participating in this exercise, someone may not have associated these stories with one another. In some cases, this may be the first time the person is suddenly recalling an experience from the past that he or she had forgotten. One story leads to the trail of another. This is the reflective power of stories.

Case Study

I was facilitating a workshop on personal effectiveness in business. Len was a nononsense, short Japanese-American, technology project manager for a nuclear research company. Len possessed exceptional communication skills. He was clear, precise, succinct, and very articulate. However, despite his technical prowess as a communicator, Len observed that he often failed to connect with people on an emotional level.

I gave Len two assignments. The first assignment was to take a complex newspaper article on a controversial topic and in thirty seconds or less provide a summary of the article's information and a recommendation. Len's second assignment was the *Magic Three*.

Len performed the newspaper exercise with the prowess of a polished politician. He was absolutely brilliant. I wanted him to serve as an example of how to deliver an effective executive sound bite. There are many times when we have thirty seconds or less to make an elevator pitch.

After appropriate accolades, I asked Len to share his three stories with us. In a matter of a few seconds, Len's body language began to transform in front of our very eyes. His erect, formal stature was replaced with a more relaxed posture. As he began to share his stories with the group, he moved to the edge of a table to sit down. Here is a recapitulation of his stories as I remember them:

> I've always been a fairly private person, so joining groups was never high on my list of things to do. About seven years ago, I decided to get more involved with my local Catholic church group. I was surprised at how

quickly I began forming a core group of friends who became a central part of my life. Weekends were filled with fishing trips, barbecue with our wives and families, and general fraternizing with my new cohorts. It had been a long time since I had experienced this kind of camaraderie and I was relishing every minute of it. As a group, we kept growing closer and closer. Even my family was caught off guard by the quality and depth of relationships I developed with a bunch of total strangers. This continued for several years. After a horrible car accident, I found myself in the hospital recovering from a life-threatening back surgery and long days of excruciating pain blunted by the constant dripping of numbing morphine. Everything was a haze. I was in a complete fog of pain, depression, and despair. During these horrific weeks, there were two pins of light that got me through these dark times: my family and my friends. Family you kind of expect to be there for you, but I was amazed at the dedication and energy my friends gave to me when I needed them the most. To this day, I believe my friends were a special gift granted to me to ensure I pulled through a very trying experience. A couple of years later my buddies wanted to go on a weekend retreat with the church. I resisted but after a lot of cajoling I agreed to go. We had a fantastic time, and the retreat was filled with lots of soulful opportunities to recharge our batteries and put the challenges of life into perspective. My friends made the retreat a special experience, and I returned home with fresh vigor and zest. A day after my return, my father died unexpectedly. I believe my friends and the retreat were granted to me as a form of preparation for my father's death. I was able to be a source of comfort and strength for my family. I had more emotional energy to give to them. To this day I am eternally grateful for friendship and all of the richness it has given me in life.

Unfortunately, my retelling is pale in comparison to Len's original account. It's missing all of the other subtle forms of communication that accompanied it, such as body language, eye contact, and tone of voice. When Len finished, there was silence in the room. People needed a moment to exit their imaginations and reenter the workshop's frame of reference. Len confessed he had never told these stories to anyone else before, and prior to the workshop he would have never dreamed of sharing them in a work environment. He reflected on the powerful connection of friendship he discovered in the three stories. Then Len made an amazing leap of insight. He concluded that he needed to be selectively more vulnerable with people at work in order to improve his personal effectiveness. Len committed to spending more time cultivating relationships in his organization. Stories, he discovered, are one of the best tools for building effective, meaningful relationships.

Summary

Stories are a fundamental part of how we communicate and learn. On some level, stories are a part of any experiential learning activity. Whether we are debriefing an activity in which people are sharing their experience in the form of stories, creating opportunities for people to reflect on their personal experiences, or encouraging people to relive an experience as they remember it, stories are operating all the time. The quickest way to use stories as an experiential learning strategy is to elicit stories during any participant collaboration activity. Under the right circumstances of trust, openness, and reflectivity, stories will naturally emerge from the conversations. The greatest challenge of working with stories is the unpredictability. Ground rules to follow and nine essential competencies to develop have been offered as a framework for supporting a facilitator's work with stories.

I'd like to leave you with a story benediction I wrote:

May stories stir your heart, inform your thoughts, and guide your actions

CHAPTER THIRTEEN

REFLECTIVE PRACTICE

Learning from Real-World Experience

Brian Remer

Brian Remer is a designer of interactive strategies for training, facilitation, and performance improvement. He blends information, discussion, games, and participant input to ensure involvement and commitment from everyone. Brian has worked with businesses and organizations in Egypt, Zaire, Ecuador, and throughout the United States. For over ten years he has consulted with organizations affiliated with the state of New Hampshire. Brian is a member of the International Society for Performance Improvement and has served on the board of directors and as chairman and president of the North American Simulation and Gaming Association. He is the founder of The Firefly Group, a training and consultation firm specializing in bringing a spark of inspiration to team building, leadership development, training of trainers, and organization development workshops.

Contact Information

The Firefly Group
339 Bullock Road
Guilford, VT 05301
(802) 257–7247
brian@thefirefly.org
www.thefirefly.org

O NE WARM SUMMER DAY, I wandered out to the screened porch to cool off. There I found an overly large housefly bouncing against the screen trying to find a way out. When it came to the outside door, I thought, "Aha! I'll simply open the door and let it fly away." But when I opened it, the fly kept bashing into the screen of the door. I pushed the door open further, yet, to my surprise, the fly didn't find its way out. Now with the door open more than 90 degrees and me waving my hand in the fly's direction, it still kept ping-ponging itself against the screen door in its futile attempt to both leave the house and avoid my hand. Finally, I gave up trying to be helpful and let the door swing shut. The fly eventually died. All the while, it could smell the fresh air but never find its way to freedom.

Sometimes we act like flies trapped behind a screen door. We don't even notice that we are making the same mistake over and over. We don't realize that a subtle change in our behavior, a simple shift in direction, will enable us to bring about the change we want. Perhaps some of us are so disempowered that we don't believe we can learn from and change our environment. Still others may be focused only on the reward at the end of their actions so that they don't pay attention to the here and now. Surely, there are other reasons we become stuck, but the point is this: When repeatedly hitting our heads against the screen door is not working, why do we believe that doing more of the same thing will make us free?

When our behavior becomes habituated and our responses conditioned, we need to reflect on what we are doing, a process that has been called "reflective practice." We don't have to be slaves to our attitudes, preconceptions, mental models, or previous behavior. Reflective practice breaks unproductive cycles and opens the door for more options for our behavior.

Reflective Practice in (and About) the Moment

There are two types of reflection that Schön (1983) has identified—reflection *in* the moment and reflection *about* the moment. The former happens in real time, on-the-fly, while the latter can be done at any time after an event or experience. Often, people initiate reflective practice in response to a problem or difficult situation. That can certainly be a valuable time to learn from experience, but reflective practice can be useful in any situation, whether it is seen as traumatic or trivial. And it is even possible to combine reflection *in* the moment with reflection *about* the moment to create a highly effective learning environment.

This past year, I taught my daughter to ride a bicycle. I wanted her to learn in a supportive environment. For me, this meant that I wanted her to be able to learn from her experiences, but I also didn't want to see her fall down and get hurt.

Now some people say you can't learn to ride a bike without falling. They say it's good to learn the right way to fall so you don't get *really* hurt. Well, I've *never* fallen from my bike "the right way," so I thought I'd help my daughter avoid that altogether. Besides, I wanted to experiment with the use of reflective practice.

We began in the deserted school parking lot one Saturday. I ran alongside my daughter, holding her up and, through my heavy breathing, hoped the day would soon come when she would be able to ride on her own. From our practice sessions, I was reminded just how long it can take to really learn to master a skill. Although we worked at it for weeks, her progress was slow and, as encouraging as I tried to be, she did not always see herself as being very successful. I found myself wondering how one actually teaches the skill of bicycle riding.

Then one day, my reflective thinking kicked in. I noticed that it was easier for my daughter to turn left than to turn right. As I thought about it, I realized that, since I was holding onto the left side of the bike, I was better able to tell when she was falling and could lend the support she needed. When she turned to the right, she was falling away from me and I was in a poorer position to support both her weight and mine. This made it very difficult to keep her from falling too far.

A light bulb went on in my head. I suddenly realized that you have to *fall* in the direction you want to turn in order to turn a two-wheel bicycle. The degree to which you let yourself fall determines the speed and tightness of the turn. Now I had a new theory and I immediately set out to test it. The next time my daughter turned right, I didn't try to keep her from falling too far. Instead, I eased up a bit to let her feel when she was falling into the turn. To my amazement, she corrected her fall and transformed it into a smooth turn. We then stopped and talked about what had happened. She described what she felt and how she reacted. I explained my new theory about falling and turning. Then she made a plan. She decided she would make three turns, right, left, right, to try it out. As I ran along beside her, we were both able to talk about what was happening and how we were experiencing it. We had made an enormous breakthrough as both learner and teacher.

My daughter and I had used reflective practice both *in* the moment and *about* the moment. *In* the moment, I noticed the difference between making left and right turns. That initiated my thinking through the phases of Kolb's Experiential Learning Cycle (Kolb, 1984). My reflection led to an analysis of turning, and I invented a theory. That theory then became the basis of an experiment. We used reflective practice *about* the moment when we stopped to rest. At that point, my daughter engaged in some observation and reflection. I told her about my theory, and she made an action plan to test it for herself.

My daughter is now a very good bicycle rider. She is confident, she has fun, and she knows *why* riding a bicycle works the way it does. She now knows some things about bike riding that I didn't know until I was over forty years old! What's more, she has learned some things about *how* to learn. She has applied those lessons about using reflective practice to situations as diverse as her weekly spelling test and to solving confrontations with her parents.

When I was my daughter's age, I remember frequent evenings of fifth-grade agony trying to memorize my weekly spelling list. But my daughter has more success with less effort. She has devised a process that includes self-quizzes, study, and making up stories and rhymes as memory devices. She uses reflection in the moment to focus her study only on the most troublesome words. And she learns from her weekly successes by reflecting after the fact about what worked best for her.

Reflective Practice with GURU

Many formal programs of study make use of reflective practice. It is common for advanced courses to have a practicum or field experience that includes keeping a journal, writing papers about critical incidents, or participating in discussion groups. In these examples, students enrich their learning by relating their field experience to classroom theory. They reflect *about* the experiences they have had.

There are also several ways to reflect *in* the moment so you can learn when you need to most—right *now*. In his book, *The Fifth Discipline Fieldbook*, Peter Senge talks about "Moments of Awareness." This means paying attention to what is happening with enough focus that you can analyze your actions and thought processes and change them while in mid-step.

I prefer to use the GURU process, which combines reflection *in* the moment with reflection *about* the moment. It's a process of self-questioning that is easy to learn and dovetails with the experiential learning cycle. It was developed by Christopher Saeger and myself and presented at a conference of the North American Simulation and Gaming Association (Saeger & Remer, 2001). As a tool of reflective practice, it is both memorable and flexible.

In the GURU process, you ask a series of questions that help the learner analyze the current situation, come to a conclusion, make a plan, and implement the first action step of that plan. GURU stands for four categories of questions: *Ground, Understand, Revise,* and *Use.* When you encounter a situation ripe for learning, a supervisor, mentor, coach, or you, yourself, can ask questions in each category.

Ground questions are meant to help the learner remember the event and recall basic data. Ask questions that will help people discover and share the common *ground* of their experiences. Your questions should zero in on people's thoughts and feelings. How can you help them identify their emotional reactions to the situation? Encourage learners to recall and report their decisions, actions, and experiences. In my situation as bicycle teacher, I asked myself what was working or not working about making turns. I got in touch with what I was feeling physically and emotionally about turning in different directions.

The second category of questions is designed to help people *understand* the situation in a larger context. Questions should encourage people to identify similarities and differences within and between events, ideas, or actions. Encourage people in this phase to articulate what they learned and make generalizations or a hypothesis. In my case, I contrasted what I had to do to support my daughter as she made right and left turns. I compared her experiences turning with my own when I ride a bike. From there, I developed the turning-is-like-falling theory of bicycle riding.

After *understand* is *revise*, in which questions are asked that will help people think of modifications they might make to their actions or attitudes. The questions should encourage people to consider how they would react if the situation or information were slightly different. The point is to encourage people to think about what aspect of their thoughts, attitudes, or behaviors they would *revise* if given the chance. After articulating my theory, I asked myself how I would support my daughter differently given this new information. How could I test it out to see if it would be helpful?

In the last phase of GURU reflective practice, questions are asked that will help people plan their next actions and *use* what they have learned. Your questions should help people think about what they want to do with the new information and ideas they have learned. Encourage them to consider how they would *use* their learning or apply it to various aspects of their lives. As a bicycle teacher, my *use* questions focused on how I could teach my new theory to my daughter. We took a rest break and I employed the GURU questioning process with her immediately after the fact to help her reflect on her riding and make a plan to try something new.

In his experiential learning cycle, David Kolb (1984) talks about four phases: Concrete Experience (doing something), Reflective Observation (thinking about what you have done), Abstract Conceptualization (adding a theory to your observations), and Active Experimentation (putting into practice what you have learned). He notes that learning is a combination of both grasping and transforming. We grasp information through Concrete Experience and Abstract Conceptualization. But then we must transform it, use it, and apply it through Reflective Observation and Active Experimentation. The result is a change in our behavior, attitudes, or knowledge level. GURU dovetails with the experiential learning cycle. When you ask GURU questions, you are initiating reflective practice and it is reflective practice that keeps people oscillating within the learning cycle between grasping new information and transforming it into usable theories and skills.

GURU for Personal Learning

GURU has been an effective tool that has kept me moving through the experiential learning cycle both personally and professionally.

A few years ago, I was living in Ecuador with my family. One thing I wanted to accomplish during our two-year stay was to learn Spanish. But that personal goal fell to pieces after seven months when Giovanni, my friend and tutor, announced he was going to take a job in Brazil. Up to that point, Giovanni had taught me all the Spanish grammar and we spent several hours every week in both practice conversations and practical use of the language. He was a resourceful and creative teacher, but suddenly he was leaving.

My initial concern was that he would be hard to replace and that I would quickly lose the skills I had worked so hard to gain. In addition, what I needed most was practice. Who would agree to listen to me speak on a regular basis? Could there ever be anyone as patient with my constant mistakes in word choice and pronunciation? How could I expect anyone else to tolerate my misuse of verb tense and gender agreement? The prospects seemed grim.

Then, while riding a crowded bus through stalled traffic one day, I realized something important. I may have been losing one Spanish teacher but, living in the largest city in Ecuador, I was surrounded by a couple hundred thousand Spanish teachers! *Everyone* there spoke Spanish! All I needed to do was start speaking to the people I would meet every day. If I were to make a plan for what I wanted to learn, I could easily try it out with a dozen people. Then, with a little analysis, a little reflective practice, about what I did right or wrong, I could improve my speaking on my own. I wouldn't need a formal teacher telling me what I needed to learn. I could use GURU questioning to decide that for myself whenever I discovered something I didn't know.

My challenge became putting this idea into practice. For me, it was difficult because I am not naturally a talkative person. I tend to listen more than speak. But I stuck to my plan and didn't hire a formal tutor. I studied regularly, practiced vocabulary, focused on subject matter that was relevant to me, and talked to people whenever I could.

I regularly asked myself *grounding* questions to stay in touch with the emotional highs and lows I experienced in my attempts to speak on the street. I used *understanding* questions to tease out relationships between the various situations when a difficult verb tense was used. *Revise* questions came in handy when I invented a clever way to remember what I had just learned, and, finally, *use* questions helped me make a plan to ensure sufficient practice of the new concepts. In the end, I surprised myself by what I was able to say in a conversation as well as what I was able to understand. I stretched both my language ability and my personal comfort zone.

The important lesson for designers and facilitators of experiential activities is simply this: If our goal is to improve workplace performance and develop continuous learning organizations, we cannot rely on classroom training to do it all. We've got to help our participants realize that they can learn from each other. They don't need to wait for the right workshop taught by an expert or the latest version of an online course to do their jobs better. They don't need scholarships or study leaves to begin to change their behavior for the better. The speed of business is fast enough that workers need to fine-tune their skills and increase their knowledge on a daily basis. And some of the best teachers they will find are the people they encounter every day: co-workers, managers, administrators, people from other departments, and of course, customers and vendors. All they need to do is commit to regular reflection about their work. They can make a plan for what they want to learn, try it out, analyze what worked and what didn't work, and try again.

GURU for Professional Learning

The need to respond in the moment is no less important professionally, and GURU questioning has been an effective way for me to handle rapidly changing information in a workshop environment as well. Imagine thinking you are teaching one group of participants when really you are educating someone totally different. This is exactly what happened in a project I coordinated in the Republic of the Congo. Local leaders of a development organization had participated in a training of trainers workshop. At the end of the fourteen days, they were to work in small groups to deliver a two-hour training, using some of the experiential techniques that they had learned about. The rest of the class would be the "learners" simulating a real group of participants for the practicing teachers.

I should have expected that something might get lost in the translation of this concept. Unfortunately, I could not even conceive how horribly it would become distorted! When the time came for the student workshops, the first group announced that they would lead a training on the control of erosion. They divided their own group of six into "trainers" and "participants" and proceeded to act out the delivery of a lesson to a group of local farmers. We were in the garden of the training center, so they scratched some lines in the sand to represent a muddy road. Then, standing on either side of their dirt etching, they acted out an elaborate role play of a training class. Meanwhile, the rest of us, nearly fifteen real participants and trainers, stood on the sidelines ignored by the "presenters," who were busy acting out their skit about a workshop.

As the lead trainer for the entire two-week event, I was stunned, knocked off balance. When I asked myself some *grounding* questions, I began to get in touch with what was going on. What was I feeling? Foolish for having assumed that the group understood my instructions and embarrassed that the rest of us had to put up with this silly show. What was happening right now? The small group was absorbed in their own performance, while everyone else appeared to be bored out of their minds—except Leon, the gardener.

When I asked *understanding* questions of myself, my insight deepened. I realized that the teachers of erosion control had worked hard and it would be inappropriate for me to simply cut them off—even if they weren't doing the assignment right. I compared this situation to other times that a workshop didn't go as planned and remembered that experiential learning is nearly always salvageable. And then I became curious about Leon. Why was he so interested when no one else was? As an employee of the retreat center, he wasn't even a member of our training of trainers program. He had simply been distracted from his weeding. Nobody else even noticed him, yet he was totally captivated by the performers.

When the "show" ended, I called a break. After a few minutes, I found Leon busily digging channels to redirect the rainwater around the steepest paths in his garden! I asked myself an important *revise* question: What if the "audience" of a workshop isn't who we think it is? What other educational possibilities might this open for us as trainers?

Asking questions about how I might *use* this new insight, I decided to invite the other participants to admire Leon's work and congratulate him on applying what he had learned. Afterward, the group of "real" trainees had a rich discussion about accidental teaching and learning, how to capitalize on the positive "fallout" from a training program, and the difference between formal and informal teaching methods. It became one of our richest learning experiences—all because the "wrong" person was being taught. And reflective practice, through the use of GURU questions, made it possible.

Teaching GURU Experientially

GURU is a very flexible tool. Ask GURU questions of yourself and you'll open the door for continuous learning. Ask these questions of the people you supervise and you'll become a mentor. Ask them of your co-workers and you'll become a team leader.

But before you begin asking GURU questions of anyone, it's important to learn and become proficient at using the questions yourself. The reflective practice of GURU can be taught in both workshop settings and on the job. I use several techniques in a workshop. If you imagine yourself a participant for a moment, I'll describe how a fictional facilitator, Jerry, would lead a session to teach GURU.

Suppose you are a participant in a workshop about techniques for improving team performance. You've arrived a couple minutes late, but that's all right because people are still settling in with introductions. You learn that the guest facilitator for today, Jerry, is from a small town more than two hours away, where you went to high school. Jerry explains that he plans to share several team performance improvement activities by having the group experience them together. He turns to his briefcase and begins rummaging through it. After several seconds, Jerry apologetically explains that he can't find the materials for the group activity. As his face grows crimson, he offers the excuse that he must have left the instructions for the activity and the accompanying handouts at his home.

You are a bit surprised that a trainer of Jerry's caliber would have made such a mistake, and you are wondering if this means that you'll be able to get back to the Simpson account sitting on your desk. Chip, from Accounting, suggests that Jerry call home and see whether his wife can fax the handouts. Jerry agrees with this great idea, but then realizes that he has left his phone at home too! Louise groans and Andrea offers her phone to Jerry, who makes the call. Louise ducks out of the room to confirm the number for the nearest fax machine. However, from listening inadvertently to one side of Jerry's call, it sounds like things are going from bad to worse. With a sigh, Jerry hangs up and reports that his wife couldn't find the necessary papers.

You are just about to chalk the whole workshop up as a total loss when Chip states that, as long as people are gathered, he would like to hear how other managers are dealing with problems in the teams they supervise. You agree that it would be productive to at least share some best practices. Others in the group come alive with this idea, and Andrea suggests that they begin by making a list of team-related problems.

As the room begins to buzz, Jerry interrupts to say that, before they start brainstorming, he would like the group to debrief the team performance activity that they have just completed. You feel a bit confused because Jerry hadn't done anything yet, but he goes on to explain that the incident of the lost training materials was not real. The whole thing was contrived to gather data about how your group might react to suddenly changing information and expectations. Even the phone call to Jerry's wife was a fake.

Jerry's deceptive practices don't feel quite right to you, but he explains that we are never in complete control of any situation and that our work conditions can change dramatically moment by moment. He says that cultivating our ability to reflect in the moment enables us to respond more effectively, and he offers a simple process for asking questions, something he calls GURU, to help people be more reflective.

Jerry begins by asking questions. What did people think when he announced that the papers were missing? How did people react to the news from his wife? What actions did people take? Jerry calls these *grounding* questions and says they are intended to help people recall what they experienced together. He explains that his next set of questions is designed to help people *understand* what happened in a wider context. What did people do that helped the group be a productive team in spite of the circumstances? How was this type of teamwork similar to or different from what happens in the workplace? What did various individuals do that helped the group solve the problem at hand? Jerry's next set of questions are designed to help people *revise* their behavior. He asks, What are the different roles individuals take upon themselves when expectations change suddenly? What can you do to help others fill the necessary roles to complete a team? What is your typical response to a leadership vacuum, and how might you choose to respond differently in the future? Finally, Jerry asks questions to help group members make a plan to *use* what they have learned. What is the most effective way you can raise the issues of changing roles and changing expectations with your own teams? What is a typical situation where GURU questions might come in handy? What would be the value of teaching your teams to use the GURU questions?

It sounds to you like this GURU thing might have some merit, if you could get the hang of it. Jerry suggests that the group spend some time writing and practicing GURU questions that will help with team building. You settle in for what turns out to be a very useful training.

As this example shows, the concept of GURU can be introduced in a way that dramatizes its value for reflecting *in* the moment. That introduction needs to be followed by practice. Role-play activities are a very effective way for participants to gain real-time experience after learning the concepts of GURU. You can begin by asking each person to write a few short sentences describing a situation when reflective practice would have been helpful. Then participants can form pairs, A and B, with A's presenting the situation and B's asking the GURU questions. To keep the learning non-threatening, you as the facilitator can play the B role for a few role plays and model how to ask the questions. Once people feel more confident, other participants can play the B role. This can also be led as a staged role play wherein the whole group watches as two participants play A and B. It this case, though, the B's are encouraged to get hints from the audience. When the B player gives a signal, anyone can shout out an idea for a GURU question.

Teaching GURU on the Job

Another way to teach GURU is during one-on-one supervision. If you are a manager, ask your supervisees to talk about a situation from their work. This can be something that went well or it can be an incident that was problematic. Then methodically work through the GURU questions until a new plan of action is agreed on. Managers who use GURU in this way report feeling less tension in situations in which ordinarily there would have been conflict. They find themselves being less judgmental and better able to address workplace issues. Supervisees say they feel listened to and that they leave the session feeling encouraged and supported to revise their work practices.

Managers can take GURU questioning from the conference room to the shop floor. They can use it to promote reflective practice among their workers and, in the process, become coaches. They can target questions to what they see is immediately happening and model how to use reflective practice in the moment. For example, a manager sees that one worker is producing a high percentage of scrap and asks questions of the worker.

> *Ground:* Describe for me the process you use to set up this particular job. How well does this job fit in with your workflow and other responsibilities?
>
> *Understand:* How does the setup of this job differ from the setup for other jobs? What makes it more complicated? What are some best practices of other workers for setting up complicated jobs?
>
> *Revise:* What can you do to ensure you are following best practices? Which specific practices will you incorporate into your work?
>
> *Use:* When will you implement your revised plan? What goal will you set for yourself to reduce your percentage of scrap? Over what time period will you achieve your goal?

The opportunities for using GURU and nurturing an atmosphere in which reflective practice flourishes are endless. The supervisor of a customer service counter can use any interaction with customers as a learning opportunity for new employees.

> *Ground:* What were the non-verbal cues that told you that last customer would be difficult? What did you see me do that helped put her at ease?
>
> *Understand:* Why do you think she might have been so vocal? What are some of the effective strategies we've talked about for responding to people when they become excited?

Revise: What are two things you could have done to help defuse the situation? What are some additional ways you can assure customers that you are genuinely interested in their concerns?

Use: How do you plan to be empathetic to overly sensitive customers while still conforming to the company's policies? What other staff are available to you as resources?

A negotiation team can revise their strategy during a fifteen-minute stretch break.

Ground: How did people react when the other negotiation team started playing hardball? What were you thinking when they added the pension clause? What made that feel unfair to you?

Understand: How is this negotiation session similar to the last time we negotiated this contract? What did we learn then that we could use now? What political pressure is the other team trying to address through the pension clause?

Revise: If the negotiation continues in the direction it is going, what can we do to make sure our most critical interests are met? What can we do to move forward, even if we think the other side has been unfair? What can we do to reduce the political pressure that's driving the disagreement about the pension?

Use: What's the best way to talk about our most important concerns without revealing our bottom line? Who is the best person on our team to respond to the pension issue? At what point, if ever, should we confront them about the issue of fairness?

A ski instructor can recharge a lesson halfway down the slope.

Ground: How did that last run feel? When did you feel most confident and what were you doing at that moment? At one point your arms were behind you. Did that make you feel more or less stable?

Understand: How did this run compare to the last? How do you account for this difference? What have you learned about the importance of keeping your arms out in front of you?

Revise: What can you do to make sure your arms stay out in front? How might you hold your poles to keep your arms and your weight shifted forward? If someone suddenly falls in front of you, how will you move your arms to maintain your balance?

Use: What are you going to work on during your next run? What can you do as a personal reminder of where to hold your arms for better balance? What would you like me to say or do that will help you as we make this next run together?

A quality improvement department at a garment factory can revise its processes during a quarterly meeting.

> *Ground:* What are all the ways we currently track quality? Why do we use these particular methods? Which of these are the best determiners of quality?
>
> *Understand:* How have our quality standards changed over the years? What new contracts are on the horizon and what types of demands will those contracts place on workers and resources?
>
> *Revise:* What changes will we need to make in how we gather data in order to be prepared for the new contracts? What revisions can we make to our quality process to catch deficiencies earlier in the production line?
>
> *Use:* What's the best timing to roll out our new quality standards? Should we consider a pilot project? Which unit is in the best position to run our pilot?

The Benefits of GURU

In these examples, reflective practice through GURU questioning has eliminated the unproductive blaming that often accompanies highly charged situations. Instead, the emphasis is on identifying problems, analyzing the situation, and inventing solutions. Learning has become a process of two-way discovery, which ultimately puts the onus of changing behavior on individuals. It is the individual who decides what skills to practice and for how long. The manager or coach, meanwhile, remains alert and ready to offer suggestions or add new ideas for the individual to try.

With GURU you can infuse any situation, incident, or event with an element of reflective practice to accomplish many different purposes.

You can . . .

- Assess a new situation to determine how to begin your interaction—entering a cocktail party, arriving late to a meeting.
- Step back from an emotionally heated encounter to begin anew—confronting your teenager, responding to criticism from your boss.
- Adjust rapidly to changing interpersonal or environmental factors—the middle page of the instruction manual seems to be missing, it's raining on your parade.
- Change course in the middle of a situation to take advantage of new information—the lost page of the instruction manual has just been found!

- Slow a process to make sure all relevant information has been considered—team members suddenly begin pointing fingers.
- Evaluate past performance to determine effectiveness—conducting a year-end review, evaluating the last meeting you facilitated.
- Make a plan for future encounters—avoiding heavy rush hour traffic next Friday afternoon, having a pleasant visit with your in-laws.

One of the difficulties of reflective practice is remembering to use it! Unfortunately, it's not enough to have a simple questioning process or a catchy name. To be effective, it has to become a habit. The good thing is that there are many strong indicators that can become reminders of when reflective practice might be helpful. Watch for them, and you will soon find opportunities to use reflective practice more often.

Cues to Consult Your GURU

- When you find yourself making the same mistake over and over—you feel like the twin of that fly trapped on the screen porch
- When you are stuck and don't know what your next move should be—your mind keeps racing over the same small circle of thoughts
- When emotions run high—anger, fear, and nervousness are especially good indicators
- When you experience cognitive dissonance—a clash of cultures or values
- When you experience a critical incident—any threshold or watershed situation
- When you fail or succeed—both have equal potential for learning
- When you've only completed a portion of the experiential learning cycle—wring the most out of every learning experience
- When you want to learn more about something—follow your interests at your own pace
- When you don't have a teacher or coach at hand—you don't need to wait for an expert
- When you unexpectedly find yourself in a teaching role—you can become the expert that others are waiting for

Get Creative

Of course, if you want to get creative, you don't have to confine yourself to the use of questions in GURU. You can keep a diary, write in a journal, or recount a critical incident to complete the initial *grounding* phase. For *understanding,* choose an object and turn it into a metaphor for what you learned or draw a picture that shows before and after images relevant to the situation. Rather than asking *revise* questions, get the same effect by making a three-dimensional model or inventing an object to represent what you will do differently. Alternatives for the questions of the *use* category include making a list, creating an action plan, or sending yourself a delayed email reminder that will arrive two weeks in the future. Any of these activities will help initiate the process of reflective practice to transform experience into learning.

However we make use of reflective practice, we need to do more than spend time thinking about what we have done. We need to be highly focused. Some people argue that "'real' reflective practice needs another person as mentor or professional supervisor who can ask appropriate questions to ensure that the reflection goes somewhere and does not get bogged down in self-justification, self-indulgence, or self-pity" (Atherton, 2005). If this is how we reflect on experience, we are no better than flies trapped on the porch. Our reflection *does* need to be purposeful. And, while a supervisor or mentor will certainly help us ask appropriate questions, it is not *absolutely* necessary to wait for an outside coach to open the screen door. Instead, we can consult our inner GURU, engage in reflective practice, and open new doors for learning ourselves.

References

Atherton, J. S. (2005). *Learning and teaching: Reflection and reflective practice.* Accessed January 30, 2006, from www.learningandteaching.info/learning/reflecti.htm

Kolb, D. A. (1984). *Experiential learning: Experience as the source of learning and development.* Englewood Cliffs, NJ: Prentice-Hall.

Saeger, C., & Remer, B. (2001). *GURU: Reflective practice for experiential learning.* Presented at a conference of the North American Simulation and Gaming Association, Bloomington, Indiana.

Schön, D. A. (1983). *The reflective practitioner: How professionals think in action.* London: Temple Smith.

Senge, P. (1994). *The fifth discipline fieldbook.* New York: Doubleday.

PART THREE

TRAINING APPLICATIONS OF EXPERIENTIAL LEARNING

THIS THIRD AND LAST SECTION of *The Handbook of Experiential Learning* contains nine chapters. Each one examines how experiential learning is used to create training success in a popular training topic:

In these chapters, the authors are recognized experts in their training areas, as well as accomplished designers and facilitators of experiential learning activities. They give us their unique perspectives on the challenges and issues facing their given training application areas and show us how they employ experiential learning to achieve results. In some instances, the author uses a wide variety of experiential methodologies. In others, the author focuses on a specific experiential strategy.

CHAPTER FOURTEEN

EXPERIENTIAL LEARNING AND TECHNICAL TRAINING

Sivasailam Thiagarajan

Sivasailam "Thiagi" Thiagarajan is CEO and "Resident Mad Scientist" of The Thiagi Group. He began his career as a teacher of physics and engineering in a high school in Chennai, India. Specializing in the application of games, simulations, and other interactive strategies for performance-based training, Thiagi has worked with trainers in high-tech, nuclear power, and other vocational education areas around the world. Thiagi served as the president of the North American Simulation and Gaming Association (NASAGA) four different times and as the president of the International Society for Performance Improvement twice, twenty-five years apart.

Contact Information

The Thiagi Group
4423 East Trailridge Road
Bloomington, IN 47408
(812) 332–1478
thiagi@thiagi.com
www.thiagi.com

A FUNNY THING HAPPENED at one of my recent training sessions with a group of technical instructors. I invited the participants to comment on the applicability of experiential learning to technical training.

Audience members were split into two opposing groups of almost equal size. One group said, "Of course, it makes sense to use experiential activities in technical training. Actually, that's the most effective way." The other group said, "You must be kidding! We have absolutely no time for experiential activities in technical training."

The ensuing debate between the two groups revealed interesting definitional issues. Those who were in favor of experiential learning were thinking of hands-on activities and lab work related to such skills as arc welding and computer programming. Those who were opposed to experiential learning were thinking of meaningless icebreakers and mindless role plays. Obviously, our perception of experiential learning in technical training depends on our mental models.

So let us begin the chapter by exploring the concepts of *technical training* and *experiential learning* and arriving at a common mental model.

Exploring Technical Training

During the past month, I scanned hundreds of books, pored over glossaries, surfed the web, and "Googled" the term, all in a futile attempt at coming up with a precise definition of *technical training*. The definitions I found took circular approaches, such as *prepare employees for technical jobs* or *ensure effective transfer of technology*. Apparently, *technical training* is one of those concepts that people have no difficulty in recognizing but find it almost impossible to define.

For the purposes of this chapter, I offer the following definition:

> Technical training is the type of training that results in performance outcomes associated with the understanding, recalling, and applying specialized skills and knowledge that are related to specific equipment, machinery, devices, procedures, methods, processes, and systems.

This definition is probably no better than the definitions that I was criticizing earlier. If you come across (or write) a better definition, please let me know. In the meantime, allow me to prop up my definition through a discussion of related concepts.

It is easy to give examples of subject-matter areas that are strongly associated with technical training. Here are some examples:

- Aeronautical engineering
- Astronautics

- Biological sciences
- Chemical engineering
- Electrical engineering
- Manufacturing
- Mechanical engineering
- Medical technology
- Nuclear power generation
- Surveying and mapping
- Working on heavy equipment

Information technology—skills and knowledge associated with the use of computer systems and the Internet—is the largest and the most rapidly growing sector in technical training. Everyone—from the occasional user learning how to manipulate a spreadsheet with a Video Professor® CD to a seasoned professional learning how to apply object-oriented analysis using the Universal Modeling Language in an elaborate high-tech computer lab—has experienced this type of technical training.

While we may not have a precise definition of technical training, it is easy to differentiate this type of training from other types of training such as *interpersonal skills training, sales training, management training,* and *basic training.* Having said that, let me dodge potential criticism by pointing out that there is probably a continuum between *basic* training (which provides generic skills applicable to different jobs) and *technical* training (which provides specific skills associated with a particular job). Here is an example of five points along this continuum.

- How to write
- How to write a proposal
- How to write a technical proposal
- How to write a technical proposal for selling a router with an integrated intrusion prevention system
- How to write a technical proposal for selling a router with an integrated intrusion prevention system to a medium-sized start-up organization

Similar continua probably exist between technical training and other kinds of training, as shown in these training topics:

- How to interact with clients at a help desk (technical and interpersonal training)
- How to make a technical presentation as a member of a sales team (technical and sales training)
- How to manage software engineers (technical and management training)

Now that we have had this nice discussion about *technical training,* let us explore the other critical term.

Exploring Experiential Learning

Several chapters in this book have emphasized different elements of experiential approaches and their impact on learning outcomes. In my perception, the key element in experiential learning is the active participation in meaningful experiences. These experiences involve interaction between the learner and other elements such as the following:

- Content presented through various media
- Equipment and materials
- Fellow learners
- Expert practitioners

Different Experiential Approaches for Technical Training

It is obvious that there are many different ways to provide meaningful learning experiences. In our technical training projects during the past four decades, my colleagues and I have used many different approaches to experiential learning. Here are brief descriptions of twenty such approaches:

Action Learning involves a combination of action and reflection by a team to solve complex technical problems in a real-world setting. Team members apply existing skills and knowledge to solve the problem and create new skills and knowledge by continuously questioning the problem definition, solution strategies, and the ensuing results.

On-the-Job Training is used both formally and informally in mastering technical skills. It includes feed-forward (guidance) before the task, coaching during the task, and feedback after the task from one or more experienced practitioners.

A-Day-in-the-Life Simulations feature a collection of in-basket exercises related to a specific technical context. Participants review a list of "to-do" items for the day (or the week or the month), along with related information. They prioritize the tasks, plan the optimal sequence for tacking them, and implement the plan.

Apprenticeship involves on-the-job training and coaching. One or more technical experts (supervisors or co-workers) support the learning and performance of a newly hired person by guiding and debriefing her activities. The learner begins by helping her mentor and then gradually takes on increasing work responsibilities.

Near-the-Job Training is especially suited to equipment-operation skills. Learners work on machines and equipment when they are idle. Alternatively, they may use a set of machines that are set aside for training purposes. Learners are given various authentic tasks and provided with guidance, coaching, and feedback, as in on-the-job training projects.

Board Games motivate learners by providing an optimum combination of cooperation and competition and a tangible scorekeeping system. In technical training, the spaces in the boards may represent milestones in a technical project. The players' progress may be accelerated or impeded by chance cards that identify the use of best practices and inefficient approaches.

Assessment-Based Learning Activities (ABLA) require learners to complete a performance test and receive feedback about their technical competencies. Whenever appropriate, ABLAs encourage interaction and discussion between learners and coaches to improve future performance.

Card Games involve pieces of technical information (such as facts, concepts, terms, definitions, principles, examples, symptoms, and questions) printed on cards. These games borrow procedures from traditional playing card games and require players to classify and sequence pieces of technical content.

Coaching Activities involve an individual practitioner (the coach) supporting the learning efforts of another individual (the coachee) through interactive questioning, guidance, and feedback. The process usually requires both people to establish technical goals and the coach to observe the coachee, debrief the activity, offer relevant feedback, and suggest suitable improvements.

Email Games are conducted through the Internet. They may involve the play of electronic versions of interactive training games or specially designed activities that permit asynchronous communication in which people receive and send messages at different times. Typical email games exploit the ability of the Internet to ignore geographic distances and involve participants pooling their ideas to solve technical problems.

Instructional Puzzles challenge the participants' ingenuity and incorporate technical training content that is to be previewed, reviewed, tested, re-taught, or enriched. Puzzles can be solved by individuals or by teams.

Interactive Lectures involve participants in the learning process while providing complete control to the instructor. These activities enable a quick and easy conversion of a passive technical presentation into an interactive experience. Different types of interactive lectures incorporate built-in quizzes, interspersed tasks, teamwork interludes, and participant control of the presentation.

Pair Learning is based on the extreme programming methodology in software design. This strategy involves two people working on the same computer, sharing a single keyboard. In addition, paired learning between an expert and a novice results in the latter learning new technical skills. Paired learning between people from different technical fields results in more effective collaboration skills.

Procedural Simulations are dress rehearsals of real-world events, such as making a technical presentation to a client, troubleshooting a piece of equipment, or providing emergency technical assistance. By working through these simulations, participants get ready for real-world events.

Production Simulations involve the design and development of a product (such as a piece of metalwork or a report from a database). Different teams may compete with each other to create the best product. The initial briefing in this strategy involves teams receiving specifications for the final product, along with a checklist of quality criteria. The final products are evaluated by a panel of outside experts who provide feedback along different technical dimensions.

Simulators are mechanical, electrical, or electronic devices that present test conditions that closely resemble actual field conditions. Most modern high-fidelity simulations include computer programs.

Structured Sharing facilitates mutual learning and teaching of best practices in some technical area. Typical structured sharing activities create a context for dialogue and brainstorming among practitioners.

Textra Games combine the effective organization of well-written technical documentation with the motivational impact of experiential activities. Learners read a handout or a manual and play a game that uses peer pressure and peer support to encourage recall and transfer of what they read.

Troubleshooting Simulations require participants to systematically find the causes of problems and to fix the problems. These activities can use simulators or computer printouts of information regarding a faulty system.

Web-Based Games are interactive activities presented on the Internet. A variety of games and simulations can be played on the web by individuals or by teams. Multi-player games permit several participants to interact with each other at the same time.

Integrating Content and Activity

An interesting and disquieting aspect of experiential learning is that people don't learn from experience alone. Hectic experiential activities may actually result in confusion and frustration rather than useful learning. To produce learning, we need to combine experiential episodes with briefing, guidance, planning, feedback, reflection, and sharing of insights. Here are three chronological contexts in which active experiencing is integrated with factual and conceptual content and deliberate and collaborative reflection.

Briefing before the experiential activity involves providing relevant facts, concepts, principles, and mental models. Learners incorporate these content elements in planning for the experiential activity.

Coaching during the experiential activity involves providing just-in time and just-enough feedback and guidance. Learners incorporate these pieces of information in revising and improving their performance.

Debriefing after the experiential activity involves providing questions and comments. Learners incorporate these elements to reflect on the experience, come up with useful insights, and share them with each other.

The secret of effective and efficient experiential learning in technical training is to integrate content and activities, participation and reflection, and the hand and the mind. This type of integration can best be illustrated through a condensed case study of a technical training session.

A Sample Integrated Technical Training Simulation Game

About fifteen years ago, I worked with Ed Finerty on applying a combination of experiential learning and other instructional techniques to train technicians on how to program complex high-tech telephone switches. The course lasted for a week (Monday to Friday) and involved a subject-matter expert and a facilitator.

Here are some details of this integrated course.

Materials

Our training design activity involved the development of the following materials:

- Five versions of authentic work orders for programming a telephone switch to perform different functions. During the final performance test, one of these work orders was randomly given to each team.
- Job aids (checklists, decision tables, and flowcharts) related to the programming procedure
- Audiotape recordings that walk the participant through the steps of different programming procedures
- Videotape demonstrations of different programming procedures, involving screen shots of the computer monitor
- Play money

Equipment

Before the training activity, we assembled the following equipment:

- Workstations for each team attached to a simulated switch and loaded with the appropriate software programs
- Audiocassette players
- VCRs and television monitors

Flow

These are the steps in the training activity that we used:

Forming teams. We organized the ten participants in our pilot group into two teams of three and one team of four. At the beginning of the five-day simulation game, we explained that each team member would be required to demonstrate the mastery of a randomly selected programming procedure at the end of the week.

Explaining the performance-test. We explained our final performance-testing procedure. On the last two days of the course, whenever a team was ready to demonstrate its mastery of the procedure, all its members would assemble at a workstation. One team member would be randomly selected to sit at the keyboard. This person would receive a simulated work order and would begin the procedure for programming the switch while the other team members observed silently. From time to time, the facilitator would replace the team member at the keyboard with another team member who would continue the procedure. The team's score would be based on the time taken to correctly complete the procedure.

Explaining other scores. In addition to the performance-test score, each team would receive three separate scores:

- **Learning Speed.** This is the time taken by the team to report for the performance test.
- **Budget Management.** On the first day, each team will be funded with equal amounts of play money. Teams can use their funds to purchase various learning materials and services. The budget-management scores will reflect how effectively they used their learning budget.
- **Collaborative learning.** Throughout the game, the facilitator will observe learning strategies used by different teams and award score points to reflect how collaboratively its members learned the procedure.

Presenting the menu of learning resources. Using a PowerPoint®
slide, we presented alternative learning resources available to the teams, along with
the cost of each resource:

- **Trial-and-error learning.** Each team will have free access to a workstation
  with the switching software. Team members can decide to learn on their own,
  using their intuition, previous knowledge of similar procedures, and the help
  screen messages.
- **Job aids.** A packet of printed reference materials is available at the cost of
  $100 per copy.
- **Audiotape walkthrough.** An audiocassette walks the listeners through the
  procedure in a step-by-step fashion. This tape (along with a cassette player) can
  be rented for $200 for thirty minutes.
- **Videotape demonstration.** A videotape demonstrates each step of the procedure. This videotape (along with a VCR and a TV monitor) can be rented
  for $500 for thirty minutes.
- **Consultant.** An experienced subject-matter expert provides answers to technical questions from a team. This consultant can be hired for the fee of $2,000
  for fifteen minutes.
- **Practice test.** The team can take a practice version of the final performance
  test at a cost of $2,000.

Using sign-up sheets. We explained that certain learning services would
be provided on a first-come, first-served basis. We created sign-up sheets for consultant services and practice-test administration on the flip chart.

Beginning the activity. We distributed $10,000 in play money to each team
and paused while the teams planned their learning strategies. After about ten minutes, we made a brief presentation about the use of the software to program a switching procedure. After the presentation, we reminded participants that all teams should
report for the final performance test not later than Friday morning.

Coordinating team-learning activities. We sold job aid packets and rented
other learning resources. We also provided consulting services and administered practice tests on demand. During quieter times, we observed and rated collaborative
learning among team members.

Administering the test. Whenever a team reported for the performance test,
we selected one member at random to be the representative. We gave an authentic
work order as the simulated test item (with input data and output specifications) to
this person. We started a stop watch and asked the person to begin programming the
required switching function. We invited other team members to silently observe
their representative. After about five minutes, we identified another team member to

replace the first representative. We repeated this replacement procedure at random intervals to ensure that all team members took a turn. When the programming procedure was completed, we announced the time taken by the team.

Concluding the session. When all teams had completed the test, we announced four different scores for each team. We identified and congratulated the winning team in each category.

Debriefing the participants. We spent a few minutes responding to questions from participants (after reassuring them that this service was free). We also commented on participants' behaviors during the performance test.

Current Status of the Integrated Simulation Approach

Learner reactions and performance outcomes from the pilot course described above were very promising. Since the original offering, our clients have successfully continued to use the integrated simulation format with several batches of new learners. We kept continuously improving the design by incorporating more experiential learning strategies from the list presented earlier. For example, we had interactive lecture sessions conducted by the expert to demonstrate different programming procedures. We currently have a new and improved template for this simulation approach that we use for different types of technical training.

Blending Experiential Learning with e-Learning

It is becoming almost impossible to find any technical equipment or device that does not include one or more microprocessors. Much of the technical work today requires skills related to the computer and the Internet. If the technical job requires the use of computers, it makes sense to deliver the training also through computers and the web. Based on this premise, we began using e-learning approaches to deliver our technical training. In our projects, we began to blend online training delivery with principles of experiential learning in a strategy that we call the *Four-Door Approach*.

Rather than presenting a case study to explain this approach, we decided to take you into a simulation in which you play the role of a learner in an e-learning technical training course.

The Four Doors

You have enrolled in a technical course called *IT Service Management*. When you log in, you see a home page that contains four doors, each with a brief description of what it contains:

Library. This is a repository of all content resources for the course. When you click here, you see a catalog. Select the piece you want and read it at your own pace, using your personal learning style. We promise not to interrupt you with annoying little questions in an attempt to force interactivity on you.

Playground. This is a collection of different web-based games (complete with graphics, animation, and sound effects) that test your mastery of the content from the library. If you are reflective, you can study in the library before playing these games. If you are impulsive (and eat dessert before the main course), you can play a game first (and probably get trounced) before reading the related content in the library.

Cafe. This is where you can hold discussions with your classmates (in an asynchronous mode, meaning that you read and respond at different times). This area also contains *OQs (Open Questions)*, where you type your answer and read other people's answers.

Torture Chamber. This is actually a fairly pleasant test center in which you are given two chances to take a performance simulation/test. You pass if your score is 80 percent or better.

Library

Being a somewhat systematic person, you visit the library and read the first resource labeled *The Service Desk*. This piece begins with a set of training objectives. The text is presented in plain language and in short paragraphs, bulleted lists, and meaningful headings and subheadings. However, the text is not dumbed-down. Initially, you are surprised by the absence of interspersed questions, because you are expecting frequent interactivity. Very soon, however, you become thankful that you can read the text in your preferred learning style and take your own notes. As you read the material, you focus on the big picture and the relationships among the technical concepts without being distracted by intruding multiple-choice questions that emphasize factual details.

Playground

Some time in the middle of reading the article about the Service Desk, you catch yourself yawning. You are getting bored with the self-imposed passivity and you decide to go play for a while. You click the playground button at the bottom of the screen.

You are given a choice of five different games. You click HANGMAN, and you are presented with a game display and initial instructions. You click the "Play" button to see a short-answer question, followed by a set of blank circles representing letters in the answer. Some of the circles are already filled in with "free" letters. You read the question and try to guess the answer. Since this question is on a technical topic that you did not encounter during your study time in the library, you are forced to make a guess. In desperation, you type the letter "E" and immediately all occurrences of this letter in the correct answer appear in the corresponding circles. A tone and a green light on the side indicate that your guess is correct. You continue by typing the letter "A." A different tone and a red light indicate that your guess is incorrect. After the next guess, you are sure of the answer. So you type all the remaining letters fourteen seconds before a timer at the bottom of the display counts down to zero. When the answer is complete, the score box displays 9 points. The next question (along with blank circles representing the answer) pops up on the play area. Since you know the answer to this question, you rapidly fill in the blank circles. Your score increases by 10 more points to 19. You use the same procedure to play through the total of ten questions in this round of play.

At the end of your first round of play, you discover that you can play the same game repeatedly. Every time you play, you are presented with a mix of new and old questions in a different sequence. You also discover that you can play the game at three levels of difficulty: If you find the game to be too easy, you can advance to the medium level of difficulty, where you play without any "free" letters. At the hardest level of difficulty, you have to spell the answer, one letter at a time, in the correct sequence.

After you get a perfect score of 100 at the most difficult level of HANGMAN, you move on to the other games.

More About the Playground

You return to the opening screen for the playground and check out four other types of web-based games:

TIC TAC. In this game, the computer presents a 3 by 3 tic-tac-toe grid, with a short-answer question in each box. When you click a question, you are presented with a text box to type your answer. You win this game if you provide the correct answers to any three questions in a straight line (row, column, or diagonal).

SEQUENCE. In this game, the computer presents you with a list of seven steps used in processing requests at the service desk. However, these steps are not presented in the correct order. You win this game if you rearrange the steps in the correct order (by dragging and dropping the steps) before the timer counts down to zero.

CATEGORIZE. In this game, the computer presents four buttons, each labeled with one of the four types of activities undertaken at the service desk.

Different items (words, phrases, or sentences) appear on the screen. Your task is to quickly read the item and click the appropriate button. Your score increases every time you classify an item correctly.

TRUE OR FALSE. This game is very similar to the CATEGORIZE game, except there are only two buttons, marked "True" and "False." Different statements appear on the screen. Your task is to quickly read the statement and decide whether it is true or false.

After playing these games (and replaying some of them), you make a mental note to work through the next module by having fun in the playground first, then studying the text resources in the library and returning to the playground again.

For the present, you return to the library and study the remaining parts of the material on the service desk. You feel confident that you have mastered the technical topics and achieved the learning objectives. So you decide to visit the cafe.

Cafe

When you visit the cafe, you are presented with an OQ (open question) that asks: *What one piece of advice would you give to a new employee who is assigned to the service desk?*

You type a facetious answer ("Ask the employee to bring a giant bottle of aspirin") and click "Send." Your answer disappears and you are presented a choice of three buttons that enable you to display

- A checklist to evaluate your answer
- Answers from different experts
- Answers from other participants

You review the earlier answers from your fellow participants and feel reassured that you could have given a good answer if you had taken the task seriously.

In the cafe, you also see a discussion forum. You visit this forum and see several discussion "threads" where other participants have made comments and asked questions. You review some of the entries and find them bland and boring. So you skip that section and visit the torture chamber.

Torture Chamber

When you enter this area, the first thing you notice is a dire warning that this is the Examination Hall, where your answers will be scored to determine whether you pass the test. You can pass out of the course by taking the test any time you want—even before you have studied the library content or completed the playground or café activities. However, you have only *two* chances to take the test. You must score at least 80 percent in order to pass.

You decide to take the test. If you pass, you can move on. If you fail, you can return to the library and study some more before taking the test again.

The test in the torture chamber contains ten scenario-based multiple-choice items. Each item presents an authentic situation related to things that happen at the service desk and asks a question. You have to select the best alternative among four plausible choices. With some difficulty, you complete the test and click "Submit." You immediately receive your score (90 percent), a congratulatory message, and a brief preview of the next module on capacity management.

Continuation

As the days roll by, you work through the other modules of the course. The format for all modules is the same, but you keep experimenting with different study strategies depending on your mood at the moment. Eventually, somewhere around the seventh unit, you work out your most efficient strategy of taking the test first, failing it, working through the library and the playground to gain mastery, and then taking the test for the second time. You know that you are living dangerously (because you cannot afford to fail the test the second time), but you enjoy the twinge of excitement.

Current Status of the Four-Door Approach

During the past five years, my colleague Matt Richter and I have successfully applied this blending of games, simulations, and e-learning procedures for creating online technical training courses. Although our clients were initially skeptical because these courses appear to be different from the "traditional" e-learning courses, performance-test results and other evaluation data have convinced them that this experiential approach is an effective one.

Key Principles of Effective Experiential Learning for Technical Training

The two examples presented above, one in the classroom and the other online, emphasize one of the key principles for the effective approach of experiential learning to technical training:

> Combine different types of experiential activities with appropriate content-presentation techniques to produce an integrated training package. Make sure that all pieces of content presented are directly related to the hands-on activities assigned to teams of learners.

Here are four additional principles that we learned from (and incorporated in) our successful technical training sessions:

- Ensure a high degree of job relevance in all experiential activities. Be extremely respectful of the learners' time. Ruthlessly remove all game-like activities that are "fun" but have nothing to do with the technical skills related to the job.
- Make sure that the training is performance-based. Require learners to demonstrate their ability to perform the technical tasks throughout the training session.
- Combine teamwork with individual accountability. Encourage mutual learning among team members during the initial stages of the training session. Conclude the session with individual performance tests.
- Resist the temptation to entrap participants into making mistakes in order to identify their errors (and suggest improvements) during debriefing. Replace the typical debriefing sessions after the experiential activity with briefing sessions before the activity or coaching sessions during the activity.

In the blended world of tomorrow, technical workers will have to master interpersonal skills (as in the case of a medical technologist interacting with a patient). At the same time, salespeople will have to master technical skills (as in the case of helping a customer reset the VCR clock). The same is true of managers (if they want to send a memo through the company's intranet). We are all going to be teaching and learning increasing amounts of technical skills.

Aren't you glad there are experiential learning approaches to make the training task more effective, efficient, and enjoyable?

CHAPTER FIFTEEN

EXPERIENTIAL LEARNING IN TEAM TRAINING

Kevin Eikenberry

Kevin Eikenberry is the Chief Potential Officer of The Kevin Eikenberry Group. He has spent the last fifteen years helping organizations all across North America on leadership, learning, teams and teamwork, creativity, and more. His client list includes the American Red Cross, Chevron, Chevron Phillips Chemical Company, John Deere, Purdue University, Southwest Airlines, the U.S. Marine Corps, and the U.S. Mint.

A former chair of the North American Simulation and Gaming Association (NASAGA), Kevin is a frequent presenter at professional conferences and a sought-after keynote speaker. He currently serves on four boards of directors in order to contribute, hone his leadership skills, and add an additional dimension to his experiences. He is the author of the book *Vantagepoints on Learning and Life*, and a contributing author to over fifteen other books. He publishes four electronic newsletters and a popular blog (www.kevineikenberry.com/blogs/index.asp), collectively read by over eighty thousand people worldwide.

Contact Information

The Kevin Eikenberry Group
7035 Bluffridge Way
Indianapolis, IN 46278
(317) 387–1424
Kevin@KevinEikenberry.com
www.KevinEikenberry.com

I T IS A COMMON REQUEST because the need is a common one.

Organizations typically arrange at least some of their work to be done by teams . . . work teams, project teams, ad hoc teams. Since this is a common way that people do work, it is normal that leaders would look for ways to improve the productivity and effectiveness of these teams. So they often ask, "What can we do to improve the effectiveness of our teams?"

While a common request, it is also a complex one because teams are complex systems.

Unfortunately, the prevalence of teams obscures the complexity and the logical request to "improve my team" leads people to assume that there is a simple, one-size-fits-all, "let's do it in an afternoon" solution.

Team-building events are being held every day, and most of them have been planned using that assumption. Unfortunately, those assumptions often lead to lackluster results back in the workplace. Don't get me wrong. Most of those events are fun in the eyes of most participants, and while deemed "a waste of time and money" by the most cynical (or those who have been through many of these events in the past), they are viewed positively by most. It's just that the transferability back to work is limited.

These facts lead to a vicious cycle in the team-building business. Budgets get built each year that include funds that will be used for team building. The events don't necessarily provide any real return on investment, but people like them, and managers get kudos for much the same reasons as cruise directors on ships are liked—they know how to put on a great event. So team-building events continue. And teams still struggle to be as effective as they could be. Why? Because the trainer or facilitator thought only about the training or facilitation (the event itself) and didn't start at the beginning.

In this chapter, I will help you think about, design, and facilitate experiential experiences to assist teams to be more successful. But before I get to design questions and exercises and approaches, I am going to start at the beginning. I am going to look at the bigger picture and how team performance fits into that picture, because it is only with this context that we have a chance to break the vicious cycle of team building described above.

Good exercises aren't enough in themselves. If they were, some of what is described above wouldn't exist. After all, if there is any area of training and development in which experiential approaches are used, it is in team building. Real results will come when good exercises are designed and facilitated from the perspective of organizational need and context. In other words, we must think like a *consultant* first to be a great *trainer* or *facilitator* of team-learning events.

Understanding the Real Situation

Often, when team building is requested, the manager or leader wants "people to get along better or get to know each other." It is assumed that team performance will improve once this happens,. While it is true that relationships are an important part of the team-building puzzle, it is far from the only piece. Let me share with you a basic model that will give you a broader perspective of the factors that will lead to highly effective teams. As you read about this model, think about how you can use it as a framework to better understand the gaps a team might be facing—and how you might design and facilitate your events accordingly. Once we have that context, we are in a position to design and deliver the best possible team-learning events.

The CARB Model

CARB is an acrostic representing the four major dimensions ultimately responsible for a team's effectiveness:

> **C**ommitment to the team and each other
>
> **A**lignment and goal agreement
>
> **R**elationships among team members
>
> **B**ehaviors and skills

The model is shown in Figure 15.1.
Let's talk about each of these components.

Commitment to the Team and Each Other

Commitment is a very powerful thing, and without it, the work of teams won't be as successful as possible. Why? Because people are busy. They have many tasks and priorities. The work of the team will just fall into that long list of priorities unless they find a reason to be truly committed to the team itself and its goals. With only so much focus and energy to spread around, without commitment they won't be fully participative and effective on the team.

There are two parts to this commitment. People must feel a commitment to the team and its purpose, and they must have some commitment to the individuals on the team, believing in them and their contributions to the team.

Of course, commitment can (and often will need to) be built. It won't pre-exist when you put people on a team. Since team formation, development, and success

FIGURE 15.1. THE CARB MODEL

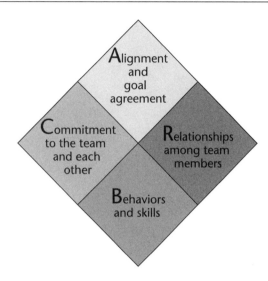

is a complex thing, several of our other CARB factors will aid in the development of this commitment. But recognizing its importance is a good first step.

How will you know when you have built a level of commitment? or What are the factors that will build that commitment? High levels of commitment correlate with several factors, including:

- *Belief*—People will believe in each other. Individual motivations are clear and generally understood. People are able to believe in the team, its individual members, and the work of the team.
- *Agreements*—People have a mutually agreed to set of behaviors that are acceptable to the team. By building a set of agreements around performance, behavior, and "how things are done," productivity is greatly improved. Why? Because effort and energy aren't spent on these distractions, effort can be directed to the work at hand.
- *Trust*—A major underpinning for team performance is trust, trust in team members and trust in leadership. It is clearly necessary for the levels of commitment required for high-performing teams.
- *Support*—Support is a critical factor, but it is also a bellwether for the rest of these factors. If people are supporting team decisions, commitment is likely present. If people are supporting each other through tough parts of a team's life, they are likely committed.

Is it possible for a team to get results with low commitment? Sure, you can get some results. But you will never approach the results that could be achieved with people who are committed to the team and to each other.

As you survey the situation of a team you will be designing an event for, make sure to think about the commitment component, asking questions to uncover any issues. There are things we can do in our designs to help here, but only if we know there is an issue.

Using the four considerations above, you can take many experiential team exercises or simulations and craft them to help a team examine or improve in the *commitment* component. Within your existing repertoire, you will find some well-suited to the trust issue. When using those exercises, make sure your goal of examining trust is prevalent in your debriefing questions. Likewise, you can craft specific questions in your debriefing of any experiential exercise to hone in on support and belief. Doing so reinforces their importance and generates valuable discussion for teams.

The *agreements* consideration can be debriefed in an exercise for awareness purposes, but in order to make a real difference more is required. In my experience, one of the most valuable things a team can do is to come to those agreements that will guide team behavior, on both the little annoyances and the big behavioral issues. This is done as a working dialogue facilitated by someone who can help the team identify their issues and help them craft agreements that everyone on the team will live with and abide by. While this approach may not be experiential training in its pure form, it is very engaging by nature and can have a very positive impact on team performance.

If you find *commitment* to be a main stumbling block for a team, consider combining an exercise in which you stress belief, trust, and/or support with a facilitated discussion on agreements.

Alignment and Goal Agreement

Teams can't succeed in a vacuum, but far too often that is what organizations expect them to do. Sometimes, this vacuum is created by omission. Leaders just aren't thinking about it or are "too busy" to set context for team success. Other times, the reason is optimism. Leaders believe in their team members and their skills. After all, they hired bright people—and bright people will figure it all out. Assumptions like these can frustrate or burn out talented people and kill teams.

And sometimes the vacuum is caused by a far more pervasive problem—a lack of clear organizational goals, objectives, or strategies. Leaders must create clear strategies, and they must create a clear line of sight throughout the organization so that people (and teams) can connect their work to the important strategies of the organization.

It takes effort to get a team in alignment with the organization's goals and strategies. It is impossible when they don't exist. Yes, strategies and goals may exist. And yes, they may have been communicated. This is a good start, but it isn't enough. Teams can't gain the clear direction they need without conversation. It is the responsibility of leadership to provide that opportunity for conversation. This conversation provides the understanding that provides the team the context they need to clarify their goals and make the decisions that come along during their work.

If you want to build stronger alignment between the team's work and the organization's goals, consider the following:

- *Start at the beginning.* Make sure the organization's goals and strategies are set. If not, there isn't much chance of the team being highly successful. At a minimum, the team needs to understand, from the start, why their work product matters in the bigger picture and how they can make a positive impact.
- *Generate conversation.* Make the time to have conversation. The alignment we are searching for needs to be deep, almost visceral. Help individuals and the team develop meaning and purpose. Help them understand how they can create work that matters.
- *Get the team's help.* Get their input. Remember that you are trying to create alignment and agreement. When people have the chance to shape the goals of the team and when they have the opportunity to have input into those decisions, they will have greater agreement with the goals.
- *Provide a connection.* Teams need someone in leadership "above" them who can provide support and resources, someone who can answer questions and keep them on track. Some people call this a team sponsor. The sponsor doesn't need to be on the team; rather he or she provides leadership, support, and connection. The sponsor keeps the team from feeling like they are all alone.
- *Make them accountable.* If the alignment is clear and the goals set, then the team needs to be held accountable for results. In organizations in which accountability has been lax in the past, this may seem like a jolt, but it won't be long before this accountability not only drives results but improves team dynamics too.

It is easy to see how these steps will help a team succeed. But more than helping them deliver a desired result, the sense of clarity, meaning, and direction that these steps create helps teams get over many other hurdles. Why? Because people want to belong to something that matters; they want things to believe in. When we give them those things, collectively they will work through many personal issues and challenges, and they will also become more committed to the end product.

Thinking about a team's situation relating to alignment will lead us to several thoughts:

- Some of the issues that might exist here aren't things that we can solve in a training session or learning event.
- Some might be able to be addressed through the conversation that might be facilitated at the end of an experience.
- Even if the specifics of alignment can't be addressed, the *need for alignment* can be exposed and understood in a learning event, if you know that is something you want people to discover.

This is a perfect example of why we need to start with our consultant's hat on. Would you have considered this as a learning objective for most team-building sessions before now?

Even more so than the *commitment* component, there are parts of the *alignment* component that you'll be hard-pressed to "solve" with any experiential exercise. That doesn't mean, however, that you can't use them as a part of the solution. Consider carefully chosen exercises as a preamble to the kinds of conversation discussed above.

Experience shows that exercises in which you provide little guidance as to the final goal are effective to help people discover the importance of alignment. In these types of exercises, people work hard based on assumptions they make (in terms of the end goal, the customer's needs, or whatever), but when/if these assumptions are incorrect, they see the results of misalignment—lots of effort for less than satisfying results. Even if the team's alignment issues don't relate to customer service issues, there are many exercises designed to illuminate the importance of customer expectations that can lead to great conversations about the need for alignment (and our general tendency to rely on our assumptions rather than asking questions).

When well run, these types of exercises can set the stage for a great conversation between leaders and teams designed to provide clear understanding and agreement goals.

Relationships Among Team Members

"We need people to get to know each other better. Once we have done that, we will be fine." As previously mentioned, this is a dangerously limiting view of teams. Relationships do matter, of course. When teams with good relationships also have the other CARB factors in large amounts, look out! Team performance can soar.

The *relationship* component has been the traditional realm of much team training. Let's get people to know each other better, let's build a sense of camaraderie. And while all of these things are important, they aren't the things that cause lasting improvement—they only set the stage for that improvement.

The best-designed relationship-focused team-building events do more than create laughs—they create learning. These events help people do more than get to know each other, they provide opportunities for teams to:

- *Learn each other's strengths.* Strong teams not only like each other, they know each other's strengths. They are collectively able to tap into the strengths and experience of the members of the team.
- *Find ways to capitalize on those strengths.* The best team-building activities give people a chance to be themselves, without all the structure and trappings of the workplace. And when people are themselves, others will see them in new and often flattering ways. This gives their strengths a chance to shine and helps others see how those strengths can be tapped by the team.
- *Get comfortable with asking for help.* Highly effective team members are willing to ask for help, regardless of their roles on the team. Team-building activities can help raise people's comfort with asking.

There are other factors about team relationships that matter that might not be addressed in traditional team building, but they are quite important. Again, these require effort and time spent to develop processes and support from leaders outside of the team. These include:

- *Initiation processes.* How new team members are added to a team, how they become oriented and acquainted with team members, norms, and expectations are typically left to chance or a quick meet-and-greet. Organizations that develop processes and plans for this will have greater success with teams that change membership frequently.
- *Role definition.* Team members need to understand where they fit in and what their roles are. When new teams are chartered or started there needs to be a format and plan for discussion of team member roles and expectations.

As you can see, even the *relationship* component of this CARB model is about more then just "liking one another." Consider all of the factors above when diagnosing a team's situation and design your events accordingly.

This area of relationship building is the traditional realm of most experiential team-building exercises. You will have little trouble finding exercises to use here. As with any exercise, the value will come from the nature and depth of your debrief. Consider the factors related to relationship building carefully as you create your debriefing plan and as you observe the exercise itself. Planning your questions through this lens will help you encourage participants to really begin to build the relationships they need for a highly functioning team.

Behaviors and Skills

The last part of the CARB model is the *behaviors and skills* component. Being a successful member of a team requires different behaviors and skills than are required of an individual contributor. Therefore, when you put people together on teams, they will perform more confidently and successfully if they have the right skills.

While the list of skills and behaviors that support success on teams is long, here is a short list to get you thinking about the types of behaviors and skills to look for when creating a team—or to develop in an existing team.

- *Strong technical skills and competence.* Having the subject-matter knowledge, industry perspective, or specific skills the team needs is critical. Of course, not everyone should bring a cloned set of skills, but it is important to identify the subject-matter needs of the team and to make sure that each team member contributes to one or more of these skills.
- *Able and willing to collaborate and share credit.* Working alone allows for people to feel the spotlight and glory when things go well. It also means those individuals will be accountable when they aren't as successful. Highly effective team members recognize that the team success will reflect on them most when they focus on team success rather than on individual accolades. The best team members are willing to collaborate.
- *Able to trust others.* Trust is something that is developed between people over time. In fact, as relationships are built, trust can blossom. The best team members are willing to start from a position of basic trust in their teammates. Certainly, this trust can deepen and grow, but the most effective team members are willing to assume the best and work together more effectively from the beginning. This behavior becomes more important as the makeup of individual teams changes more quickly.
- *Able to participate in and lead effective meetings.* Meetings are an important component of team success. Whether the team meets every day, on remote conference calls, or meets only quarterly, the ability to contribute ideas and insights, to help the team move toward the desired results, to provide feedback when needed, and the ability to and willingness to stay focused are critical skills for effective teams.

- *Comfortable and competent at group problem solving.* Some problems a team faces can be solved by individuals. Sometimes a subteam will tackle a problem, and sometimes it requires the entire team. In every case, effective team members know how to work together to solve problems, how to listen to the ideas of others, how to ask questions without being condescending, and how to make sure that the strengths, experiences, and insights of each team member are taken into account in the problem-solving process.
- *Willing to continuously learn.* The work of today is more complex and demanding than it has ever been. This means that each individual on the team needs to continuously improve his or her individual skills for teams to succeed.

This short list of team-member skills should also be a starting point for you when considering the exercise to use or modify for your needs. You will be most successful when you select, create, or modify your experiential exercise based on the behavioral or skills gaps you have identified or discovered.

What Type of Team Are You Working With?

Beyond having a larger model to give you some context for team performance, there is another challenge that gets in the way of successful team-building events—team type.

To keep things simple, I believe there are two basic types of teams. There are basketball teams and there are track and field teams.

Basketball Teams

Basketball teams (or soccer or hockey) are teams that require, by the nature of their task, that everyone play as one unit. On teams in these sports, the players are *interdependent*. At any moment of any game, the entire team needs to be working in harmony in order to be successful. The role of each player is designated by his or her position (which takes into account innate strengths and acquired skills). However, the situation at any moment during the flow of the game may require any player to take any role.

And on good teams of this sort, all players are willing to be flexible, to assist, to change roles, to "do what it takes." They know that they can't achieve their team goals of victory without working together, because the nature of the game forces interdependency among the team members.

Track and Field Teams

Players on track and field teams, on the other hand, except in a few relay events, are not interdependent. They are *independent*. Shot putters have a skill set that is largely unrelated to the sprinters. And the high jumpers can be personally skilled and successful without any tangible help or support from the distance runners.

At the end of the day (or meet), the team can win if enough of the individuals do well. In other words, if enough individuals win, the team will win. The most successful of these teams will have highly talented individual contributors, supporting each other to reach their common goal of winning. In this way, they are definitely a team. They may feel allegiance to the group. They certainly can have pride in being a part of the group. They want each other to be successful. They know that they can all be more successful when each individual is more successful. They can have a common goal (to win the meet or championship). But the fundamental relationship between the players isn't the same as it is on a basketball team.

Most organizations will likely have both sorts of teams. They have teams that work in a process flow or project for which the outputs of one person directly affect the work of the next, in which the work and the people are highly interdependent.

They also have teams that look more like the track and field team. In these situations, people are working toward a common mission and goal, but their work doesn't intersect in nearly the same ways as for the highly interdependent teams.

In my experience, leaders (and team members) tend to think that all teams should be like basketball teams. If the work or project dictates that focus, great. You can quickly see that the needs of each type of team are different. This difference can have a significant impact on the way you design a given learning event. Keeping these types in mind, along with your observations provided by the CARB model, will put you in the position to design the right kind of event.

In short, you do not help the team or organization if you build your exercise(s) around the basketball model of interdependency if the team operates independently. This is a critical design consideration. If you have the perfect exercise to illustrate or teach a concept from the CARB model above, and it requires teams operating in the exercise differently than they are required to on the job, then make sure to discuss those differences during your debriefing.

The Team or the Individuals?

There is one more factor to consider before getting on with your design. Will the event contain a single (or several) intact teams, or will it be made up of people who are on teams, but not necessarily the same team? This is an important consideration.

In general, if you have intact teams participating, you will be able to design in more components from the CARB model. If you have members from a variety of teams, you are most likely going to have to focus on the *behaviors* section. Or, if you do talk about other factors, they may not be able to be applied to the full team at that time. (Through additional dialogue and conversation at a later time, you may be able to affect these types of changes.) Again, recognizing who will be in your audience will help you set a realistic goal for what you can achieve and will help you set a focus for the experience you are designing.

After thinking about the context the team is operating in, and after gaining some understanding of the team's situation and needs, after determining what kind of team you are dealing with, and after understanding who will be participating and why, you can *finally* begin thinking about design. With this background, you are in the position to design something extremely successful. The next section of this chapter will help you think about your design.

Types of Experiential Team Learning Events

Experiential team learning events fall into one of four categories:

- Traditional events
- Outdoor events
- Real work events
- Other activities

Let's talk about each type briefly.

Traditional Events. They may be in a classroom or hotel conference room, but regardless of where they are, they are the traditional team-building events done indoors. It might include some exercises, games, or simulations, and it might include some other more traditional learning components (I mean lectures and corporate pep talks on PowerPoint). These situations are probably the ones you've been thinking about most as you have been reading this chapter. These are events with great opportunities for improvement with experiential approaches. Indoor events can be used to help a team gain confidence, awareness, and/or skills in any of the CARB model components. In this case, the venue has less to do with results than the nature of the exercise itself.

Outdoor Events. Known often as adventure learning courses, these events are already experiential in nature. Like any type of learning event, their effectiveness will hinge on design, applicability to the needs of the team, and the skill of the facilitator. When these three things are in alignment, these events can be very effective and successful. When they aren't, they can become expensive playtime. There are many sources for deeper discussion of this genre. While this genre is discussed in-depth in Chapter 10 in this handbook, recognize that the design and debriefing sections to come are as applicable to these events as to any other. Use these sections to help you build better outdoor events, even if you are hiring your facilitator.

Outdoor events lend themselves to addressing trust and support issues from the *commitment* component especially well. Beyond that, skilled facilitators of outdoor events can design experiences that can meet nearly any of your learning needs. An important consideration is adequate debriefing. Sometimes there are many distractions in an outdoor environment that can take away from the effectiveness of your debriefing. Since the debriefing is the most critical component of the learning event, plan for this accordingly.

Real Work Events. Often overlooked, there can be excellent opportunities to use experiential learning with intact teams in conjunction with real work events and projects. Consider combining an experiential training event within an actual project meeting or planning session as a way to invigorate team discussion. When they are designed well, you might do some skills work by giving the team specific guidelines to apply in the work they are doing at that time. Or use the real work activity as a chance to see how the team functions without any prior guidance. In either case, be sure to debrief the real work activity after it has concluded so that participants assess how it went and what changes they would make the next time they engage in such an activity back on the job. A real work activity is also an opportunity for a team to evaluate its current goals—with or without your assistance.

I have described some important times to use real work as a part of applying the CARB model. Beyond these examples, you can use popular (or craft your own) short experiential exercises at the start of a major team meeting that jolt participants into awareness of the team concept. A good example is Ball Warp, a brief exercise in which team members must exchange a ball in a particular sequence. Challenging them to do the exchange at higher speeds requires them to strategize together. If they don't, their speed will not increase significantly. Such an exercise can provide the team with a key experience and learning point that they can carry throughout their meeting. Often, this approach can show significant impact as a team immediately uses something they have learned in their real work.

Other Activities. Anything that doesn't fall neatly into one of the categories above falls into "other activities." These can include a mini-golf outing, bowling, or other types of events. (See Chapter 6.) While teams often do these types of events, seldom are they designed to provide more than the relationship aspects. If you determine to use one of these activities, consider that there is a great opportunity to debrief the activity to draw important lessons from the experience.

In addition to these four categories, remember that your event might contain a combination of these events. In fact, your experiential design will be more effective as it combines approaches and becomes less of an event and more a part of the fabric of people's work.

Design Questions

Now that we have talked about the types of events we can consider, let's dive into some specific questions we should ask. We can use these questions to design a brand new exercise or event or to modify and adjust one we have experienced or read about.

These questions are meant to be a starting point. Some of these questions are obvious, perhaps some less so, but all are crucial to making your design process both easier and more effective. The clearer your answers to these questions, the easier it will be for you to design a powerful experiential team-building activity.

1. *What is the organizational goal?* Why are you even embarking on this design? What are the performance gaps or issues that you want to simulate and improve? The CARB model discussed above will help you structure the specific questions you need to answer. While your client may have asked for some "team building," you will likely have to dig a bit deeper—as we discussed in the first portion of this chapter.

2. *What is the instructional goal?* This goal (or goals) comes from the organizational goals of course. It is important to think of them as two separate questions though. First, it keeps our designs rooted in the real world. Second, it allows us to drill into the most important components of learning for the team and the team members—be they attitudes, skills, or knowledge.

3. *What are the critical components?* Your answers to the first two questions may give you a long laundry list! Determine the most critical pieces, knowing that you likely won't be able to solve everything in one event. Sometimes, simulations and exercises become too big and unwieldy because people try to simulate *everything*. Stay focused and clear on the most critical pieces.

4. *Who plays/who needs to play?* With answers to the first three questions, you can now think about this question. Who are the participants in the event going to be? Given the goals and objectives, are the right people here? Perhaps the client wants you to do an event with multiple intact teams. Your analysis might be is that it would be much more successful doing the training one team at a time to allow the team to work on very individual (and perhaps private) issues. Or perhaps you have determined that having several teams participate together might break down some communication or "silo" issues. Use your answers to these questions to influence your client on this point, if appropriate.

5. *What is my approach?* You need to decide what kind of experience you want to build. Are you going to design something during which people do something or build something? Are you going to use a board-type game? Are you going to have people manipulate things? Is your exercise going to focus more on thinking and discussion? Effective design doesn't start with this question. Contrary to popular practices, effective design asks this question when it is almost obvious (with the information you have gained from questions 1 through 4).

6. *How real does it need to be?* Some experiences mirror real life very closely, others hardly at all (at least on the surface). This is an important question for you to consider in your design process.

7. *How elaborate does it need to be?* Your client's organizational culture and the expectations you set will play a role in your answer to this. Does your simulation or game need to have fancy components, glossy handouts, etc.? Or can you work with more simplicity and elegance?

8. *How much time is available?* You can't squeeze a four-hour simulation into a forty-five-minute lunchtime session. This is an important question! Again, you may need to put your consulting hat on and build a case for more time, or perhaps you just need to be creative and design your product into the time expectations.

9. *How much money/resources do you have?* Knowing your budget and what other resources you have available are important to your design. Keep these things in mind and work within these constraints.

10. *How flexible does the experience need to be?* Are you designing something to put into one workshop situation, or will you need to be able to scale this activity over different sizes of groups, different audiences, different lengths of time, and so forth? While this may not be an important consideration when you are initially designing for a given situation, it is critical to your productivity over time. Thinking up-front about how you might continue to use or adapt something as you build it will be time well spent.

11. *What about the experience?* Early in the design process, spend some time thinking about the participants and their experience. Make a list of adjectives you would like them to use in describing the experience. This will help you design in the levels of competition, fun, laughter, reflection (and a hundred more things) that you want.

12. *How will you debrief?* A good design includes a design for the debriefing. The codification and application of the learning come during the discussion that follows the experience, so you must design it carefully and completely. There are a variety of ways to do this and a number of questions you must plan. You will find an extended discussion of debriefing in Chapter 3 in this handbook.

This chapter has taken you through a full cycle for the development and use of experiential exercises for team building and team development—from request or need through consultation, design, facilitation, and debriefing.

While almost everyone will use some sort of experience when "teaching" team building, I hope this bigger picture and broader view will allow you to assure yourself, your client, and the participants that the events you design and lead will be more than just engaging and fun—that they will have a real impact on the skills, behaviors, and results required back on the job.

CHAPTER SIXTEEN

EXPERIENTIAL LEARNING IN INTERPERSONAL SKILL DEVELOPMENT

Mel Silberman

Mel Silberman is the author of numerous books in the field of training and development, including *Active Training* (3rd ed.) (Pfeiffer, 2006), *PeopleSmart* (Berrett-Koehler, 2000), *Working PeopleSmart* (Berrett-Koehler, 2004), *101 Ways to Make Training Active* (2nd ed.) (Pfeiffer, 2005), and *Training the Active Training Way* (Pfeiffer, 2006). Mel is professor emeritus of adult and organizational development at Temple University and president of Active Training, a provider of seminars and publications in adult learning, training techniques, coaching, team facilitation, and interpersonal intelligence. He is a frequent presenter at conferences of the American Society for Training and Development (ASTD), the International Society of Performance Improvement (ISPI), and the North American Simulation and Gaming Association (NASAGA). His clients encompass corporate, educational, governmental, and human service organizations worldwide. Recent clients include the U.S. Senate Office of Education and Training, BMW, Linens N' Things, Consolidated Edison, Nationwide Insurance, the Federal Reserve Bank, and the Stockholm School of Economics.

Contact Information

Active Training
303 Sayre Drive
Princeton, NJ 08540
(609) 987–8157
mel@activetraining.com
www.activetraining.com

NO MATTER WHAT SOMEONE'S FUNCTION IS, everyone in today's workplace is in the people business! It used to be said that some people were in the business of working with people and some were in the business of working with facts, figures, and machinery. But the people business is no longer the domain of the few. It now includes everyone.

Ask the person on the street what it means to be skilled with people, and you are bound to hear many who have this picture: "Oh, that's a person who is really a smooth operator . . . a person who knows how to get others to join his side." A different picture you might get is someone who is "personable . . . friendly . . . fun to be with."

While few people would complain about having those two attributes, they represent a very limited view of what it means to be gifted with people. Interpersonal success is a multi-faceted competence. It is not limited to political skills or social graces, but includes a wide range of abilities.

As I have written in my book *PeopleSmart: Developing Your Interpersonal Intelligence* (2000), there are eight skill areas that should be considered in any interpersonal skills training effort.

1. Understanding People

Interpersonally skilled people listen actively, empathize with someone's feelings, and acknowledge his or her viewpoint. That not only helps them to be appreciated but also works to draw out information they need to figure out what makes the other person tick. They ask questions to clarify what someone is saying when the person is confusing. They also realize that understanding others goes beyond the words they speak. They know how to interpret the unspoken. Finally, they are expert at reading other people's style and motives.

2. Expressing Yourself Clearly

Interpersonally skilled people know how to get their message across so it's understood. When people go on and on to make a point, they simply have no effect on other people. Effective communicators get to the point when brevity is required, yet give enough detail so that other people are not confused. They can also sense when the other person has not understood and can quickly rephrase what they are saying. Above all, they include the listener in the conversation by asking questions and obtaining reactions.

3. Asserting Your Needs

Interpersonally skilled people know that they've got to be their own person. They have to have limits, and they have to establish those limits. If they try to be all things to all people, they'll wind up disappointing them. They also are straight-forward with their wishes. They realize that hinting at what they need from others only leads to disappointment and frustration. Assertive individuals are also able to remain calm and confident, even when others try to provoke them and push their emotional buttons.

4. Seeking and Giving Feedback

Interpersonally skilled people are open about their reactions to others. They are able to give feedback easily and do it in such a way that the other people don't become defensive. They also know that it is smart to get in the habit of asking for feedback themselves. If feedback is withheld, it's as though the person has blind-ers on. Without feedback, a person is always left wondering what the other person is thinking.

5. Influencing Others

Interpersonally skilled people have the ability to motivate others to action. They are also people others come to for advice. Moreover, they are able to connect with others, unearth their needs, reduce their resistance to new ideas, and persuade effectively.

6. Resolving Conflict

Interpersonally skilled people are exceptional conflict resolvers. They get the sub-ject right out on the table. They figure out what's bothering the other person. They are especially adept at negotiating differences and working out creative solutions to problems.

7. Being a Team Player

Interpersonally skilled people are team players. They work more to advance the group's goals, rather than their own. They also know how to complement the styles of others, coordinate the efforts of team members without bossing them around, and build consensus.

8. Shifting Gears When Relationships Are Stuck

Finally, interpersonally skilled people are flexible and resilient. While they have an inner core and a predominant style of dealing with people, they also understand that there are different strokes for different folks. They realize that one of the ways you can get a stuck relationship to change is to change the way you behave in it. They know how to get out of old patterns and unfreeze situations that have previously been frozen shut.

Developing Interpersonal Skills Is Challenging

While some people believe that the ability to relate well to others is something you have or don't have, interpersonal skill can be increased beyond anyone's present ability level. That's the good news. However, expect a rocky road! That's because adults don't change very easily.

Consider these factors:

*   The comfort zones of adults are very well-established. If you don't believe this, do this simple experiment:

    Fold your arms without thinking. Now, fold them the opposite way so that you switch which arm is on top. Feel awkward? You bet. Well, stay that way for a minute. Now, cross your legs without thinking about it. Yep, the upper part of your body is still uncomfortable, but your lower part is nice and comfortable. Now . . . cross your legs the opposite way. All of you is now out of your comfort zone. So go right back to the way you fold your arms and cross your legs. Feel better now? Yep, that's the real you. Comfortable, but doing something the same way all the time!

    Well, for better or worse, adults have gotten used not only to the ways they fold their arms or cross their legs, but also to the ways they relate to other people. And it would be uncomfortable to change their ways.
*   By the time adults are grown up, they have tried a lot of times to change some things in their lives and haven't succeeded. Compared to children, they've stopped dreaming and become deeply pessimistic about their ability to change. After all, look at how many times they have failed to lose weight, exercise regularly, spend more quality time with loved ones, donate blood, or do a host of other actions they know are important.
*   Perhaps the most stubborn source of resistance comes from the fact that, by now, they have a highly developed interpersonal style. The temperament with which they were born, the environments to which they've been exposed, and the relationships they have formed all contribute to the creation of a preferred way to relate to others. This style is so dominant that it will probably not change for the rest of their lives.

Because someone's style is somewhat set, no one should expect or desire a *complete makeover*. But we can get adults to look in the mirror, take pride in their strengths and take stock in their weaknesses, and look for ways to work with and around them.

The challenge is to get adults to think of becoming interpersonally fit just as they would think of getting physically fit. While their body type, their genetic makeup, and their age place considerable restrictions on what physical prowess they can achieve, they can still become more physically fit than they presently are. The same is true with interpersonal fitness.

The Four Steps to Developing People Interpersonally

As you undertake the task of developing interpersonal skills in your workforce, consider these four steps as you proceed with your plan. Don't pass over any of them.

1. *Get them to "WANT IT."* From the start, people must be honest with themselves and determine whether they want to develop their people skills. The first thing to do is to have participants take stock of their strengths and weaknesses with each of their skills. To assist them with this process, provide them with a short survey that assesses their current ability level in each skill area. Urge them to rely not just on their own perceptions. Push them to find the courage to ask others how they see them as well. Taking a candid look at themselves is a critical step along the road to self-improvement.

In addition, don't expect them to change without a lot of motivation. Provide them with a list of benefits that they might receive if they improve their people skills now. What they need to do is select one or two benefits and use them as their personal inspiration to get out of their comfort zones and do something different. They are also more likely to be motivated if they are aware of when and where they need the skill most. To help them make this connection, provide them with a list of situations in which they might find the skill in question to be particularly relevant in their immediate jobs.

2. *Get them to "LEARN IT."* Interpersonally gifted people do certain things very well. Invite participants to become familiar with the core skills possessed by people who exemplify each of the eight components of interpersonal competence. While they don't need a whole course in each area to make some changes, it is important to acquire a few basics. Of course, some people may already be familiar with this material. If that describes the people you are training, you should still urge them to review it just the same to refresh themselves before taking any action. Better yet, use experiential strategies that help these ideas come alive.

3. *Get them to "TRY IT."* Most people make the mistake of going for broke and then fizzle out when results don't come quickly. With each interpersonal skill,

encourage your employees to conduct an "experiment in change." You want them to try on a small change in behavior "for size" and to see whether they like what happens. Don't kid yourself: they won't persist unless they find that there is something "in it for them." By offering them some "experiments in change" for their consideration, they will able to test their wings and find the initial successes to sustain themselves for further practice.

4. *Get them to "LIVE IT."* One of the reasons that changes don't last is that, after people get pumped up about doing something, they try to make it on sheer inspiration and will power. They may have some initial success, but then quickly relapse. Real change only comes by overcoming obstacles that are in the way in daily life, not by jumping over buildings in leaping bounds. Help your employees to confront *their* difficulties with each interpersonal skill. The skill may be difficult for them for reasons that are different than for someone else. If they face the reasons why the skill is difficult for them, they will have a greater chance for incorporating the skill into their lives.

The Role of Experiential Learning

As I noted in Chapter 1 of this handbook, experiential learning activities play a vital role in any training effort in which attitude and behavior change are sought. No better case in point can be found than in the arena of interpersonal skill development.

With Freda Hansburg, I have developed a comprehensive training program called the *PeopleSmart Workshop* (Silberman & Hansburg, 2006). Created to fit a variety of training contexts, this modular workshop can be used to supplement existing skills training programs as a foundation of an entirely new interpersonal skills development program. Key to the success of this workshop is the use of a wide array of experiential learning methodologies. What follows are examples from each of the eight skill areas previously mentioned.

Understanding People

When frustrated by a person whose behavior they find challenging, people often cope with that frustration by writing off that person as a "difficult person." This labeling process, whether conscious or not, interferes with a proactive attempt to understand the challenging behavior and find an effective response. To help participants experience this tendency, they are asked to read a description of a hypothetical person whose behavior has been "written off" by a co-worker. (The labeling in the description is not mentioned at this point by the facilitator.) Participants are then asked to write their own description of someone whose behavior they find difficult. Invariably, their descriptions are ridden with labels ("he is arrogant, opinionated, and sloppy"). Having witnessed their own tendency to label difficult behavior, participants are paired up and asked to help each other understand rather than label challenging behavior. To help them in the exercise, they are given five guidelines to understand other people.

Expressing Yourself Clearly

In this skill area, five steps are highlighted in order to communicate clearly to another person:

1. Orient the receiver before going into details.
2. Limit the information to key points.
3. Feed information in chunks.
4. Use listener-friendly references.
5. Allow the receiver to talk.

These steps are difficult when a person is a "one-way" rather than a "two-way" communicator. In order to help participants gain awareness of their tendency to be "one-way" communicators and to practice being "two-way communicators," they first participate in a classic exercise. In pairs, participants are seated back-to-back. One of the pair, the "communicator," is given a diagram and asked to "communicate" it to his or her partner, the "receiver," so that he or she is able to draw it accurately. However, the "receiver" is not allowed to ask questions of the "communicator." Key to the "communicator's" success is the ability to use the five steps just highlighted. Especially important is Step 5: *allow the receiver to talk*. Most "communicators" assume that the receiver cannot talk in the exercise and fail to realize that they can ask questions of the receiver (e.g., "Can you describe to me what you just drew?"), even though he or she cannot initiate questions. With the insights gained from this classic exercise, participants are then given the opportunity to practice the five steps in a realistic situation in which the information is complicated (e.g., the features of new operating system).

Asserting Your Needs

In this skill area, participants are urged to use confident phrases to introduce their needs, such as:

- I will not. . . .
- I would prefer that. . . .
- It works best for me if. . . .
- I've decided to. . . .

They are also warned not to become defensive or caught up in power struggles. Needless to say, such recommendations are easier said than done. To help them out, the facilitator invites one of the participants to assist in a role play. The participant is asked to portray a person toward whom he or she has found it difficult in real life to be assertive while the facilitator attempts to be calm, confident, and clear about that participant's needs. Rather than beginning a conventional demonstration, the facilitator immediately asks fellow participants for advice on how to start off on the right foot. After listening to a few proposals, the facilitator then acts on one of those suggestions. The role play proceeds for a few sentences (the original participant is urged to be difficult), and then the facilitator stops the action again and invites suggestions on how he or she can avoid becoming defensive or caught up in a power struggle. Continuing this stop-and-restart pattern, the role play is eventually completed. In effect, the participants are "coaching" the facilitator on assertive behavior. After debriefing the "coached" role play, participants are engaged in further skill practice.

Seeking and Giving Feedback

One of the key skills of highly effective people is their ability to encourage feedback from colleagues who may be reluctant to provide it. Most people are more willing to *receive* feedback than to *volunteer* it to someone else. A clever two-phase exercise that helps to make this point and gives participants a chance to act in new ways involves the use of animal metaphors. In the first phase, participants are paired and asked to select, but not reveal, the animals that most resemble their partners from a list that includes a lion, a bear, a cat, a dog, and a bird, among other choices. After a minute of reflection, participants are polled: *How many of you are eager to tell your partner what animal you selected?* (followed by) *How many are eager to hear what animal your partner selected?* You can expect that far more people will want to hear than tell. So participants realize from this simple exercise that people may often withhold feedback from each other . . . even though they have some feedback that can be shared. In the second phase of the exercise, participants are told that they can now share their animal selections with their partners, but only if the partner successfully convinces him or her that he or she really wants the feedback. (Suggested phrases are given to participants as guidelines.) Thus, participants simulate what it's like to encourage feedback from others rather than merely waiting for it to be given. Finally, participants practice asking for feedback in real-life scenarios.

Influencing Others

Asking questions to better understand another person's viewpoint is an important skill in being able to get someone to change his or her mind. A volunteer is recruited and enlisted to portray a person who is opposed to a course of action, such as becoming a vegetarian. The audience is told that the facilitator is operating under a specific constraint in his or her attempt to change the other person's mind and that their job is to figure out what the constraint is. (The constraint is that the facilitator is not allowed to ask the person any questions.) During the role play, the facilitator does everything he or she can to urge the volunteer to change his or her mind about a course of action, except for asking ANY questions to better understand the concerns, needs, or objections of the party to be persuaded. After the role play, it is evident to the audience what the constraint is. After debriefing, the participants realize that the influencer is always in a better position to change someone's mind if he or she stops preaching and starts asking questions. At the end of the design, participants are given the following challenge: *With a partner who resists your advice, ask a series of questions. See how long you can go without inserting your own point of view.*

Resolving Conflict

In conflict situations, people often overlook the possibility of win-win solutions. A well-known exercise, The Case of the Ugli Oranges, jolts participants' awareness on this point. One volunteer is assigned the role of Dr. Roland and another the role of Dr. Jones. Each party is given a fact sheet about his or her role. (The audience is given both fact sheets.) It turns out that both Dr. Roland and Dr. Jones need to possess the world's only supply of three thousand ugli oranges in order to cope with a biological crisis each is responsible for averting. It will do them no good to split the oranges. Each party requires all the available oranges to accomplish his mission. They are asked to negotiate with each other, a task that seems absurd given that it appears that one must "win" and other must "lose." Each party typically overlooks that fact that they can share the three thousand oranges because Dr. Roland only needs the orange rinds and Dr. Jones only needs the juice from the oranges. Usually, the role players get bogged down in arguing the righteousness of their causes and fail to inquire what each needs from the oranges. The audience is spellbound by the needless conflict that takes place. The real challenge, however, lies ahead for them as the entire group is engaged in a negotiation in which the win-win solution is not as obvious.

Being a Team Player

During the time a team works together to solve any problem, its success depends on the degree to which members see themselves as part of a "dialogue" rather than a "debate." The purpose of dialogue is to enlarge ideas, not diminish them. This occurs when people listen to each other, react to and build on each other's ideas, acknowledge real differences, and look for common ground. There are numerous team exercises that can help to drive home this point. Our choice is to use the classic exercise Winter Survival. A plane has crash-landed in the woods of northern Minnesota in the middle of January. In these brutally cold conditions, a survival plan must be figured out. The simulation poses great questions: Do we remain where we are or do we attempt to travel to the nearest known habitation? How do we stay warm? How can we build a fire? What creative uses can we find for the resources at our disposal? The scenario tempts participants into persuading each other ("I know we can use the whiskey to build a fire!"), rather than exploring, assessing the available options, and seeking as much information from each other as possible. In the design, the participants first read about the nature and benefits of "dialogue" and then work out their survival plan. Before learning whether the plan will work or not, they are asked to evaluate how well they "dialogued" with each other. If they did, chances are they survived. If not, they "died" rather than "dialogued."

Shifting Gears

Shifting gears is all about not getting stuck in one place. Think of a car in deep snow where the driver keeps gunning the accelerator, spinning the wheels, rather than rocking the car by shifting from forward to reverse. A simple exercise that drives home this point is one similar to the classic nine-dot problem (where the solution is to "think outside the box"). Participants are each given six toothpicks (of equal length) and told to create four equilateral triangles with them. Participants become bogged down because they attempt the solution with the toothpicks flat on a surface. The only way to achieve the solution is to make a three-dimensional structure (the base triangle is flat, but the other three are upright). Once the point is made, the trick is to transfer the principles of shifting gears into the interpersonal arena. This is accomplished with an improv exercise in which participants brainstorm and dramatize a number of ways to change direction in a case situation in which a person keeps repeating the same behavior in a work relationship, even though it goes nowhere.

Maximizing the Impact of Experiential Activities in Interpersonal Skill Training

Even though there are numerous classic activities and newer ones appearing all the time, just conducting each one and hoping it will have a lasting impact is naïve. From my years designing and facilitating interpersonal skills training, I have taken away many valuable lessons:

- The most important thing to keep in mind is what you want each activity to accomplish. The strategy is secondary to the objective. Take, for example, a training on the roles people play in teams. Is the goal to help participants become aware of the roles they currently play? Is the goal to help them decide what changes they want to make? Is the goal to be skilled at performing different roles? Or is it to understand why teams need members to perform different roles? I could go on and on. Needless to say, you're not limited to one objective. At the same time, you can overwhelm your design with too many. The critical process is to think carefully about what may happen as a result of a given activity. Is that what you want to achieve? If not, the best activity in the world is worthless if it doesn't get the results you are seeking.
- The activity must be suited to the size of the group and the time available. Some activities don't work well with large groups, while other activities require a critical mass. In my experience, for example, conducting the *PeopleSmart Workshop*, role-playing practice in pairs is very hard to monitor when a group has more than sixteen participants. Some activities take a long time, and the group is too tired to debrief afterward. This often happens with complex games and simulations.
- Always keep in mind who the participants are. Some have been through similar interpersonal awareness and skill activities in previous training and complain, "I've already done this." Some activities may be premature for a less-experienced group. Others may not be sufficiently challenging. (*Note:* I would not avoid rich experiential activities simply because the participants are cerebral, "techie," or some other similar characteristic.)
- Buy-in is all-important. Give participants a reason for an activity before starting. (That's not necessarily the same as revealing the main point of the activity.) Explain how the activity connects to substantive issues and events in their professional lives. If the activity makes a point by analogy, make sure the analogy is solid. Sell the benefits of the activity. Express confidence in the activity.
- Virtually all experiential activities in the arena of interpersonal skill development involve the need for clear directions. What exactly are participants to do? With whom? Where? When? Sometimes, it is important for participants to have

a mental picture of what they are to do. Provide a brief sample of what the activity looks like. Use yourself and/or a few participants to illustrate the directions. If the directions are complex, don't give them all at once. Set up the activity (e.g., grouping participants) before launching into directions.

- Keep participants involved in the experience. Don't de-energize the activity by speaking very slowly, endlessly recording participants' contributions on flip charts, or letting a debriefing drag on too long. Challenge the participants by making sure the activity has a moderate level of tension. Show interest in the participants as they engage in the activity. Don't stand off or busy yourself with other things.

- When an activity is over, the learning begins. Debriefing is critical to any experiential activity concerning interpersonal skills training. A model I use for debriefing is called: *What? So What? Now What?*

  - *What?* Take participants through an experience that is appropriate to the skill area on which you are focusing. These experiences might involve a game or simulation exercise, an outdoor event, a role play, a story, an action learning task, or a host of other methodologies.

    Ask participants to share what happened to them during the experience: What did they do? What did they observe? Think about? What feelings did they have during the experience?

  - *So What?* Next, ask participants to ask themselves so what? What benefits did they get from the experience? What did they learn? Relearn? What are the implications of the activity? How does the experience (if it is a simulation or role play) relate to the real world?

  - *Now What?* Finally, ask participants to consider now what? How do you want to do things differently in the future? How can you extend the learning you had? What steps can you take to apply what you learned?

Applying Interpersonal Skills Training Back on the Job

The bottom line for all interpersonal skills training is whether it is applied back on the job. Many training efforts never get off the ground because they are not integrated into the workplace. What truly separates effective from ineffective training is the explicit attention given to back-on-the-job application. Without it, the benefits of even the best interpersonal skills training are not realized.

Happily, there are many ways to design your interpersonal skills training so that the training sticks and back-on-the-job application occurs. My suggestions will cover three time periods: *before the training event begins, while it is in progress, and after it concludes.*

Prior to the Training Program

Perhaps the single best insurance policy you might obtain to ensure that participants will transfer what they have learned from classroom to job is to pre-train their supervisors. When they receive such training, supervisors are able to serve not merely as managers but also as mentors, coaches, role models, and encouragers. When training sessions are followed up with on-the-job support, up to a 300 percent return is realized on every dollar invested. Conversely, little retention of skills occurs after training if management fails to reinforce it.

Of course, such an insurance policy is initially expensive, time-consuming, and hard to come by. If you cannot pre-train supervisors, you will frequently have the chance to brief them about the training their employees are receiving. In such briefings, it is important for you to discuss the following:

- The objectives of the training program
- The course outline
- The kinds of training activities utilized in the program
- Course materials
- Suggestions for facilitating further practice and application of skills

This approach will work well if you have built your interpersonal skills training program with organizational objectives in mind. That way, management will trust that trainees will find a connection between their new skills and the organization's goals and priorities.

Another way to make supervisors your allies is to enlist their cooperation with regard to any pre-course preparation you may ask of their employees. Giving the participants time off from their regular responsibilities to read advance materials or complete pre-course assignments is a real contribution. It is even better when supervisors sit down with their employees and help them define a personal case problem or two to bring to the training program. This problem then becomes the basis for real-life problem solving in your instruction.

Prior to the training program, it is also possible to ask participants and their supervisors to select a project to undertake as a result of what the participants learn. When participants come to the training program with a project in mind that has already been discussed with upper management, back-on-the-job application is built into the program design.

During the Training Program

As you teach new skills, you can do certain things to promote retention and on-the-job application. A first tip is to allow enough practice time for skill mastery.

Some trainers have a tendency to move quickly from skill to skill without enough rehearsal. For example, they may give participants the opportunity to role play a win-win negotiation and provide (or have peers provide) feedback on their performance, but neglect to provide a chance for participants to redo the role play based on the feedback received. Some degree of over-learning is required in order for participants to feel confident about exercising a new skill. Skill mastery is like the process of breaking in new shoes. At first, it feels unnatural but, with enough wear, the shoes begin to feel comfortable. Confidence grows even more when participants master exercises of increasing levels of difficulty. Eventually, they feel that they truly own the skill.

Participants are more apt to use skills back on the job if they have been able to practice them realistically. The more similar the training situation is to the back-on-the-job situation, the more likely it is to last. Even re-creating the physical environment of the job can be helpful. For example, call center training is greatly enhanced if recordings of actual customer calls are used and the training takes place in an actual call center.

As participants learn new skills, they should be encouraged to express their attitudes about the skills being taught and their feelings about their performance. Paradoxically, participants are less likely to resist changes if they have the chance to express their reservations and trepidation about them. Some trainers hard-sell the value of the skills, ideas, and procedures they are advocating. It is far better to encourage participants to draw their own conclusions. Ultimately, they are the ones who will decide whether to use what you have taught them.

A final tip can be implemented if you are able to arrange for time back on the job in between training sessions. Give assignments to be completed in the participants' own work settings. When you resume the training, you can ask the participants to share how well the real-life practice went and to pose any questions they may still have about the skills they have been learning.

At the End of the Training Program

Before ending the training program and after it concludes, you can employ several strategies to encourage application back on the job.

1. Ask participants to evaluate what they have learned about themselves, including their knowledge, behavior, and attitudes. Taking stock of oneself is a great motivator of change. A wide variety of techniques can help participants with their self-assessments. Make use of questionnaires, post-tests, and final role-playing performances.

2. Use job aids (both hard copy and electronic) such as checklists and worksheets. These aids provide a structure that helps participants to remember and apply what they have learned in the course. Job aids are most effective when they are explained and tried out first in the course itself.
3. Ask participants to select actions they will try to do more frequently back on the job. Below is a process that is used at the conclusion of the *PeopleSmart Workshop.*

Look over the checklist below and select one action from each category that is the most important for you to take.

To Understand People Better

☐ Ask more questions
☐ Avoid labeling
☐ Look beyond surface behavior
☐ Evaluate how I compare to another person (style, gender, age, culture)

To Express Myself More Clearly

☐ Think before I talk
☐ Provide more/less detail
☐ "Give up the microphone"
☐ Be straightforward and direct

To Assert My Needs Better

☐ Get clearer about what I want
☐ Say no when I must
☐ Speak up and ask for what I need
☐ Remain calm and confident under fire

To Exchange Feedback Better

☐ Invite others to give me feedback
☐ Listen to the feedback others give me
☐ Don't withhold feedback I can give
☐ Offer suggestions instead of criticism

To Become More Influential

☐ Temporarily drop my agenda and connect
☐ Find out more about the opinions of others

☐ Explain the benefits others may obtain
☐ Give people time to mull over my advice

To Resolve Conflicts More Effectively

☐ Bring concerns out into the open sooner
☐ Find out what the other party needs
☐ Seek solutions, not victory
☐ Persevere despite initial negative reactions

To Become a Better Collaborator

☐ Find out what teammates need
☐ Express appreciation
☐ Use the talents of others
☐ Keep others informed about my activity

To Shift Gears When Necessary

☐ Accept when a relationship is in a rut
☐ Look for the patterns we fall into
☐ Take the initiative in shifting gears
☐ Do something different

References

Silberman, M. (2000). *PeopleSmart: Developing your interpersonal intelligence.* San Francisco: Berrett-Koehler.

Silberman, M., & Hansburg, F. (2006). *PeopleSmart workshop.* San Francisco: Pfeiffer.

CHAPTER SEVENTEEN

EXPERIENTIAL LEARNING
IN DIVERSITY TRAINING

Julie O'Mara

Julie O'Mara is president of O'Mara and Associates, an organization development consulting firm specializing in leadership, facilitation, and the managing diversity process. She is co-author of *Managing Workforce 2000: Gaining the Diversity Advantage,* a best-seller published by Jossey-Bass, and author of *Diversity Activities and Training Designs,* a manual of activities, lecturettes, and guidelines for effective diversity training, published by Pfeiffer. In 2001, Prime-Learning developed five e-learning diversity modules based on her work. She is currently writing a book on global diversity best practices. A former national president of the American Society for Training and Development (ASTD), Julie has been a volunteer leader for ASTD since 1977 and currently is a reviewer for the Workplace Learning Awards. Among Julie's professional honors are ASTD's Torch Award for outstanding service; the ASTD Women's Network Professional Leadership Development Award; the 1993 Honored Instructor Award for outstanding service from the University of California Extension, Berkeley; the 1995 Ben Bostic Trainer of the Year Award from ASTD's Multicultural Network; and ASTD's Valuing Differences Award for 1996, presented to the Royal Bank of Canada and Julie O'Mara.

Contact Information

O'Mara and Associates
5979 Greenridge Road
Castro Valley, CA 94552
(510) 582–7744
Julie@omaraassoc.com
www.omaraassoc.com

THINK OF A TIME IN YOUR LIFE when you felt different from other people around you. It could be recent or a long time ago—personal or professional. Recall and relive the situation.

Now think of a word that describes how you felt in that moment of feeling different. Focus on the feeling in the moment, rather than on your reflection or analysis of what you learned from it.

The above two paragraphs are the opening instructions to an experiential learning activity called *When I Felt Different.* It is used frequently in diversity training. The next step is to meet with a partner and, in two minutes, share the story and the word. Then the facilitator asks participants to call out the word and charts all the words that describe the feelings. Typically, words like angry, uncomfortable, alienated, alone, sad, isolated, hurt, and left out are given. Participants soon grasp that they interpreted the word "different" as a negative, even though the instructions gave no such definition of the word. Smiles indicating insight that the connotation of "different" is generally negative come across participants' faces. The debriefing discussion reinforces the point that most people think of being different as negative, even though organizations emphasize how they value differences and welcome different perspectives and viewpoints. In our heads, we believe that being different can be an asset, but our emotions tells us that we don't usually want to be the person who's different and who doesn't fit. This experiential activity achieves a key insight that helps explain the need to address diversity in organizations.

Impacting Individuals, Teams, and Organizations

Today, most U.S. organizations and many around the world have diversity as an organizational value, have business goals related to diversity, a business case for diversity, an entire department or at least one manager with diversity as part of his or her job title, or a series of business-related interventions led by management. Although there are a variety of ways and degrees to which organizations practice diversity—some calling it diversity management, some referring to it as inclusion—most will agree that diversity work must focus on development of the individual, the team, and the organization.

Experiential learning is a critical process for educating and advancing diversity with individuals, teams, and organizational systems. The use of experiential learning may be more important for diversity work than for any other arena addressed by organizations.

For individual development, some degree of empathy, "getting it" or "personal work" is needed to appreciate diversity issues. Empathy is a key skill because it is important to understand that various stakeholders, including employees, suppliers, and customers, have needs and see situations from different viewpoints and perspectives. Marilyn Loden, diversity author and consultant in Tiburon, California, says that employees at all levels may be actively managing various dimensions of diversity. By this she means that they are acutely aware of a dimension of diversity such as race, level in the organization, family status, or sexual orientation, because others may make assumptions about or stereotype them based on that dimension. Thus, they are continuously striving to counter that bias. A first step in appreciating different experiences and viewpoints is to understand how your own experience and viewpoint may be just one of many that can help an organization thrive. Experiential learning can help you "walk two moons in someone's moccasins," as the Native American saying goes.

For team development, experiential learning helps team members learn how others operate in group settings. Although more research on the effective functioning of diverse teams needs to be done, the common belief is that diverse teams are more innovative and better at solving problems than homogeneous teams. Diverse teams, however, sometimes take longer to function well. Thus, there's a need for team building that uses experiential learning to increase the depth of understanding of how each member functions in a group—and what adjustments the group can make so that each member can operate at peak performance. This is an arena in which intercultural learning (see Chapter 20 in this handbook), work on communications and interpersonal style—all diversity dimensions—is especially important.

For organization development, experiential learning can help management appreciate the need for how their biases may have institutionalized hiring practices that unintentionally screen out candidates who may not look like or operate like the current executives. Or how management may be overlooking market segments or making incorrect judgments about how to advertise to potential customers. Or how some policies, benefits, and practices may create an environment that causes some people to leave an organization.

Making Progress on Diversity Goals

The California State Automobile Association (CSAA), the second-largest affiliate of AAA, representing 4.4 million members in Northern California, Nevada, and Utah and headquartered in San Francisco, achieved a 3 percent increase from 2004 to 2005 on the Diversity Index of its annual Employee Engagement Survey. The Diversity Index is a sub-set of questions that measures diversity and inclusion. "Of course, there are many factors that contributed to this significant one-year increase. We believe our use of experiential learning in both our vision and values and our Winning with Diversity courses contributed significantly to this increase. We are committed to asking our employees at all levels to become aware of and own any assumptions they make or biases they have. We do this so they can become aware of these biases and assumptions and strive to make work-related decisions based on fact, not colored by assumptions and bias. We believe experiential learning helps reach that goal," says Patrick Vitale, manager of diversity and inclusion.

One of the experiential learning activities used by CSAA, Safeway, Inc., and other organizations involves watching a film and debriefing it. That process is not always experiential, even though it might be useful learning. What makes the process experiential and effective diversity learning is that participants personally experience something similar to what the film shows. This is an activity Steve Hanamura, principal of Hanamura Consulting headquartered in Beaverton, Oregon, and I co-designed and use frequently. We show the first twenty-five minutes of the film, *Frontline: A Class Divided,* one of the most frequently used films in diversity training in the United States. The film is a documentary of an experiment in prejudice that a third-grade Riceville, Iowa, teacher began shortly after Martin Luther King, Jr., was killed. Known as the blue-eyed, brown-eyed experiment, she treated the blue-eyed students better than the brown-eyed students one day and reversed the treatment the next. In this classic experiential activity, we see the children respond by calling each other names, becoming spiteful, angry, hurting each other, and being hurt. And we see their performance in a testing activity decline on the day they are in the poorly treated group and increase on the day they are in the well-treated group, and then we learn that the overall scores were much higher for all on an ongoing basis after the experiment.

After viewing the film, small groups of participants spend fifteen minutes in discussion guided by three questions. We begin the large group debriefing by asking for their reactions, processing those, and elaborating on various diversity principles and practices. When participants begin to describe how the children were programmed to be prejudiced, Steve moves into a fun segment that has a big "ah ha!" He asks the group to repeat after him and say the word "silk" six times with vigor. The group responds and quickly says "silk" six times. Then as the last "silk" is said, Steve asks: "What do cows drink?" Most participants quickly respond with "milk!" But that's incorrect. Cows drink water. We hear laughter and see smiles on their faces, because they know they were programmed to respond without thinking. Steve then announces that they get to try again. This time the word is "roast." They repeat it six times and then Steve asks: "What do you put in the toaster?" Most participants respond by saying "toast." But the correct answer is "bread." Once again, they were programmed. This segment is followed by definitions, principles, and a discussion on how we are programmed to have biases and prejudices by the media, family, school, communities, and others. Next, I tell a personal example of a bias. Then, reminding participants of our confidentiality ground rule, we ask them to voluntarily identify a bias or prejudice they have and tell partners. We debrief that, but we do not ask participants to share their prejudices or biases in the large group. Participants usually state that they were uncomfortable sharing their biases or prejudices, but felt it worthwhile to "name it and claim it." Owning it is the first step to stopping our unintentionally allowing bias and prejudice to influence decisions.

Safeway Inc., headquartered in Pleasanton, California, and one of the largest food and drug retailers in North America, uses the *Frontline: Class Divided* film and a version of the Silk Six Times activity, as well as several other experiential learning activities, in its diversity training. Safeway has been repeatedly named to *Fortune* magazine's America's fifty best companies for minorities and in 2006 received the prestigious Catalyst Award for Outstanding Initiatives to Advance Women in Business. About the value of experiential learning in its diversity efforts, Kim Farnham, director, human resources planning, says, "Experiential learning breaks down patterns of thinking and biases in a non-threatening way. It provides a self-reference point as we discuss the impact of stereotypes."

Setting Tougher Stretch Goals and Increasing Communication

Wells Fargo Card Services, a business group within Wells Fargo Bank, N.A., credits the use of experiential learning in helping achieve an increase in the communication between its Card Services Leadership Diversity Council and its five site diversity councils and the managers at each site. The results were tougher stretch goals than had been set in prior years.

"We knew we needed to help council members and managers understand diversity issues at a deeper level," explains Brenda Hardy, human resources manager. "Not all council members had personal experience with diversity issues. Most had a grasp of the importance of diversity to the business, but lacked the depth of understanding we felt was needed to make significant contributions to the diversity effort. I believe the use of experiential learning contributed significantly to setting the tougher, stretch goals."

Through the use of pre-session reading, brainstorming personal privileges in small groups, watching a powerful video that demonstrates the historical construction of privilege in this country, council members and managers then applied this knowledge to real workplace case studies and an interactive strategic planning model. These experiential learning exercises helped both managers and council members understand how privilege can undermine critical business goals around recruitment and retention of a diverse workforce. Carol McHuron, president of Prep-Inc., a San Francisco diversity consulting firm, who collaborated with Wells Fargo Card Services to design and then facilitate the training and strategic planning sessions, added, "Council members and managers in all five locations then understood the need for significant diversity goals at a deep and more complex level. The sharing of stories also helped the five site councils bond as a team, increasing their conviction to pursue advocating for these tougher, stretch goals."

Creating Epiphanies and a Critical Mass of Diversity Champions

Sodexho Inc., the leading provider of food and facilities management in North America, with $6 billion in annual revenue and over 120,000 employees, has a multiyear, "Building Block Diversity Learning Strategy," which includes developing its sixteen thousand managers to achieve seven diversity competencies. Experiential learning is embedded throughout all elements of the strategy. Rohini Anand, senior vice president and chief diversity officer, says, "At Sodexho, experiential learning is a cornerstone of our learning strategy. We have seen the benefits of engaging participants' minds and hearts through simulations, dialogues, and role plays. Our experiential diversity workshops have helped us create epiphanies for participants and develop a critical mass of diversity champions at Sodexho."

Building Block Number 3, Heightening Awareness of Self and Others, which includes the Spirit of Diversity one-day course, contains several experiential learning activities. One activity has also been used by other organizations over several decades and in many variations. It is commonly known as "The Staff Meeting" (O'Mara, 1994) and helps participants gain insight on how their assumptions and stereotyping cause them and others to behave in meetings.

The Staff Meeting is often done fishbowl style with five or six volunteer participants sitting in chairs in a circle to simulate a staff meeting. The remaining workshop participants form an outer circle and serve as observers, with some participants designated responsibility to observe specific inner-circle participants. The facilitator designates these roles for persons in the inner circle by giving them a hat or necklace with the role name and a short line telling the other meeting participants how to treat them. The persons wearing the hats or necklaces don't know what roles they've been assigned. Typical roles are expert—ask my opinion; clown—laugh at me; lower-level employee—patronize me; boss—agree with me; new team member—discount my suggestions; your protégé—encourage me.

Each Staff Meeting participant is instructed to participate in the meeting by interacting with the other participants and treating them according to the labels they are wearing without directly disclosing what the labels say. A simple task that all participants would have skill and knowledge to contribute, such as how to reward and recognize employees for doing a good job or planning a company social event, is given by the facilitator. The facilitator then simply tells the participants that, whenever they are ready, they should start the meeting. What often happens is that someone starts by asking the person wearing the "expert" label to share his or her ideas. This starts the conversation flow, with participants interacting with others according to their labels. We find that the "expert" contributes many ideas and often leads the conversation, the "boss" becomes more and more lively and contributes process points and managing ideas, and the "protégé" is also actively engaged and contributing ideas. Soon the "clown," "lower-level employee," and "new team member" stop contributing and begin to withdraw. Of course, there can be a rogue participant who doesn't respond to how the others are treating him or her, but usually this activity goes as planned. There's a lot of laughter as the meeting progresses, especially if the volunteers are outgoing and good sports.

After five or seven minutes, the facilitator stops the meeting and asks the volunteers one by one to guess what their labels say. Most get it correct—or close enough. Then the facilitator hears from the observers, who amplify what has happened. Participants literally see and feel how, when someone is treated a certain way—either "positively" or "negatively"—he or she soon begins to behave as he or she is being treated. This is a critical learning in diversity work. The debriefing of this activity focuses on the pressure and stress that the expert, boss, or protégé may feel and the ramifications of this; that the expert, boss, and protégé may not have the best ideas, but because they are in certain roles we assume they do; how others may withdraw from conversation and thus the organization loses their productivity.

In some organizations, the debriefing also includes a discussion of internalized oppression. This is an important foundational concept in diversity and inclusion work. Often people who are in the minority of any identity group may internalize oppression. This means that they come to believe that the negative messages they receive are true. That changes their behavior—sometimes permanently—and they may become less productive or need to "work twice as hard" to be fully included.

The facilitator then leads a discussion on what can be done to help everyone be alert to the assumptions and stereotypes we make that impact how we treat others. The discussion focuses on behaviors such as listening, suspending judgment, being attentive, how to provide opportunities to others so that they can contribute fully, and how to recognize and, if needed, manage your assumptions and behavior patterns in meetings.

Helping Participants Understand Their Own Prejudices and Biases

In diversity work, experiential learning is key to helping learners understand various "isms," such as racism, sexism, heterosexism, and adultism.

YouthBuild USA (YB) uses an experiential activity to help the staff and youth it serves understand and become committed to countering the effects of adultism—the systematic mistreatment and disrespect of young people by adults. Headquartered in Somerville, Massachusetts, YouthBuild USA is a national nonprofit organization that helps unemployed and undereducated young people ages sixteen to twenty-four work toward their GEDs or high school diplomas while learning job skills by building affordable housing for homeless and low-income people.

Tanya Cruz Teller, formerly YB associate director of the Academy for Transformation and currently senior manager: training and development, Umsobomvu Youth Fund, a YB international project partner in South Africa, says they are committed to using experiential processes in their training because it helps achieve the results they need. One activity addressing adultism begins with the facilitator asking participants to think of a time when they felt disrespected or mistreated just because they were young. They either think to themselves or journal their thoughts answering the questions: What were the main messages of this treatment? How did this make me feel?

Then, in a small group, they post the messages on a chart. Common messages are: "I put you into this world, I can take you out"; "Children are meant to be seen not heard"; "You're stupid and won't amount to nothing"; "You're just like your X, no good"; and "You don't know nothing yet." The facilitator then reads the messages aloud and elicits feelings participants associate with the different messages. Common feelings reported are depression, anger, hopelessness, low self-esteem, desperation, rebelliousness, and inferiority. After participants reflect on these messages for a moment, the facilitator elicits behaviors that result from the feelings. Common behaviors are suicide, substance abuse, withdrawal, promiscuity, stealing, aggression, and eating disorders.

In the debriefing discussion that follows, the facilitator emphasizes that messages bring feelings and that feelings can lead to actions. Next, the facilitator links comments often made about the behaviors of young people with the feelings and messages behind those behaviors: "The kids just don't care"; "They have no respect"; "All they want to do is sex and drugs"; and "They just can't be trusted." As the discussion continues, the facilitator helps participants link their experiences—the messages on the charts—with the feelings and behaviors they listed. The activity ends with explanations of adultism and identifies similarities that can be made to young people today.

This activity, one of many experiential learning processes used by YouthBuild USA, serves as a foundation for staff and the youth it serves to recognize and counter the effects of adultism. "With this learning on adultism, and the recognition that everyone is in the power-less position and grows into the power-full position, we believe staff and students are then able to move quickly to embrace the mission and goals of the organization," Tanya summarizes.

Another example of experiential learning that helps participants understand their own prejudices, biases, and racism and be more effective against racism in their work, communities, and daily life is a public program in Northern California. The UNtraining: Untraining White Liberal Racism (www.untraining.org) has as its mission providing tools and resources to white people who are motivated to investigate their white conditioning. White conditioning is both conscious and unconscious training or socialization we learn through family, community, social institutions, and culture. It includes reactions and behavior based on racist prejudices and assumptions and acting from the position of dominance and privilege as a white person. This process was founded in 1994 by Robert Horton and is facilitated by him and several colleagues. Phases 1 and 2 of the multi-phase process consist of six, five-hour monthly meetings limited to ten participants who commit to being fully present at all sessions.

Nancy Arvold, social worker and MFT with the San Mateo County (California) Mental Health Department and an UNtraining facilitator, describes how helpful the training was when she was involved in a fender-bender car accident. Nancy explains, "I was impatient with the driver of the car in front of me, an Asian woman. She was moving too slowly, so I beeped the horn and then unintentionally hit her bumper. Perhaps sensing racism, she jumped out of the car and started yelling at me for doing it on purpose. I realized that I had been hooked by my white conditioning, being impatient and wanting to get my own way. Because of the UNtraining I was able to be polite to her, stay non-defensive, calm, understand her reaction, and not be rude, like a white person can be in these circumstances. Before the training, I probably would have yelled back or been very defensive. I'm also less reactive and more culturally appropriate with clients and colleagues at work."

One of the experiential processes in the UNtraining is called Tracking Your Racism. It helps participants understand various aspects of white conditioning, particularly the power dynamics around race. White people are usually blind to the racism in subtle situations. Tracking is a practice whereby white people learn to see for themselves how racism is involved in situations people of color would readily call racist. The interaction with other "isms" and how much the experience of race is held in our bodies and emotions is also tracked. The process of tracking involves asking a series of probing questions about a personal experience we suspect may have racist elements. The exercise helps to uncover this conditioning by naming the behaviors, attitudes, and assumptions involved, which are the first steps in being able to address and change them.

Bill Blackburn, a diversity consultant living in Camp Meeker, California, who will soon complete Phase 2, says, "This second phase has been an intense experience. It pushed me to the edge of my tolerance of intensity and conflict and enabled me to see how caught up I was in my white niceness. This experience has enabled me to understand how avoiding conflict and wanting to be liked prevent me from confronting intolerant behavior and being an ally to others. It will encourage me to be bolder in the future. The process was professional, supportive, and non-shaming."

Strengthening Diversity Leadership

Diversity councils, committees, affinity groups, and networks are part of the structure that advances diversity work in many organizations. And while they are "official," sanctioned, supported groups in organizations, members usually participate more on a "volunteer" basis, as the diversity work is typically outside the boundaries of their regular work. Often members are not rewarded or held accountable for their work in diversity, and it is expected that their individual passion for diversity work will motivate them to perform well in these roles. And, indeed, that is frequently the case. However, some organizations train, support, and reward these groups well.

One organization using experiential learning to assist in the development of its seven diversity networks is Amgen, a global biotechnology company headquartered in Thousand Oaks, California. The leadership team of each network is invested in seeing its group succeed and evolving to become business partners in support of the company's mission. Each network has an executive sponsor to help champion its efforts and to provide informal mentoring. Executive sponsors coach and encourage the groups on how to link their goals with Amgen's goals. Recently, Amgen decided to provide even more support by piloting the executive leadership program with the network leaders. Teaming with their executive sponsors, Latino Employee Network leaders are participating in developing core competencies and receiving 360-degree feedback, with added sessions on efficacy for Latino leaders and taking charge of one's career. Nadia Younes, global diversity manager, says that results of this experiential process are already evident. She says, "Managers of some of the network leaders have commented on the increased abilities and competencies that they see being applied to their daily work. The entire sponsorship and leadership development processes use the network issues at hand to help develop leaders. And the other benefit is that executives find that they are learning more about diversity from the network leaders. So it's truly mutual mentoring."

Mentoring Contributes to Diversity Learning

Mentoring, a process through which two or more people exchange knowledge over an extended period of time, is frequently used in many development processes and diversity initiatives. Mentors, who are the more senior members of a mentoring partnership, share their expertise and knowledge with the mentees, who are typically less knowledgeable in terms of career, profession, or role in the organization.

Rita Boags, Ph.D., Leadership Technologies, headquartered in Castro Valley, California, and an expert in mentoring, says, "I believe mentoring is the ultimate form of experiential learning, since the mentoring partners have a broad range of information to share, mostly drawn from their own experiences."

When mentoring partnerships are formalized, they embody a number of distinct benefits that would not have occurred in the more spontaneous or so-called "natural" forms of mentoring. Facilitated matches of a mentor and a mentee can encompass many forms of diversity. The mentoring partners can be composed of differences in gender, race, cultures, country of origin, regions of the country, and one that is frequently overlooked, lines of business within an organization.

When Quest Diagnostics, the leading provider of diagnostic testing, information, and services in the United States, headquartered in Lyndhurst, New Jersey, started a formal mentoring program as a part of its leadership development program, it took advantage of the many levels of diversity available to the company. The mentoring program, GENESIS, included only employees at the supervisory level and above, so some of the mentees were quite senior in terms of years of experience within their disciplines. Like so many professions, this creates a silo effect in terms of competencies—not the broad range and view desired for up-and-coming leaders.

One of the mentoring pairs consisted of a mid-career professional who had considerable experience on the scientific side of the company. She was matched with a vice president who had a broad range of experience, having worked in many different venues within the business. Through their mentoring partnership, the mentee was able to collaborate on a project that rescued over $3 million in business that was in jeopardy. Carol Blacken, director of learning and development, explains, "How did they do that? Through their planning and monthly interactions, they had built a trusting relationship that allowed them to collaborate on a critical project."

Facilitating Life-Changing Moments

While well-designed diversity experiential activities and tools are crucial to achieve the desired results, so is the skill of the facilitator to process real-time session experiences to enhance participant learning and achieve those "life-changing moments." Heather Price, The Diversity Consulting Company (www.diversityconsultingcompany.com), with offices in Australia and New Zealand, provides this example, which she calls The Matumelo Story.

She was conducting a diversity management workshop for twenty-one- to twenty-five-year-old MBA students at the University of Pretoria in South Africa. Of the thirty-one students, thirty were white Afrikaans-speaking men and one was an African woman. Heather was not surprised that the class was predominantly white, even though this was four years after the dismantling of apartheid. Pretoria had been the seat of the nationalist government, the architects of apartheid, and was a conservative environment in which transformation and integration had been decidedly slower than the rest of the country. She decided, in light of this, that she could quite safely make some assumptions about the group. Most of the Afrikaans-speaking white male students were likely to have had very little knowledge about or meaningful interaction with blacks, other than with domestics or laborers who worked for their families at home. They would also be likely to view their one female African classmate as "an Affirmative Action appointment," admitted only because of the color of her skin to meet the requirements of the "new South Africa."

With these assumptions in mind, Heather decided to use The Diversity Game for South Africa in a way that would ensure the students would experience the consequences of their prejudices and stereotypical views toward Africans, if they held them. The Diversity Game, developed by Alan Richter, Ph.D., QED Consulting, New York, and customized by Heather for South Africa, Australia, and New Zealand, is an experiential learning board game designed to sensitize and educate participants about workplace diversity and how best to manage it. Teams compete against each other, winning and losing points as they are challenged to deal with various scenarios addressing issues of age, race, gender, ethnicity, multiculturalism, language, disability, sexual orientation, and so forth. For the MBA class, Heather selected twenty of the one hundred scenarios contained in the South African game. She heavily loaded the scenarios to include those on African culture or black issues in the South African workplace.

When it came to playing the game, instead of dividing the students into four teams with a predetermined composition, she asked them to form into four teams themselves. Hearing that this was a competition to see which team knew the most about diversity in the South African workplace and how best to handle it, these competitive MBA students fought for whom they regarded as "the brainiest and best" in their respective teams and left Matumelo, the female African student, standing alone unselected. Heather then allocated Matumelo to a team and, although it would have spared Matumelo the awkwardness to do so earlier, Heather decided she needed to let the dynamics play themselves out and make sure everyone had noticed that Matumelo was not invited onto any team.

As Heather predicted, the only team that answered these scenarios knowledgeably and won the points each time was the team with Matumelo on it. It did not take long for her team to be way ahead of the pack. When one of the all-white teams drew another scenario on African culture, they called out in distress, "That's not fair! How can we answer another question on African issues? We don't have HER (pointing at Matumelo) on our team!"

Heather then capitalized on the opportunity offered by their behavior. She declared Matumelo's team the winners and asked the other teams to consider how they had begun playing The Diversity Game by treating Matumelo as a liability. She also gave Matumelo the opportunity to address this. Matumelo shared, saying, "This has been the first opportunity I had to show you, my fellow students, that I am good at something and worth having on your team. Whenever we are given group work, you always treat me, as you did today, as a liability." Heather then encouraged Matumelo to say more, and she responded with, "Perhaps today you learned that, although I am African and female and different to you, I have some value to offer. But I would like you all to know that I also know about a lot of things other than African culture and blacks in the South African workplace. Stop and consider that I had to do twice as well as all of you to be selected for this MBA degree, being both a woman and black."

Not only had The Diversity Game taught them a great deal about diversity issues impacting on the South African workplace, but the students had undergone a direct experience illustrating how lack of respect for diversity had considerably hampered their performance. They saw that they had not shown respect for diversity while playing The Diversity Game. It was an experience that challenged the mindset of the MBA students about diversity and was instantaneously internalized.

Years later, Heather bumped into one of the male students and he told her that The Diversity Game experience was a life-changing moment that confronted him and his fellow students with their inability to value difference and allowed them to see the consequences thereof.

A Site Visit

Although not used nearly as often as they could be in diversity work, excursions to museums, such as The Museum of Tolerance in Los Angeles, the United States Holocaust Memorial Museum, or the National Museum of the American Indian in Washington, D.C., can be effective experiential learning, if debriefed well. An example is a visit to Hector Peterson Memorial and Museum to the student protests during apartheid in Soweto, South Africa, that the Umsobomvu Youth Fund (UYF) includes as part of its youth development basic program.

UYF was established by the South African government in January 2001 with the mandate of promoting the job creation and skills development and transfer among young South Africans between the ages of eighteen and thirty-five, 65 percent of whom are unemployed.

Youth development practitioners must know the contributions and sacrifices of youth in the country's emancipation from apartheid, as this sets the context for the current challenges faced by young people. As the youth development sector is newly formalized since the new democracy of 1994, it is important for practitioners to understand the policies, frameworks, and structures that underpin and guide the sector, as well as the theories, models, and practices of youth development. The foundation of UYF's capacity-building initiatives is the Youth Development Basic course, designed by Ntombizandile Tshabalala, lead trainer, and Tanya Cruz Teller, senior manager, training and development.

Instead of asking youth development practitioners to memorize policies or read about frameworks and structures, participants learn and internalize the information by experiencing it first. After a brief opening, participants are taken to the heart of Soweto, a former black township during the apartheid era, where the student protests of June 16, 1976, marked a turning point in the fight against apartheid. For most young South Africans today, the June 16 public holiday is a day off from work or school. One visit to the Hector Peterson Memorial and Museum changes that perspective. This excursion and the debriefing afterward help participants to gain first-hand information on this history and cement young people as the key catalysts for change. It helps personalize the government's youth development policies and frameworks.

Participants are given a few questions to reflect on while they walk around the museum: Where was I (or my parents if I was not alive then) and what was I doing on June 16, 1976? What has been the legacy of June 16, 1976? How do I feel about what I am observing? As this revisiting of the days of oppression and children getting shot and wounded while peacefully protesting against the newly mandated teaching and learning in the Afrikaans language is quite emotional and disturbing, all participants are paired up with process buddies.

After a ninety-minute visit, participants return to the training center and debrief. All participants have a chance to speak. The debriefing covers the history, participants' thoughts and feelings, and new perspectives. The questions used during the site visit are mostly "heart." During the debriefing, there's a shift to the "head" and "hands," with questions like: How does this legacy inform our current definition of youth development? (*Note:* The Head-Heart-Hands Model, by Armida Mendez-Russell, shows that effective diversity work focuses on three areas—the head represents thinking and facts, the heart represents compassion, and the hands represent taking action.)

For participants of all ages, this visit is moving. The older generation is able to relive its commitment and actions toward reaching South Africa's new democracy. The younger generation is able to develop a better understanding of what their predecessors did that now enables them to live a life filled with choices.

The following days continue to build on the "so what" of the site visit and the "so what" of June 16, 1976. Now when the National Youth Development Policy Framework, which mentions June 16, 1976, in the preface, is discussed, it is experientially understood by the participants. When the data on the status of South African youth in 2003 is analysed, the historical effects of apartheid can be linked more concretely to the findings.

One participant, Shamiema McLeod, had this to say about learning the history, frameworks, and structures in an experiential manner: "In my work, the government's National Youth Development Framework is our manual, but we've only engaged with it through the traditional learning means. The visit to the Hector Peterson Memorial and discussions surrounding it are transformative in that they create a foundation for understanding, using our own memories and experiences. Visiting the museum has a way of landing the why and the depth of the framework in a way that reading and studying it hasn't. I feel renewed clarity and confidence in my work and the vision of youth development in my country."

Be Aware of Fine Lines and Limitations

Although most diversity practitioners agree that effective diversity training includes helping learners recognize and own their prejudices and biases so that they can make decisions based as much as possible on facts and clear judgment, a line must be drawn to protect an individual's privacy, minimize stress and embarrassment, and honor confidentiality. When diversity work is done in organizations in which people are employed, it must focus on what the individual needs to know and do to perform his or her current or future job.

While Public Law 105–277 and EEOC Notice N-915.022 don't apply to all types of organizations, they serve to alert diversity practitioners to some areas of caution. While experiential learning is not mentioned directly, I believe we need to be more cautious with experiential learning in diversity than with other methods. Here are some things covered in the Public Law:

- Training must be provided for identified needs for knowledge, skills, and abilities bearing directly on the performance of official duties.
- Training must not contain elements likely to induce high levels of emotional response or psychological stress in some participants.
- Employees must receive prior notification of the content and methods to be used in the training.
- Training must not contain any methods or content associated with religious or quasi-religious belief systems or new age belief systems as defined in EEOC N-915.022, dated September 2, 1988.
- Training must not be offensive to, or designed to change, participants' personal values or lifestyles outside of the workplace.

One of the best ways to be sure planned diversity activities and other interventions do not cross the line on appropriateness is to have an organization's legal department review them before building them into a program. While this requires extra time and could result in some redesign work, I've found legal departments very accommodating and not too restrictive. I've appreciated this review, and it causes me to feel more comfortable using certain activities.

Assure Full Participation

Whether your topic is diversity or not, you will need to assure your activities accommodate people with disabilities. The goal is not only that everyone can achieve the learning objectives, but that he or she can fully participate in all the activities. The accommodation may mean that someone participates in a slightly different way, but he or she can participate without it being awkward, uncomfortable, or embarrassing. The Americans with Disabilities Act and similar legislation in other countries is clear about the need to accommodate. But, more importantly, and especially in diversity work, accommodation is both the right thing to do and it is important for business reasons that everyone be able to achieve performance goals safely.

Because there are a variety of visible and invisible disabilities, the best—perhaps only—process is to ask participants before the session in enough time for you to alter the activity or replace it. During the registration process, ask participants to notify you if they need any accommodation or ask the group manager whether any employees need accommodations.

Once you know someone needs an accommodation, it is best to talk with that person directly, describe your design and activities, and learn his or her abilities and preferences in participating in the activities. Don't assume you know what accommodation to make. For example, some people who are deaf read lips and some don't. Some use interpreters and some don't. Some persons with mobility challenges can easily steer a wheelchair to form small groups or read things posted on the wall, and others will not be able to. Some blind or sight-impaired persons will want to receive workshop materials in advance so they can determine whether any activities will be problematic or so they can translate the materials into Braille and read them prior to the session; others will have a colleague read the materials to them; and others will expect you to have them translated into Braille.

Just like everyone else, people with disabilities have a variety of styles and personalities. Some will be accommodating to your activities and others will expect adjustments; some will be easy to work with and others not so easy.

Creativity may be called for when adjusting activities to meet the needs of various persons with disabilities. Activities that involve posting information on charts as it is brainstormed is challenging for someone who is blind. But it can still be done as a process if someone reads aloud what is on the chart as it is posted and then again as the lists are reviewed, sorted, or whatever the activity. Here's another example. There is a diversity activity called The Line. The way it works is that participants walk forward or backward as various questions pertaining to advantages, privilege, or access are asked. Participants who have had advantages and access step forward, and those who haven't step backward. It is important that all participants make note of the direction people are going and can see the results of who is where at the end. Most people in wheelchairs can do this and won't mind the use of the term "step." But that should be checked out, as you can easily say, "Move fifteen inches forward or backward." The activity is more challenging with someone who is blind or deaf. After talking with a blind participant prior to the activity, we decided that a co-facilitator would walk with him and describe what was happening to others as each statement was called out. I slowed the pace of calling out the statements, and the blind participant felt included.

For someone deaf or hearing impaired, an interpreter may need to walk with her, or the facilitator may put the statements on cards, slides, or a chart and unveil them as well as read them. These are just examples. Usually, you can figure out an accommodation, but as you can see, advance planning and some creativity are required.

There might be a situation in which you do not know someone with a disability is in your session until it starts. In that case, you will need to pause and talk with that person privately about what that person needs to participate fully and problem solve from there. It may not be easy to accommodate, but you will have to do the best you can. Remember that the goal is full participation to achieve the learning objectives without creating discomfort.

Adjust for Cultural, Personality, and Language Differences

Some participants may not be comfortable learning in the language in which you are training because that language is not his or her native or first language. It is, of course, best if you can find this out prior to the session. To accommodate, you can:

- Talk slower, not louder.
- Use more visuals to augment what you say in the session. Thus, participants can both hear and see the information. While this strategy is especially important for non-native speakers, it is also helpful to everyone.
- Definitely use slides, charts, or handouts with activity instructions. Yes, this can be more work in preparation for the facilitator, but it will help most participants more easily understand the instructions.
- Translate materials into a person's native language.
- Show respect by not singling out a non-native speaker, embarrassing anyone, or being obvious in your accommodations.

Conclusion

Experiential learning helps with individual, team, and organizational development. Diversity work may be the most important arena in which to apply experiential learning.

Reference

O'Mara, J. (1994). *Diversity activities and training designs.* San Francisco: Pfeiffer.

CHAPTER EIGHTEEN

EXPERIENTIAL LEARNING
IN LEADERSHIP DEVELOPMENT

Ellen Van Velsor and Joan Gurvis

Ellen Van Velsor is a senior fellow at the Center for Creative Leadership in Greensboro, North Carolina. She also serves as R&D group director of individual leader development. In this capacity, she is responsible for the development of knowledge in the area of leader development and its conversion to programs, products, and services. She has expertise in the use and impact of feedback-intensive programs and 360-degree feedback, gender differences in leader development, how managers learn from experience, and the dynamics of executive derailment. Ellen is an editor of the Center for Creative Leadership's *Handbook of Leadership Development* (1998, 2003), and she is co-author of *Breaking the Glass Ceiling: Can Women Reach the Top of America's Largest Corporations?* (1987, 1991). She has authored numerous book chapters, articles, and reports, including *Gender Differences in the Development of Managers* (CCL, 1990); *Feedback to Managers, Volumes I and II* (CCL, 1992); "Why Executives Derail: A Cross-Cultural Perspective "(*Academy of Management Executive*, 1995); and *Choosing 360* (CCL, 1997). She serves on the editorial board of *Leadership Quarterly* and co-edited a special double issue of the journal focused on leadership and diversity. Before joining the staff at the Center for Creative Leadership, Ellen was a postdoctoral fellow in adult development at Duke University.

Joan Gurvis is the campus director at the Center for Creative Leadership in Colorado Springs, Colorado. In that capacity, she manages the faculty and support functions of the campus in addition to the adjunct faculty. Prior to this, Joan was the group manager of individual leader development. In that role, she had overall responsibility for CCL's flagship public offering, the Leadership Development Program (LDP), as well as The Looking Glass Experience. Her expertise in human resource development and competency-based learning is an asset to the wide variety of clients she works with at CCL. She is a certified feedback specialist, has coached action learning teams, and has co-authored publications on resiliency, adaptability, and balance. Prior to joining the Center, Joan was an assistant vice president of U.S. Trust Company, a wealth-management firm. Joan also has extensive experience in the healthcare field. As founder and principal of Medi-Legal Consulting, she provided legal consultation to North Carolina law firms and developed custom programs for healthcare provider organizations throughout the state. A published author on healthcare, she also worked as a clinician, educator, and administrator. Her CCL Press publications include *Adaptability: Responding Effectively to Change* and *Finding Your Balance*.

Contact Information

Ellen Van Velsor, Ph.D.
Research & Innovation
Center for Creative Leadership
One Leadership Place
Greensboro, NC 27410
(336) 286–4433
vanvelsor@leaders.ccl.org
www.ccl.org

Contact Information

Joan Gurvis
Group Director
Colorado Springs Campus, CCL
850 Leader Way
Colorado Springs, CO 80906
(719) 633–3891
gurvisj@leaders.ccl.org
www.ccl.org

THIS CHAPTER FOCUSES ON Looking Glass, Inc.®, a leadership development simulation originally developed at the Center for Creative Leadership (CCL) more than twenty years ago. This robust, person-centered, interactive simulation is a good example of the kind of exercise that can create powerful experiential learning for leaders. We will describe the key features of the simulation itself and will discuss characteristics of the accompanying debriefings—facilitated sessions that serve to turn the action experience of the simulation into real and powerful learning for participants (Van Velsor, Ruderman, & Phillips, 1989). We will also describe the complementary features of the program in which this simulation is often embedded at CCL, because the modules leaders experience in that program surround provide additional vital assessment, challenge, and support that heighten the impact of the experiential learning from the simulation and debriefing processes.

Learning from Experience

We know from our research that leaders believe the majority of their most significant development experiences occur not from formal developmental experiences such as classroom training, but from challenging on-the-job assignments, relationships with other people, and hardships, both work-related and personal (Douglas, 2002; McCall, Lombardo, & Morrison, 1988; Morrison, White, & Van Velsor, 1991; Van Velsor & Hughes, 1990). This preference should not be surprising. Although leaders tend to be action-oriented individuals who learn best from direct experience, much of the classroom training in which leaders participate is not experientially based.

While classroom learning experiences don't top leaders' lists of key developmental events, well-designed experiential learning exercises can provide what most leaders lack on the job—a structured environment in which the challenge of action is supported by the opportunity for facilitated reflection and intensive, constructive feedback on both strengths and areas for development (Guthrie & King, 2003). It is our experience that, whenever people are provided with opportunities to be interviewed or otherwise prompted to reflect on their experiences, they often find the exercise to be a helpful one. Until leaders are asked to reflect on their "key events," they often have not fully realized what they learned from those experiences or how much they had benefited from that learning. While leaders in any organization certainly face a good deal of challenge, and often encounter situations in which they need to stretch and change their perspectives or develop new skills, seldom do they have or take the opportunity to reflect on those experiences to fully understand and appreciate what they have learned. And even when people do take the time to reflect, learning from one's experience is hard.

Learning is difficult because, at all levels of management, good, balanced feedback is often lacking in organizational environments. As leaders move higher in organizations, relationships may become broader and more superficial, information is more filtered, and the amount of feedback decreases, requiring that leaders develop new skill sets. Asking for feedback becomes a critical competency. Yet, in this hectic and chaotic world, everything else can seem more urgent than seeking out feedback or taking the time to reflect on one's experience. Even when given the assignment to step back and reflect in a structured classroom exercise, leaders frequently have difficulty untethering themselves from the pull of technology (that is, stepping away from cell phones or email devices) long enough to take advantage of the learning opportunity. We have found that encouraging program participants to "slow down in order to speed up" is a helpful way to avoid the tendency to engage in the learning experience with partial attention.

Another reason learning from experience is hard is that past successes can get in the way, creating a sense of inertia. Being rewarded for a certain pattern of behavior often makes it difficult to recognize when new behaviors or attitudes are necessary. Learning signals risk and often triggers anxiety, as people don't want to move from feeling more competent to feeling less competent in how they go about managing their work or the work of others.

Personal orientations and preferences frequently get in the way as well. We all have certain set ways of going about things, some of which are rooted in personality-based orientations, cultural preferences, or habit. Doing things differently feels like going against one's grain, an uncomfortable experience for most. While in the midst of a hardship or an intense learning experience, performance actually dips, frequently producing anxiety and a desire to revert to comfortable behavior and old habits. Finally, support for learning and change is often missing or inadequate in work environments, raising the risk/anxiety factor even further (Van Velsor, Moxley, & Bunker, 2003).

Despite these difficulties, and perhaps because of them, simulations can be a particularly powerful tool for leadership development. Well-designed simulations can capture the circumstances that evoke and elicit managerial action and—if realistic enough and accompanied by debriefing sessions rich in assessment, challenge, and support—can provide a credible basis for powerful feedback, reflection, and learning (McCall & Lombardo, 1978; Van Velsor & McCauley, 2003).

The Looking Glass Simulation

The context for the Looking Glass Inc.® (LGI) simulation is a glass manufacturing company with over 4,500 employees, three major divisions, and locations in the United States, Europe, and Asia, recording $590 million in sales. The glass industry was chosen for the simulation case because its products are relevant and identifiable to everyone and are not overly complex or technical. Very rarely will participants attend LGI with glass industry experience and, if they do, we find that they experience the case as challenging and relevant. Those who do not have glass industry experience draw many parallels from the case to their own industries.

The simulation was developed through field research that focused on the actual problems faced on the job by managers in three large glass companies. The case contains seventy-two major problems, comprised of one hundred sixty-seven issues on which action can be taken. In-basket materials in the form of company memos were developed for each position, based on the actual in-baskets of managers at the research sites. In the three divisions, there are twenty-four positions that span four organizational levels (president, vice president, director, and plant manager). The design of the case is such that the organization's three divisions function in different business conditions and face unique external environments, ranging from the large, traditional, stable "cash cow" Commercial Glass Division (CGD) to the volatile, somewhat entrepreneurial Advanced Products Division (APD). The third division, Industrial Glass Division (IGD), is a mix of volatility and stable product lines and illustrates the challenges of production processes colliding with unstable market conditions.

Looking Glass, Inc.® is a behaviorally based, organizational simulation, not a role play. It is a form of assessment for development and not a traditional assessment center in-basket type exercise. It is important to differentiate between a behavioral simulation like Looking Glass, a role play, and a traditional assessment center exercise in order to call out the features that make this type of simulation developmentally powerful. A key differentiating feature is the debriefing methodology that must accompany the simulation. Much will be said about this later in the chapter.

Another important factor that distinguishes this type of simulation is how compelling and realistic it is. This simulation draws participants quickly and much more powerfully into their roles and into the larger organizational setting than does the average experiential exercise. Unlike a role play, actions in the simulation are not scripted. Participants are instructed to bring their "whole selves" into their positions and behave as they normally would "back home." The feedback managers receive is enriched because it is focused on behavior that is most likely experienced by others in their own work settings.

Different from assessment center simulations and very much like real life, there is not one set of right answers in the Looking Glass simulation. Instead, the case is constructed to help leaders re-experience and more deeply understand both the choices and tradeoffs of managerial decisions and the impact of those decisions on others. While it would be easy to position the simulation as a competition among the three divisions, that is not the design. Instead, the learning experience focuses on individual, group, and organizational performance. However, a natural competition does occur internally for resources and commitment to new products. Individual leadership style emerges in the simulation, and participants get to see the impact of their own ways of operating on those around them.

In writing the Looking Glass in-basket materials, several devices were used to make the simulation more closely replicate reality. According to McCall and Lombardo (1978), these included:

- Hiding the critical issues among the irrelevant ones
- Throwing in minor annoyances among more significant issues
- Making memos pithy and fun to read
- Keeping the in-basket materials relatively simple—relying on the complexity of human interaction and the uncertainty associated with many of the problems as the source of difficulty
- Spreading information around within the organization and outside of it
- Creating a financial system that reflects the problems embedded in the organization, rather than designing one that creates its own problems

There are no restrictions placed on participant behavior, with the exception of the emphasis on the fact that this is a "key day" in the life of Looking Glass Inc.® because it is the day that all the plant managers and executives have been brought together for their bimonthly meeting at corporate headquarters. The instructions given to participants are to run the company for the day in any way they choose. Short of *not* running the company that day, they are free to structure their meetings, conversations, communications, and decisions however they see fit. They are told to make decisions, take action, and imagine as if they "really are the plant manager" or whatever position they hold. There are no tricks in the simulation and only one forced decision involving an offer to sell off a plant. If a decision has not been made by a certain time, the "president" is prompted for his or her decision by the staff and forced to respond to the offer. Throughout the day, participants are able to take breaks at their discretion and schedule a working lunch. The simulation culminates in an all-hands meeting. Facilitators are present during the simulation but are essentially invisible, as they do not engage the participants or respond to requests for help or coaching.

Because participants lose themselves in the simulation, and tend to act naturally, it produces a representative and reasonably accurate sample of how they normally perform (Drath & Kaplan, 1984). They tend to take seriously the impact of their actions in running the company. While it is relatively easy to dismiss mistakes in choosing survival items in a moon crash, it is quite another matter for managers to deny the significance of permitting a major plant to close down unnecessarily. Assessment and debriefing are primarily centered around how managers go about interacting with each other to get the work done and the impact of their behaviors and decisions on effective performance—as individuals and as a group.

The simulation itself is six hours long and is person-centered. That is, it is neither computer-based nor computer-driven. Laptops are used sparingly in the simulation to provide the participants with a simple search engine to gather additional information about the case and PDAs are used to collect self-report quantitative data at the completion of the simulation. It uses a telephone system and a written communications system (i.e., paper memo forms) to aid participants' interactions, but these are optional and not required.

The use of a paper system was intentional during the design phase of the simulation because designers found that "real time" delivery of information by telephone created a "trainer-driven" sense of urgency that compromised the abilities of individuals to work together on problems they had decided were important. In more recent years, the addition of computers for email communication has been discussed, but always discarded.

A main desired outcome of the simulation is feedback, based on behavioral actions observed during the exercise. If participants spend much of their time on email, the assumption is that face-to-face interaction would be significantly limited and email interactions would be substantially less valuable for the feedback on which the follow-up debriefing sessions are based (more about this later). However, the real need for written forms of communication is minimal, as participants sit in close enough proximity to one another during the simulation that face-to-face interaction is always a viable, and preferred, mode. It is interesting to observe some participants sitting together at the same table inches apart and communicating by phone and not talking directly to each other, simply because the phone is available to them. In setting up the physical space for the simulation, status differences between positions are emphasized by office differences for more senior roles.

The simulation has been updated every few years. While the problems have shifted to keep pace with the current business context, the underlying principles used to create the original case remain unchanged.

From Experience to Development: The Simulation Debriefing

As a simulation, Looking Glass Inc.® is a stimulus for behavior rather than a development experience in and of itself. It is the vessel in which actions are taken or not taken, commitment to align around a direction is achieved or not achieved, and leadership is enacted or not enacted many times over during the course of a day. The action-reflection framework on which most experiential learning is based clearly underlies our use of this simulation. Looking Glass creates a controlled setting in which leaders can both *have* challenging experiences and *examine* them. The simulation itself provides the context for action. A set of three structured debriefings that follows provide an intense period of challenging and supportive feedback, as well as a context for deep reflection on both group process and individual effectiveness. The debriefings are linked to the simulation in that they provide an opportunity to review and examine leadership actions within the organizational context.

The purpose of debriefing is to create shared understanding and to make meaning, individually and collectively, of what happened in the simulation experience. Debriefings are a way of reconstructing the events of the day, providing an overview of what has usually seemed quite chaotic and often fragmented, and bringing out much of what was experienced privately or unexpressed. The impressions and feelings about events and people that remained hidden have great potential for learning when surfaced and discussed during these group sessions. Intense bonding occurs as a result of the debriefing process, which is structured in three small groups throughout the week. In fact, participants spend more time with their small groups than as a large collective. As shared understanding is achieved, the full complexity of the day's events is revealed and the task is to discover the causes and consequences of people's actions (Drath & Kaplan, 1984).

The simulation becomes the basis for the entire debriefing process. Following the experience of running Looking Glass for a day are three subsequent debriefings. Prior to the simulation, participants spend time discussing their learning goals and areas for feedback and describing their "back home" organizational context. This information helps the staff focus their observations during the simulation and make pertinent connections during the debriefings. Norms are established for the debriefing process. Among the key norms are (1) debriefing is a process of discovery, (2) disagreement is okay, (3) confidentiality, and (4) it is not about "right" or "wrong"; rather it is about the consequences of decisions.

Debriefing 1 immediately follows the simulation and is focused on airing immediate reactions and gaining an initial grasp of the groups' experiences within the three divisions. This discussion is stimulated not only by reactions to the simulation itself but also from the fact that, between the end of the simulation and the start of the first debriefing, participants are asked to complete the Problems and Issues Questionnaire (PIQ), a rather lengthy survey that captures what information each participant knew and what decisions each participant believes were made during the course of the day. The survey is designed as a list of all possible information that could have been uncovered during the day and all decisions that could have been made. For many participants who leave the simulation feeling less than satisfied with their own performance and/or the performance of their units, the exercise of completing this questionnaire can add another level of frustration and feeling of inadequacy. As such, Debriefing 1 serves as a beneficial catharsis. The discussion that ensues during this initial debriefing offers reassurance by showing participants they are not alone in feeling inadequate and can serve to boost morale by bringing out what they did accomplish. It is also an opportunity to surface differing perspectives about how the day was approached and to discuss underlying assumptions people held throughout the simulation.

An example of a methodology to surface differing perspectives is a technique known as a *graffiti wall*. The wall is a powerful way of visually capturing these assumptions. Flip-chart paper is posted on a wall, and participants are asked to think about their experiences in preparing for the simulation, starting with the in-basket review all the way to the PIQ. They are then asked to use a visual image, metaphor, or short phrase to depict their thoughts and feelings at key points in the day. Each participant takes a turn recording his or her images on the graffiti wall and sharing his or her story with the group. Collectively, the group is able to see different perspectives and assumptions and begin to make meaning of their interactions as a group. For instance, because Looking Glass, Inc.® is structured hierarchically, some participants enact strongly hierarchical orientations in their own behavior and do not hold meetings with skip level managers. Others disregard the structure and walk freely into the president's office. Tension in the simulation may emerge about different approaches to power distance, but without context. The wall helps in surfacing and providing context for discussion of those differences.

Debriefings 2 and 3 occur the following day and are the most challenging. Number 2 is an analysis, by division, of its functioning and performance as a team in the context of the larger organization. In this session, participants who have spent the day together in a single division (i.e., Commercial Glass, Industrial Glass, Advanced Products) work together in separate breakout rooms with CCL faculty, who serve as facilitators and have spent their entire time observing that particular division in depth during the simulation. In this session, they focus on how the team functioned as a whole. They differentiate between strategic and tactical decisions they made, explore the differences between their management and leadership behaviors, and receive group-level feedback on group performance measures. Specifically, these include the number of actions taken during the day (as a proportion of all possible actions), as well as influence and effectiveness rankings made by members of each participant's division. Participants also learn whether their decisions were collaborative, individual, strategic, tactical, or solution-expansions (decisions that involved creative or unusual decision making). The team receives feedback on the quality of their decisions compared to a norm group of other runs of LGI. These data serve as a way to unfreeze the group's perspectives and prepares them for individual feedback later in the day, as well as providing a context for rich discussion of leadership effectiveness. The success of the second debriefing is important from a facilitator perspective in readying the participants to receive individual feedback later on. It is important to work with individuals in a way that acknowledges what was realistic and not realistic in the simulation and to make connections to real-life situations. Participants frequently push back on aspects of the simulation that they perceive to be not realistic and can discount important feedback as a result. Facilitators emphasize the importance of learning from mistakes in this debriefing.

Finally, the second debriefing turns to a discussion and analysis of the process by which teams achieved these results and often includes a dissecting of their handling of specific problems during the day or a review of how their personal preferences played out in how they enacted their positions. For example, if the head of the division is extraverted and leads very relationally, and her team has different preferences (such as introversion), communication may be an issue. The team may have gravitated toward one-on-one meetings or communicated primarily via memo, while the leader may have been pushing for emergent face-to-face interactions. This debriefing session typically takes half of the day following the simulation.

The third debriefing focuses in on each individual participant's performance, with the emphasis on behavioral feedback. Each individual's performance is discussed within the context of the divisional team. The "president" has the opportunity to move among the three small groups and receive feedback from the entire company. Feedback is structured according to CCL's feedback model of "Situation, Behavior, Impact" and is given and received in a group setting—a process very different from many intensive feedback experiences and adding unique elements of challenge and support. Each member of the group prepares peer feedback based on his or her recollection of interactions during the simulation. The feedback session lasts approximately four hours and is a very powerful component of the experience. It is in this session that participants learn the impact of their behavior and actions on others.

The experience provides a unique opportunity to receive feedback in a climate of trust and respect. Participants are very candid and open with each other and learn not only about receiving feedback, but about how to construct and deliver quality, objective, and behaviorally oriented feedback. It is a skill that they can apply directly to their own direct reports when they return home. The feedback is recorded so that they can listen to the session later in the program. As they consolidate information they have collected, they set goals or plan to do so back home. The facilitator also participates in the feedback process and integrates his or her behavioral observations of the participant into the feedback process, incorporating specific comments about areas that participants earlier identified that they wanted to improve, such as verbal tone, body language, decision making, or conflict avoidance. Facilitators are trained in behavioral observation and are able to hone in on very specific actions, making powerful learning connections for the participants. At the end of the feedback session, participants are asked to think of something they learned about themselves and about leadership effectiveness. This insight often becomes the basis for the action-oriented goal-setting session that concludes the program.

The Roles of Assessment, Challenge, and Support

The simulation and debriefings exemplify a model of learning and development that underlies much of CCL's leader development work. That is, CCL sees the best leader development activities as having three interrelated components: *assessment, challenge,* and *support* (Van Velsor & McCauley, 2003).

As part of any learning experience, assessment can be formal (e.g., psychological tests, 360-degree instruments) or informal (e.g., asking a peer for feedback, observing others' reactions to one's behavior or ideas). It can come from a variety of sources (e.g., peers, direct reports, superiors, customers, instruments, simulations, surveys). Assessment plays an important role in development because it gives the individual a sense of where he or she is now in terms of current strengths and weaknesses, performance, or effectiveness. Some forms of assessment can also give people insight on how they are perceived by others and the extent to which those perceptions differ from one's own self-assessment. Good assessment can point out gaps between one's current behavior and skills and desired behavior states or skill levels, and as such, it can point to key areas for learning and change (Browning & Van Velsor, 1999).

In our model of leader development, challenge is the element of any experience that forces an individual out of his or her comfort zone. The aspect of any experience that stretches an individual creates disequilibrium and motivation for change by calling for skills he or she does not have or perspectives not yet developed. Common sources of challenge in any experience are novelty, ambiguity, difficult goals, conflict, competing demands, loss, and failure. Challenge provides both the motivation and the opportunity to develop skills.

Support, on the other hand, provides safety and a sense of equilibrium in the midst of development and change. Support can come from people (co-workers, bosses, coaches, mentors, family, program facilitators, fellow program participants), or it can come from systems and processes built into organizations or into development experiences. Support is a crucial factor in maintaining a person's willingness to learn, and, in the best development experiences, is in good overall balance with the challenges to be faced.

Both assessment and challenge are key components of the Looking Glass simulation and the debriefings that follow. Data are generated during both the simulation and the debriefings and provide ample opportunity for assessment. Assessment strategies include the use of facilitators as observers during the simulation, self-report, quantitative data (generated just after the simulation concludes), and performance norms against which participants and divisional groups are compared. Discussion of these data during that debriefing generates even more assessment data from the group on the strengths and weaknesses of participants' collective approach to the challenges they faced. The peer feedback session also provides an element of assessment, enabling participants to get a "fix" on their strengths and opportunities for development—as seen through the eyes of their peers in the learning experiences. Because each division is observed by one trained facilitator, who will later work with that divisional group during all the debriefing sessions that follow, the role of facilitator serves as an additional source of assessment.

The Looking Glass simulation is also full of challenge for participants. The experience of challenge starts with position selection after the group has been together for only a few hours. The group is asked to fill the president's position first via self-nomination. Individuals who self-nominate are then asked to provide the group with a brief statement of "why" they believe they would be the best choice for president. Elections follow. Participants are pre-assigned to one of the three divisions and meet to divide up the remaining division positions among themselves. Facilitators are present during this process and observe group dynamics and individual interactions, but do not intervene in the selection process. Observations from the position selection are often incorporated into individual feedback. Facilitators may set up the position selection process by emphasizing that there are learning opportunities in all positions and that participants may want to consider assuming positions quite dissimilar from the work they do back home. For instance, a sales and marketing manager may want to take on the position of director of research so that he or she can experience the role that the individual normally would have conflict with in the real work setting. In doing so, the participant experiences the challenge of working in unfamiliar territory and is quickly pushed out of his or her comfort zone.

After positions are chosen and the logistics of the simulation are reviewed, inbasket materials are distributed by role. Participants take these with them for the evening and are given the assignment to read over the materials, but are asked not to meet with others in their groups prior to the start of the simulation the next morning. The challenge of reading and trying to piece together an initial set of personal and potential group priorities from the fragmented information in one's given in-basket is a task at which some individuals work for as little as one hour in preparation, while others take as many as three or four hours to feel prepared. The degree to which an individual preps for his or her position often correlates with the ability to manage and digest complex and ambiguous information, which then plays out behaviorally in the simulation. For most participants, this "homework" provides a significant source of challenge. Additionally, the simulation often begins without the president engaging in activities such as setting direction for the day or outlining actions to be accomplished. For many participants, this further adds to the challenge of operating in the midst of significant ambiguity.

There is little in the way of support designed into the simulation itself. As mentioned earlier, the simulation is a stimulus and a tool for producing behavior and collecting observations for feedback. Facilitators' only activity during the simulation itself is to observe the actions of the participants and record notes relevant to the debriefings that will follow. In fulfilling their roles during the course of the day, participants are free to be as supportive of others as they choose or not, as the case may be. The climate participants create in running the company is all up to them. This often becomes a significant point of conversation in the debriefing, with direct connections made to the importance of the element of support in the "real world" of work. The simulation is never run without the accompanying debriefings, which provide a significant source of support, and both the simulation and debriefings are often embedded in a longer program, providing both another source of support and an environment that encourages participants to support each other. The structure of the feedback session also lends an element of support to what initially feels like challenge to the participants. Participants reap the benefit of feedback given in a totally kind and honest way.

It is to the integration of the simulation and debriefings with this larger program surround that we now briefly turn. Support is present as part of the goal-setting activity that occurs on the last day of the program. Participants are asked to develop an actionable goal and identify measures as well as sources of support. The goal is shared in the small group, and a brainstorming process ensues, with each person having an opportunity to hear tips, useful approaches, and strategies from peers. This is a powerful opportunity for participants to expand their thinking about their goals and to partner with someone in the group for support post-program. Additionally, the facilitators are available for short one-on-one coaching sessions with participants prior to the conclusion of the program, serving as a way of addressing specific feedback or concerns. Participants report this aspect of the program as very useful and supportive.

In order to enhance the overall impact of the simulation and the power of the learning experience, we have found that the addition of program modules focused on personality preferences, 360-degree feedback from "back home," and goal setting is beneficial. The beauty of this surround is that it can be customized to meet specific client objectives when run in a custom setting. Organizational dynamics emerge and can be debriefed accordingly. A program surround can provide additional opportunity for assessment as well as a broader framework for integrating support into the challenges of the experiential learning. Pre-program assessments (such as the Myers-Briggs Type Indicator® and Fundamental Interpersonal Orientation—Behavior [FIRO-B], and multi-rater leadership assessments) facilitate the integrated understanding of how personality preferences relate to behavior as rated on the 360-degree instrument and as observed during the simulation. The ratings of participants' actual bosses, peers, and direct reports often provide strong support for observations and feedback provided during simulation debriefings, creating a powerful set of data that are hard to ignore. While it is relatively easy to dismiss feedback from a simulation, no matter how realistic the experience, it is quite a bit more difficult to deny feedback when it comes from both simulated experience and real associates back home.

We also sometimes include a module on managing complex challenges following the simulation and debriefings. This step allows participants the opportunity to try new behaviors based on feedback that they receive in the final debriefing. The experience of being thrust into a situation in which they must revisit the simulation and have an opportunity to lead a change-oriented experience is a powerful opportunity for participants to incorporate their insights into actionable behaviors. We know from our research that one of the factors contributing to executive derailment is difficulty in changing or adapting (Leslie & Van Velsor, 1996). The change activity is often unexpected. Participants learn what it is like to drive change in an organization as well as experience the personal impact of change by being immersed in a disruptive experience and collectively debriefing that experience afterward.

Looking Glass remains a powerful example of a simulation that provides rich experiential learning through repeated and well-integrated opportunities for assessment, challenge, and support. The richness of the case and its bias for action allow participants to fully immerse themselves in a developmental experience that has direct application to the challenges they face in their own work environments. While no two runs of Looking Glass are ever the same, participants typically leave the Center having had a significant and impactful learning experience. The robust design of the simulation has withstood the test of time and continues to serve as a reminder of the power of combining a shared learning experience, an action-oriented methodology, and reflection that is catalyzed by a feedback-rich and well-facilitated debriefing process.

References

Browning, H., & Van Velsor, E. (1999). *Three keys to development: Defining and meeting your leadership challenges.* Greensboro, NC: Center for Creative Leadership.

Douglas, C. (2003). *Key events and lessons for managers in a diverse workforce.* Greensboro, NC: Center for Creative Leadership.

Drath, W., & Kaplan, R. (1984). *The Looking Glass experience: A story of learning through action and reflection.* Greensboro, NC: Center for Creative Leadership.

Guthrie, V., & King, S. (2003). Feedback intensive programs. In C. McCauley & E. Van Velsor (Eds.), *The Center for Creative Leadership handbook of leadership development* (2nd ed.). San Francisco: Jossey-Bass.

Leslie, J., & Van Velsor, E. (1996). *A look at derailment today: North America and Europe.* Greensboro, NC: Center for Creative Leadership.

McCall, M., & Lombardo, M. (1978). *Looking Glass, Inc.®: An organizational simulation.* Greensboro, NC: Center for Creative Leadership.

McCall, M., Lombardo, M., & Morrison, A. (1988). *The lessons of experience: How successful executives develop on the job.* New York: The Free Press.

Morrison, A., White, R., & Van Velsor, E. (1991). *Breaking the glass ceiling: Can women reach the top of America's largest corporations?* Reading, MA: Addison-Wesley.

Van Velsor, E., & Hughes, M. (1990). *Gender differences in the development of managers: How women managers learn from experience.* Greensboro, NC: Center for Creative Leadership, Technical report #145.

Van Velsor, E., & McCauley, C. (2003). Our view of leadership development. In C. McCauley & E. Van Velsor (Eds.), *The Center for Creative Leadership handbook of leadership development* (2nd ed.). San Francisco: Jossey-Bass.

Van Velsor, E., Moxley, R., & Bunker, K. (2003). The leader development process. In C. McCauley & E. Van Velsor (Eds.), *The Center for Creative Leadership handbook of leadership development* (2nd ed.). San Francisco: Jossey-Bass.

Van Velsor, E., Ruderman, M., & Phillips, D. (1989, November). The lessons of Looking Glass: Management simulation and the real world of action. *Leadership and Organization Development Journal, 10*(6), 27–31.

CHAPTER NINETEEN

EXPERIENTIAL LEARNING IN CHANGE MANAGEMENT

James Chisholm and Greg Warman

James Chisholm is the co-founder of ExperiencePoint, a global simulation design and development company with offices in Toronto and San Francisco (www. experiencepoint.com). A pioneer in the design of web-based business simulations, James has authored numerous leadership simulations that have been used by tens of thousands of executives and managers worldwide. Over the past decade, James has worked with senior leaders at hundreds of organizations and business schools, including the United Nations, GlaxoSmithKline, AstraZeneca, Bombardier, and the Carlson Group. James is inspired by the challenge to create, whether a world-class simulation or a world-class organization. From ExperiencePoint's Toronto office, he leads a development team whose work has been recognized for excellence by a variety of organizations, including the Stanford Research Institute, the American Society for Training and Development, and leading technology providers such as Macromedia. James is a member of the Entrepreneurs' Organization, The Toronto Board of Trade, The Association for Business Simulation and Experiential Learning, and The International Simulation and Gaming Association.

Greg Warman is the co-founder of ExperiencePoint. An expert in business games, Greg has led numerous competitive simulation workshops for senior managers at organizations such as CIBC, SAP, Bell Canada, and U.S. Steel. He has also assisted numerous clients with the creation and implementation of highly engaging and effective custom simulations. He is passionate about the intersection of management development and technology, specifically how video games can create superior learning experiences. His opinions on this subject have been featured in *The Globe and Mail,* the *Ottawa Citizen, Canadian Business* and on Toronto's *Citytv.*

Contact Information

ExperiencePoint
47 Colborne Street, Suite 203
Toronto, ON M5E 1P8
(416) 369–9888 x22
james.chisholm@experiencepoint.com

Contact Information

ExperiencePoint
(415) 816–3749
greg.warman@experiencepoint.com

R AY ANDERSON WAS SIXTY when he "got religion."

As founder and chairman of Interface Flooring, Anderson has achieved every entrepreneur's dream—namely building and leading a market-dominant company. Interface focuses on what's under your feet—the company designs, manufacturers, markets, and installs flooring solutions throughout the world. If you've wandered the halls of a school, government building, or corporate tower, chances are you've encountered Interface's products. Today, the scope of the company's operations is enormous. Nine manufacturing facilities on four continents and 110 offices worldwide serve Interface's ever-expanding global client base.

Back in 1995—at the time of Ray's epiphany—this bright future was uncertain. Indeed, the construction market was flagging and competitive forces were intensifying. While these conditions would drive most executives to focus on cost containment, Anderson decided a new goal for the business must supplant all others—environmental sustainability.

"There is not an industrial company on earth," states Anderson in his inspiring book, *Mid-Course Correction,* "that is sustainable, in the sense of meeting its current needs without, in some measure, depriving future generations of the means of meeting their needs. When earth runs out of finite, exhaustible resources and ecosystems collapse, our descendants will be left holding the empty bag."

And so began the single greatest organizational transformation in Interface's history. Anderson intended to imbue every facet of the company's operations with a new sense of responsibility to the environment and society. In his words, Interface would "be the first company that, by its deeds, shows the entire industrial world what sustainability is in all its dimensions: People, process, product, place, and profits—by 2020—and in doing so, become restorative through the power of influence."

Everything would change—not just the products, manufacturing methods, installation, and disposal techniques, but also the structures, systems, and culture required to support Interface in this audacious pursuit. And as is the case in all major enterprise programs, success would hinge on human acceptance, adoption, and ultimately advocacy of these changes. Ray Anderson needed superior *change management capability* to win the full support of the men and women of Interface who would ultimately make his dream a reality.

Change Management: A Competitive Advantage

Change management—the ability to mobilize people to adopt new ways of doing things—has unequivocally become a key organizational capability. The recognition of its importance has driven leading organizations and business schools to integrate change management as part of their core development curricula.

The effects of globalization and the dawn of the information age have profoundly accelerated the pace of change in all aspects of our personal and professional lives. The advent of new technologies, business processes, government regulations, and ever-changing consumer tastes combine to create an environment that requires innovation and dexterity to survive. For companies, this means that an advantage gained in one corner of the world is quickly felt by competitors and consumers in another. Indeed, Ray Anderson foresaw leveraging this pace of change to quickly force new realities on the flooring market, thus improving Interface's competitive footing while simultaneously influencing other organizations to adopt sustainable practices. This ambition would have seemed laughable only twenty-five years ago.

The "global economy" and its effects became real in the 1980s as the North American auto industry was seriously challenged by lower-cost, higher-quality Japanese imports. Forced to change to survive, the industry's response was to benchmark and adopt Japanese manufacturing processes such as just in time, kanban, and kaizen.

This was only the beginning. Process benchmarking spread from intra-industry to inter-industry, with cross-fertilization of ideas taking place across seemingly unrelated businesses. New processes often required supporting technologies, and the advent of automation and communication technologies created a virtuous, or vicious, cycle—depending on your perspective.

Today, organizations that adapt survive. Organizations that innovate thrive. But even innovators need to keep moving in this Darwinian environment. An organizational adaptation that enhances one organization's competitive ability is relatively quickly emulated by nimble competitors.

How Change Efforts Succeed

The stark reality is that, while some changes succeed, most change initiatives fail. In fact, should the stock market ever adopt the conventions of Las Vegas bookies, it should, based on the research, put a given change initiative's odds of success at less than one in four.

In today's business environment, these odds are clearly unacceptable. Good change management skills are no longer a "nice to have," but rather a "need to have." And while the stakes of failure are high, the good news is that change management skills can be learned. Moreover, they are best learned through experience.

So what is the secret? What differentiates success from failure? In short, it's all about people. Leading organizations recognize that it is not enough to change processes and technologies, but it is also critical to change the knowledge, skills, and behaviors of those individuals who will be operating in the new environment. (See Figure 19.1.) This is the crux of change management.

FIGURE 19.1. ALL SYSTEMS MUST BE INVOLVED IN CHANGE EFFORTS

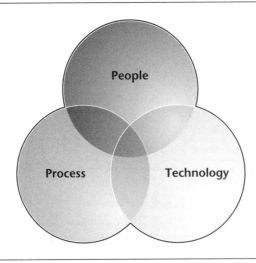

This is something that Ray Anderson knew, too. His pioneering vision for Interface needed to permeate the culture. He needed to win the hearts and minds of his employees. He recognized the challenge and approached it in a disciplined manner to educate, motivate, and support key stakeholders inside and outside of the company.

While the discipline of change management has gained prominence over the last decade, the field's underlying principles are over fifty years old. Kurt Lewin, widely recognized as the father of organizational development, outlined a simple three-stage approach in the 1940s to achieving behavioral change: unfreeze current behaviors, change the behaviors, and then refreeze them in the desired state. (See Figure 19.2.)

Of particular import was his recognition of the challenges of unfreezing current behaviors and beliefs. He suggested a force-field model based on the observation that individuals seek out a current state of emotional balance—a comfort zone. The forces driving or pushing against the current state are counter-balanced by restraining forces. (See Figure 19.3.) At the core of change management practice is Lewin's key insight that, in order to change, it is far more effective to reduce the restraining forces than to increase the driving forces. In short, people don't respond well to a "hard sell," but rather prefer a "soft sell" approach that includes information, incentives, and involvement.

The involvement aspect is why experiential learning is such a powerful tool for managing change. Change is not a purely rational exercise. If all behavioral change required was a presentation of facts, the tobacco industry would be in serious trouble! Change requires, at its core, an emotional transformation. Experiential approaches to teaching change are the most effective way of connecting on both a rational and emotional level.

Building organizational change capability necessitates enhancing the skills of two equally important groups: leaders/managers and employees. For leaders and

FIGURE 19.2. LEWIN'S CHANGE MODEL

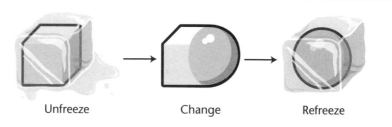

Unfreeze   Change   Refreeze

FIGURE 19.3. LEWIN'S FORCE FIELD MODEL

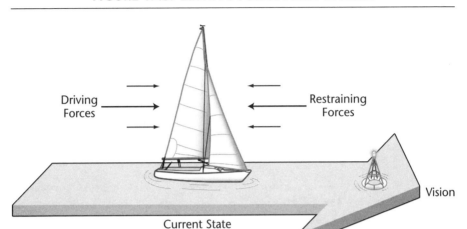

managers setting the direction for the organization, this means adopting best practice models for change planning and implementation. It also means enhancing the interpersonal skills critical to influencing others in tumultuous times. For employees affected by change, this means learning to support specific change and increasing personal resiliency. The following sections explore a variety of powerful experiential learning approaches—at both the leader and employee level.

The Leadership Perspective

Leadership is, by definition, a process whereby an individual or group influences and controls a larger group toward a common goal. Considering that an organization's common goal or direction is in a relentless state of flux, all leadership is change leadership. Developing leaders is about more than building knowledge and skills. It's about developing good judgement. Good leaders are wise leaders. Management guru Peter Drucker, in his book *Management in Turbulent Times*, may have said it best when he surmised that "[good] leaders know the right things to do, [good] managers know how to do things right."

The DIKW (data, information, knowledge, wisdom) framework (see Figure 19.4) suggests that progress from knowledge (doing things right) to wisdom (knowing the right things to do) requires a deeper understanding of the fundamental

FIGURE 19.4. THE DIKW FRAMEWORK

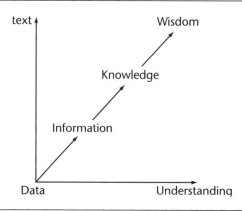

principles informing a decision. Experiential methods such as simulation are particularly powerful means of imparting these core principles.

Good simulations can challenge participants to do the right things at the right time while operating within a realistic high-stress and emotionally charged environment. The following sections describe several experiential exercises designed to develop the two key change leadership dimensions: influencing and controlling and setting a direction.

The ExperienceChange Simulation

ExperienceChange is a web-based change management simulation developed by ExperiencePoint and launched in 2000. It has been used by over twenty thousand leaders and managers at organizations as diverse as the U.S. Navy, the United Nations, U.S. Steel, and Habitat for Humanity. It has also become a mainstay of executive education and MBA programs at numerous leading business schools such as UNC, Rotman, Georgia Tech, Cornell, Carlson, and Kellogg.

ExperienceChange helps leaders and managers learn and adopt a best-practice approach to leading change. It provides participants with a practical framework for planning and implementing their own change initiatives. The underlying principles that inform the simulation are based on research of what works from such change thinkers as Kurt Lewin, Edgar Schein, David Nadler, and John Kotter. The result is the ExperienceChange seven-stage model for change, shown in Figure 19.5.

FIGURE 19.5. THE EXPERIENCECHANGE SEVEN-STAGE MODEL

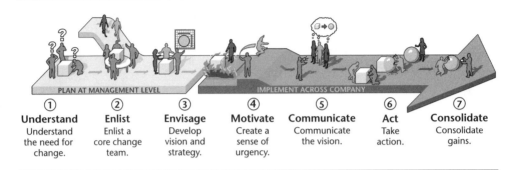

① Understand	② Enlist	③ Envisage	④ Motivate	⑤ Communicate	⑥ Act	⑦ Consolidate
Understand the need for change.	Enlist a core change team.	Develop vision and strategy.	Create a sense of urgency.	Communicate the vision.	Take action.	Consolidate gains.

The ExperienceChange model has two phases: (1) planning for change and (2) implementation. Planning for Change teaches participants to (a) understand the forces driving and restraining the change; (b) enlist key stakeholders to lead and support the change; and (c) develop a vision and strategy with their input. The second phase of the model, Implementation, deals with rolling out the change throughout the organization. Implementation teaches participants to (d) motivate employees by creating dissatisfaction with the status quo; (e) communicate the vision and strategy; (f) take action by changing systems and structures; and (g) consolidate gains by capitalizing on momentum.

The ExperienceChange simulation works because it re-creates many of the dynamics of leading real change, but in a safe, no-risk environment. Typically in a one-day workshop, participants are challenged to apply the seven-stage model to turn around Global Tech—an ailing high-tech company. Participants operate in teams of four to six individuals all working together around one computer to first understand, then plan, and finally implement the change for Global Tech. Teams must work quickly to synthesize a large volume of information, correctly identify the forces driving and restraining the change, and build an effective plan. Each team's objective is to achieve a critical mass of stakeholder support for the change. Stakeholder support is increased by making the right decisions at the right time as advocated by the seven-stage model.

Participants' emotional commitment to the experience is increased through a combination of time pressure, imperfect information, and competition. With regard to the competitive dimension, each team is scored based on the effectiveness (success) and efficiency (use of resources) of their change program. These conditions make the simulation fascinating to watch. Otherwise constructive team behaviors quickly come grinding to a halt as team members struggle with information overload, tight timeframes, and a fear of failure. Only an experiential approach to learning change can test both the process by which a decision is made as well as the core principles that inform this decision.

Unlike most business games, which are traditionally based on economic models of the firm, the evaluative model within ExperienceChange is leadership-oriented. The model rewards making the right decisions at the right time and in a logical sequence. Furthermore, some of these decisions also need to be executed. For example, once participants have decided when it is appropriate to build a change team, they must also decide on the composition of that team.

The underlying leadership engine uses fuzzy logic principles. There are no single right answers or a "golden path" to success. In fact, an astronomically large number of different combinations are possible (over 1.5×10^{56}), and only a small subset of these will yield success. Teams that adhere to the principles of the seven-stage ExperienceChange model will achieve this success.

Participants describe ExperienceChange as an intense, realistic, but very fun experience. At the end of the workshop, participants leave recharged with a new language and approach for managing change. Not only is the seven-stage model firmly engrained in their minds, but they've also gained practical experience using it.

In the ExperienceChange simulation, one tactic that can be used to build motivation for change is "Departmental Q&A Sessions":

> Conduct Q&A sessions in each department to discuss competitive and financial information. These sessions are led by the president and CEO, the change agent, and an appropriate member of the core change team.

To choose this tactic in the simulation, participants click the "Implement" button and the activity is performed. Evaluation is based on whether or not it was timed well and sequenced with appropriate activities, two substantive components of a good leadership decision. Participants, however, are not required to execute. Imagine the real-world implementation of this activity. How would the president handle a challenging question from the audience? What if the change agent is asked directly about workforce reduction rumors? What if a key departmental manager excuses herself from the session, citing workload?

As leaders contemplate the best tactics for influencing during times of change, they will quickly recognize that interpersonal skills are critical to good execution. Whether a manager is communicating the benefits of change for a specific employee audience, delivering bad news, or confronting managers who undercut needed change, the change management soft skills required are those best learned through experience.

Reading, quiet reflection, or standard training presentations are ultimately insufficient methods for enhancing soft skills for the simple reason that the "doing" component is absent. In-the-moment interpersonal interactions are replete with nuance. The combination of cognition and emotion at play in any interpersonal interaction can manifest in surprising ways. For example, communicating is a combination of verbal (content, intonation, cadence, etc.) and non-verbal (posture, stance, arm placement). Therefore, the best way to build such skills is through experiential approaches such as simulation.

To Compute or Not to Compute, That Is the Question!

Computer-based simulations focused on soft skills development are increasingly available. They follow a fairly standard form. The user is positioned across from a character who has just uttered the catalyst to a conversation. The user then has four to five options of things to say back—some strikingly bad, others ostensibly harmless, and still others that are somewhat attractive. The user's response elicits the character's next statement, and so the process continues.

It is important to recognize that these types of exercises have significant limitations. Although they can provide hints as to the "types of things" one could say in these situations, such exercises ultimately fail because they simply cannot allow for the permutations of real-world human-to-human conversation. Worse, computers cannot yet recognize and/or appropriately express the non-verbal component of interpersonal interactions. Currently, at the MIT media lab, research is underway to enable computers to "read" human emotion. By collecting user data like "position in chair" (e.g., leaning back or sitting forward), the "conductivity of skin" (i.e., degree of perspiration), eye movement, and even the pressure with which one squeezes the mouse, the researchers hope to determine the configuration of input representative of different emotions. This may eventually enable powerful interpersonal skill-building exercises, but today no such exercises exist.

Where computer-based simulations *can* be effective in building interpersonal skills is by teaching a process or approach. As a simple example, consider a five-step approach to confronting the manager who excused herself from the "Departmental Q&A Sessions" in our example above:

1. Create interest in having discussion.
2. Determine rationale for opposition to change.
3. Explore possibilities for support through dialogue.
4. Position benefits of change to meet needs.
5. Gain commitment to specific next steps.

Computer-based simulation can certainly bring this process to life and in so doing cement it in a learner's mind. Executing the process effectively though, requires something more.

Role Play: Live Simulation

Unlike the computer simulations described above, role plays are open-ended and the dialogue can accurately reflect the scope and breadth of a real-world interpersonal interaction. Moreover, verbal and non-verbal, cognitive and emotional facets of interpersonal communications are reflected. Unfortunately, many people have an instant bias against role play because they fear potential embarrassment or find it inescapably artificial. The following elements are important to promote successful role-play exercises (see Chapter 11 in this handbook for an in-depth discussion of role playing):

- *Simple scenarios; clear instructions*—Keep the scenarios simple. Scenarios that are overly complex for the time available (too many characters, issues, or background details) can dilute the focus of the exercise as participants expend excessive energy complying with the parameters. Clear instructions will minimize the confusion which can instantly derail the exercise.
- *Relevance*—Create familiar situations for participants. This will not only ensure participants are more comfortable and can lend credibility to their roles, but will also facilitate the transfer of learning to back-on-the-job scenarios.
- *Progressive difficulty*—Ease participants into the exercise by staging the various challenges in the role play. Build confidence early to gain acceptance.
- *Shared, structured evaluation*—Let participants know in advance how they are being evaluated so that they feel set up for success.

Role playing the "Departmental Q&A" tactic described above is a simple way of building change management interpersonal skills.

More detailed role plays, properly facilitated and debriefed, can be exceptionally powerful. Examples include the behavioral simulations of Park Li.

Park Li Behavioral Simulations

Whereas the ExperienceChange simulation tackles the principles of effective change management while operating in a team setting, another category of simulation delves deeply into the behavioral dimension of group interaction. These behavioral simulations are designed to identify how leaders and managers interact with their colleagues and to provide course-correcting coaching as required. One of the leaders in this field is the New York-based company Park Li.

Experiencing a Park Li simulation is like filling a test tube with all of the ingredients required for conflict and then stepping back to see what emerges. Throw into the "test tube" eight to fifteen participants. Add a liberal dose of role-specific information via memos, faxes, and emails to describe individual goals, motivation, and background. Finish it off with an overarching problem that needs to be solved. Shake, and leave to observe for two to five days.

Participants quickly fall into their natural patterns of interaction and behavior as they are challenged by realistic demands on their time. Facilitators, meanwhile, seek to meld into the background and observe how participants manage both themselves and those around them—identifying coaching points throughout.

At the end of the process, participants gain invaluable insight into how they interact, manage, and influence those around them and how they respond to the management of others. The safe and supportive learning environment encourages deep reflection. Participants leave the process with a richer understanding of what they need to do to improve their own ability to influence and motivate, especially in times of change.

Scenario-Planning Exercises

Change requires leaders to chart new destinations for their organizations. An experiential exercise known as scenario planning has become an important tool for many business and military organizations to help anticipate change and map out a direction for the future. This approach was pioneered by military planners in the 19th century and was arguably first adopted in industry by the Shell Group in response to the oil shock of the early 1970s. Scenario planning remains a very popular tool within the military and continues to gain support in the corporate boardroom.

Scenario-planning exercises immerse participants in a game-like environment to help them explore the outcomes of various future hypothetical situations. More open-ended than pure computer simulations, scenario planning is a consensus-building experience that harnesses the collective knowledge of an organization to better understand and prepare for a changing environment.

Before participants are ready to play, a great deal of preparatory work is required to build the scenarios. A variety of research methods, including interviews, are used to gather a wide range of information about key stakeholders, driving forces, trends, and uncertainties. The objective is to describe two to four scenarios of what is possible in the future. Occasionally, these scenarios are then further supported with computerized business models that capture key quantitative factors.

Scenarios are typically played out in a workshop format by a small group of four to twelve key decision makers and/or analysts in the organization.

The scenarios provide a platform for participants to debate the implications of each scenario in a safe "What if?" format. Participants are encouraged to explore possible competitive and consumer reactions to the changing environment described in each scenario. The outcome of the process often yields new strategic insights for immediate implementation or fosters the development of contingency plans in the event that a scenario actually materializes.

The Employee Perspective

For those under leadership's sway in times of change, a different set of knowledge and skills is required for success. Once again, experiential learning proves the most effective and efficient solution. It can facilitate the development of both employee *support*—the willingness to adopt and advocate a specific set of changes—and *resilience*–the willingness and ability to quickly adapt to change in general.

Interface's "Global Village": Building Support for a Specific Change

How can one ensure a corporate audience understands global population and resource distribution and the inevitable consequences of an imbalance? A Power-Point presentation laden with statistics and pie charts seems the natural choice. However, to really help *his* people understand, Ray Anderson recognized the need for something more.

Building the case for Interface's new environmental sustainability strategy required employees to expand their worldview. So Anderson and his national conference team devised a simple but extremely powerful exercise. As eleven hundred employees gathered at an off-site meeting to learn of Interface's new direction, each was given a numbered card. Anderson's representative Bill Browning began explaining the story of "spaceship earth," providing memorable analogies to describe our planet's cosmic insignificance and, paradoxically, local import.

"Each one of you represent five million citizens of spaceship earth," Browning intoned. He then called out a number, asking individuals to stand if it matched their cards. Fifty-nine people stood in the massive room. "You are North America," Browning said. He continued to call out numbers, each new standing group representing a different part of the world. When "Asia" stood, it clearly represented greater than half the audience. The participants began to appreciate the world's population distribution. But that was just the beginning. Using this technique, Browning's audience were soon participating in visual demonstrations of the prevalence of diseases worldwide, the maldistribution of wealth, and non-sustainable population growth.

Because the exercise was experiential, the magnitude of looming international crises was suddenly and excruciatingly palpable. Consequently, the information registered with employees more meaningfully than statistics or charts ever could.

Recall that stages four through six of the ExperienceChange model focus on minimizing employee resistance and building broad support for a specific change. Experiential exercises are unparalleled in their capacity for achieving the objectives of each stage and contributing to successful implementation. Stage four, "Motivate," is dedicated to helping employees understand why the need for change is urgent. Stage five, "Communicate," paints a desirable and clear vision of the future. Stage six, "Act," tackles the very transformation itself, including the development of new employee skills and know-how.

Interface's Global Village addressed the critical stage of "motivation." Anderson's exercise helped build a sense of urgency, and in turn helped build support for Interface's new way of doing business.

Other experiential exercises focus on "Communicate," and still others on "Act." Simulation can in fact address all three stages.

Going to the Circus

In the fall of 2003, ExperiencePoint was approached by a company seeking a highly effective intervention. A significant—and significantly expensive— organizational transformation was afoot. At the time, many of the company's technologies were antiquated, and there was little automated integration between client-facing representatives and back-office functional groups. The result was an unacceptable backlog of customer support inquiries and, not surprisingly, customer satisfaction levels were beginning to suffer. What's more, to maintain even these levels of service, the company required ad hoc solutions: employees worked overtime and temporary contractors were hired to assist.

A new customer relationship management (CRM) strategy was developed to address these and other challenges. A substantive component of this strategy was the integration of leading-edge technologies into the company's operations. When introducing enterprise-wide technologies in the workplace, organizations soon discover that the scope and breadth of change is redoubtable. Reporting relationships and structures, business processes, and specific work tasks are all subject to change. Success clearly depends on employees supporting and competently adopting the new systems and resulting processes.

And what were the potential barriers to success? The company's situation was not dissimilar to the majority of organizations on the cusp of a major change initiative. Some employees believed, a priori, that their role and importance would diminish under the new system. Others felt, based on the history of the organization, that the initiative was the CEO's pet project and would disappear at the end of his tenure (which, also predicated on historical standards, was likely to be exceedingly brief). In sum, there was no strongly felt sense of urgency, despite the highly visible flaws in the existing system.

What's more, the vision of the future of the company, once the CRM strategy was fully implemented, was known only to a select group of executives and project management leaders. Finally, the new system was to confer benefits that could in fact only be realized if employees significantly expanded their skill sets.

The company quickly accepted ExperiencePoint's proposed solution for building support—a customized simulation exercise for all employees and managers.

A custom simulation reflects a company's transformation process. It presents the organization's current state (highlighting the strengths to build on and the challenges to overcome), alludes to an appropriate solution and its associated rollout, and succinctly demonstrates the form and benefits of the future state.

To some extent, these objectives can be accomplished with another experiential technique, the "Conceptual Map." Such visuals communicate metaphorically the rationale for and direction of change and can be highly engaging and compelling. The maps are often used as the focal point of an experiential workshop wherein employees "bring the maps to life" through interpreting and describing what they see. Two of the better-known providers of custom conceptual maps are Root Learning (www.rootlearning.com) and XPLANE (www.xplane.com). Custom simulations build on this method.

Custom simulations communicate the what, how, and when of a specific project in an engaging and memorable way. More importantly, however, they allow participants to *discover for themselves* both the rationale for change and the appropriate direction, thus creating significant buy-in. It is analogous to giving a map to a driver skeptical of directions you've provided and asking him to plot the shortest route to a destination. In other words, participants see, given the same information, constraints, and resources, that they would make the same decisions as management. Motivation to change (stage 4) and commitment to the vision (stage 5) are both generated.

Custom simulations also initiate the performance training that employees and managers require to build future-state skills. The simulation can incorporate the types of decisions, relationships, and tools (or reasonable abstractions of those tools) that will play a role in the future organization. The result is a reduced time-to-competency once the organization's new systems and structures are implemented.

Designing and developing custom simulations is no easy task. For the exercise to be truly meaningful, good decisions are required at each step of the process. The considerations described in Table 19.1 are the most critical in the design process of a simulation called "Big Top: Serving Circus Performers."

TABLE 19.1. GUIDING PRINCIPLES FOR BIG TOP SIMULATION

	Guiding Principles	Client Company Example
Desired Outcomes	Gain consensus early regarding the desired outcomes of the exercise. Determine the knowledge, skills, behaviors, and attitudes required for success.	Employees had to know: • The high-level CRM strategy, the specific technologies to be implemented, and the supporting process changes Employees had to develop: • Proactive service skills; new teaming skills Employees had to feel: • The status quo was unacceptable • The proposed CRM solution would confer benefits to both customers and employees • The solution was realistic and worthy of everyone's support
Constraints	Know the parameters within which the solution must fit. When is the simulation required to roll out? How should it be delivered? (e.g., online single user? in multiple class sessions? team-based? at a single, large-group event?) Who are the subject-matter experts? What is their availability? What facilities and technology are available? What is the budget?	• The simulation had to roll out prior to the introduction of any new systems (six months) • The simulation had to be delivered in small sessions, team-based, to avoid major disruptions to operations • A classroom with non-Internet computers arranged in close proximity was available • A budget of $150K for simulation design, development, and delivery
Audience	Know who the primary stakeholders are. Also determine secondary stakeholders and the extent to which a role exists for them in the simulation.	• Primary stakeholders were those employees tasked with using the new system • Secondary stakeholders were employees asked to support the first group
Messaging	Once the audience is known, determine the key messages they must understand. How will they be affected by the change? What is their role in the change's success? What fears/concerns might they have? What benefits will accrue to them in the future state? What other things do they need to know?	• Employees need to understand timeline for new systems rollout, the specific areas impacted, and how they could support the successful implementation

TABLE 19.1. (*Continued*)

Complexity	Constraints may limit the complexity reflected in the simulation's scenario (story line) and model (decisions, evaluation, and feedback), but ultimately complexity should be driven by the desire to capture the essence of an organization's situation. If an exercise is too complex, the links between participant decisions and outcomes achieved will be lost. Conversely, exercises that are too simple do not provide a meaningful challenge or opportunity for discovery. Striking the right balance is key!	• The company's key metrics for success became the simulation's metrics . . . all decisions would influence (positively or negatively) these measures • The multiple functions of the organization were distilled into five key areas; the types of customer requests were reduced to three most common • The decisions available related to ad-hoc management of the backlog (through increasing overtime or hiring contract workers) or leading the implementation of new technologies
Proximity to reality	Manufacture a fantasy world in the simulation one step away from participants' work realities. Ensure the environment is visually and emotionally engaging. Keep it close enough to reality to ensure the lessons learned are applicable. Keep it distant enough to limit participants' a priori conclusions.	• Participants worked at a company serving circus performers, "Big Top" • While the issues faced were similar to their own, participants encountered fictitious colleagues and customers
Game play process	Consider how participants will interact with and within the simulation. How do you minimize "time-to-first-decision" to gain immediate engagement? How can you ensure ease-of-use? What must be communicated in the simulation's pre-briefing? What lessons must be debriefed and how?	• The simulation was computer-based and required multiple decisions; to facilitate decision making, a legend card was provided • Participants were eased into the decision-making process; for the first round, only simple decisions designed to familiarize participants with the interface were required; successive rounds introduced greater complexity

(*Note:* In addition to ExperiencePoint, other suppliers of custom simulation solutions include Accenture Consulting [www.accenture.com], BTS [www.bts.com], Imparta [www.imparta.com], and Forio [www.forio.com].)

Factors Influencing the Success in Change Management

Resilience

Personal change is both necessary and challenging. The environment is dynamic, so people must be adaptable to succeed. Paradoxically, people need stability to discern patterns in the world that enable surviving and thriving. It can be argued that human abilities to adapt and determine patterns evolved in simpler times, and therefore the majority are perplexed by today's pace of change. Human genetic programming simply has not yet optimized for today's rate of shift. Consequently, at a primal level, people will be slow to move away from the fundamental patterns on which they have come to rely.

Imagine the multiplicative affect of this trait in organizations of hundreds, thousands, or potentially ten's of thousands of employees. The rapid deployment of a new system, structure, or process designed to confer competitive advantage can be significantly frustrated by a welter of natural, unintended resistance. Therefore, it behooves an organization to ensure employees flex their adaptability. By helping employees recognize reactions to change in general, a company takes the first step toward ensuring they make better choices about their actions during change programs. Once again, experiential techniques are extremely effective.

Creating Dissonance

As previously stated, change is more than a rational exercise. People have great difficulty foreseeing the emotional and psychological reactions that are natural when trying something unfamiliar. Methods that can help create dissonance (show that, indeed, there is something to learn) include:

- *Body bends:* Ask participants to fold their hands in their laps or sit and cross their legs. Each will default to a natural or comfortable way of doing this. For example, someone may always place her left thumb over her right and, conversely, her right leg over her left. Ask participants to try the opposite way and ask them to describe their feelings. Invariably, this new way will be possible, but less familiar and therefore less comfortable. This is the emotional reaction to change.
- *Stories that are fun and familiar:* In *Blink,* Malcolm Gladwell describes the immediate and unconscious reaction humans have to the unfamiliar by highlighting the intriguing behind-the-scenes stories from familiar products. He discusses the launch of the Aeron chair and how it nearly suffered death at the hands of focus groups. Its visible mechanics, mesh covering, and overall strange design were so dissimilar from the common understanding of a luxury chair that test customers instantly dismissed the Aeron outright. Nonetheless, the manufacturer, Hermann Miller,

chose to stick with the Aeron and gave the market a chance to adapt. Consequently, the Aeron became the greatest selling chair of all time. Gladwell also provides the examples of "The Mary Tyler Moore Show" and "All in the Family," two very successful sitcoms that again tested badly in focus groups for the simple reason that they were radically different from what an audience had come to know and expect from TV. Such stories affect an audience viscerally and can demonstrate effectively how people emotionally react to change.

Helping Employees Understand and Manage Reactions

Once employees know that emotional reactions are natural, it is important to delineate these reactions and suggest methods for managing or coping.

- *The power of the parable:* Fables have been part of human culture for thousands of years. Parables help explain and diffuse seemingly complex or threatening issues and provide memorable lessons that can be applied to life. The stories become experiential because participants will read through and, typically in a workshop setting, discuss the application of the concepts introduced in the context of their own change challenges. The change management field has benefited greatly from this technique:
  - *Who Moved My Cheese?* by Spencer Johnson. In this story, two human characters and two mice living in a maze must cope with the loss of their cheese.
  - *It Happens* by Julie Smith. This tells the story of two squirrels and their human friends and how a forest fire forces them to face change for the first time.
  - *Our Iceberg Is Melting* by John Kotter and Holger Rathgeber. A penguin colony in Antarctica faces imminent doom unless the entire group agrees to fundamental change.
- *Exercises in reframing:* Often, in times of change, people become narrowly focused on what is being lost versus what can or will be gained. Gains can be of two types: (1) the change may be moving the individual toward something potentially good and/or (2) the change may be moving the individual away from something that was, at least in part, bad. Helping individuals practice reframing thoughts to focus on gains is a useful exercise to build resiliency. One experiential approach is to practice with famous movie lines:
  - *Finding Nemo,* Disney/Pixar (2003): Marlin: "Now what's the one thing we have to remember about the ocean?" Nemo: "It's not safe." Marlin: "That's my boy!"
  - *Apollo 13,* MCA/Universal (1995): Henry Hurt: "Whata we got? The parachute situation, the heat-shield, the angle of trajectory, and the typhoon; there's just so many variables. I'm a little at a loss. . . ." NASA Director: "I know what the problems are Henry. This will be the worst disaster NASA's ever experienced."

Enabling Experimentation

To build comfort and competence with change, an organization should seek opportunities to enable employees to safely experiment with new ways of doing things. At a very basic level, this experimentation can take the form of a personal commitment to practice a new behavior, for example, communicating more positively with co-workers by saying "yes and" instead of the more common "yes but." Employees can engage in simple action learning projects and assess their successful compliance themselves.

More elaborate opportunities for experimentation can also be provided. Back in 1996 when Ray Anderson was determining the first contours to Interface's fledgling environmental sustainability strategy, he learned that the annual employee off-site meeting had been scheduled to occur at a luxurious resort hotel in Hawaii. At first glance it seemed disastrous—a hotel dedicated to catering to the whims of its affluent guests hardly would send a message consistent with Anderson's new vision. But Ray and his management team were creative and turned the event into an opportunity for experimentation. Working with the hotel, Anderson collected figures on energy usage, water consumption, and total waste produced. He then challenged employees at the meeting to work in teams with hotel staff to develop tactics for reducing all three. The ideas generated and implemented ended up saving the hotel over a million dollars a year in operating costs. As importantly, employees experienced (and embraced) the very principles that were to become intrinsic to Interface's operational strategy.

Conclusion

As the year 2020 approaches, the prognosis for Interface is good—very good. On a series of self-imposed measures, the company is fast approaching its goal of having a "negative environmental footprint." In his book, Ray Anderson praises his management team and employees alike for their dedication, creativity, and hard work. The company's culture has irrecoverably changed, with employees finding their identity in Interface's environmentally sustainable operations. Moreover, the company's financial statements tell the business story: Interface is "doing well by doing good."

And yet, had Interface been like most organizations, this new strategy would have died long before it gained traction. At some level in the organization, resistance would have surfaced and thwarted this noble effort. Without its strong change management capability—enhanced through the experiential tactics used in the strategy's implementation—Interface would likely have remained a regular player in an obscure industry. Instead, it is the apotheosis of a modern corporation.

CHAPTER TWENTY

EXPERIENTIAL LEARNING
IN INTERCULTURAL TRAINING

Sandra Fowler and Judith Blohm

Sandra M. Fowler has been an intercultural program manager, consultant, researcher, and trainer for over three decades. Her training experience began in 1973 on the research team for the U.S. Navy that developed BaFa' BaFa', a classic simulation game for cross-cultural training. She was president of the International Society for Intercultural Education, Training, and Research (SI) from 1986 to 1988 and was selected as one of only four people during SI's history to receive the Prima Inter Pares Award. She recently received the Optime Merens de Collegis Award from SIETAR USA. She also served on the board of directors for the North American Simulation and Gaming Association (NASAGA). Sandra has conducted workshops all over the world, including the Summer Institute for Intercultural Communication in Portland, Oregon. Also a writer and editor, her body of work includes the two-volume set: *Intercultural Sourcebook: Cross-Cultural Training Methods.* These books cover all training methods effective for intercultural training. For the past decade, she has served as the art editor for the *American Psychologist,* flagship journal of the American Psychological Association.

Judith M. Blohm has teaching and curriculum development experience at all pre-collegiate levels as a teacher and at professional training institutes in the United States and abroad. Her training and training design experience include all phases of foreign sojourns, multinational staff development, and international development for professional, development, and educational organizations and non-profits and the Peace Corps, State Department, and other government agencies. She has written and edited numerous educational and training materials, including teaching games and simulations, pamphlet series, training manuals, culture-specific study guides, self-study workbooks, and handbooks for various audiences. She has contributed to various published works on cross-cultural training methods, authored *Where in the World Are You Going?*, a workbook for children making international transitions, and co-authored *Kids Like Me: Voices of the Immigrant Experience* for American and immigrant youth. Judith has served on the executive and governing board of SIETAR International and on the board of NASAGA. She has lived and worked for extended periods of time in Africa, South America, and the Caribbean.

Contact Information

Sandra M. Fowler
8276 Caminito Maritimo
La Jolla, CA 92037 USA
(858) 546–1326
sfowler@apa.org

Contact Information

Judith M. Blohm
2311 N. 18th Street
Arlington, VA 22201
(703) 527–0499
judeeblohm@msn.com

THE FIELD OF INTERCULTURAL TRAINING provides fertile ground for experiential methods. After all, the whole idea behind intercultural training is to improve the odds for a successful experience with someone from a culture different from one's own. Increasing the chances for a successful experience implies that participants are alerted to potential misunderstandings because of differences in behaviors, including communication styles. Unless one is already in a multicultural situation, there can be no better way to learn than with experiential activities that replicate important components of such an experience.

This chapter explores the contribution of experiential methods to intercultural training. After we introduce how culture impacts training, a very brief history of intercultural training provides the background in which cross-cultural learning activities have occurred over time. We provide our rationale for using experiential exercises, which focuses on the well-known training outcomes: knowledge, skills, and attitude. We also discuss the difference between training across cultures and between cultures. Additional context in the form of some answers to who, what, when, and where intercultural training happens is followed by some ideas for designing, selecting, and facilitating the experiential methods most often used in intercultural training. We conclude the chapter with a short, select list of resources for readers interested in knowing more about using experiential activities for intercultural training.

All training events can be considered cultural events. The style of trainer, expectations of participant behavior, and activities chosen all carry cultural values. Intercultural trainers are perhaps unique in that they often use the training itself as a way to explore culture. Beginning with participant introductions that start many training sessions, intercultural trainers may step back after everyone has introduced themselves and ask, "In what way were the responses cultural?" Names certainly are culturally based. Ruth Lambach (1996, p. 53) describes an exercise called What's in a Name? that specifically focuses on names to break the ice and establish rapport. No matter how similar or different the participants are, each has had a family who named them, and the name always has a story behind it.

Asking participants to introduce themselves in terms of what they do is also culturally based. Americans are "doing" oriented, so this seems quite natural and necessary. More traditional cultures are "being" oriented, so who one is in terms of family and place would seem much more natural and necessary. In some cultures, such as many of the European cultures, one's titles and educational background would be essential parts of the introductions.

A further step back would address the use of introductions in a training session and what that says about the culture in which it is happening. It may be hard for many Americans to believe, but there are cultures in which participant introductions would seem unnecessary—or even quite inappropriate and intrusive.

This illustrates one element of intercultural training: taking something participants are familiar with and giving it new meaning—a cultural meaning. Typical behaviors or ways of looking at the world can be analyzed and understood as reflecting cultural values. Once participants begin to get the idea that the way things go in their own culture is not necessarily how they will go in a different culture (or with someone from another culture), then they are on their way to intercultural understanding. Their expectations have been sharpened and shaped.

Another element of intercultural training is the practice effect. To learn any behavior requires practice; to learn to do something outside of one's comfort zone requires a great deal of practice. Experiential exercises offer the opportunity to practice. In times of stress, one usually reverts back to the comfortable, familiar way of reacting. Practice can make a difference. Sometimes, an initial meeting can be anxiety-provoking. Going back to introductions, Americans are likely to stick out their hands to shake hands, but in Japan they may be greeted by a bow from the waist. When the Japanese person then goes to shake hands, the American is bowing from the waist (hopefully, in the correct gender manner), and a series of comical behaviors can ensue. Pre-departure preparation and practice can make the bowing greeting more familiar and comfortable and avoid some embarrassment. Going in the other direction, pre-departure training for the Japanese businessperson can help him or her feel comfortable with the handshake as well as understanding how hard to press, how long to hold, and all the other nuances that Americans who grew up shaking hands take for granted.

As another example, for someone from an individualist culture who needs to be able to resolve a conflict with someone from a collectivist culture, it will not come naturally to make saving face for the other person the most important outcome. Learning how to do this effectively in a workshop may lead to a successful business contract. Without this skill, perhaps there will be no contract.

A Very Brief History of Intercultural Learning

The influence of classic experiential methods such as simulation games on intercultural understanding and cross-cultural communication has been profound. According to Pusch (2004): "[Edward T.] Hall noted in 1956 that adequate training materials were lacking, and this continued to be the case until research and experimentation began in the 1960s that produced many of the training techniques commonly used today" (p. 15). A watershed in intercultural training occurred in 1961 with the formation of the U.S. Peace Corps. Bennhold-Samaan (2004, pp. 363–394) traces the evolution of cross-cultural training in the Peace Corps, showing how the university model eventually yielded to an experiential approach to training.

Although cross-cultural training had existed prior to the 1960s, it was most often known as "area studies" and was by and large cognitive training. Several things in addition to the advent of the Peace Corps happened in the 1960s that prompted the move toward experiential training. Research played a big part in the adoption of experiential techniques. A project conducted from 1962 to 1966 by the Human Resources Research Organization (HumRRO) led to the creation of the contrast-American exercise. (For a full description of this method, see the three chapters on the contrast culture method in the *Intercultural Sourcebook* [Fowler & Mumford, 1995, pp. 47–80].) Also in the 1960s, Navy chaplains in Vietnam saw a need and began to conduct some cross-cultural training for in-country Marines. Their work became known in Washington, and further research was funded to expand on what the chaplains were doing. This research led, among other things, to the culture assimilator. (See Fowler & Mumford, 1995, pp. 157–186, for a full explanation of this project and culture assimilators).

Also in the 1960s, the field of education began to take a serious look at the relationship between international students and their American counterparts. After studying how these relationships actually worked, David Hoopes and Stephen Rhinesmith developed a series of intercultural communication workshops (Pusch, 2004). The School for International Training (SIT) was created by the Experiment in International Living (EIL) in 1964 as its academic arm. They developed and used many experiential strategies for intercultural training, and even though many intercultural trainers obtained fugitive copies, it was not until 1977 when the materials were published in the edited volume *Beyond Experience* (Batchelder & Warner, 1977).

In the early 1970s the Navy contracted with R. Garry Shirts to develop a simulation to teach Navy personnel something about specific cultures in which unpleasant incidents had occurred. It was soon decided that learning about specific cultures was not the answer, as naval personnel needed to learn about the nature of culture itself, its impact on human interaction, and how to apply this understanding to behavior. Shirts felt that a simulated cross-cultural experience would motivate participants to learn how to act in any culture and to further realize that what seems irrational, contradictory, and unimportant can be understood in the other culture as rational, consistent, and very important (Shirts, 1995). The result was the development of *BaFa BaFa*. Initially, *BaFa BaFa* was to be used for selection purposes, and research was conducted to establish behaviorally anchored rating scales but, in its wisdom, the Navy recognized a good training tool and abandoned the idea of grading sailors and officers on their behavior during play of the game.

Although *BaFa BaFa* is a classic and among the first of the intercultural simulation games, there have been others over the years. Youth for Understanding International Exchange (YFU) developed *Markhall* in 1983 to be used for re-entry or follow-up training for American students returning from Japan. *Markhall* is described in Volume 1 of the *Intercultural Sourcebook*. Intercultural resource outreach centers such as Stanford Programs on Intercultural and Cross-Cultural Education (SPICE) and books such as *Experiential Activities for Intercultural Learning* (Seelye, 1996) published simulations that can be used in the classroom as well as adapted for other cross-cultural training settings. Other simulation games such as *Barnga* (Steinwachs & Thiagarajan, 1990) and *Ecotonos* (Nipporica, 1993) have been developed and enjoy widespread use. (These last two simulation games are described in the section on simulation games in the first volume of the *Intercultural Sourcebook*.)

Simulation gaming is not the only method used to foster intercultural understanding. Many of the methods are familiar and have long been used in a variety of training settings. Role plays, case studies, critical incidents, and video/film have also played a vital role in helping people learn to be more effective intercultural communicators. A host of intercultural exercises and activities have been developed to meet specific needs. There is not an intercultural trainer alive today who has not developed or adapted an exercise to answer a client's need. As technology advances and more technologically savvy trainers appear, each will play an increasing role in intercultural learning. The use of interactive CD-ROMs has been used for a number of years, and intercultural training via e-learning is being explored and improved continually. Where we go with computerized training in the future remains to be seen.

In summary, intercultural learning profited greatly from the recognition that experiential techniques were the most effective way to prepare people to interact successfully across cultures. Without experiential methods, intercultural training would still be focusing on knowledge gained from area studies alone, instead of building skills and developing attitudes necessary to work effectively across cultures.

Why Use Experiential Methods for Intercultural Learning?

Intercultural training has been defined by Jack Levy (1995, p. 1) as a "cohesive series of events or activities designed to develop cultural self-awareness, culturally appropriate behavioral responses or skills, and a positive orientation toward other cultures . . . To achieve these outcomes, trainers use experiential, workshop-type designs." In other words, intercultural training needs to address knowledge, skills, and attitudes—concepts familiar to every trainer. Each of these outcomes is enhanced by providing an engaging session that involves learners, using their current or past experiences to inform and be readily applicable to their new experiences.

Knowledge

As we have noted in our chapter in the *Handbook of Intercultural Training* (Fowler & Blohm, 2004), trainees can be assigned reading, listen to a panel, watch a video, or do research on the Internet when acquisition of knowledge is the desired outcome (such as history of race relations, the economic development of a particular country, how meetings are conducted in another culture, or what a culturally appropriate hostess gift is when invited to someone's home for dinner). While knowledge-based objectives do not depend on experiential activities, they are certainly enhanced by them. Acquisition of knowledge may or may not mean hands-on training, but when accompanied by a chance to use the knowledge and debrief it, the training will be more meaningful. This is true for speakers, panels, video/film, and even reading. Thiagi has experiential templates that make the experience of acquiring knowledge seamlessly interactive (Thiagarajan, 2003). Experiential learning has taken the rather dry lectures that characterized area studies and turned them into interactive, dynamic activities that engage the learner.

Skills

We are in agreement with other intercultural trainers and research that there are three general skills or abilities essential to intercultural effectiveness, the ability to (1) manage psychological stress, (2) communicate effectively, and (3) establish interpersonal relationships. These skills or abilities do not occur in a vacuum and need to be related to the business at hand to make the training relevant. This can be accomplished by setting the experiential activities in the day-to-day realm of the trainee—whether an employee, family member, or volunteer.

Each of the three main skills can be broken down into several components. For example, managing psychological stress has culture shock written all over it. Understanding the causes, symptoms, and some solutions for culture shock can be a big help for people being transferred overseas. A simple exercise that can make a difference is to have trainees draw a picture of the thing they fear most about moving to another culture. One participant drew his cat Fluffy on her back with her legs in the air. He was afraid Fluffy would die. After the group helped him plan for Fluffy's transition to the new culture, we were able to turn the drawing upside down so Fluffy's legs were down to earth.

Strategies for adjusting to a foreign culture and maintaining self-esteem are also part of this ability. Case studies are particularly useful for helping participants understand what can happen in a foreign culture, particularly when they are followed by a role play that gives them a chance to try out different behaviors. These subsequent activities can lead learners to develop their own action plans for culture entry and dealing with highly stressful situations throughout their stay.

Communication activities abound and are useful in improving effective communication skills. While *BaFa BaFa* and *Barnga* (Thiagarajan & Steinwachs, 1990) are classic simulations that raise awareness of cultural differences, two more-recent games provide practice in different aspects of communication. *Piglish* (Hartley & Lapinsky, 1999) gives participants an opportunity to try speaking in another language (not only vocabulary and grammar, but unusual sounds and gestures as well), experience any resistance they may have to speaking another language, and achieve a perspective on the process. *Redundancia* (Saphiere, n.d.) provides experience in some of the difficulties in speaking in another language, even when participants are using their own.

The third skill, establishing intercultural relationships, begins by first understanding oneself and how relationships are formed and maintained in one's own culture. Such understanding rarely happens without seeing a contrast. Cultural assimilators, critical incidents, and values clarification activities are all useful for this purpose in training settings. Learning contrasting values in the target country provides the basis on which to practice. Role plays, simulated classrooms and meetings, and other relevant settings provide the method and environment. When possible, pairing a trainee with a mentor from another culture and practicing greetings, conversation, and other components of establishing a relationship will help somewhat.

Attitudes

The final piece in the K/S/A triumvirate is attitude, and when the desired outcome of the training is for trainees to modify their attitudes, experiential methods that touch the trainees' belief systems—often intensely—are required. An exercise in which the group will score higher than any individual (most survivor exercises work this way) will give participants the feel for group process that some cultures value over individual decision making. Video/film clips often provide strong images that can be debriefed from a values perspective, such as the comical first encounter of the American auto worker with a Japanese board of directors in *Gung Ho* or the emotional scene of decision making for the young Guatemalan at his sister's deathbed in *El Norte*. By role playing relevant situations, participants not only feel the emotion but have to act on it.

Almost every exercise can be used to make several points. *Piglish* was mentioned as a means to helping people overcome their resistance to speaking a foreign language. *Piglish* can also be used to help participants develop empathy for new-language learners. Exchange programs in the United States often have monolingual parents hosting a child who speaks limited English. It is helpful for them to experience what the child may be going through as he or she adjusts to a new family and a new culture. Such an exercise also can help all first-language users to understand some of the challenges of their colleagues or employees who are working in a second, third, or even fourth language.

Training Across Cultures

Intercultural trainers need to consider whether they being asked to design and conduct training *across* cultures or *about* cultures. Of course, training can be both, but generally one will predominate. The difference is that training about a specific culture "refers to the preparation of trainees to encounter and function in a different culture." Training across cultures refers to "situations in which the trainer and trainees are of different cultures, or, most commonly, where trainees are a multicultural group in and of themselves" (Blohm, 2005).

Training about cultures may be culture-general (that is, applicable to any culture) or culture-specific. It is often preparation for future encounters, such as individuals or families from one culture moving into a different one or medical students preparing to be part of "doctor culture" encountering "patient culture." We use *BaFa BaFa* on the first day of the academic year to help first-year medical students at the Uniformed Services University of the Health Sciences confront their reactions to different-ness. In addition, the medical students are introduced to some of the concepts of cultural difference and how being a military doctor has its own culture. Sometimes trainees already are in a different cultural setting; in this case, training can assist them in making sense of their surroundings and their roles there. Examples include a business manager working in a foreign environment, student exchange students living with host families, or development workers doing pre-service training after arriving in their country of assignment.

Training across cultures happens when a multicultural group needs to acquire knowledge and skills. For example, the training may be about such things as peer feedback or other business practices in specific cultures, or it may be more culture general and concern such concepts as culture shock or cultural adjustment strategies. When the audience is from various cultures, this makes it training across cultures, even when the trainer may be teaching one thing such as team building or computer programming. Experiential activities for multicultural groups provide the practice effect as well as opening trainees' eyes to the differences among cultures for a task that they take for granted in a monocultural group. It seems these days that the norm has become multicultural groups; monocultural groups are becoming less frequent, so trainers need to learn ways of introducing experiential methods and debriefing techniques that do not offend, are not threatening, and facilitate multicultural learning.

Goals

There are many goals for intercultural training—perhaps as many as there are training programs—because it is essential for the training to be done in the context of the trainees' world. We did a training session for teachers who were embarking on a Fulbright exchange program in which they would be living and teaching in a foreign culture. Had we not set all our examples and all the exercises in the teaching arena, we might have lost many of those trainees right at the beginning.

Making intercultural training immediately relevant is especially important in business. Most businesspeople feel that they do not have the time for something "soft" like intercultural training. Therefore, one has to set the training in the business setting for it to be successful. For example, a large American chemical company was hosting a consortium of chemical companies from around the world. This group had met before, and the company officials said that they had not been satisfied with the way the meeting had gone in the past. They wanted the meeting to be more open, for a greater sharing of information and for more solid relationships to be formed. Tall order? Yes, but not too tall for the classic cross-cultural simulation *Bafa Bafa* (Shirts, 1974). Some changes in emphasis to focus on the host/guest relationship opened the Americans' eyes to how they might view the guests with a different perspective, respecting their goals and accommodating their differing ways of communicating. The report from the meeting was that it had a completely different feeling and that all the goals of the company officials had been met and exceeded.

Elements of Context: Who, What, When, Where

We have discussed why experiential methods are useful for intercultural learning but, to better understand the intercultural training arena, it is important to touch on context. It stands to reason that the context or circumstances surrounding a training program play a major role in how well the training is accepted and used. For example, a real key for intercultural training to be accepted and supported is for both employers and employees to see the training as recognizing and enhancing potential, and not as a punishment.

Among others, *who* should receive intercultural training ranges from diplomats to youngsters in bicultural schools to families being sent abroad because of military, government, business, educational, or missionary postings. Much intercultural training in the United States is conducted for people coming to the United States for business, education, or other purposes and for those who will work with or host those individuals. Diversity trainers often make use of components of intercultural training (see Fowler, 2006). When designing or choosing an experiential exercise, intercultural trainers need to take into account the personal and cultural backgrounds of the trainees as well as their ages, educational levels, learning styles, cognitive styles, and communication styles. Training has been compared to working with the layers of a multi-layered cake. The diversity of the trainees comprises one of the layers.

Experiential activities work especially well with families who are moving overseas. They can work on projects together and learn from how they worked together as well as from what they did. Sample tasks for a family might be to work on a description of their transfer location, drawing a picture of what it might be like to live there, and developing lists of things the family will miss and what equivalents exist in the new culture.

What the training should consist of is another layer of the cake. The content versus process controversy has been laid to rest. A good, integrated training program uses both—usually in balance. But in the case of intercultural training, there is often more process than content in the training room. Content may be gained by self-study prior to using limited and valuable face-to-face training time for practicing and debriefing. Both culture-specific and culture-general goals need to be addressed. Whether the training program is designed from scratch or uses packaged materials, clearly the program has to be customized to the client's needs. Most trainers customize their training by selecting and modifying existing exercises and simulations that meet the goals of the training, and they design specific activities when nothing appropriate exists. We realize that clients often do not want to hear about the hours that have been spent customizing a piece of training. They just want the trainer to make it relevant, do it, and do it well.

When the training should take place depends on what kind of training is being conducted. Pre-departure training is best done fairly close to the time of departure. Of course, this is the time of maximum chaos for transferring persons and their families, but the training can be framed as a time out from all the rigors of moving and a time to focus on what is ahead. There is validity in preparation before the encounter. One participant in a State Department training wrote back to say that, when she got off the plane in Thailand, her *BaFa* experiences began. Also, immediately prior to departure may be the only time a group can be assembled, such as teachers or students from various cities going to various locations in the host country.

In-country training has some advantages, if it is possible. The differences are real: communication is limited or exasperating, how to get things done is a mystery, and why people behave the way they do is unexpected and unnerving. In-country training can focus on immediate needs and therefore feel more relevant for participants than pre-departure training. In business, intercultural training is done more and more via a coach who works by phone as the need arises after the participant is already in the foreign country. The Peace Corps' pre-service training of eight to twelve weeks after arriving in the country of service is perhaps the most extensive and well-known example of in-country training. Their program historically combined a variety of interactive training activities and now relies heavily on the total immersion model, with strong emphasis on debriefing what is actually happening in the new culture (Bennhold-Samaan, 2004, pp. 363–394).

Re-entry training is best done before leaving to come home and if it is a part of the overseas program. People are sure everything is the same at home and rarely realize that they have changed, perhaps more than those at home have. Once home, the symptoms of re-entry problems are often very diffuse and not recognized as being related to the overseas sojourn. It is difficult to convince people that attending a training program would be useful. Depending on what they come home to, their foreign experience may be ignored and even depreciated—they may have lost a year of school or missed promotion opportunities. Different family members will experience different stresses. Young people in particular find re-entry very distressing, as they are out of step with their former peers, who would normally provide a sense of identity and be their closest support. The interactive exercises that have been developed for re-entry training are among the best experiential activities in the intercultural field.

"When" is an important factor for trainers addressing diversity—at work, in the classroom, or in communities. There are few monocultural settings left in the United States; opportunities arise continually to introduce a relevant exercise or to debrief an actual experience. "Three key concepts—learning, connecting, and belonging—are interdependent and critical to making sense of a new, complex, and even frightening world environment. Hearing and reading about different values and beliefs may challenge us. If we learn more about ourselves, our roots, and our history, we are better able to understand, interact, and connect with people who have a different history from our own. This is a key step toward building a strong community where all people are valued, included, and given opportunities to belong and contribute" (Blohm & Lapinsky, 2006). Teachers and community members, like trainers, have a constant flow of real events and circumstances that provide the experience; helping students and neighbors learn from them is the ultimate application of experiential learning. Many trainers find the most effective diversity training to be tied to actual work requirements. When a multicultural team is faced with a task, multicultural team building is a *real time* event.

Where the training takes place makes a difference in the exercises a trainer chooses. For example, if the training is in the foreign country, the total immersion in the new culture makes exercises not as important as debriefing what is happening on a daily basis. This is the epitome of experiential training, with the experience being provided by the culture. If the training takes place in the home location, simulations and experiential exercises can bring some of the same challenges and gut feelings one has when in another culture.

Facilitating Intercultural Learning

To conduct successful intercultural training, one must know about design, know how to select the right experiential exercise, and possess keen facilitation skills.

Design

Designing intercultural training is much like designing any effective training program. Typical of any training, intercultural training design must take into consideration the desired outcomes and personal preferences of both trainer and trainee. However, in intercultural training, the cultural norms of trainer and trainees are of much greater importance. Culture influences both content and process, so effective intercultural trainers must design with that fact firmly in mind.

Even though experiential learning activities have been seen to be effective in various cultural settings, there are several design factors to consider. For example, *where* exercises are placed in the training sequence may determine their overall acceptance and effectiveness. Participants who by cultural background or personal preference are accustomed to learning theory and factual information will need to start with what they know about the theory on which an activity is based. An exercise like a game or simulation may be introduced as a way to practice or apply what has been learned through lecture, reading, video, or other method. For participants who prefer interactive and experiential learning, using a game or simulation to start a session may be more energizing and encourage them to value the theoretical parts of the training to solve problems or explain what was not clear in the interactive activity.

Experiential learning is an important component of training that is intercultural in nature but not in name. We have been focusing mainly on cultural differences because of ethnic or national boundaries, but cultural differences occur also by occupation, age, gender, status, and so forth. Consequently, the training design needs to take into consideration similar or different preferences in learning styles inherent in functional groups, gender groups, or age groups. For example, diplomats or bankers may prefer more abstract theory to active learning. In a diverse group with multiple learning styles, the solution is likely to be the appropriate sequencing of cognitive and experiential activities to achieve the best results.

Selection

One way to take culture into account when selecting exercises for intercultural training is to ask if a particular method would likely offend a cultural norm. Controlling for fear of shame and loss of face is a major factor in the success of training for trainees from cultures where this is a powerful norm.

Another good question to pose is: Does the exercise or activity fit cultural preferences for communication and learning? To answer this question, the training designer must be knowledgeable about the Experiential Learning Cycle (abstract conceptualization, active experimentation, concrete experience, and reflective observation) as well as very familiar with the cultures of the trainees— or at least in touch with someone who has long experience in the culture. Communication styles also vary between direct and indirect, linear and circular, and detached and attached. Despite variation within cultures, certain communication styles predominate, so it is important to take them into consideration.

It is difficult to think of an experiential exercise that does not have cultural factors in it through its premise, definitions, or artifacts. Some exercises are specifically designed for intercultural learning, but others—originally designed for another purpose—may also be used for focusing on and clarifying intercultural issues. When selecting or designing an exercise for intercultural training, designers should always focus on the desired outcomes so the primary goal is in the forefront. But secondary goals can be achieved simultaneously. These often can be built into the processing of an exercise. Sometimes they arise spontaneously; other times the trainer wants to introduce the ideas or begin a discussion when participants seem to be heading in that direction. When reviewing a method to determine whether it should be included in a training design, the following lists (based on Blohm, 2005) suggest some of the possible factors that carry cultural implications. They should be considered to make sure they will not interfere with the desired learning and may be addressed as spinoff outcomes of intercultural learning activities.

Concepts

- leadership
- fairness
- power
- success
- rules
- rewards
- winning
- confidentiality
- punishment
- decision making (consensus, majority rule, etc.)

Knowledge

- one culture's historical concepts, heroes, anecdotes, proverbs
- one culture's daily "tools" (money, transportation, housing, etc.)
- rituals

Value Systems

- respect
- competition, cooperation
- time
- group, individualism
- status
- absolute versus relative values (right/wrong)

Language and Communication Styles

- first and second languages
- symbols
- non-verbals
- acceptable terminology (slang, acronyms, jargon)
- linear versus circular
- direct versus indirect
- high versus low context

Cultural Advantage

- rules of game may favor one culture's problem-solving style
- goal or mission of the game may exclude a particular group

Any of these items can, of course, be the primary goal of an exercise. On the other hand, they may take the form of spinoff discussions that take trainees where they need to go in learning about themselves and about people from another culture.

Facilitation

Effective facilitation of experiential intercultural learning relies on trainer competencies. R. Michael Paige (1993) has described trainer competencies for international and intercultural training programs and, despite his list having been developed over a decade ago, it remains one of the best and most comprehensive lists available. Paige points out that exceptional competencies are required by the demands and complexities of intercultural learning. He categorizes trainer competencies by cognitive knowledge, behavioral skills, and personal attributes and states that no single trainer will possess all of the skills and attributes to the fullest extent. However, he cautions that intercultural trainers should continually strive to improve their knowledge base, behavioral performance, and personal qualities. In each of the domains, Paige lists competencies that pertain specifically to experiential learning.

The *cognitive domain* provides the conceptual base for intercultural training. According to Paige, there are eight knowledge areas that break down into thirty-two knowledge specifics. He says that intercultural trainers must know, among many other things, the psychological and social dynamics of the intercultural experience. They must have a realistic understanding of the relationship of training to performance in the target culture, debriefing principles and strategies, ethical issues such as proper handling of the transformation imperative of training, international issues, multicultural issues, and their own strengths and limitations as trainers. Pertaining to experiential training, Paige declares that developing intercultural training programs requires a detailed understanding of content and process alternatives as well as debriefing principles and strategies.

The trainer competencies in the *behavioral domain* are also organized into eight areas with thirty-two specific behavioral skills or capacities. Paige includes such skills as the capacity to promote learner acquisition of skills, knowledge, and personal qualities relevant to intercultural effectiveness, the ability to articulate a clear, theory-and research-based training philosophy, an ability to debrief learning activities with individuals and groups, the capacity to secure appropriate information about and resources on the target culture, the ability to present theories of development, social change, and transfer of technology, and the capacity to provide instruction about cultural pluralism and diversity and to handle the controversy and tension associated with extremely sensitive issues such as racism. Specifically, Paige says that the competent trainer must be able to construct activities that will enable learners to think about, feel, and behaviorally react.

Paige lists twelve *personal attributes* that include cultural self-awareness, patience, interpersonal sensitivity, tolerance of differences, openness to new experiences and to people who are different, and a sense of humor. (To read the entire list, see Paige, 1993, pp. 190–193.) Cognitive and behavioral flexibility are also on the list. These attributes pertain directly to experiential learning activities, since the complex, unpredictable nature of training as a learning enterprise demands the ability to respond and adjust learning activities when plans go awry. New conceptual explanations may be required, and expectations often need to be adjusted. The dynamics of training of all kinds (but especially intercultural training) predicate flexibility on the part of the trainer and a large tool bag of experiential exercises to call upon.

It has been our experience that as trainers we are often modeling the behaviors and attitudes we hope to encourage in our trainees. It is important to be realistic about the challenges intercultural experiences are guaranteed to provide—if it were easy there would be no need for intercultural training. But it is equally important to communicate a sense of enthusiasm for intercultural encounters and express a dedication for doing it well.

Conclusion

Intercultural training offers ample opportunities to use experiential methods. In fact, it is hard to imagine an intercultural training program without the experiences that exercises and activities offer to make learning fun and central to the needs of the participants. Experiential exercises are indeed the gateway to the exciting path of intercultural learning.

A Few Selected Resources

Fantini, Alvino E. (Ed.). (1997). *New ways in teaching culture.* Alexandria, VA: Teachers of English to Speakers of Other Languages (TESOL).www.tesol.edu. This volume provides background and activities that explore how language, culture, and intercultural work belong together. Activities are at various levels.

Stanford Programs on Intercultural and Cross-Cultural Education (SPICE). http://spice.stanford.edu. This outreach center has various simulations and units, for example, "Heelotia: A Cross-Cultural Simulation" and "Living in a Global Age" simulation, and classroom units on "Why Do People Move: Migration from Latin America" and "Historical Legacies: The Vietnamese Refugee Experience." Sessions are referenced to standards.

Simulation Training Systems. www.simulationtrainingsystems.com. This company produces experiential learning modules for various audiences. "Rafa Rafa" (for younger students) and "Bafa Bafa" (for older students and adults) are simulations that quickly put participants into different cultures where they must behave according to cultural norms, as well as interact with yet a different culture.

The North American Simulation and Gaming Association (NASAGA). www.nasaga.org.

The Peace Corps, 1111 20th Street, NW, Washington, DC 20026. www.peacecorps.gov.

- World Wise Schools is an office of the Peace Corps that links Peace Corps volunteers with classrooms and provides materials to classrooms. *Looking at Ourselves and Others* and *The Bridge* are two good general sources for cross-cultural activities for the classroom.
- Online library, found through the website, has many other downloadable Peace Corps resources. These are particularly relevant to classrooms: *Culture Matters*—cultural concepts with activities.

The Society for Intercultural Education, Training, and Research USA (SIETAR USA). www.sietarusa.org. or email info@sietarusa.org.

References

Batchelder, D., & Warner, E. G. (1977). *Beyond experience: The experiential approach to cross-cultural education*. Brattleboro, VT: Experiment Press.

Bennhold-Samaan, L. (2004). The evolution of cross-cultural training in the Peace Corps. In D. Landis, J. M. Bennett, & M. J. Bennett (Eds.), *Handbook of intercultural training* (3rd ed., pp. 363–394). Thousand Oaks, CA: Sage.

Blohm, J. M. (1995). Markhall: A comparative corporate-culture simulation. In S. M. Fowler & M. G. Mumford (Eds.), *Intercultural sourcebook: Cross-cultural training methods, Vol. 1* (pp. 109–115). Yarmouth, ME: Intercultural Press.

Blohm, J. M. (2005). Using simulations and games in intercultural training. *SIMAGES: Newsletter of the North American Simulation and Gaming Association (NASAGA)*, *5*(1), 21–22. www.NASAGA.com.

Blohm, J. M. (2005). Using simulations and games in intercultural training, Part II. *SIMAGES:* Newsletter of the North American Simulation and Gaming Association (NASAGA), *5*(2), 6–10. www.NASAGA.com.

Blohm, J. M., & Lapinsky, T. (2006). *Kids like me: Voices of the immigrant experience*. Yarmouth, ME: Intercultural Press.

Fowler, S. M. (1986). Intercultural simulation games: Removing cultural blinders. In L. H. Lewis (Ed.), *Experiential and simulation techniques for teaching adults* (pp. 71–82). San Francisco: Jossey-Bass.

Fowler, S. M. (2006). Training across cultures: What intercultural trainers bring to diversity training. *International Journal of Intercultural Relations, 30*(3), 401–411.

Fowler, S. M., & Blohm, J. M. (2004). An analysis of methods for intercultural training. In D. Landis, J. M. Bennett, & M. J. Bennett (Eds.), *Handbook of intercultural training* (3rd ed., pp. 37–84). Thousand Oaks, CA: Sage.

Fowler, S. M., & Mumford, M. G. (Eds.). (1995). *Intercultural sourcebook: Cross-cultural training methods, Vol. 1*. Yarmouth, ME: Intercultural Press.

Fowler, S. M., & Mumford, M. G. (Eds.). (1999). *Intercultural sourcebook: Cross-cultural training methods, Vol. 2*. Yarmouth, ME: Intercultural Press.

Hartley, C., & Lapinsky, T. (1999). Piglish: A language learning simulation. In S. M. Fowler & M. G. Mumford (Eds.), *Intercultural sourcebook: Cross-cultural training methods, Vol. 2* (pp. 131–142). Yarmouth, ME: Intercultural Press.

Lambach, R. (1996). What's in a name? In H. N. Seelye (Ed.), *Experiential activities for intercultural learning, Vol. 1* (pp. 53–56). Yarmouth, ME: Intercultural Press.

Levy, J. (1995). Intercultural training design. In S. M. Fowler & M. G. Mumford (Eds.), *Intercultural sourcebook: Cross-cultural training methods, Vol. 1* (pp. 1–16). Yarmouth, ME: Intercultural Press.

Nipporica Associates. (1993). *Ecotonos: A multicultural problem-solving simulation*. Yarmouth, ME: Intercultural Press.

Paige, R. M. (1993). Trainer competencies for international and intercultural programs. In R. M. Paige (Ed.), *Education for the intercultural experience* (pp. 169–200). Yarmouth, ME: Intercultural Press.

Pusch, M. D. (2004). Intercultural training in historical perspective. In D. Landis, J. M. Bennett, & M. J. Bennett (Eds.), *Handbook of intercultural training* (3rd ed., pp. 13–36). Thousand Oaks, CA: Sage.

Saphiere, D. H. (n.d.). *Redundancia.* Nipporica Associates. www.nipporica.com/prod.htm.

Seelye, H. N. (Ed.). (1996). *Experiential activities for intercultural learning, Vol. 1.* Yarmouth, ME: Intercultural Press.

Shirts, R. G. (1974). *BaFa BaFa: A cross-cultural simulation.* Del Mar, CA: Simulation Training Systems.

Shirts, R. G. (1995). Beyond ethnocentrism: Promoting cross-cultural understanding with BaFa BaFa. In S. M. Fowler & M. G. Mumford (Eds.), *Intercultural sourcebook: Cross-cultural training methods, Vol. 1* (pp. 93–100). Yarmouth, ME: Intercultural Press.

Thiagarajan, S., & Steinwachs, B. (1990). *Barnga: A simulation game on cultural clashes.* Yarmouth, ME: Intercultural Press.

Thiagarajan, S., with Thiagarajan, R. (2003). D*esign your own games and activities: Thiagi's templates for performance improvement.* San Francisco: Pfeiffer.

CHAPTER TWENTY-ONE

EXPERIENTIAL LEARNING IN EMOTIONAL INTELLIGENCE TRAINING

Marcia Hughes

Marcia Hughes is president of Collaborative Growth, author of *Life's 2% Solution* (Nicholas Brealey, 2006), and co-author of *Emotional Intelligence in Action* (Pfeiffer, 2005). Marcia weaves her expertise in emotional intelligence throughout her leadership and team development, strategic design, and conflict resolution training and consultation. Her clients include Medtronic, American Express, and the Department of the Interior. Marcia is a certified trainer in the Bar-On EQ-i® and EQ-360™. Together with her partner, James Terrell, she provides train-the-trainer training and coaching in EQ. She led Collaborative Growth's development of the International EQ Symposium, which focused on distilling effective strategies for behavioral change from emotional intelligence theory.

Contact Information

Collaborative Growth

P.O. Box 17509

Golden, CO 80402

(303) 271–0021

contact@cgrowth.com

www.cgrowth.com and www.lifes2percentsolution.com

EMOTIONAL INTELLIGENCE (EI) is a constant factor governing success in all parts of our lives—professional and personal. Recognition of the critical influence EI has on success is gaining increasing momentum throughout the workplace and beyond. When doing his work on IQ and the Wechsler Adult Intelligence Scale, David Wechsler wrote about the need for understanding other forms of intelligence, especially emotional intelligence. EI is here to stay, and the exciting differentiation from IQ is that EI is based on skills that can be learned and grown.

There is an inseparable link between EI and experiential learning. The two go hand-in-hand. One of the best growth strategies organizations have available is to identify the most important EI skills for their type of operation and then establish a well-thought-out training program to enhance those critical skills. That training program has to be based in experiential learning. One of our favorite phrases at my company, Collaborative Growth, is that the learning has to "get in the bones" so it's a natural application for the individual. Skill development in areas such as self-regard and empathy requires experiential practice. Sitting down and hearing about optimism, for example, can trigger valuable interest, but to actually grow our optimism, we must practice. Expanding our EI and experiential practice go hand-in-hand.

For example, I write about the success Carlos found in growing his assertiveness in my book, *Life's 2% Solution*. His progress was based on an astute combination of experiential strategies. He was concerned that his softspoken nature limited his ability to be fully influential at work and at home. Carlos made a commitment to speak up at least twice a day in situations in which he would otherwise be quiet at work during the week and at home on weekends. His strategy included that he would do this for at least a month; every night he would take a few minutes to note how well it worked for the day; and once a week he would meet with two respected peers to hear their feedback on how he was doing. Carlos told me that he gained increased respect and influence at work and at home. I was touched when he told me how surprised he was to find that people really wanted to hear what he had to contribute.

There are many ways to increase EI skills, yet all of them have to include direct experiential practice or people will just be learning about EI instead of growing their skills.

Emotional Intelligence: An Overview

While emotional intelligence may be defined in a variety of ways, there are actually four key components: understanding your own emotions and managing them and understanding the emotions of others and responding well to them.

Contrary to personality measures, which are viewed as being essentially permanent reflections of who we are, emotional intelligence is based on skills that can be developed. Personality measures such as the Myers-Briggs Type Indicator® and Emergenetics® present a picture of someone's preferences for being extroverted or introverted, preferring social or analytical thinking, and so on. Their popularity with groups indicates the desire our clients have to know more about themselves. Emotional intelligence training provides many rich opportunities to meet this desire and takes it to a much more powerful level, given the potential of significant skills enhancement.

One of your first choices when working with EI is whether or not to use an assessment such as the BarOn EQi®, the ECI, or the MSCEIT™. You can be successful either way, although an assessment allows you to more specifically identify the needs of your clients. Thus, you can choose the focus of your experiential training with more precision. Each of these measures is described in *Emotional Intelligence in Action* (Hughes, Patterson, & Terrell, 2005). At Collaborative Growth, we primarily use the BarOn EQi®, as the results clients receive are clear, practical, and an excellent source for initiating experiential learning. Additionally, the measure is based on decades of research documenting the fifteen EI competencies identified. This is particularly relevant, as working with EI is still new enough that many clients aren't clear just what we're talking about. *Emotional intelligence* or *emotional quotient* are terms used interchangeably, thus we interpret EI or EQ as referring to the same concept.

The five scales and fifteen competencies in the EQi create a handy list of critical factors for your training focus, whether or not you are using a measurement instrument. (More information can be found in Bar-On's *Technical Manual* [1997, 2002].) The competencies are

Intrapersonal

> Self-Regard
>
> Emotional Self-Awareness
>
> Assertiveness
>
> Independence
>
> Self-Actualization

Interpersonal

> Empathy
>
> Social Responsibility
>
> Interpersonal Relationships

Stress Management

> Stress Tolerance
>
> Impulse Control

Adaptability

> Reality Testing
>
> Flexibility
>
> Problem Solving

General Mood

> Optimism
>
> Happiness

Illustrating the Experiential Application of EI Skills Development

Self-Regard

One strategy we use to expand awareness of one's own self-regard is to ask the people in the room to form pairs. Then one member of the pair is given a card. Half of the room will receive guidance to compliment the other person in a genuine way—about clothing, recent work, or a comment made during the training. The other half is instructed to nicely criticize the other person. The same topics can be used. Then the recipients of the message in the pairs are asked to talk with the group as a whole about their experience. The key point is that self-regard is about accepting ourselves, warts and all. The discussion centers on the fact that we don't always hear positive comments. When we don't, what happens? This can be taken into multiple applications with the pairs so that the participants have a chance to focus on their ability to make their own decisions about themselves while giving appropriate consideration to comments by others.

The skill of maintaining a healthy self-regard is based on an individual's ability to accept him- or herself fully. I often describe it as embracing the good, the bad, and the ugly. This acceptance is a significant skill, one that people often act as if it is more fully developed than is really the case. It matters both in the sense of the individual's peace of mind and daily happiness. It deeply colors the way one treats others. If one doesn't accept him- or herself, direct reports, family, and others are likely to pay a price. This may be expressed as intolerance for mistakes, perfectionism, or an unwillingness to speak frankly. These behaviors are likely generated from a sense of not being good enough, and possibly some defeatism associated with shame or hopelessness.

Several experiential strategies can help your clients first understand their level of self-regard and then develop their skill. Key components that will support any exercise you do include:

- *Knowledge:* They have to understand what they are working on. Many people don't realize that accepting their challenge areas (some might call it their shadow side) is a vital part of exercising healthy self-regard.
- *WIIFM:* Changing this emotional engagement with life can be done, but habits aren't changed easily. Your clients have to really believe this work is worth their effort or it won't happen.
- *Self-inquiry:* They have to be guided in poking and prodding around their current lives. The tools you may tap into to accomplish this process are discussed in this chapter. Overall, you may have them answer questions you've developed by writing in quiet by themselves, discussing the questions in pairs with someone they trust, or, if you're near an open area, set them loose to walk outside while contemplating the questions you have posed.
- *New behavioral engagement:* They need to do something specifically new in order to hard-wire this new habit and for it to replace the old way of engagement.

An exercise I frequently use draws on the need for participants to be aware of their current levels of self-regard. I pose specific questions for them to contemplate and give them guidance, such as:

- Think of a time when things went really well.
- Think of a time when things went really poorly.
- How did you respond in each scenario? Take time and write at least three elements of your response in each circumstance.
- Get together with one other person and discuss what each of you wrote.

Have the group debrief the matter together. Follow the debriefing guidance provided in this article as you conduct the discussion.

The purpose of this exercise is to have the participants take time to think about *themselves* (not tasks, the stock market, or whatever else). They are guided to begin paying attention to specifics of their responses in successful, as compared to unsuccessful, situations. From this each group member can begin to understand his or her strengths and weaknesses in the regard he or she gives to him- or herself.

Giving Negative Feedback

Most of us need to give constructive criticism or feedback to be successful at work and home. Yet many of us shy away from telling the truth. We use many experiential exercises to guide the development of this skill. One example is a role play during which one is the boss and the other a direct report. The boss is to give a performance review and find many things right, but two or three specific concerns that need to be addressed. The instructions are for the boss to deliver the full message in a way that the staff person feels respected, resourceful, and understands how to change. The staff person can be given a variety of instructions, from "Your mom is seriously ill and you can barely listen" to "You are a highly resourceful person who can easily respond to suggestions for improvement." It is interesting that this can raise the awareness of the need to improve self-regard for both participants. If the "boss" doesn't feel strong about his or her own capabilities, the person is likely to be defensive in discussing the idea with others. The group discussion after the role play can focus on the application of several EI skills in addition to self-regard, such as assertiveness and optimism.

Another exercise I use to build this skill is to ask participants to role play giving a key person they are in a relationship with negative feedback. I guide them to draw on a real situation from their lives, not a role play I construct. The person can be a direct report, a child, or a boss. The key is that *the relationship matters* and they care enough to give some unpleasant information. Then I ask them to go into a "meta" state—to stand back and access their responses. I pose questions such as:

- How did it feel?
- How successful were you?
- Did you avoid any hard discussions?
- What do you notice about the similarity between the expectations you place on yourself and what you're asking of the other?
- If you're an over-achiever or prefer to keep low and not give much, do you impose the same expectation on others?

I then have the group develop the questions from this point.

Positive Emotions: Happiness

Research is abundant in demonstrating the critical importance of positive emotions. They guide us to live longer, be healthier, and reach more of our goals at work. They support us in endurance in hanging in there with challenging situations. While I used to encounter resistance when I discussed this topic with some groups, the resistance is diminishing. I'm not sure whether the enhanced receptiveness is due to increased education about the benefits of these positive factors in our lives or if it is because of the hunger for change given the fast-paced, taxing lifestyle so many live. It may be a combination of the two. What is important is that groups are increasingly receptive to learning about these skills.

One way I seek to work with these emotions is to first get the group into a positive state. This can be done by asking them to remember and discuss a positive occurrence they've enjoyed recently. Another way is to show movie clips of positive events. (If you do this, be sure to comply with copyright requirements.)

When the group is in a positive state, I frequently follow this process:

Growing Happiness

- Ask them to reflect on how they are enjoying their lives.
- To measure this, ask them how happy they are today on a scale of 1 to 10, 10 being highest.
- Ask them to reflect on why they gave themselves that number and whether it's the number they want to live with.
- If they want a change, ask them to identify two steps to begin a lasting change. If they're happy where they are, ask them to identify two steps to maintain this positive level of happiness.
- Guide them to have examples in both categories of physical action and attitudinal change. Ask whether they want to address the area of the biggest drag on their happiness or to be strategically incremental.
- Explore the decisions and the recognitions with the group as a whole.

The purpose of this exercise is multi-fold. Happiness is probably the key driving force for all human behavior. As they gain recognition that their happiness is directly related to workplace or whole life success (depending on which framework drives them), they will be excited to recognize that they can change their experiences. Happiness is contagious! They will feel good as they begin implementing a specific strategy, and that positive feeling will be reinforced by positive feedback from others.

Take It Home

Another way to expand positive emotions that I use is to give a homework assignment. Tell everyone in the group to find partners and make commitments to their partners about some action they will take that night to be intentionally positive. It must take at least fifteen minutes and be purposeful. They are told to report back to their partners in the morning, and then we have a group discussion about what happened. Benefits include that the participants integrate this skill into their real lives. Furthermore, it just about guarantees that the group will start the day in a positive, upbeat mood, which promotes learning and certainly is more fun for everyone.

Self-Actualization

This is the big "Wow" of EI. It is about motivation at the simplest level and about truly giving our gifts to the world at the highest level. It has been found to be the number one factor for overall business success. Unquestionably, experiencing this skill helps us know that life is worth living. If you choose to work in this area, you have a lot of positive outcomes available. However, it can be challenging at times to get people to understand and focus on the concept. Paradoxically, they may think it's too lightweight.

I believe so strongly in this concept that I've written a book that presents a ten-step action plan for bringing our gifts to life. *Life's 2% Solution* (2006) is based on research I've conducted for years with professionals in many walks of life. I've interviewed many who have implemented a strategy that I call a 2 percent project and found significantly increased meaning in their lives. Simply put, a 2 percent project calls for us to spend 2 percent of our time—thirty minutes a day—on an activity or in a manner that helps us sing our heart's song. It's about giving that deep longing many are putting off until some future day some air time right now. It's a manageable amount of time for people who want to have a fully rewarding life, and the focus required makes the time powerful.

Experiential Training Considerations to Support EI Growth

When you are designing emotional intelligence training, whether an introduction to EI or a full-scale intervention, a few key considerations are important to take into account. Best practices I strongly recommend and that you will find in the above-referenced resources are discussed below. (This discussion is drawn from *Emotional Intelligence in Action* [Hughes, Patterson, & Terrell, 2005, pp. 116–117]).

- *Include a small amount of theory with a lot of application.* Most clients have a desire to know something about EI, what it is, why it is important for them, and how they should use it. However, a little theory goes a long way. Get them out of their seats and applying the concepts quickly. It's hard to find a training subject more amenable to experiential learning.
- *Develop your own skills so you are ready to work with emotional issues.* Pay careful attention to the necessary training skills and to the best practices recommended

when working with emotional intelligence. You are working in a complex area and can stir up many emotions. Furthermore, you can't assume everyone will respond the same to any particular exercise. What will be easy for some clients may be difficult for others. Thus, you will need to apply your own judgment and knowledge about the specific situation you are using in your training. Working in this field requires that the trainer be particularly attentive to his or her client's skills, capabilities, and needs. Fortunately, there are two excellent sources of best practices for training and development with emotional intelligence. The Consortium for Research on Emotional Intelligence in Organizations provides Guidelines for Best Practice, which are found at www.eiconsortium.org and *Promoting Emotional Intelligence in Organizations* by Cherniss and Adler (2000).

Follow these best practices:

1. Provide a safe environment. Work at a pace that is comfortable for your clients. Use strategies to empower them to influence their learning process; acknowledge their concerns and their successes.
2. Establish and observe rules governing confidentiality and disclosure. From the first time your client(s) become aware of the work they will be doing, they should know what, why, and how any information about them will be used. Be certain that you are clear about what you will discuss and with whom after your interventions. The norm is that you will not discuss any information with anyone else. This creates an environment of trust that is essential for the deep work of change. If you are working with a team or group, the first ground rule is usually "What is said here stays here."
3. Get the learning in the body. Surely you agree, given your interest in experiential learning, that it takes concrete experience to make change. Cognitive understanding of new concepts complements this work, but sustainable behavioral change is based on a repeatedly reinforced experiential process. Practice number 16 in the EI Consortium (www.eiconsortium.org) list states: "Active, concrete, experiential methods tend to work best for learning social and emotional competencies. Development activities that engage all the senses and that are dramatic and powerful can be especially effective."
4. Pace your clients. To successfully guide transformative EI development, you need to pace, pace, pace your clients. If they are concerned about doing the work and don't have any experience, go slowly. Start with simple challenges and move to more difficult ones as understanding and trust grow. If they already have considerable experience in this area, keep your work at a more challenging level to maintain their interest.

5. Establish support systems that are commiserate with the level of intervention you will be conducting. Especially if your experiential activities are very deep or personal, be sure to understand the organization's EAP system or have a list of referrals so you are able to help them find support if needed.

6. Follow through. Longlasting behavioral change happens only when there is a neuronal change. Old habits must be extinguished and new ones developed. This is possible, but it doesn't happen overnight. It takes repeated practice, reinforcement, and, most of all, a big desire to make the change. Challenge your clients as they say they'll make certain changes about the specifics of their learning process because, without this clarity, the good intentions are likely to be just that. They may never see the light of day.

7. Evaluate your work. Some of the first questions to ask when you begin working with your client(s) are: "How will you know your objectives have been accomplished." "What specifically will be different?" Check in at the end to determine whether you accomplished your goals as well as theirs.

Critical Decisions

- Make it fun. This is truly all about them, and people love that. However, for it to be fun, it must be safe. Manage the number of expectations as to how much they are expected to explore or disclose. In general, I invite participants to work on matters of moderate importance to them and then say, with a chuckle, to not go into an area requiring Kleenex. Of course, if you have a small group and you're ready to explore deeper, then you won't need this restriction. Be careful and aware at all times of what you're stirring up.

- Don't ask the people who are quite introverted to present in front of a group if you're only pulling a few people up as a demonstration. It's painful for many people with this preference, and they may not be able to help you make your point.

- If you're going to ask a few people to do a special task, ask them in advance so they are prepared to cooperate well.

- Invite questions throughout the training; help your group be involved and participate. Keep your eye on them so you're ready to call on participants to add their points of view or questions to the discussion.

- Keep your examples as practical for them as possible. That means that, when you're talking with salespeople, you use sales examples, and when you're working with engineers, tie your examples to their profession, and so on.

Enrollment Strategies

Start with a simple, short exercise, something fun. One I use sometimes is to have people name their favorite character when they were young. Then talk to a friend and identify Goofy's (or whichever character was chosen) key EQ skill.

Then get feedback from the group as a whole. If the group is small enough, you can go around and ask who each of them named and the characteristic. If you have a large group, ask for some examples. The purpose is to get them engaged and applying the concept. Before you move on, give them the teaching point as to why you asked them to do the exercise. My teaching point for the favorite character exercise is to demonstrate how much they already know and their ability to recognize EQ characteristics, even though they haven't yet had formal training in the subject.

Getting Active Involvement in Exercises

One of the trickiest parts of the training can be to get participants to actually do what you're asking them to do. The second-biggest challenge is to manage the activity so that they gain the learning you intend. I find the following steps are particularly important when asking people to build their emotional intelligence skills.

1. Explain what you want them to do *before* they leave their seats to begin the exercise. You may have the instructions on a handout for them, listed on a flip chart or PowerPoint slide you keep on the screen. Go through the steps in a linear fashion and ask whether there are any questions. Only after they have an understanding of the assignment should you free them up to begin the exercise. If you have pre-assigned groups, I recommend you gain their understanding before showing the list of group assignments; otherwise, the more socially oriented people will start moving out of their seats. Then it can be a real struggle to organize them.

2. Depending on the exercise, it may be helpful for you to role model it in front of the group. For example, if you are training them to match non-verbal behaviors to build empathy, bring a willing participant up front to move through the exercise with you so the group can understand what you're asking.

3. Create an expectation that they will be reporting back on their experience and that it has value for their lives after the training. This helps create buy-in and gains greater long-term learning. You can create this expectation by asking them for examples of current life circumstances for which they are already using EI skills, even though they don't think of the skills in that context. This

will help your trainees recognize practical value and believe that it is possible for them to connect successfully with these skills.

4. After the exercise, explain why you had them engage in the activity. Take time to explain in a variety of ways so that you can engage the attention of those who think differently. I refer to this as a "whole brain approach."

Feedback

You are a role model for your training participants. They will decide whether you have any credibility in training in EI largely based on your demeanor, so pay close attention. A great deal will be learned from watching you. After all, "monkey see, monkey do" is a critical part of how humans learn.

Your clients are likely to be more vulnerable when working on an EI issue than on most other areas, especially as compared to a basic technical issue at work. They need a balance of responses from you. Show them regard and proceed at a respectful pace. However, don't be so safe that you just give nice platitudes in your feedback. True skills development requires meaningful, on-point feedback, delivered in a way that the participant can listen and work with your advice.

Key steps I recommend in giving EI feedback are:

1. *Listen*—truly, actively, and with the ears of your heart. Pay attention when they are speaking.
2. *Don't resist*—their experiences really are their experiences. Listen, acknowledge, and prepare to suggest changes as appropriate, without framing your response as resistance. It just doesn't work to tell people they aren't feeling the way they report.
3. *Ask for more information*—this is a way to expand your own awareness and can be quite helpful to the participants. Guided and focused questions can help them gain much more understanding.
4. *Reframe*—most behaviors aren't all good or all bad. Help them find practical and useful contexts for key behaviors. Perhaps explore what is useful about the behavior and what gets in the way. With a developed understanding, you can then lead them to a focused behavior change to expand the skill in question.
5. *Make connections*—Tie your comments and theirs to the main teaching points.

Selecting Exercises

A broad range of exercises is available to assist your clients in growing their EQ. You may have some in your files, you will find forty-six exercises in our book, *Emotional Intelligence in Action,* and you can find other sources by searching for information about the particular skill online. Whatever exercises you use, I recommend you follow the following tips:

- Know your group. Are they high-flying executives, new hires just out of college, in sales, engineering, and so on.
- Determine their background. Are they totally new to EI or looking for advanced training?
- Know what they want and what they need. Take time to conduct outcomes identification before you design your training.
- Choose a limited number of skills to develop. If you have a day, limit yourself to two or three skills for the group.
- Consistently emphasize how important it is that each individual in the training select one area to begin to grow. If some of your group are eager to take on more than one growth challenge, have them prioritize and begin first with the one they believe will provide the most benefit. Pace your group to recognize that, with some success under their belts, they can move on to their next priorities.
- Decide whether you want to guide the group to expand areas of strength or to address areas that are a drag on their success. Determine whether you are engaged in team building, and thus expanding the skills of the whole group and how they act collectively, or focusing on assisting each individual to become individually stronger.

As an example of applying some of these considerations, if I'm working with a group of strong executives, I might choose to emphasize development of self-regard, positive emotions (happiness or optimism), and self-actualization. These skills have been found to be among the top five critical to workplace success. If I'm working with a group of new hires, I might focus on emotional self-awareness and empathy, because they need skills in building relationships and connecting in the workplace.

An exercise I use in a group to help participants get a personal sense of their self-actualization and to set a goal for maintaining or increasing their success follows:

- Ask each of them to draw a circle and label it "My life today."
- Ask them to create spaces in the circle to represent the areas they feel they are living well or partially well today. This isn't about perfect pie wedges, but shapes that represent different areas of importance and different levels of success. For example, there may be a work picture that is 70 percent on track, a family picture that's 80 percent on track, and so on.

- Then ask how much of the circle isn't filled in and have them write about or talk with partners about what is needed to continue filling in the circle and to celebrate how much is already in place.

The purpose of the exercise is to increase people's personal awareness about their satisfaction with their lives right now, as well as to take stock of where they are headed given how they are living. As with any EQ exercise, it is vital to continuously relate the exercise to their lives now and to practical outcomes so you maintain their buy-in and focus.

Conclusion

Learning skills that promote emotional intelligence in one's life requires experiential learning. You have several well-researched areas from which to choose as you seek to guide your clients in expanding their emotional intelligence. Side-by-side with the tremendous possibilities are the important responsibilities of the trainer. We must pay attention to the personal impact of this work on each member of the groups with which we work. Throughout the engagement, it is important to pace the development of their competencies with respect and to provide needed support.

References

Bar-On, R. (1997, 2002). *Bar-On emotional quotient inventory (EQ-i) technical manual.* Toronto, Ontario: Multi-Health Systems, Inc.

Cherniss, C., & Adler, M. (2000). *Promoting emotional intelligence in organizations.* Alexandria, VA: American Society for Training and Development.

Hughes, M. (2006). *Life's 2% solution: Simple steps to achieve happiness and balance.* Boston, MA: Nicholas Brealey.

Hughes, M., Patterson, B., & Terrell, J. (2005). *Emotional intelligence in action.* San Francisco: Pfeiffer.

INDEX

A

Abelson, R. P., 45

ABLA (assessment-based learning activities), 245

Abma, T. A., 47

Abrams, L., 47

Abstract Conceptualization phase, 228

Academy for Transformation, 295

Action learning: applications of, 105–109; described, 95; emerging trends, 109; example of, 104–105; guiding principles of, 96–98; history of, 96; multiple-problem and single-problem groups, 100; questions used in, 97, 98–99; stages of, 100–104; technical training using, 244; theoretical foundations of, 95; two group norms/ground rules for, 98–99

Action Learning in Action (Marquardt), 94

Action learning applications: 1. problem solving, 106; 2. leadership development, 106–107;

3. building teams, 107; 4. creating learning organizations, 107; 5. individual professional growth and development, 107–108

Action learning coach, 98, 99

Action Learning in Practice (Pedler), 96

Action learning problems: centering around, 96; experiential learning imbedded in, 6; reframing, 102; solving, 106; taking action on the, 97

Action Learning Research and Practice (journal), 96

ACTION PLAN (example), 30–31

Action Replay model, 69, 74–75

Active Experimentation phase, 228

Active Training (Silberman), 13, 272

Adams, L. T., 37, 38

Adaptability Effectively to Change (Gurvis), 307

Adenzato, M., 37

Adler, M., 368

Adventure in the Amazon workshop (Ukens), 127, 133

Adventure learning: blending with other activities, 180–181; description of, 174–175; future

of, 183; how it works, 176–178; making a difference on the individual level, 181–183; origins of, 175–176; processing experience of, 178–180. *See also* Project Adventure

Affective learning, 8

AFR Midnight Rambler (1998 Sydney-Hobart sailing race winner), 181

African American History Game (video game), 51, 52–53*fig*

African-American History Education and Culture, 52

An Alien Among Us (Powers), 126

"All in the Family" (TV show), 339

"All-2-1" debriefing pattern, 64

Alpha testing simulation, 92–93

American Psychologist (journal), 341

American Society for Training and Development (ASTD), 13, 94, 155, 202, 272, 288

Analogy, 212

Anand, R., 293

Anderson, R., 322–323, 325, 333, 340

helping participants to understand their prejudices/biases, 295–297; making progress towards goals of, 291–292; mentoring contributions to, 298–299; setting tougher stretch goals/increasing communication, 292–293; site visit as part of, 301–302; strengthening diversity leadership, 297–298. *See also* Intercultural training

Douglas, C., 308

Dramatic readings (role playing), 26

Drath, W., 311, 313

Drone Zone, 182*t*

Drucker, P., 326

Durlach, N. I., 39

Dynamic debriefing: benefits of effective, 61–62; described, 61; methods of, 73–79

Dynamic debriefing models: Action Replay, 69, 74–75; Horseshoe, 77–78; Metaphor Maps, 76–77; Missing Person, 77; Objective Line, 75–76; overview of, 73–74; Turntable, 78–79

E

E-learning, 250–254

ECI assessment, 362

Ecotonos (simulation game), 345

EDNA-E (Event-Driven Narrative Analysis Engine), 50*fig*–51

EEOC Notice N-915.022, 303

Eikenberry, K., 119, 256

Elimination Lists (improv activity), 169

Elliott, L. R., 39

Email games, 245

Embodied cognition, 37

Emergenetics, 362

Emotional Intelligence in Action (Hughes, Patterson, & Terrell), 360, 362, 367, 371

Emotional intelligence (EI): competencies of, 362–363; experiential applications of, 363–367; experiential training to support growth of, 367–373; importance of, 361; overview of, 361–363; training feedback on, 371

Emotional intelligence (EI) skills: categories of competencies, 362–363; giving negative feedback, 365; positive emotions: happiness, 365–367; self-actualization, 362, 367; self-regard, 362, 363–364

Employees: enabling experimentation by, 340; facilitating understanding/reactions to change, 339; leadership development of, 106–107, 297–298, 308–319; managing change perspective by, 333–337*t*; professional development by, 107–109, 230–231

Engaging Learning, Designing e-Learning simulation Games (Quinn), 138

Entin, E. B., 39

Epstein, S., 68

Evaluating simulation design, 150–152

Evolutionary prototyping, 149

Exchange feedback skills: checklist for improving, 286; experiential learning for, 279; as interpersonal skill, 274

Executive coaches. *See* Coaches

Experience: action replay to rerun, 69, 74–75; debriefing, 65, 66–69, 72–73; learning role of, 2–3, 68–69, 308–309; link between stories and, 203–205; processing an adventure learning, 178–180; reflective learning from real-world, 224–238; systematic design of simulated, 146–153

Experience economy, 154

Experience and Education (Dewey), 3

ExperienceChange (simulation), 327–330, 328*fig*, 334

ExperiencePoint, 321, 322, 334

Experiential activities: considering new attitudes/behaviors through, 21–27; creating openness using, 18–19; examples of stories used as, 218–222; experimenting through, 27–28; improvisation, 24, 163–170; maximizing impact in interpersonal skill training, 282–283; obtaining support through,

28–32; promoting understanding through, 19–21. *See also* Games; Simulations

Experiential Activities for Intercultural Learning (Seelye), 345

Experiential learning (EL): blending e-learning with, 250–254; change management, 323–340; description of, 6–9; diversity training for, 289–305; facilitating, 132–136; growth of, 3–4; intercultural training, 342–357; interpersonal skill development, 273–287; Kolb's cycle of, 226; leadership development, 308–319; methodologies used in, 8–9; role of debriefing in, 70; using stories to promote, 211–214; in team building, 257–271; technical training application of, 241–255. *See also* Learning

Experiential Learning (Kolb), 3

Experiential simulation: learning benefits of, 84; ten secrets of, 84–93. *See also* Simulations

Experiential simulation secrets: 1. don't confuse replication with simulation, 84–85; 2. choose the right subject to simulate, 85–86; 3. develop a design plan, 86–87; 4. design simulation so participants take responsibility for actions, 87–90; 5. use symbols/metaphors for emotionally charged ideas, 90–91; 6. don't play games with participants, 91; 7. use non-participants to add realism, 91–92; 8. develop appropriate performance assessment model, 92; 9. alpha test simulation in low-risk circumstances, 92–93; 10. set your own standards for success, 93

Experiential training: adventure learning used for, 174–184; change management, 323–340; diversity, 289–305; for emotional intelligence growth, 367–373; improv contribution to art of, 24, 155–170; intercultural,

381

Pfeiffer Publications Guide

This guide is designed to familiarize you with the various types of Pfeiffer publications. The formats section describes the various types of products that we publish; the methodologies section describes the many different ways that content might be provided within a product. We also provide a list of the topic areas in which we publish.

FORMATS

In addition to its extensive book-publishing program, Pfeiffer offers content in an array of formats, from fieldbooks for the practitioner to complete, ready-to-use training packages that support group learning.

FIELDBOOK Designed to provide information and guidance to practitioners in the midst of action. Most fieldbooks are companions to another, sometimes earlier, work, from which its ideas are derived; the fieldbook makes practical what was theoretical in the original text. Fieldbooks can certainly be read from cover to cover. More likely, though, you'll find yourself bouncing around following a particular theme, or dipping in as the mood, and the situation, dictate.

HANDBOOK A contributed volume of work on a single topic, comprising an eclectic mix of ideas, case studies, and best practices sourced by practitioners and experts in the field.

An editor or team of editors usually is appointed to seek out contributors and to evaluate content for relevance to the topic. Think of a handbook not as a ready-to-eat meal, but as a cookbook of ingredients that enables you to create the most fitting experience for the occasion.

RESOURCE Materials designed to support group learning. They come in many forms: a complete, ready-to-use exercise (such as a game); a comprehensive resource on one topic (such as conflict management) containing a variety of methods and approaches; or a collection of like-minded activities (such as icebreakers) on multiple subjects and situations.

TRAINING PACKAGE An entire, ready-to-use learning program that focuses on a particular topic or skill. All packages comprise a guide for the facilitator/trainer and a workbook for the participants. Some packages are supported with additional media—such as video—or learning aids, instruments, or other devices to help participants understand concepts or practice and develop skills.

- *Facilitator/trainer's guide* Contains an introduction to the program, advice on how to organize and facilitate the learning event, and step-by-step instructor notes. The guide also contains copies of presentation materials—handouts, presentations, and overhead designs, for example—used in the program.

- *Participant's workbook* Contains exercises and reading materials that support the learning goal and serves as a valuable reference and support guide for participants in the weeks and months that follow the learning event. Typically, each participant will require his or her own workbook.

ELECTRONIC CD-ROMs and web-based products transform static Pfeiffer content into dynamic, interactive experiences. Designed to take advantage of the searchability, automation, and ease-of-use that technology provides, our e-products bring convenience and immediate accessibility to your workspace.

METHODOLOGIES

CASE STUDY A presentation, in narrative form, of an actual event that has occurred inside an organization. Case studies are not prescriptive, nor are they used to prove a point; they are designed to develop critical analysis and decision-making skills. A case study has a specific time frame, specifies a sequence of events, is narrative in structure, and contains a plot structure—an issue (what should be/have been done?). Use case studies when the goal is to enable participants to apply previously learned theories to the circumstances in the case, decide what is pertinent, identify the real issues, decide what should have been done, and develop a plan of action.

ENERGIZER A short activity that develops readiness for the next session or learning event. Energizers are most commonly used after a break or lunch to stimulate or refocus the group. Many involve some form of physical activity, so they are a useful way to counter post-lunch lethargy. Other uses include transitioning from one topic to another, where "mental" distancing is important.

EXPERIENTIAL LEARNING ACTIVITY (ELA) A facilitator-led intervention that moves participants through the learning cycle from experience to application (also known as a Structured Experience). ELAs are carefully thought-out designs in which there is a definite learning purpose and intended outcome. Each step—everything that participants do during the activity—facilitates the accomplishment of the stated goal. Each ELA includes complete instructions for facilitating the intervention and a clear statement of goals, suggested group size and timing, materials required, an explanation of the process, and, where appropriate, possible variations to the activity. (For more detail on Experiential Learning Activities, see the Introduction to the *Reference Guide to Handbooks and Annuals*, 1999 edition, Pfeiffer, San Francisco.)

GAME A group activity that has the purpose of fostering team spirit and togetherness in addition to the achievement of a pre-stated goal. Usually contrived—undertaking a desert expedition, for example—this type of learning method offers an engaging means for participants to demonstrate and practice business and interpersonal skills. Games are effective for team building and personal development mainly because the goal is subordinate to the process—the means through which participants reach decisions, collaborate, communicate, and generate trust and understanding. Games often engage teams in "friendly" competition.

ICEBREAKER A (usually) short activity designed to help participants overcome initial anxiety in a training session and/or to acquaint the participants with one another. An icebreaker can be a fun activity or can be tied to specific topics or training goals. While a useful tool in itself, the icebreaker comes into its own in situations where tension or resistance exists within a group.

INSTRUMENT A device used to assess, appraise, evaluate, describe, classify, and summarize various aspects of human behavior. The term used to describe an instrument depends primarily on its format and purpose. These terms include survey, questionnaire, inventory, diagnostic, survey, and poll. Some uses of instruments include providing instrumental feedback to group members, studying here-and-now processes or functioning within a group, manipulating group composition, and evaluating outcomes of training and other interventions.

Instruments are popular in the training and HR field because, in general, more growth can occur if an individual is provided with a method for focusing specifically on his or her own behavior. Instruments also are used to obtain information that will serve as a basis for change and to assist in workforce planning efforts.

Paper-and-pencil tests still dominate the instrument landscape with a typical package comprising a facilitator's guide, which offers advice on administering the instrument and interpreting the collected data, and an initial set of instruments. Additional instruments are available separately. Pfeiffer, though, is investing heavily in e-instruments. Electronic instrumentation provides effortless distribution and, for larger groups particularly, offers advantages over paper-and-pencil tests in the time it takes to analyze data and provide feedback.

LECTURETTE A short talk that provides an explanation of a principle, model, or process that is pertinent to the participants' current learning needs. A lecturette is intended to establish a common language bond between the trainer and the participants by providing a mutual frame of reference. Use a lecturette as an introduction to a group activity or event, as an interjection during an event, or as a handout.

MODEL A graphic depiction of a system or process and the relationship among its elements. Models provide a frame of reference and something more tangible, and more easily remembered, than a verbal explanation. They also give participants something to "go on," enabling them to track their own progress as they experience the dynamics, processes, and relationships being depicted in the model.

ROLE PLAY A technique in which people assume a role in a situation/scenario: a customer service rep in an angry-customer exchange, for example. The way in which the role is approached is then discussed and feedback is offered. The role play is often repeated using a different approach and/or incorporating changes made based on feedback received. In other words, role playing is a spontaneous interaction involving realistic behavior under artificial (and safe) conditions.

SIMULATION A methodology for understanding the interrelationships among components of a system or process. Simulations differ from games in that they test or use a model that depicts or mirrors some aspect of reality in form, if not necessarily in content. Learning occurs by studying the effects of change on one or more factors of the model. Simulations are commonly used to test hypotheses about what happens in a system—often referred to as "what if?" analysis—or to examine best-case/worst-case scenarios.

THEORY A presentation of an idea from a conjectural perspective. Theories are useful because they encourage us to examine behavior and phenomena through a different lens.

TOPICS

The twin goals of providing effective and practical solutions for workforce training and organization development and meeting the educational needs of training and human resource professionals shape Pfeiffer's publishing program. Core topics include the following:

Leadership & Management

Communication & Presentation

Coaching & Mentoring

Training & Development

E-Learning

Teams & Collaboration

OD & Strategic Planning

Human Resources

Consulting